International Tourism Today

International Tourism Today

Ramesh Kant Rajput

RANDOM PUBLICATIONS
NEW DELHI (INDIA)

International Tourism Today

ISBN 978-93-5111-548-9

Published in 2015 in India by

RANDOM PUBLICATIONS

4376-A/4B, Gali Murari Lal, Ansari Road
New Delhi-110 002
Phone : +9111-43580356, 011-23289044, 011-43142548
e-mail: sales@randompublications.com,
info@randompublications.com, randomexports@gmail.com

Reprinted 2021

Type Setting by : Friends Media, Delhi-110089
Digitally Printed at : Replika Press Pvt. Ltd.

Preface

Tourism is travel for recreation, leisure, religious, family or business purposes, usually for a limited duration. Tourism is commonly associated with international travel, but may also refer to travel to another place within the same country. The World Tourism Organization defines tourists as people "traveling to and staying in places outside their usual environment for not more than one consecutive year for leisure, business and other purposes". Tourism has become a popular global leisure activity. Tourism can be domestic or international, and international tourism has both incoming and outgoing implications on a country's balance of payments. Today, tourism is a major source of income for many countries, and affects the economy of both the source and host countries, in some cases being vital importance. International tourism receipts grew to US$1.159 trillion in 2011, corresponding to an increase in real terms of 5.3% from 2012.

The World Tourism Organization reports the following countries as the top ten tourism earners for the year 2013, with the United States by far the top earner. Tourism suffered as a result of a strong economic slowdown of the late-2000s recession, between the second half of 2008 and the end of 2009, and the outbreak of the H1N1 influenza virus. It then slowly recovered, with international tourist arrivals surpassing the milestone of 1 billion tourists globally for first time in history in 2012. International tourism receipts grew to US$1.03 trillion in 2011, corresponding to an increase in real terms of 3.8% from 2010. In 2012, China became the largest spender in international tourism globally with US$102 billion, surpassing Germany and United States. China and emerging markets have significantly increased their spending over the past decade, with Russia and Brazil as noteworthy examples.

I would like to thank my team for standing beside me throughout my career and writing this book. My special thanks go to "Random Publications" who have published the book.

– Ramesh Kant Rajput

Contents

1

International Tourism

DEFINING TOURISM

Tourism is the act of travel for predominantly recreational or leisure purposes, and also refers to the provision of services in support of this act. Tourists are people who travel to and stay in places outside their usual environment for not more than one consecutive year for leisure, business and other purposes not related to the exercise of an activity remunerated from within the place visited. The distance between a place of origin and a tourism destination is immaterial to this definition. Tourism has become an extremely popular, global activity. In 2004, there were over 763 million international tourist arrivals.As a service industry, tourism has numerous tangible and intangible elements. Major tangible elements include transportation, accommodation, and other components of a hospitality industry. Major intangible elements relate to the purpose or motivation for becoming a tourist, such as rest, relaxation, the opportunity to meet new people and experience other cultures, or simply to do something different and have an adventure.

Tourism is vital for many countries, due to the income generated by the consumption of goods and services by tourists, the taxes levied on businesses in the tourism industry, and the opportunity for employment and economic advancement by working in the industry. For these reasons NGOs and government agencies may sometimes promote a specific region as a tourist destination, and support the development of a tourism industry in that area. The contemporary phenomenon of mass tourism may sometimes result in overdevelopment, however alternative forms of tourism such as ecotourism seek to avoid such outcomes by pursuing tourism in a sustainable way.

The terms tourism and travel are sometimes used interchangeably. In this context travel has a similar definition to tourism, but implies a more purposeful journey. The terms *tourism* and *tourist* are sometimes used pejoratively to imply a shallow interest in the cultures or locations visited by tourists.

Definition, Classification and Prerequisites of International Tourism

One of the earliest definitions of tourism was provided by the Austrian economist Hermann Von Schullard in 1910, who defined it as, "sum total of operators, mainly of an economic nature, which directly relate to the entry, stay and movement of foreigners inside and outside a certain country, city or a region."

Hunziker and Krapf, in 1942, defined tourism as "the totality of the relationship and phenomenon arising from the travel and stay of strangers, provided that the stay does not imply the establishment of a permanent residence and is not connected with a remunerative activities". In 1976 Tourism Society of England defined it as "Tourism is the temporary, short-term movement of people to destination outside the places where they normally live and work and their activities during the stay at each destination. It includes movements for all purposes.

"In 1981 International Association of Scientific Experts in Tourism defined Tourism in terms of particular activities selected by choice and undertaken outside the home environment.

United Nations classified 3 forms of tourism in 1994 in its Recommendations on Tourism Statistics as follows:

1. Domestic tourism, involving residents of the given country traveling only within this country;
2. Inbound tourism, involving non-residents traveling in the given country;
3. Outbound tourism, involving residents traveling in another country.

UN also derived different categories of tourism by combining the 3 basic forms of tourism:

1. Internal tourism, which comprises domestic tourism and inbound tourism;
2. National tourism, which comprises domestic tourism and outbound tourism;
3. International tourism, which consists of inbound tourism and outbound tourism.

Prerequisites of Tourism

Before people are able to experience tourism they usually need at least:

1. Disposable income, *i.e.* money to spend on non-essentials
2. Leisure time
3. Tourism infrastructure, such as transport and accommodation

Individually, sufficient health is also a condition, and of course the inclination to travel. Furthermore, in some countries there are legal restrictions on travelling, especially abroad.

Certain states with strong governmental control over the lives of citizens (notably established Communist states) may restrict foreign travel only to trustworthy citizens. The United States prohibits its citizens from traveling to some countries, for example, Cuba.

DIFFERENT TYPES OF TOURISM

Wealthy people have always travelled to distant parts of the world to see great buildings or other works of art, to learn new languages, to experience new cultures, or to taste new cuisine. As long ago as the time of the Roman Republic places such as Baiae were popular coastal resorts for the rich.

The terms *tourist* and *tourism* were first used as official terms in 1937 by the League of Nations. Tourism was defined as people travelling abroad for periods of over 24 hours.

The history of European tourism can perhaps be said to originate with the medieval pilgrimage. Although undertaken primarily for religious reasons, the pilgrims in the Canterbury Tales quite clearly saw the experience as a kind of holiday (the term itself being derived from the 'holy day' and its associated leisure activities). Pilgrimages created a variety of tourist aspects that still exist - bringing back souvenirs, obtaining credit with foreign banks (in medieval times utilising international networks established by Jews and Lombards), and making use of space available on existing forms of transport (such as the use of medieval English wine ships bound for Vigo by pilgrims to Santiago De Compostela). Pilgrimages of one sort or another are still important in modern tourism - such as to Lourdes or Knock in Ireland. But there are modern equivalents - Graceland and the grave of Jim Morrison in Pere Lachaise Cemetery.

In the course of the sixteenth century, it became fashionable in England to undertake a Grand Tour. The sons of the nobility and gentry were sent upon an extended tour of Europe as an educational experience. The eighteenth century was the golden age of the Grand Tour, and many of the fashionable visitors were painted at Rome by Pompeo Batoni. The modern equivalent of the Grand Tour is the phenomenon of the backpacker, although cultural holidays, such as those offered by Swann-Hellenic, are also important.

Health tourism has always existed, but it was not until the eighteenth century that it became important. In England, it was associated with spas, places with supposedly health-giving mineral waters, treating diseases from gout to liver disorders and bronchitis. Bath was the most fashionable resort, but Buxton, Harrogate, and Tunbridge Wells, amongst others, also flourished. Of course, people visited these places for the balls and other entertainments, just as much as 'the waters'. Continental Spas such as Karlsbad attracted many fashionable travellers by the nineteenth century.

It could be argued that Britain was the home of the seaside holiday. In travelling to the coast, the population was following in the steps of Royalty. King George III made regular visits to Weymouth when in poor health. At the time, a number of doctors argued the benefits of bathing in sea water, and sea bathing as a widespread practice was popularised by the Prince Regent (later George IV), who frequented Brighton for this purpose. Some English travellers, after visiting the warm lands of the south of Europe, decided to stay there either for the cold season or for the rest of their lives. Leisure travel was a British invention due to sociological factors. Britain was the first European country to industrialize, and the industrial society was the first society to offer time for leisure to a growing number of people. Initially, this did not apply to the working masses, but rather to the owners of the machinery of production, the economic oligarchy, the factory owners, and the traders. These comprised the new middle class. Cox and Kings were the first official travel company to be formed in 1758.

The British origin of this new industry is reflected in many place names. At Nice, one of the first and best-established holiday resorts on the French Riviera, the long esplanade along the seafront is known to this day as the Promenade des Anglais; in many other historic resorts in continental Europe, old well-established palace hotels have names like the Hotel Bristol, the Hotel Carlton or the Hotel Majestic - reflecting the dominance of English customers.

Winter Tourism

Winter sports were largely invented by the British leisured classes, initially at the Swiss village of Zermatt (Valais), and St Moritz in 1864.

The first packaged winter sports holidays (vacations) followed in 1903, to Adelboden, also in Switzerland.

Organized sport was well established in Britain before it reached other countries. The vocabulary of sport bears witness to this: rugby, football, and boxing all originated in Britain, and even Tennis, originally a French sport, was formalized and codified by the British, who hosted the first national championship in the nineteenth century, at Wimbledon. Winter sports were a natural answer for a leisured class looking for amusement during the coldest season.

Mass Travel

Mass travel could not really begin to develop until two things occurred.

- Improvements in technology allowed the transport of large numbers of people in a short space of time to places of leisure interest, and
- Greater numbers of people began to enjoy the benefits of leisure time.

The father of modern mass tourism was Thomas Cook who, on 5 July 1841, organized the first package tour in history. He arranged for the rail company to charge one shilling per person for a group of 570 temperance campaigners from Leicester to a rally in Loughborough, eleven miles away. Cook was paid a share of the fares actually charged to the passengers, as the railway tickets, being legal contracts between company and passenger, could not have been issued at his own price. There had been railway excursions before, but this one included entrance to an entertainment held in private grounds, rail tickets and food for the train journey. Cook immediately saw the potential of a convenient 'off the peg' holiday product in which everything was included in one cost. He organised packages inclusive of accommodation for the Great Exhibition, and afterwards pioneered package holidays in both Britain (particularly in Scotland) and on the European continent (where Paris and the Alps were the most popular destinations).

He was soon followed by others (the Polytechnic Touring Association, Dean and Dawson etc.), with the result that the tourist industry developed rapidly in late Victorian Britain. Initially it was supported by the growing middle classes, who had time off from their work, and who could afford the luxury of travel and possibly even staying for periods of time in boarding houses.

The Bank Holiday Act of 1871 introduced a statutory right for workers to take holidays, even if they were not paid at the time. By the last quarter of the nineteenth century, the tradition of the working class holiday had become firmly established in Britain. These were largely focussed upon the seaside resorts.

The spread of the railway network in the nineteenth century resulted in the growth of Britain's seaside towns by bringing them within easy distance of Britain's urban centres. Blackpool was created by the construction of a line to Fleetwood, and some resorts were promoted by the railway companies themselves - Morecambe by the Midland Railway and Cleethorpes by the Great Central Railway.

Other resorts included Scarborough in Yorkshire, servicing Leeds and Bradford; Weston-super-Mare in Somerset, catering for the inhabitants of Bristol; and Skegness, patronised by the residents of the industrial East Midlands. The cockneys of London flocked to Southend-on-Sea, mainly by Thames Steamer, and the South Coast resorts such as Broadstairs, Brighton, and Eastbourne were only a train ride away, with others further afield such as Bournemouth, Bognor Regis and Weymouth.

For a century, domestic tourism was the norm, with foreign travel being reserved for the rich or the culturally curious. A number of inland destinations, such as the English Lake District, and Snowdonia appealed to those who liked the countryside and fine scenery. The holiday camp began to appear in the 1930s, but this phenomenon really expanded in the post-war period. Butlins and Pontins set this trend, but their popularity waned with the rise of overseas package tours and the increasing comforts to which visitors became accustomed at home. Towards the end of the 20th century this market has been revived by the upmarket inland resorts of Dutch company Center Parcs.

Cox and Co, the forebear of Cox and Kings were in existence from 1758 largely entwined with the travel arrangements for the British Army serving around the Empire. While acting as 'agents' for various regiments, they organised the payment, provision, clothing and travel arrangements for members of the armed forces. In the 19th century their network of offices contained a banking and also travel department. The company became heavily involved with affairs in India and its Shipping Agency had offices in France and the Middle East.

Other phenomena that helped develop the travel industry were paid holidays:

- 1.5 million manual workers in Britain had paid holidays by 1925
- 11 million by 1939 (30% of the population in families with paid holidays)

International Mass Tourism

Increasing speed on railways meant that the tourist industry could develop internationally.

To this may be added the development of sea travel. By 1901, the number of people crossing the English Channel from England to France or Belgium had passed 0.5 million per year. Shipping companies were anxious to fill cabin space that was under utilised. For example, PandO found that the majority of their passengers for India and the Far East joined the ship at Marseilles. Consequently, they marketed holidays based upon sea trips from London to Lisbon and Gibraltar. Other companies diverted their older ships to operate cruises in the summer months.

However, the real age of international mass travel began with the growth of air travel after World War Two. In the immediate post-war period, there was a surplus of transport aircraft, such as the popular and reliable Douglas Dakota, and a number of ex military pilots ready to fly them. They were available for charter flights, and tour operators began to use them for European destinations, such as Paris and Ostend.

Vladimir Raitz pioneered modern package tourism when on 20 May 1950 his recently founded company, Horizon, provided arrangements for a two-week holiday in Corsica. For an all inclusive price of £32.10s.-, holiday makers could sleep under canvas, sample local wines and eat a meal containing meat twice a day - this was especially attractive due to the continuing austerity measures in post-war United Kingdom. Within ten years, his company had started mass tourism to Palma (1952), Lourdes (1953), Costa Brava (1954), Sardinia (1954), Minorca (1955), Porto (1956), Costa Blanca (1957) and Costa del Sol (1959).

However it was with cheap air travel in combination with the package tour that international mass tourism developed. The postwar introduction of an international system of airline regulation was another important factor. The bilateral agreements at the heart of the system fixed seat prices, and airlines could not fill blocks of empty seats on underused flights by discounting.

But if they were purchased by a tour operater and hidden within the price of an inclusive holiday package, it would be difficult to prove that discounting had taken place - even though it was obvious that it had! This was the origin of the modern mass package tour. These developments coincided with a significant increase in the standard of living in Britain. At the end of the 1950s, Harold Macmillan could say "you've never had it so good."

Another significant development also happened at the end of this decade. The devaluation of the Spanish peseta made Spain appear a particularly attractive destination. The cheapness of the cost of living attracted increasing numbers of visitors. Mass package tourism has at times been an exploitative process, in which tour operators in a country with a high standard of living make use of development opportunities and low operating costs in a country with a lower standard of living. However, as witness the development of many tourist areas in previously poor parts of the world, and the concomitant rise in standards of living, when there is equality of bargaining power, both parties can gain economic benefits from this arrangement. Spain and the Balearic Islands became major tourist destinations, and development probably peaked in the 1980s. At the same time, British tour operators developed the Algarve in Portugal. The continuing search for new, cheaper, destinations spread mass tourism to the Greek Islands, Italy, Tunisia, Morocco, parts of the coast of Turkey, and more recently Croatia. For the worker living in greater London, Venice today is almost as accessible as Brighton was 100 years ago. Consequently, the British seaside resort experienced a marked decline from the 1970s onwards. Some, such as New Brighton have disappeared. Others have reinvented themselves, and now cater to daytrippers and the weekend break market.

Recent Developments

There has been a discernible upmarket trend in tourism over the last few decades, especially in Europe where international travel for short breaks is commonplace. Tourists have higher levels of disposable income and greater leisure time. They are also better educated and have more sophisticated tastes. There is now a demand for a better quality product in many quarters. This has resulted in the following trends:-

- The old 'sun, sea, and sand' mass market has fragmented. People want more specialised versions of it, such as 'Club 18-30', quieter resorts with select hotels, self-catering, etc.
- People are taking second holidays in the form of short breaks/city breaks, ranging from British and European cities to country hotels.
- There has been a growth in niche markets catering for special interests or activities, including growth of destination hotels.

The developments in technology and transport infrastructure (particularly the advent of jumbo jets) have placed some types of holiday in the affordable mainstream:-

- The development of a mass cruise holiday market.
- The advent of affordable holidays to long-haul destinations such as Thailand or Kenya.
- The phenomenon of the low budget airline, utilising a new generation of small regional airports.

There have also been changes in lifestyle, which may call into question the current definitions of tourism. Some people (particularly the 45+ and retired) may be adopting a tourism lifestyle, living as a tourist all the year round - eating out several times a week, going to the theatre, daytripping, and indulging in short breaks several times a year.

Much of this results in impulse purchasing. This is facilitated by internet purchasing of tourism products. Some sites have now started to offer dynamic packaging, in which an inclusive price is quoted for a tailor- made package requested by the customer upon impulse.

There have been a few setbacks in tourism, such as the September 11, 2001 attacks and terrorist threats to tourist destinations such as Bali and European cities. Some of the tourist destinations, including the Costa del Sol, the Baleares and Cancún have lost popularity due to shifting tastes. In this context, the excessive building and environmental destruction often associated with traditional "sun and beach" tourism may contribute to a destination's saturation and subsequent decline. This appears to be the case with Spain's Costa Brava, a byword for this kind of tourism in the 1960s and 1970s. With only 11% of the Costa Brava now unblemished by low-quality development (Greenpeace Spain's figure), the destination now faces a crisis in its tourist industry.

Sustainable tourism is becoming more popular as people start to realize the devastating effects tourism can have on communities.

Receptive tourism is now growing at a very rapid rate in many developing countries, where it is often the most important economic activity in local GDP.

In recent years, second holidays or vacations have become more popular as people's discretionary income increases. Typical combinations are a package to the typical mass tourist resort, with a winter skiing holiday or weekend break to a city or national park.

On December 26, 2004 a tsunami, caused by the 2004 Indian Ocean earthquake hit Asian countries bordering the Indian Ocean, and also the Maldives. Tens of thousands of lives were lost, and many tourists died. This, together with the vast clean-up operation in place, has stopped or severely hampered tourism to the area.

SPECIAL FORMS OF TOURISM

Adventure Tourism

Adventure tourism is a type of tourism involving exploration or travel to remote areas, where the traveler should expect the unexpected. Adventure tourism is rapidly growing in popularity as tourists seek unusual holidays, different from the typical beach vacation.

Adventure tourism typically involves traveling into remote, inaccessible and possibly hostile areas. It may include the performance of acts that require significant effort and grit and may also involve some degree of risk. Adventure Tourism becoming more and more Famous specially among youth. India is not a country but a world in itself. Here one can find World's biggest river for rafting and endless mountains for trekking. It is a country who have somthing for every kind of Adventure lover.

For Mountainerring and Trekking one can go to Sikkim, the home of mighty Kunchnjanga and situated within eastern himalayas. Jummu and Kashmir the heaven on earth.The place for Ski loversand wonderful for backpackers.Himachal one of the best sites for Pargaliding in World and famous for beautiful gentle hills and Where glaciers are not far from mainland. Uttranchal a place where every single person wants to go, famous for valley of flowers and for Shiva Dhams and Last but not least Leh and Ladakh the cold deasert of India a place where one cannot find Trees and find really cold and different culture much closer to Tibtian clutre and a starting point for Extreame tourism lovers who want to travel beyond the main land towards zanskar and nubra velleys.For Rafting India is heaven the rivers like Ganga,Teesta,and Brahamaputra provide rafters a real thrill and challange. Rafting is becoming very popular among the corporates combined with Stay in riverside resorts and team building exercises.

Mountaineering

Mountaineering is the sport, hobby or profession of walking, hiking and climbing up mountains. It is also sometimes known as alpinism, particularly in Europe. It may be said to consist of two main aspects, rock-craft and snow-craft, depending on whether the route chosen is over rock or over snow and ice. Both require great gymnastic and technical ability, but experience is also a very important part of the latter. Training in these areas for several months enhances a person's abilities and increases their chances for survival while climbing.

Hazards

The craft of climbing has been developed to avoid two main types of danger: the danger of things falling on the traveller and the danger of the climber falling himself. The things that may fall include rocks, ice, snow, other climbers or their gear; the mountaineer may fall from rocks, ice or snow, or into crevasses in ice or snow. There are also dangers from weather. In all, there are eight chief dangers: falling rocks, falling ice, snow-avalanches, falls from difficult rocks, falls from ice slopes, falls down snow slopes, falls into crevasses and dangers from weather. To select and follow a route avoiding these dangers is to exercise the climber's craft.

Falling Rocks

Every rock mountain is slowly disintegrating due to erosion, the process being especially rapid above the snow-line. Rock faces are constantly swept by falling stones, which are generally possible to dodge. Falling rocks tend to form furrows in a mountain face, and these furrows (couloirs) have to be ascended with caution, their sides often being safe when the middle is stoneswept. Rocks fall more frequently on some days than on others, according to the recent weather. Ice formed during the night may temporarily bind rocks to the face but warmth of the day or direct sun exposure may easily dislodge these rocks. Local experience is a valuable help on determining typical rockfall on such routes.

The direction of the dip of rock strata often determines the degree of danger on a particular face; the character of the rock must also be considered. Where stones fall frequently debris will be found below, whilst on snow slopes falling stones cut furrows visible from a great distance. In planning an ascent of a new peak mountaineers must look for such traces. When falling stones get mixed in considerable quantity with slushy snow or water a mud avalanche is formed (common in the Himalaya). It is vital to avoid camping in their possible line of fall.

Falling ice

The places where ice may fall can always be determined beforehand. It falls in the broken parts of glaciers (seracs) and from overhanging cornices formed on the crests of narrow ridges. Large icicles are often formed on steep rockfaces, and these fall frequently in fine weather following cold and stormy days. They have to be avoided like falling stones. Seracs are slow in formation, and slow in arriving (by glacier motion) at a condition of unstable equilibrium. They generally fall in or just after the hottest part of the day, and their debris seldom goes far. A skillful and experienced ice-man will usually devise a safe route through a most intricate ice-fall, but such places should be avoided in the afternoon of a hot day. Hanging glaciers (*i.e.* glaciers perched on steep slopes) often discharge themselves over steep rock-faces, the snout breaking off at intervals. They can always be detected by their debris below. Their track should be avoided.

Avalanches

The avalanche is the most underestimated danger in the mountains. People generally think that they will be able to recognise the hazards and survive being caught. The truth is a somewhat different story. Every year, 120 - 150 people die in small avalanches in the Alps alone. The vast majority are reasonably experienced male skiers aged 20-35 but also include ski instructors and guides. There is always a lot of pressure to risk a snow crossing. Turning back takes a lot of extra time and effort, supreme leadership, and most importantly there seldom is an avalanche to prove the right decision was made. Making the decision to turn around is especially hard if others are crossing the slope, but any next person could become the trigger.

There are different types of avalanche:

1. The slab avalanche: This type of avalanche occurs when a plate of snow breaks loose and starts sliding down; these are the largest and most dangerous.
2. Hard slab avalanche - formed by hard-packed snow in a cohesive slab. The slab will not break up easily as it slides down the hill, resulting in large blocks tumbling down the mountain.
3. Soft slab avalanche - formed again by a cohesive layer of snow bonded together, the slab tends to break up more easily.
4. The loose snow avalanche: This type of avalanche is triggered by a small amount of moving snow that accumulates into a big slide. Also known as a "wet slide or point release" avalanche. This type of avalanche is deceptively dangerous as it can still knock a climber or skier off their feet and bury them, or sweep them over a cliff into a terrain trap.

Dangerous slides are most likely to occur on the same slopes preferred by many skiers: long and wide open, few trees or large rocks, 30 to 45 degrees of angle, large load of fresh snow, soon after a big storm, on a slope 'lee to the storm'. Solar radiation can trigger slides as well. These will typically be a point release or wet slough type of avalanche. The added weight of the wet slide can trigger a slab avalanche. Ninety percent of reported victims are caught in avalanches triggered by themselves or others in their group.

When going off-piste or travelling in alpine terrain, parties have a moral responsibility to always carry:

1. Avalanche beacons
2. Probes
3. Shovels (retrieving victims with a shovel instead of your hands is five times faster)

Paradoxically, expert skiers who have avalanche training make up a large percentage of avalanche fatalities; perhaps because they are the ones more likely to ski in areas prone to avalanches.

Even with proper rescue equipment and training, there is a one-in-five chance of dying if caught in a significant avalanche, and only a 50/50 chance of being found alive if buried more than a few minutes. The best solution is to learn how to avoid risky conditions.

Falls from Rocks

The skill of a rock climber is shown by one's choice of handhold and foothold, and his adhesion to those one has chosen. Much depends on a correct estimate of the firmness of the rock where weight is to be thrown upon it.

Many loose rocks are quite firm enough to bear a person's weight, but experience is needed to know which can be trusted, and skill is required in transferring the weight to them without jerking. On rotten rocks the rope must be handled with special care, lest it should start loose stones on to the heads of those below. Similar care must be given to handholds and footholds, for the same reason. When a horizontal traverse has to be made across very difficult rocks, a dangerous situation may arise unless at both ends of the traverse there be firm positions. Mutual assistance on hard rocks takes all manner of forms: two, or even three, people climbing on one another's shoulders, or using for foothold an ice axe propped up by others. The great principle is that of co-operation, all the members of the party climbing with reference to the others, and not as independent units; each when moving must know what the climber in front and the one behind are doing. After bad weather steep rocks are often found covered with a veneer of ice (verglas), which may even render them inaccessible. Crampons are useful on such occasions.

For travel on slopes consisting of ice or hard snow, crampons are a standard part of a mountaineer's equipment. While step-cutting can sometimes be used on snow slopes of moderate angle, this can be a slow and tiring process, which does not provide the higher security of crampons. However, in soft snow or powder, crampons are easily hampered by balling of snow which reduce their effectiveness. In either case, an ice axe not only assists with balance but provides the climber with the possibility of self-arrest in case of a slip or fall. On a true ice slope however, an ice axe is rarely able to effect a self-arrest. As an additional safety precaution on steep ice slopes, the climbing rope is attached to ice screws buried into the ice.

True ice slopes are rare in Europe, though common in mountains located in the tropics, where newly-fallen snow quickly thaws on the surface and becomes sodden below, so that the next night's frost turns the whole mass into a sheet of semi-solid ice.

Snow Slopes

Snow slopes are very common, and usually easy to ascend. At the foot of a snow or ice slope is generally a big crevasse, called a bergschrund, where the final slope of the mountain rises from a snow-field or glacier. Such bergschrunds are generally too wide to be stepped across, and must be crossed by a snow bridge, which needs careful testing and a painstaking use of the rope. A steep snow slope in bad condition may be dangerous, as the whole body of snow may start as an avalanche. Such slopes are less dangerous if ascended directly than obliquely, for an oblique or horizontal track cuts them across and facilitates movement of the mass. New snow lying on ice is especially dangerous. Experience is needed for deciding on the advisability of advancing over snow in doubtful condition. Snow on rocks is usually rotten unless it is thick; snow on snow is likely to be sound. A day or two of fine weather will usually bring new snow into sound condition. Snow cannot lie at a very steep angle, though it often deceives the eye as to its slope. Snow slopes seldom exceed 40°. Ice slopes may be much steeper. Snow slopes in early morning are usually hard and safe, but the same in the afternoon are quite soft and possibly dangerous; hence the advantage of an early start.

Crevasses

Crevasses are the slits or deep chasms formed in the substance of a glacier as it passes over an uneven bed. They may be open or hidden. In the lower part of a glacier the crevasses are open. Above the snow-line they are frequently hidden by arched-over accumulations of winter snow. The detection of hidden crevasses requires care and experience. After a fresh fall of snow they can only be detected by sounding with the pole of the ice axe, or by looking to right and left where the open extension of a partially hidden crevasse may be obvious. The safeguard against accident is the rope, and no one should ever cross a snow-covered glacier unless roped to one, or even better to two companions. Anyone venturing onto crevasses should be trained in crevasse rescue.

Weather

The primary dangers caused by bad weather centre around the changes it causes in snow and rock conditions, making movement suddenly much more arduous and hazardous than under normal circumstances. Whiteouts make it difficult to retrace a route while rain may prevent taking the easiest line only determined as such under dry conditions. In a storm the mountaineer who uses a compass for guidance has a great advantage over a merely empirical observer. In large snow-fields it is, of course, easier to go wrong than on rocks, but intelligence and experience are the best guides in safely navigating objective hazards.

Summer thunderstorms may produce intense lightning which are attracted to the highest points on the ground. If a climber happens to be standing on or near the summit, they may now in fact be the highest point. There are many cases where people have been struck by lightning while climbing mountains. In most mountainous regions, local storms develop by late morning and early afternoon. Many climbers will often begin ascents "alpine style"; that is before or by first light so as to be on the way down when storms are intensifying in activity and lightning and other weather hazards are a distinct threat to safety.

Altitude

Rapid ascent can lead to altitude sickness. The best treatment is to descend immediately. The climber's motto at high altitude is "climb high, sleep low", referring to the regimen of climbing higher to acclimatize but returning to lower elevation to sleep. In the South American Andes, the chewing of coca leaves has been traditionally used to treat altitude sickness symptoms.Common symptoms of altitude sickness include severe headache, sleep problems, nausea, lack of appetite, lethargy and body ache. Mountain sickness may progress to HACE (High Altitude Cerebral Edema) and HAPE (High Altitude Pulmonary Edema), both of which can be fatal within 24 hours.

In high mountains, atmospheric pressure is lower and this means that less oxygen is available to breathe. This is the underlying cause of altitude sickness. Everyone needs to acclimatize, even exceptional mountaineers that have been to high altitude before. Generally speaking, mountaineers start using bottled oxygen when they climb above 7,000 m. Exceptional mountaineers have climbed 8000-meter peaks (including Everest) without oxygen, almost always with a carefully planned Programme of acclimatization.

In 2005, researcher and mountaineer John Semple established that above-average ozone concentrations on the Tibetan plateau may pose an additional risk to climbers.

Backpacking

Backpacking (also tramping or trekking or bushwalking in some countries) combines hiking and camping in a single trip. A backpacker hikes into the backcountry to spend one or more nights there, and carries supplies and equipment to satisfy sleeping and eating needs.

A backpacker packs all of his or her gear into a backpack. This gear must include food, water, and shelter, or the means to obtain them, but very little else, and often in a more compact and simpler form than one would use for stationary camping. A backpacking trip must include at least one overnight stay in the wilderness (otherwise it is a day hike). Many backpacking trips last just a weekend (one or two nights), but long-distance expeditions may last weeks or months, sometimes aided by planned food and supply drops.

Backpacking camps are more spartan than ordinary camps. In areas that experience a regular traffic of backpackers, a hike-in camp might have a fire ring and a small wooden bulletin board with a map and some warning or information signs. Many hike-in camps are no more than level patches of ground without scrub or underbrush. In very remote areas, established camps do not exist at all, and travelers must choose appropriate camps themselves.

In some places, backpackers have access to lodging that are more substantial than a tent. In the more remote parts of Great Britain, bothies exist to provide simple (free) accommodation for backpackers. Another example is the High Sierra Camps in Yosemite National Park. Mountain huts provide similar accommodation in other countries, so being a member of a mountain hut organization is advantageous (perhaps required) to make use of their facilities. On another trails (*e.g.* the Appalaichian Trail) there are somewhat more established shelters of a sort that offer a place for weary hikers to spend the night without needing to set up a tent. Most backpackers purposely try to avoid impacting on the land through which they travel. This includes following established trails as much as possible, not removing anything, and not leaving trash in the backcountry. The Leave No Trace movement offers a set of guidelines for low-impact backpacking ("Leave nothing but footprints. Take nothing but photos.").

Why People Backpack

People are drawn to backpacking primarily for recreation, to explore places that they consider beautiful and fascinating, many of which cannot be accessed in any other way. A backpacker can travel deeper into remote areas, away from people and their effects, than a day-hiker. However, backpacking presents more advantages besides distance of travel. Many weekend trips cover routes that could be hiked in a single day, but people choose to backpack them anyway, for the experience of staying overnight.

These possibilities come with disadvantages. The weight of a pack, laden with supplies and gear, forces backpackers to travel more slowly than day-hikers would, and it can become a nuisance and a distraction from enjoying the scenery. In addition, camp chores (such as pitching camp, breaking camp, and cooking) can easily consume several hours every day.

Backpackers face many risks, including adverse weather, difficult terrain, treacherous river crossings, and hungry or unpredictable animals. They are subject to illnesses, which run the gamut from simple dehydration to heat exhaustion, hypothermia, altitude sickness, and physical injury. The remoteness of backpacking locations exacerbates any mishap. However, these hazards do not deter backpackers. Some simply accept danger as a risk that they must endure if they want to backpack; for others, the potential dangers actually enhance the allure of the wilderness.

Equipment

Almost all backpackers seek to minimize the weight and bulk of gear carried. A lighter pack causes less fatigue, injury and soreness, and allows the backpacker to travel longer distances. Every piece of equipment is evaluated for a balance of utility versus weight. Significant reductions in weight can usually be achieved with little sacrifice in equipment utility, though very lightweight equipment is often more costly.

A large industry has developed to provide lightweight gear and food for backpackers. The gear includes the backpacks themselves, as well as ordinary camping equipment modified to reduce the weight, by either reducing the size, reducing the durability, or using lighter materials such as special plastics, alloys of aluminium, and titanium, or making them consumable such as sleeping bags made of processed paper which can be burned. Designers of portable stoves and tents have been particularly ingenious. Homemade gear is common too, such as the beverage-can stove.

Some backpackers use lighter and more compact gear than do others. The most radical measures taken in this regard are sometimes called ultralight backpacking.

Due to the emphasis on weight reduction, a practical joke common in some circles is to secretly pack a small but relatively heavy luxury item, such as a soft drink, into another backpacker's pack. Then, once the group stops for a rest, the perpetrator retrieves the item, thanks the bearer for carrying it, and consumes it.

Backpackers always carry some water from the trailhead, to drink while walking. For short trips, they may carry enough to last the whole trip, but for long trips this is not practical. A backpacker needs anywhere from two to eight liters or more per day, depending on conditions, making a water supply for more than a few days is prohibitively heavy.

Backpackers typically carry two to four liters of water depending on conditions and availability. Although some backpacking camps in heavily-used areas provide potable water, it must usually be obtained from lakes and streams.

Drinking and cooking water nearly always needs treatment with a filter or purifier to protect against bacteria and protozoa. If water is unavailable, or if the only water available is irreparably filthy, backpackers may need to carry large amounts of water for long distances.

Water may be stored in bottles or in soft, collapsible hydration packs (bladders). Some backpackers store water in ordinary plastic beverage bottles, while others use special Lexan bottles or metal canteens. For accessibility they may be carried by a shoulder strap or attached to the outside of a pack.

Bladders are typically made of plastic, rubber, and/or fabric. They are light, easily stored and collapsible. They may be equipped with drinking hoses for easy access while hiking. In spite of this convenience, bladders are more prone to leaking than bottles, particularly at the hose connections. Hoses also allow the hiker to lose track of the water supply in the bladder and to deplete it prematurely.

Some backpackers enjoy cooking elaborate meals with fresh ingredients, particularly on short trips, and others carry the gear and take the time to catch fish or hunt small game for food. However, especially for long expeditions, most backpackers' food criteria are roughly the same: high energy content (particularly protein), with long shelf life and low mass and volume.

Ordinary household foods used on backpacking trips include cheese, bread, sausage, fruit, peanut butter, and pasta. Popular snack foods include trail mix, easily prepared at home; convenient and nutritious energy bars; and chocolate and other forms of candy, which provide quick energy and flavor. Traditional outdoor food includes dried foodstuffs such as jerky or pemmican, and also products like oatmeal (which can also be consumed raw in emergency situations).

Most backpackers avoid canned food, except for meats or small delicacies. Metal cans and their contents are usually heavy, and, like all trash, the empties must be carried back out.

For dinners, many hikers use specially manufactured, pre-cooked food that can be eaten hot. It is often sold in large, stiff bags that double as eating vessels. One common variety of special backpacking food is freeze-dried food, which can be quickly reconstituted by adding hot water.

One can also purchase a commercial food dehydrator which removes the majority of water from a pre-cooked meal. To eat, water is mixed in with the meal several hours before eating and allowed to rehyrdate before heating. Some various distributors of this are Backpackers Pantry and Mountain Outfitters. Another kind of special backpacking food is UHT-packaged without dehydration, and can be reheated with a special, water-activated chemical heater. This technology originated with the U.S. military's Meal Ready-to-Eat ("MRE"), but is now produced also for the commercial market. The small chemical heater obviates the need for a portable stove and fuel, but the meals and packaging weigh so much that, for more than a few meals, there is no weight advantage.

Winter Backpacking

Although backpacking in the winter is rewarding, it can be dangerous and generally requires more gear. Backpackers may need skis or snowshoes to traverse deep snow, or crampons to cross ice. Cotton clothing, which absorbs moisture and chills the body, is particularly dangerous in cold weather, so backpackers stick to synthetic materials or materials that won't hold moisture. Special low-temperature sleeping bags and tents can be expensive, but will be more comfortable than many layers of warm clothing.

However when hiking in cold weather it is always better to hike with varying layers of clothing so that as the body heats up layers can be taken off without causing to wearer to sweat or become very chilled.

Skills and Safety

- Survival skills are handy for peace of mind: In case the weather, terrain or environment is more challenging than prepared for, or for dealing with shortcomings in.
- Navigation and orienteering are useful to find the trailhead, then find and follow a route to a desired sequence of destinations, and then an exit. In case of disorientation, orienteering skills are important to determine where you are and formulate a route to somewhere more desirable. At their most basic, navigation skills allow you to choose the correct sequence of trails to follow.

- First Aid: effectively dealing with minor injuries (splinters, punctures, sprains) is considered by many a fundamental backcountry skill. More subtle, but maybe even more important, is recognizing and promptly treating hypothermia, heat stroke, dehydration and hypoxia, as these are rarely encountered in daily life.
- Leave No Trace is the backpacker's version of the golden rule: To have beautiful and pristine places to enjoy, help make them. At a minimum, don't make them worse.
- Distress signaling is a skill of last resort.

Agritourism

Agritourism is a style of vacation in which hospitality is offered on farms. This may include the opportunity to assist with farming tasks during the visit. Agritourism is often practiced in wine growing regions, as in Italy, France and Spain. In America, Agritourism is wide-spread and includes any farm open to the public at least part of the year.

Tourists can pick fruits and vegetables, ride horses, taste honey, learn about wine, shop in gift shops and farm stands for local and regional produce or hand-crafted gifts, and much more. Each farm generally offers a unique and memorable experience suitable for the entire family.

Agritourism is being developed as a valuable component of a business model to support many agricultural entities when the farm products they produce are no longer economically competitive otherwise.

To help promote the single agritourism operations, farms get together and form festivals or tours, such as Agri-tours, a two-weekend festival in September celebrating the lower Ottawa Valley's unique farms. This festival includes over a dozen non-traditional farms that specialize in everything from deer and pheasant, to apples and wine.

People are more interested in how their food is produced and want to meet the producers and talk with them about what goes into food production. Children who visit the farms often have not seen a live duck, or goat, and have not picked an apple right off the tree. This form of expanded agri-tourism has given birth to what are often called "entertainment farms." These farms cater to the pick-your-own crowd, offering not only regular farm products, but also food, mazes, open-pen animals, train rides, picnic facilities and pick-your-own produce.

Dude ranches offer tourists the chance to work on cattle ranches and sometimes include cattle drives.

CULTURAL TOURISM

Cultural tourism tourism and ecotourism, the number of living cultural areas is continually droping off. For an indigenous culture that has stayed largely separated from the surrounding majority culture, tourism can present both advantages and problems on to it. On the positive side are the unique cultural practices and arts that attract the curiosity of tourists and provide opportunities for tourism and economic development. On the negative side is the issue of how to control tourism so that those same cultural amenities are not destroyed and the people do not feel violated.

Destination Planning Resources

Planning Guides

It is important that the destination planner takes into account the diverse definition of culture as the term is subjective. Satisfying tourists' interests such as landscapes, seascapes, art, nature, traditions, ways of life and other products associated to them -which may be categorized cultural in the broadest sense of the word, is a prime consideration as it marks the initial phase of the development of a cultural destination.

The quality of service and destination, which doesn't solely depend on the cultural heritage but more importantly to the cultural environment, can further be developed by setting controls and policies which shall govern the the community and its stakeholders. It is therefore safe to say that the planner should be on the ball with the varying meaning of culture itself as this fuels the formulation of development policies that shall entail efficient planning and monitored growth *(e.g. strict policy on the protection and preservation of the community)*.

Local Community, Tourists,the Destination and Sustainable Tourism

While satisfying tourists' interests and demands may be a top priority, it is also imperative to ruminate the subsystems of the destinatons (residents). Development pressures should be anticipated and set to their minimun level so as to conserve the area's resources and prevent a saturation of the destination as to not abuse the product and the residents correspondingly. The plan should incorporate the locals to its gain by training and employing them and in the process encourage them to participate to the travel business. Keep in mind that the plan should make travellers not only aware about the destination but also concern on how to help it sustain its character while broadening their travelling experience.

Planning Tools

Sources of Data

The core of a planner's job is to design an appropriate planning process and facilitate community decision. Ample information which is a crucial requirement is contributed through various technical researches and analyses. Here are some of the helpful tools commonly used by planners to aid them:

1. Key Informant Interviews
2. Libraries, Internet, and Survey Research
3. Census and Statistical Analysis
4. Spatial Analysis with Geographical Information System (GIS) and Global Positioning System (GPS) technologies

Key Institutions

Participating structures are primarily led by the government's local authorities and the official tourism board or council, with the involvement of various NGOs, community and indigenous representatives, development organizations, and the academe.

Tourism is coming to the previously isolated but spectacular mountainous regions of Central Asia, the Hindu Kush and the Himalayas. Closed for so many years to visitors from abroad, it now attracts a growing number of foreign tourists by its unique culture and splendid natural beauty. However, while this influx of tourists is bringing economic opportunities and employment to local populations, helping to promote these little-known regions of the world, it has also brought challenges along with it: to ensure that it is well-managed and that its benefits are shared by all.

As a response to this concern, the Norwegian Government, as well as the UNESCO, organized an interdisciplinary project called the Development of Cultural and Eco-tourism in the Mountainous Regions of Central Asia and the Himalayas project. It aims to establish links and promote cooperation between local communities, national and international NGOs, and tour agencies in order to heighten the role of the local community and involve them fully in the employment opportunities and income-generating activities that tourism can bring. Project activities include training local tour guides, producing high-quality craft items and promoting home-stays and bed-and-breakfast type accommodation.

As of now, the project is drawing on the expertise of international NGOs and tourism professionals in the seven participating countries, making a practical and positive contribution to alleviating poverty by helping local communities to draw the maximum benefit from their region's tourism potential, while protecting the environmental and cultural heritage of the region concerned.

HERITAGE TOURISM

Cultural heritage tourism is a branch of tourism oriented towards the cultural heritage. Culture has always been a major object of travel, as the development of the Grand Tour from the 16th century onwards attests. In the 20th century, some people have claimed, culture ceased to be the objective of tourism: tourism is now culture. Cultural attractions play an important role in tourism at all levels, from the global highlights of world culture to attractions that underpin local identities.

According to the Weiler and Hall, culture, heritage and the arts have long contributed to appeal of tourist destination. However, in recent years 'culture' has been rediscovered as an important marketing tool to attract those travellers with special interests in heritage and arts. According to the Hollinshead, cultural heritage tourism defines as cultural heritage tourism is the fastest growing segment of the tourism industry because there is a trend Towards an increase specialization among tourist. This trend is evident in the rise in the volume of tourists who seek adventure, culture, history, archaeology and interaction with local people.

Cultural heritage tourism is important for various reasons; it has a positive economic and social impact, it establishes and reinforces identity, it helps preserve the cultural heritage, with culture as an instrument it facilitates harmony and understanding among people, it supports culture and helps renew tourism.

Cultural heritage tourism has a number of objectives that must be met within the context of sustainable development such as; the conservation of cultural resources, accurate interpretation of resources, authentic visitors experience, and the stimulation of the earned revenues of cultural resources. We can see therefore, that cultural heritage tourism is not only concerned with identification, management and protection of the heritage values but it must also be involved in understanding the impact of tourism on communities and regions, achieving economic and social benefits, providing financial resources for protection, as well as marketing and promotion.

Heritage tourism involves visiting historical or industrial sites that may include old canals, railways, battlegrounds, etc. The overall purpose is to gain an appreciation of the past. It also refers to the marketing of a location to members of a diaspora who have distant family roots there.

Heritage tourism is distinct from visiting a family member in a faraway place because the connection to the original homeland is removed; a recent Irish immigrant to the US, for example, may return home to see relatives but would probably not be considered a heritage tourist.

On the other hand, an Irish-American whose family emigrated in the 19th century, also going to Ireland but rather to see the country generally, would be partaking in heritage tourism.

This is particularly relevant to European areas where large numbers of people emigrated to North America in the 19th century and early 20th century. People from Quebec have been moving back and forth to France for centuries in fairly significant numbers, as have their counterparts with ties to the British Isles and other countries for more recent immigrants. Other examples include Black/African Americans who visit Africa and Hispanics who visit Spain.

The purpose can be education, fun, marriage, employment, etc. Permanent emigration tied to heritage tourism is less common but increasing.Decolonization and immigration form the major background of much contemporary heritage tourism. Falling travel costs have also made heritage tourism possible for more people.

Another possible form involves religious travel or pilgrimages. Many Catholics from around the world come to the Vatican and other sites such as Lourdes or Fatima. Large numbers of Jews have both visited Israel and emigrated there. Many have also gone to Holocaust sites and memorials. Islam commands its followers to take the hajj to Mecca, thus differentiating it somewhat from tourism in the usual sense, though the trip can also be a culturally important event for the pilgrim.

Heritage Tourism can also be attributed to historical events that have been dramatised to make them more entertaining. For example a historical tour of a town or city using a theme such as ghosts or vikings.

ECOTOURISM

Ecotourism means ecological tourism, where ecological has both environmental and social connotations. It is defined both as a concept-tourism movement and as a tourism (specifically sustainable tourism) section.

Born in its current form in the late 1980's, Ecotourism came of age in 2002, when the United Nations celebrated the "International Year of Ecotourism". The meeting was a watershed event, but it was not created with those who had pioneered the niche.

There are various definitions as this is a vibrant movement and ecotourism may be defined by its lack of definition.

Generally speaking, ecotourism focuses on local cultures, wilderness adventures, volunteering, personal growth and learning new ways to live on the planet. It is typically defined as travel to destinations where the flora, fauna, and cultural heritage are the primary attractions. Responsible ecotourism includes programs that minimize the adverse effects of traditional tourism on the natural environment, and enhance the cultural integrity of local people. Therefore, in addition to evaluating environmental and cultural factors, initiatives by hospitality providers to promote recycling, energy efficiency, water re-use, and the creation of economic opportunities for local communities are an integral part of ecotourism.

Many global environmental organizations and aid agencies favour ecotourism as a vehicle to sustainable development.

Ideally, true ecotourism should satisfy several criteria, such as

- Conservation (and justification for conservation) of biological diversity and cultural diversity, through ecosystems protection
- Promotion of sustainable use of biodiversity, by providing jobs to local populations
- Sharing of socio-economic benefits with local communities and

indigenous people by having their informed consent and participation in the management of ecotourism enterprises.

- Increase of environmental and cultural knowledge
- Minimisation of tourism's own environmental impact
- Affordability and lack of waste in the form of luxury
- Local culture, flora and fauna being the main attractions

For many countries, ecotourism is not so much seen as a marginal activity intended to finance protection of the environment than as a major sector of national economy and as a means of attracting tourists. For example, in countries such as Costa Rica, Ecuador, Nepal, Kenya, Madagascar and Antarctica, ecotourism represents a significant portion of the gross domestic product (or in Antarctica's case, economic activity).

The concept of ecotourism is widely misunderstood and, in practice, is often simply used as a marketing tool to promote tourism that is related to nature. Critics claim that ecotourism as practiced and abused often consists of placing a hotel in a splendid landscape, to the detriment of the ecosystem.

According to them, ecotourism must above all sensitize people with the beauty and the fragility of nature. They condemn some operators as "green-washing" their operations — that is, using the label of "ecotourism" and "green-friendly", while behaving in environmentally irresponsible ways.

Although academics argue about who can be classified as an ecotourist, and there is precious little statistical data, some estimate that more than five million ecotourists — the majority of the worldwide population — come from the United States, with other ecotourists coming from Europe, Canada and Australia.

Currently there are various moves to create national and international ecotourism certification programs, although the process is causing controversy. One example of ecoturism certificates has been put into place at Costa Rica, though the Programme has been dismissed as green-washing by others.

One criticism against ecotourism is that the air travel to often remote places is not included in the "environmental impact calculation". A journey to a place 10,000 kilometers away and home consumes about 700 litres of fuel per person. Another problem is that some of the destinations visited by ecotourists are extremely sensitive to environmental impact from human use (*e.g.* Antarctica, Amazonian Rain Forests, bird breeding colonies) and can be damaged even by careful travellers. A new form of tourism is called Clean Tourism.

ECOLOGICAL MASS TOURISM

When people think about the word 'Ecological Mass Tourism' they normally link it with negative thoughts of mass tourism that is associated with environmental degradation. The truth is we believe that Ecological Mass Tourism is beneficial for everyone, but in essence we must first understand what Ecological Mass Tourism actually encompasses: Mass Tourism: "refers to the steady stream of large numbers of tourists to holiday destinations." Ecotourism "nature based tourism involving the education and interpretation of the natural environment and is managed to be ecologically sustainable. This definition also recognises that 'natural environment' includes cultural components and that 'ecologically sustainable' involves an appropriate return to the local community and long term conservation of the resource" Ecotourists: are tourists who participate in different sorts of nature based tourism.

Furthermore "most ecotourists are often found to be residents of the developed world with above average incomes and educations." By integrating all 3 words into 1 we have constructed our definition of Ecological Mass Tourism or (EMT) for short. Ecological Mass Tourism or (EMT): are large numbers of educated tourists and ecotourists participating within the realms of diversified forms of managed ecotourism. EMT also attracts tourists who not only participate in ecotourism, but also recognise its cultural components and its involvement with giving a fitting return to the local community and long term conservation of the resource.

In properly defining EMT we believe that it is beneficial to all parties involved, and more importantly it can also be perceived to be sustainable. In addition to this EMT also has the ability to be managed properly and has definite infrastructure, cultural and social benefits linked Ecological Mass Tourism does not go against the principle of mass tourism on the basis that it contains financial, cultural and social benefits associated with its concept.

EnvirOnmentally Responsible Hotels

One component of ecotourism travelers can consider is environmentally responsible hotels. The concept of "green hotels"—hotels, motels, bed and breakfasts, lodges, and inns that use energy and other natural resources in environmentally responsible ways—is one that can be adopted not only by ecotourists but by anyone who travels, whether for business or pleasure. Hotels that adopt green practices help reduce the negative impact that hotel use has on the environment when they utilize renewable resources whenever possible, make efficient use of nonrenewable resources, and ensure that any byproducts that result from their operations are reused or recycled.

Examples of green practices some hotels have adopted include rerouting waste water to irrigate their golf courses and salvaging the sludge to use as fertilizer; reducing laundry water temperatures from 90 °C to 60 °C, replacing incandescent lights with compact fluorescent lamps, installing low-flow shower head and low-flow toilets, offering a sheet and towel reuse Programme whereby guests have their linens exchanged every two to three days instead of daily, installing solar panels to heat water, implementing a hotel-wide recycling Programme, and replacing individual soaps and lotions with wall dispensers.

Adoption of green practices typically helps hotels realize considerable savings that can range from several thousand to hundreds of thousands of dollars per year.

Although the number of hotels adopting green practices is growing, many have not yet embraced the concept. All travelers can support green hotels, encourage Non-green hotels to adopt environmentally responsible practices, or engage in such practices themselves whenever they are hotel guests.

Tourism event organizers can also distinguish themselves by explaining the criteria of where they stage events. Sadly, most ecotourism events have been held at hotels which have not distinguished themselves with green building, eco-efficient technology or community-friendly relations.

HERITAGE TOURISM

Cultural heritage tourism is a branch of tourism oriented towards the cultural heritage.

Culture has always been a major object of travel, as the development of the Grand Tour from the 16th century onwards attests. In the 20th century, some people have claimed, culture ceased to be the objcctive of tourism: tourism is now culture. Cultural attractions play an important role in tourism at all levels, from the global highlights of world culture to attractions that underpin local identities.

According to the Weiler and Hall, culture, heritage and the arts have long contributed to appeal of tourist destination. However, in recent years 'culture' has been rediscovered as an important marketing tool to attract those travellers with special interests in heritage and arts. According to the Hollinshead, cultural heritage tourism defines as cultural heritage tourism is the fastest growing segment of the tourism industry because there is a trend Towards an increase specialization among tourist. This trend is evident in the rise in the volume of tourists who seek adventure, culture, history, archaeology and interaction with local people.

Cultural heritage tourism is important for various reasons; it has a positive economic and social impact, it establishes and reinforces identity, it helps preserve the cultural heritage, with culture as an instrument it facilitates harmony and understanding among people, it supports culture and helps renew tourism.

Cultural heritage tourism has a number of objectives that must be met within the context of sustainable development such as; the conservation of cultural resources, accurate interpretation of resources, authentic visitors experience, and the stimulation of the earned revenues of cultural resources. We can see therefore, that cultural heritage tourism is not only concerned with identification, management and protection of the heritage values but it must also be involved in understanding the impact of tourism on communities and regions, achieving economic and social benefits, providing financial resources for protection, as well as marketing and promotion. Heritage tourism involves visiting historical or industrial sites that may include old canals, railways, battlegrounds, etc. The overall purpose is to gain an appreciation of the past. It also refers to the marketing of a location to members of a diaspora who have distant family roots there. Heritage tourism is distinct from visiting a family member in a faraway place because the connection to the original homeland is removed; a recent Irish immigrant to the US, for example, may return home to see relatives but would probably not be considered a heritage tourist. On the other hand, an Irish-American whose family emigrated in the 19th century, also going to Ireland but rather to see the country generally, would be partaking in heritage tourism.

This is particularly relevant to European areas where large numbers of people emigrated to North America in the 19th century and early 20th century. People from Quebec have been moving back and forth to France for centuries in fairly significant numbers, as have their counterparts with ties to the British Isles and other countries for more recent immigrants. Other examples include Black/African Americans who visit Africa and Hispanics who visit Spain.The purpose can be education, fun, marriage, employment, etc. Permanent emigration tied to heritage tourism is less common but increasing.

Decolonization and immigration form the major background of much contemporary heritage tourism. Falling travel costs have also made heritage tourism possible for more people.

Another possible form involves religious travel or pilgrimages. Many Catholics from around the world come to the Vatican and other sites such as Lourdes or Fatima. Large numbers of Jews have both visited Israel and emigrated there. Many have also gone to Holocaust sites and memorials. Islam commands its followers to take the hajj to Mecca, thus differentiating it somewhat from tourism in the usual sense, though the trip can also be a culturally important event for the pilgrim.

Heritage Tourism can also be attributed to historical events that have been dramatised to make them more entertaining. For example a historical tour of a town or city using a theme such as ghosts or vikings.

MEDICAL TOURISM

Medical tourism is the act of traveling to other countries to obtain medical, dental, and surgical care. The term was initially coined by travel agencies and the media as a catchall phrase to describe a rapidly growing industry where people travel to other countries to obtain medical care while at the same time touring, vacationing and enjoying the attractions of the countries which they are visiting. A combination of many factors has led to the recent increase in popularity of medical tourism: the high cost of Health care in industrialized nations, the ease and affordability of international travel, and the improvement of technology and standards of care in many countries of the world. A large draw to medical tourism is the convenience in comparison to that of other countries. Some countries that operate from a public health-care system are so taxed that it can take a considerable amount of time, sometimes even years, to get needed medical care.

The time spent waiting for a procedure, such as a hip replacement, can be a year or more in Britain and Canada; however, in Bangkok or Bangalore, a patient could feasibly have an operation the day after their arrival.

Above all else, the real lure to medical tourism is saving money on costly procedures. According to research found in an article by UDaily: the cost of surgery in India, Thailand or South Africa can be one-tenth of what it is in the United States or Western Europe, and sometimes even less. A heart-valve replacement that would cost US$200,000 or more in the U.S., for example, goes for $10,000 in India—and that includes round-trip airfare and a brief vacation package.

Similarly, a metal-free dental bridge worth $5,500 in the U.S. costs $500 in India, a knee replacement in Thailand with six days of physical therapy costs about one-fifth of what it would in the States, and Lasik eye surgery worth $3,700 in the U.S. is available in many other countries for only $730. Cosmetic surgery savings are even greater: A full facelift that would cost $20,000 in the U.S. runs about $1,250 in South Africa."

Medical tourists are generally residents of the industrialized nations of the world. The countries to which they travel are typically less developed and have a lower cost of medical care. This is, in some cases, due to favorable currency exchange ratios. Currently, many of the procedures accessed are considered "elective procedures," such as cosmetic surgery. Because elective procedures are rarely covered through health insurance plans, there may be greater incentive to find such care at lower costs.

The list of countries currently promoting medical tourism include:Bolivia, Brazil, Cuba, Costa Rica, Hungary, India, Israel, Jordan, Lithuania, Malaysia, The Philippines, and Thailand with the Joint Commission International accredited Bumrungrad Hospital. Belgium, Poland and Singapore are also breaking into the business. South Africa is taking the term "medical tourism" very literally by promoting their "medical safaris": Come to see African wildlife and get a facelift in the same trip. [2] However, feelings towards medical tourism are not always positive. In places like the US, where most have insurance and access to quality health care, medical tourism is viewed as risky.

While the tourism component might be a big draw for Southeast Asia countries that focus on simple procedures, India is positioning itself the primary medical destination for the most complex medical procedures in the world. India's commitment to this is demonstrated with an ever growing number of hospitals that are attaining the US Joint Commission International accreditation. Singapore has made international news for providing complex neurosurgical procedures. Currently Singapore boasts the largest number of US Joint Commission accredited hospitals in the region.

There are companies emerging to offer global Health care options that will allow North American patients to take full advantage of dramatic reductions in air travel and access world class Health care at a fraction of the cost. Companies that focus on 'Medical Value

Travel' typically will have experienced nurse case managers to assist patients with pre- and post-travel medical issues. They will also help provide resources for follow-up care upon the patient's return. While these services will initially be of interest to the self-insured patient, several studies indicate that the rapid growth of Health Savings Accounts will also drive interest to Health care in other countries.

India

India is one of the most touted destinations in the world for medical tourists. It is known in particular for heart surgery and hip resurfacing, areas of advanced medicine in which India is generally considered a global leader.

Probably no country has been in the news for medical tourism than India in 2005-06, and the government and private hospital groups both seem committed to a goal of making the subcontinent a world leader in the industry. Indian medical industry's main appeal is low-cost treatment. Most estimates claim treatment costs in India start at around a tenth of the price of comparable treatment in America or Britain. Morever Indian Hospitals also provides more personalized care than available in west.

For example, in April Madras Medical Mission, a Chennai-based hospital, successfully conducted a complex heart operation on an 87-year-old American patient at a reported cost of $8,000 (□7,000, £4,850) including the cost of his airfare and a month's stay in hospital.

The patient claimed that a less complex operation in America had earlier cost him $40,000. Take the rising popularity of "preventive health screening". At one private clinic in London a thorough men's health check-up that includes blood tests, electro-cardiogram tests, chest x-rays, lung tests and abdominal ultrasound costs £345. By comparison, a comparable check-up at a clinic operated by Delhi-based Health care company Max Health care costs $84.

Escorts Heart Institute and Research Center in Delhi and Faridabad, India performs nearly 15,000 heart operations every year, and the post-surgery mortality rate is only 0.8 percent, which is less than half of most major hospitals in the United States.Estimates of the value of medical tourism to India go as high as $2 billion a year by 2012. In 2003, Indian finance minister Jaswant Singh called for India to become a "global health destination".

Thailand

Medical tourism is a growing segment of Thailand's tourism and health-care sectors. Lower Labour costs translate into significant cost savings on procedures, compared to hospitals in the United States, and a higher, more personalized level of nursing care than Westerners are accustomed to receiving in hospitals back home. In 2005, one Bangkok hospital took in 150,000 treatment seekers from abroad. In 2006, medical tourism was projected to earn the country 36.4 billion baht.

One patient who received a coronary artery bypass surgery at Bumrungrad Hospital in Bangkok said the operation cost him US$12,000, as opposed to the $100,000 he estimated the operation would have cost him at home in the US.

Hospitals in Thailand are a popular destination for other Asians. Another hospital that caters to medical tourists, Bangkok General Hospital, has a Japanese wing. When Nepal Prime Minister Girija Prasad Koirala needed medical care in 2006, he went to Bangkok.

While it is not commonly known outside Thailand, the modern Thai medical system had its origins in the United States when Prince Mahidol of Songla, the King's father, earned his MD degree from Harvard Medical School in the early 20th century. Prince Mahidol and another member of the Thai Royal Family paid for an American medical education for a group of Thai men and women. Prince Mahidol also convinced the Rockefeller Foundation to provide scholarships for Thai citizens to study medicine and nursing. Funds from the Rockefeller Foundation were also used to help build modern medical training facilities in Thailand. The men and women who studied medicine and nursing as a result of Prince Mahidol's efforts became the first educators for the modern Thai medical system.

Today many Thai physicians hold US professional certification. A number of Thai hospitals have relationships with facilities in the US. The US Consular information sheet gives the Thai Health care system high marks for quality, particularly facilities in Bangkok. In Thailand, there is modern infrastructure, with clean, safe streets. According to the US Consular information sheets, the crime rate in Bangkok is lower than that of many US cities. Personal safety is another factor to consider when traveling abroad both for vacation as well as Health care. Thailand offers everything from cardiac surgery to organ transplants at a price much lower than the US or Europe, in a safe, clean environment.

Thailand has long been known as a preferred destination for medical tourists, and has a growing number of hospitals with JCAHO accreditation. Over one million people per year travel there for everything from cosmetic surgery to cutting edge cardiac treatment. Don Ho, the famous Hawaiian entertainer, recently received cutting-edge adult stem cell cardiac treatment at a Bangkok hospital. Six weeks later he had recovered sufficiently from his Non-ischemic cardiomyopathy and was able to return to the stage.

POP-CULTURE TOURISM

Pop-culture tourism is the act of traveling to locations featured in literature, film, music, or any other form of popular entertainment. Popular destinations have included the Iowa cornfields featured in Field of Dreams, New Zealand after The Lord of the Rings was filmed there, and The Louvre in which the book and movie The Da Vinci Code takes place. Prince Edward Island, in which the Canadian novel Anne of Green Gables takes place, is a popular attraction for tourists, notably from Japan.

Pop-culture tourism is in some respects akin to pilgrimage, with its modern equivalents of places of pilgrimage, such as Elvis Presley's Graceland and the grave of Jim Morrison in Père Lachaise Cemetery.

PILGRIMAGE TOURISM

A pilgrimage is a term primarily used in religion and spirituality of a long journey or search of great moral significance. Sometimes, it is a journey to a sacred place or shrine of importance to a person's beliefs and faith. Members of every religion participate in pilgrimages. A person who makes such a journey is called a pilgrim.

Secular and civic pilgrimages are also practiced, without regard for religion but rather of importance to a particular society. For example, many people throughout the world travel to the City of Washington in the United States for a pilgrimage to see the Declaration of Independence and the Constitution of the United States. British people often make pilgrimages to London for public appearances of the monarch of the United Kingdom.

Pop culture has also sought to redefine pilgrimages, defining a demoscene party as a pilgrimage.

History

Early Pilgrimage

Some of the oldest destinations for pilgrimages are in India. On the sacred river Ganges lies Benares, the holy city of Brahminism. Buddhism offers four sites of pilgrimage: the Buddha's birthplace at Kapilavastu, the site where he first preached at Gaya, where the highest insight dawned on him at Benares, and where he achieved Nirvana at Kusinagara.

In the kingdoms of Israel and Judah the visitation of certain ancient cult-centers was repressed in the 7th century BC, when the worship was restricted to Jahweh at the temple in Jerusalem. In Syria, the shrine of Astarte at the headwater spring of the river Adonis survived until it was destroyed by order of Emperor Constantine in the 4th century AD.

In mainland Greece, a stream of individuals made their way to Delphi or the oracle of Zeus at Dodona, and once every four years, at the period of the

Olympic games, the temple of Zeus at Olympia formed the goal of swarms of pilgrims from every part of the Hellenic world. When Alcxander the Great reached Egypt, he put his whole vast enterprise on hold, while he made his way with a small band deep into the Libyan desert, to consult the oracle of Ammun. During the imperium of his Ptolemaic heirs, the shrine of Isis at Philae received many votive inscriptions from Greeks on behalf of their kindred far away at home.

Pilgrimage in the Middle Ages

In the Middle Ages, even as early as the 4th century AD, Christian pilgrimage was regarded as a sacred obligation and a trial of one's faith, since travel was dangerous, expensive and time-consuming. A returning pilgrim was called a palmer, as they would wear two crossed palm leaves to show they had made the pilgrimage.

The anonymous "Pilgrim of Bordeaux" has left an itinerary of a pilgrimage to the Holy Land in 333. Empress Helena's discovery of the True Cross outside Jerusalem was the result of a pilgrimage. The Seven Sleepers of Ephesus attracted pilgrims, who left their graffiti in the catacomb.

In the West, Saint Martin of Tours and Martial of Limoges inspired building projects and an industry catering to pilgrims' requirements, including, in Martial's case, elaborately faked pious documentation (see Adhemar of Chabannes). The shrine of Santiago de Compostela in Spain lay at the end of the Way of St. James and a long connected string of pilgrims' sites. The city of Rome was also the destination of pilgrimage, by routes such as the Via Francigena, as the center of the Western Church. Popular destinations for pilgrimage in England included Bury St. Edmunds and Thomas Beckett's shrine at Canterbury, the destination of Chaucer's 14th century pilgrims in The Canterbury Tales. In the north, many pilgrims headed to the shrine of Saint Cuthbert of Lindisfarne.

Effects on Trade

Pilgrims contributed an important element to long-distance trade before the modern era, and brought prosperity to successful pilgrimage sites, an economic phenomenon unequalled until the tourist trade of the 20th century. Encouraging pilgrims was a motivation for assembling (and sometimes fabricating) relics and for writing hagiographies of local saints, filled with inspiring accounts of miracle cures. Lourdes and other modern pilgrimage sites keep this spirit alive.

Modern Pilgrimage

Pilgrimages are still made throughout the world: modern-day pilgrimages include the Way of St. James, the Hajj, and the pilgrimage to Mount Kailash. In modern usage, the terms pilgrim and pilgrimage can also have a somewhat devalued meaning as they are often applied in a secular context. For example, fans of Elvis Presley may choose to visit his home, Graceland, in Memphis, Tennessee. Similarly one may refer to a cultural center such as Venice as a "tourists' Mecca".

Pilgrimage Centres In Various Times and Cultures

Many ancient religions had holy sites, temples and groves, where pilgrimages were made.

- Karnak, Egypt.
- Thebes, Egypt.
- Kurukshetra, India
- Delphi, Greece. Oracle.
- Dodona, Epirus, Greece. Oracle.
- Ephesus Temple of Diana.
- Baalbek Lebanon.

Ayyavazhi

The prilgrim centers of Ayyavazhi is Panchappathis. But nowadays in addition the Avatharappathi and Vakaippathi were also becoming important though not equal to Panchappathis. All of them but Avatharappathi is situated in Kanyakumari district, Tamil Nadu.

- Swamithoppe - where Vaikundar performed The Great Tavam.
- Ambalappathi - where Ayya unified into him, the seven Deities.
- Muttappathi - where Ayya was given second as well as third Vinchai.
- Tamaraikulampathi - where Akilattirattu Ammanai, the scripture of Ayyavazhi was written down.
- Pooppathi - where Ayya unified into him Poomadanthai, the goddess of Earth.
- Vakaippathi - where 700 families were send to tavam by Ayya Vaikundar.
- Avatharappathi - where Ayya after the incarnation in the sea, arose in the world.

Baha'i Faith

A Baha'i pilgrimage currently consists of visiting the holy places in Haifa, Akka, and Bahji in Northwest Israel. Baha'is do not have access to other places designated as sites for pilgrimage.

Baha'u'llah decreed pilgrimage in His Motherbook (Kitab-i-Aqdas) to two places: the House of Baha'u'llah in Baghdad, Iraq, and the House of the Bab in Shiraz, Iran. In two separate Tablets, known as Suriy-i-Hajj, He prescribed specific rites for each of these pilgrimages (lifting the injunction regarding the shaving of one's head for pilgrimage in the Kitab-i-Aqdas). It is obligatory to make the pilgrimage, "if one can afford it and is able to do so, and if no obstacle stands in one's way". Baha'is are free to choose between the two Houses, as either has been deemed sufficient. And although women are not bound to perform pilgrimage, they are certainly not prohibited to do so.

Later, 'Abdu'l-Baha designated the Shrine of Baha'u'llah at Bahji (the Qiblih) as a site of visitation. No rites have been prescribed for this.

Buddhism

Gautama Buddha spoke of the four sites most worthy of pilgrimage for his followers to visit:

- Lumbini: birth place (in Nepal)
- Bodh Gaya: place of Enlightenment
- Sarnath: (formally Isipathana) where he delivered his first teaching
- Kusinara: (now Kusinagar, India) where he died

Other pilgrimage places in India and Nepal connected to the life of Gautama Buddha are: Savatthi, Pataliputta, Nalanda, Gaya, Vesali, [Sankasia]], Kapilavastu, Kosambi, Rajagaha, Varanasi.

Other famous places for buddhist pilgrimage in various countries include:

- India: Sanchi, Ellora, Ajanta.
- Thailand: Sukhothai, Ayutthaya, Wat Phra Kaew, Wat Doi Suthep.
- Tibet: Lhasa (traditional home of the Dalai Lama), Mount Kailash, Lake Nam-tso.
- Cambodia: Angkor Wat, Silver Pagoda.
- Sri Lanka: Polonnaruwa, Temple of the Tooth (Kandy), Anuradhapura.
- Laos: Luang Prabang.
- Myanmar: Bagan, Sagaing Hill.
- Nepal: Bodhnath, Swayambhunath.
- Indonesia: Borobudur.
- China: Yung-kang, Lung-men caves.
- Japan: Kyoto, Nara.

Christianity

Pilgrimages were first made to sites connected with the birth, life, crucifixion and resurrection of Jesus. Surviving descriptions of Christian pilgrimages to the Holy Land date from the 4th century, when pilgrimage was encouraged by church fathers like Saint Jerome. Pilgrimages also began to be made to Rome and other sites associated with the Apostles, Saints and Christian martyrs, as well as to places where there have been apparitions of the Virgin Mary. The crusades to the holy land are also considered to be mass armed pilgramages. The second largest single pilgrimage in the history of Christendom was to the Funeral of Pope John Paul II after his death on April 2, 2005. An estimated four million people travelled to Vatican City, in addition to the almost three million people already living in Rome, to see the body of Pope John Paul II lie in state.

World Youth Day is a major Catholic Pilgrimage, specifically for people aged 16-35. It is held internationally every 2-3 years. In 2005, young Roman Catholics visited Cologne, Germany. In 1995, the largest gathering of all time was to World Youth Day in Manila, Philippines, where four million people from all over the world attended.

The major Christian pilgrimages are to:

- Jerusalem. Site of the crucifixion and resurrection of Jesus.
- Rome on roads such as the Via Francigena. Site of the deaths of Saint Peter, Saint Paul and other early martyrs. Headquarters of the Catholic Church.
- Constantinople (today Istanbul, Turkey). Former capital of the Byzantine Empire and the see of one of the five ancient Patriarchates and spiritual see of the Eastern Orthodox Church. Hagia Sophia, former cathedral and burial place of many Ecumenical Patriarchs.
- Santiago de Compostela in Spain on the Way of St James (Spanish: El Camino de Santiago). This famous medieval pilgrimage to the shrine of aint James is still popular today.

Other important Christian pilgrimage sites include:

- Avila, Spain, St Theresa of Avila, relics
- Bethlehem, in Israel, Birthplace of Jesus and King David.
- Canterbury associated with Saint Thomas à Becket.
- Cap-de-la-Madeleine, Quebec, Canada in honour of Our Lady of the Cape.
- Cathedral of Chartres, France.
- Miercurea Ciuc, Transylvania, Romania. Whit Sunday gathering of (mostly ethnic Hungarian) Catholics.
- Croagh Patrick, Ireland. Saint Patrick.
- Conques, France
- Cologne, Germany. Relics of the Three Kings.
- Czêstochowa, Poland. Virgin Mary image.
- Glastonbury, England. St Joseph of Arimathea.
- Goa, India. St. Francis Xavier
- Hill of Crosses, Lithuania
- Kapel in 't Zand, Limburg
- Kevelaer, Germany
- Lisieux, France. Saint Therese of Lisieux, burial place.
- Lourdes, France. Apparition of the Virgin Mary. Place of healing.
- Mariazell, Austria. Marian Shrine to Austria and Hungary
- Mount Athos, Greece. Orthodox monastic centre.

- Mount Nebo, Jordan. Traditional site of the death of Moses.
- Mount Sinai, Egypt, holy mountain to the ancient Hebrews, traditional site has been commemorated since time of Constantine
- Nazareth, Israel, hometown of Jesus
- Fatima, Portugal. Apparition of the Virgin Mary.
- Guadalupe, Spain.
- Sea of Galilee, Israel, site of Jesus' early ministry.
- Shrine of Our Lady of Guadalupe, Mexico City. Apparition of the Virgin Mary.
- St. Patrick's Purgatory, Donegal, Ireland
- St. Thomas Mount, India. Place where St. Thomas was martyed.
- Taize Community, France, modern monastery that actively encourages pilgrimages to it
- Nidaros Cathedral, Norway
- Turin, Italy. Holy Shroud.
- Vailankanni, India. 16th-century Mary apparition site.
- Vierzehnheiligen, Germany.
- Walsingham, England. Virgin Mary apparition site.
- Wittenberg, Germany. Church of Martin Luther and centre of the Protestant Reformation.

Hinduism

- Kedarnath
- Gangotri
- Yamunotri
- Rishikesh
- Haridwar
- Benares
- Mandher Devi temple in Mandhradevi
- Vrindavan
- Mayapur

The first four sites in the list above together comprise the Chardham, or four holy pilgrimage destinations. It is believed that travelling to these places leads to moksha, the release from samsara (cycle of rebirths). Vrindavan is most important place of pilgrimage for every Vaishnava, especially for the followers of Gaudiya Vaishnavism who regard Krishna as the original Personality of Godhead (God). Here one can attain love of God (prema).

Islam

Pilgrimage to Mecca – the hajj – is one of the Five Pillars of Islam. It should be attempted at least once in the lifetime of all able-bodied Muslims. In addition to that most of the Shiite Muslims undertake a pilgrimage to the holy city of

Mashhad in northeastern part of Iran. The Hajj is an inward journey to the Kab'ah of heart and soul. Local Pilgrimage traditions - those undertaken as ziarah visits to local graves, are found throughout Muslim countries. In some countries, the graves of saints and heroes have very strong ziarah traditions as visiting the graves at auspicious times is a display of national and community identity. Some traditions within Islam have negative attitudes towards grave visiting.

Judaism

Within Judaism, the Temple in Jerusalem was the center of the Jewish religion, until its destruction in 70 AD, and all who were able were under obligation to visit and offer sacrifices known as the korbanot, particularly during the Jewish holidays in Jerusalem.

Following the destruction of the Second Temple and the onset of the diaspora, the centrality of pilgrimage to Jerusalem in Judaism was discontinued. In its place came prayers and rituals hoping for a return to Zion and the accompanying restoration of regular pilgrimages (see Jerusalem, Jews and Judaism).

Until recent centuries, pilgrimage has been a fairly difficult and arduous adventure. But now, Jews from many countries make periodic pilgrimages to the holy sites of their religion.

The western retaining wall of the original temple, known as the Wailing Wall, or Western Wall remains in the Old City of Jerusalem and this has been the most sacred site for Zionist Jews. Pilgrimage to this area was off-limits from 1948 to 1967, when East Jerusalem was controlled by Jordan.

Some Reform and Conservative Jews who no longer consider themselves exiles, still enjoy visiting Israel even if it is not an official "pilgrimage."

2

Important Aspects in Tourism

TOURIST ATTRACTION

A tourist attraction is a place of interest where tourists visit. Some examples include historical places, monuments, zoos, museums and art galleries, botanical gardens, buildings and structures (*e.g.*, castles, libraries, former prisons, skyscrapers, bridges), national parks and forests, theme parks and carnivals, ethnic enclave communities, historic trains, cultural events and oddities.

Tourist attractions are also created to capitalise on unusual and unexplained, even perhaps sensational, phenomena such as a supposed UFO crash site near Roswell, New Mexico and the alleged Loch Ness monster sighting near Inverness, Scotland. Reported ghost sightings also make tourist attractions.

Ethnic communities may become tourist attractions, such as Chinatowns, the Vietnamese community of Little Saigon in southern California in the United States and the black British neighborhood of Brixton borough of London.

Owners and marketers of attractions usually advertise tourist attractions on billboards along the side of highways and roadways, especially in remote areas. Also, many tourist attractions have free promotional brochures and flyers in information centres, fast food restaurants, hotel and motel rooms or lobbies, and rest areas.

While some tourist attractions provide visitors a memorable experience for a reasonable admission charge or even for free, others can have a tendency to be of low quality and to overprice their goods and services (such as admission, food, and souvenirs) in order to profit from tourists excessively. Such places are commonly known as tourist traps.

Many tourist attractions have a higher concentration of hotels and motels located nearby.

PACKAGE HOLIDAY

A package holiday or package tour consists of transport and accommodation advertised and sold together by a vendor known as a tour operator. Other services may be provided like a rental car, activities or outings during the holiday. Transport can be via charter airline to a foreign country.

Package holidays are organised by a tour operator and sold to a consumer by a travel agent. Some travel agents are owned by tour operators, others are independent.

Organised Tours

The first organised tours dated back to Thomas Cook who, on 5 July 1841, chartered a train to take a group of temperance campaigners from Leicester to a rally in Loughborough, twenty miles away. Thomas Cook - the company - grew to become one of the largest and most well known travel agents before being nationalised in 1948. With the gradual decline of visits to British seaside resorts after the Second World War, Thomas Cook began promoting foreign holidays (particularly Italy, Spain and Switzerland) in the early 1950s. Information films were shown at town halls throughout Britain. However they made a costly decision by not going into the new form of cheap holidays which combined the transport and accommodation arrangements into a single 'package'. The company went further into decline and were only rescued by a consortium buy-out on 26 May 1972.

Package Tours

Vladimir Raitz, the co-founder of the Horizon Holiday Group, pioneered the first mass package holidays abroad with charter flights between Gatwick airport and Corsica in 1950, and organised the first package holiday to Palma in 1952, Lourdes in 1953, and the Costa Brava and Sardinia in 1954. In addition, the amendments made in Montreal to the Convention on International Civil Aviation on June 14, 1954 was very liberal to Spain, allowing impetus for mass tourism using charter planes.

By the late 1950s and 1960s, these cheap package holidays - which combined flight, transfers and accommodation - provided the first chance for most people in the United Kingdom to have affordable travel abroad. One of the first charter airlines was Euravia, which commenced flights from Manchester Airport in 1961 and Luton Airport in 1962. Despite opening up mass tourism to Crete and the Algarve in 1970, the package tour industry declined during the 1970s. On 15 August 1974, the industry was shaken when the second-largest tour operator, Court Line which operated under the brand names of Horizon and Clarksons, collapsed. Nearly 50,000 tourists were stranded overseas and a further 100,000 faced the loss of booking deposits.

Recently a growing number of consumers are avoiding package holidays and instead are travelling with budget airlines and booking their own accommodation. In the UK, the downturn in the package holiday market led to the consolidation of the tour operator market, which is now dominated by a few large tour operators. The major operators are Thomson Holidays, part of the TUI AG, Thomas Cook AG, MyTravel, and First Choice. Under these umbrella brands there exists a whole range of different holiday operators catering to different markets, such as Club 18-30 or Simply Travel.

Passport

A passport is a travel document issued by a national government that usually identifies the bearer as a national of the issuing state and requests that the bearer be permitted to enter and pass through other countries.

Passports are connected with the right of legal protection abroad and the right to enter one's country of nationality. Passports usually contain the holder's photograph, signature, date of birth, nationality, and sometimes other means of individual identification. Many countries are in the process of developing biometric properties for their passports in order to further confirm that the person presenting the passport is the legitimate holder.

Types

Ordinary Passports are the normal passports issued to most citizens and have no special connotations.Diplomatic Passports are issued to Diplomats and diplomatic representatives of a home country, or can be issued for any state employees who serve on long-term (resident) duty, and in other cases official passport holders may be granted visa-free entry, while normal passport holders are required to get a visa.Official or Service Passports are issued to employees of a goverment travelling for work related reasons who either do not qualify as Diplomats or are not entiled to Diplomatic Status under the Vienna Convention.

Alien's passports are documents issued by some countries to non-citizen residents.A collective passport may be issued, for example, for a school trip. All children on the trip would be covered by the group passport for the duration of the trip.Internal passports have been issued by some countries, as a means of controlling the movement of the population. Examples include the Soviet internal passport system and the hukou residency registration system used in the People's Republic of China.

Emergency or Temporary Passports are issued to persons whose original passport has been lost or stolen and who need to urgently travel.

Business Passports are passports with extra pages issued to frequent travellers. Laisser Passer are documents issued by organisations such as the United Nations for their officials. Family Passports are passports that are not issued to individuals but to family units (parents and children).

Standards

Historically there were no agreed standards for passports because they were not generally required for international travel until the First World War. After the war the League of Nations Paris Conference on Passports and Customs Formalities and Through Tickets (1920) agreed the first set of standards that were expected of all passports issued by members of the League. The establishment of the International Civil Aviation Organisation (ICAO) in 1947 with 188 contracting states saw the responsibility for setting passport standards fall to that authority.

Passports now have a standardised format. They begin with a cover identifying the issuing country, then have a title page also naming the country. This is usually followed by pages giving information about the bearer and the issuing authority, (although some European Union member state passports provide this information on the inside back cover of the document). Then, a number of blank pages are given for foreign countries to affix visas, or stamp the passport on entrance or exit. Passports are provided with a serial number by the issuing authority.It is usual for a passport to have a note (usually near the front of the booklet) requesting and requiring help for its holder. For example, the note in an Israeli passport states:

The Minister of the Interior of the State of Israel hereby requests all those whom it may concern to allow the bearer of this passport to pass freely without let or hindrance and to afford him such assistance and protection as may be necessary.

Some passports include the note bilingually, for example, New Zealand passports has the note in English:The Governor General in the Realm of New Zealand requests in the Name of Her Majesty The Queen all whom it may concern to allow the holder to pass without delay or hindrance and in case of need to give all lawful assistance and protection.

Passports used to carry information (family name, given names, date of birth, place of birth, etc.) only in textual form. In recent years, however, passports issued by many countries have become more complex.

Machine-readable passports are standardized world-wide standard by the ICAO.They bear a zone where some of the information otherwise written in textual form is written as strings of alphanumeric characters, printed in a manner suitable for optical character recognition. This enables border controllers and other law enforcement agents to process such passports quickly, without having to input the information manually into a computer.

Biometric passports with RFID chips will carry supplemental information about the bearer, in a digitised form. These passports have already been introduced many years ago in Malaysia and more recently in Australia, New Zealand, Japan, Sweden, United Kingdom, the United States, Germany, the Republic of Ireland and Poland. These new passports were primarily introduced to prevent identity fraud. When technology improves, the embedded chips may also allow rapid clearance through immigration controls with quicker confirmation of identity. Facial Maps are popular for use in Biometric passports as the data (the distances between key facial features) can be gathered from the holder's passport photo without any other information. The irony is that although many countries now have biometric passports very few have introduced the equipment to read them at ports of entry and in the absence of an international standard it is not currently possible for one country to read the biometric information of another one.

Languages

In 1920 the International Conference on Passports, Customs Formalities and Through Tickets mandated that passports be issued in French and at least one other language. Now, many countries issue passports in English and the language of the issuing country.

- Belgium allows its citizens to choose which of its three official languages (Dutch, French, or German) should appear first in the individual's passport.
- The face page of the Hungarian passports ("Útlevél" in Hungarian, lit. "Roadletter") is in Hungarian only, though on the inside there is a second, Hungarian-English bilingual page mentioning "Passport" as well. The personal information page offers Hungarian, English and French explanation for the details. An additional page including the explanations in English, French, Chinese, Russian, Spanish and Arabic has been added in recent years.
- Passports issued by European Union member states bear all of the official languages of the European Union. These are not printed in each location, however. A number of languages (2 or 3) will be printed in the relevant point, followed by a number, which is used as a reference for a page on the passport dedicated to translations into all the remaining languages.
- United States passports, once issued in English and French only, are now issued in English, French, and Spanish since the second Clinton administration, due to the fact that they are used in Spanish-speaking Puerto Rico.
- Soviet internal passports were only printed in Russian and the language of Republic of the USSR, foreign passports were printed bilingual Russian and English, though they used French transliteration for names. The same situation exists in the present-day Russia except that in the newest version of the passports, names are no-longer transliterated according to the French method.

Common Designs

The member states of the European Union are perhaps the best-known countries to have a common format for their passports. European Union (EU) member state passports have standardised layouts and designs, although the photo page can be at the front or in the back of the booklet and small differences in design indicate which member state is the issuer.

Ordinary EU member state passports are burgundy-red, with the words "European Union" written in the national language or languages (*e.g.* Dutch, French, Finnish, Maltese) on the front, below which is the official name of the country, the national seal, and the word for "passport", in the respective language(s), can be found at the bottom. Malta was the first country of the new EU states from Central Europe and the Mediterranean to issue EU format passports. Estonia and Slovakia began issuing EU format passports in 2005. Slovenia and Poland started issuing biometric EU format passports in 2006. Others such as Latvia and Cyprus are likely to follow in the coming years.

In Central America, the members of the CA-4 Treaty (Guatemala, El Salvador, Honduras and Nicaragua have adopted a common design passport also called the Central American Passport. Although the design has been in use by Nicaragua and El Salvador since the mid-1990's, it will be the norm for the CA-4 area effective January 2006. The main features are its navy blue cover with the words "América Central" and a map of Central America with the territory of the issuing country highlighted in gold.

This effectively replaces the national seals of the different countries with one single element, the map. At the bottom of the cover, the name of the issuing country and the passport type. As of 2006, the Nicaraguan passport (which will be used as the model for the other three countries) is issued in Spanish, French and English. It also has 89 security features, including bidimensional barcodes, holograms and watermarks, ranking it as one of the most secure passport models in the world.

The Caribbean Community (CARICOM) recently began issuing passports to a common design, featuring CARICOM's symbol along with the national seal and official name of the member state in its official languages (*i.e.* English, French, Dutch). The first member state to issue CARICOM passports was Suriname, and currently four other member states use the common design: St. Kitts and Nevis, Dominica, St. Vincent and the Grenadines and Antigua and Barbuda. These five countries are to be followed by the other countries in CARICOM.

The declaration adopted in Cusco, Peru, establishing the South American Community of Nations signalled an intent to establish a common passport design, but this appears to be a long way away. Already, some member states of regional sub-groupings such as Mercosur and the Andean Community of Nations issue passports that bear their official name and seal along with the name of their regional grouping. Examples include Paraguay and Ecuador. Member states of the Andean Community of Nations have agreed to phase in new Andean passports bearing the official name of the regional body in Spanish by January 2005, although previously issued national passports will be valid until their expiry date.

Government Restrictions and Special Cases

Although most countries recognise the passports of most other countries, there are a number of exceptions. Generally these exceptions are due to circumstances where one country does not recognise another territory's administration as a sovereign state. Some countries also decline to accept passports that do not afford the bearer the right to live in the issuing country.

Most countries make it a policy not to accept passports issued by authorities they do not recognise as states. The usual one-off exceptions are persons involved in negotiation between authorities (analogous to diplomatic talks) and those offering humanitarian relief. Standing exceptions include passports issued by the Hong Kong and Macau Special Administrative Regions of China. In Brazil, citizens of such countries must apply for a Brazilian laissez-passer, a type of travel document usually allowing only a single entry into the issuing country.

In most countries, passports are state property which may be withdrawn at any time. In some countries the executive authorities may declare a passport void, although such cases may be subject to judicial review; judicial decision may be needed for other countries. For instance, typically, a person on bail must temporarily surrender their passport while awaiting trial if they pose a flight risk.

Many countries issue only one passport per person. Once the passport is expired, the applicant is required to surrender the expired passport, or have the issuing authority punch holes through the passport to invalidate it. A growing number of countries, including the United Kingdom and the United States, are allowing their citizens to hold more than one passport per person. It may be useful for a person who travels frequently to many countries while one passport is used to obtain a visa, the person may travel abroad with another passport.

Some countries issue passports and exit visas only to those who meet particular political and ideological requirements.

China (PRC and ROC) and Colonial Passports in Hong Kong and Macau

Under the auspices of their Basic Laws, Hong Kong and Macau SARs have the authority to issue passports, to contract agreements, to abolish visa requirements with other countries, and to exercise immigration control on foreign nationals. Passports issued by the respective SAR governments state that the bearer is a Chinese national with a right of abode in the issuing SAR. The National People's Congress has also delegated powers to the Hong Kong and Macau governments to administer Chinese nationality laws in their respective regions. The PRC does not recognise the Republic of China (ROC) as a sovereign state and considers Taiwan a part of its territory. The ROC based in Taiwan since 1949 has not renounced claims to mainland China. Despite presence of mutual immigration control, neither side of the Taiwan Strait considers travelling to and from the mainland and Taiwan international travel. The PRC and the ROC never stamp passports issued from the other side.

A Taiwan resident entering mainland China uses a special permit issued by mainland public security authorities and usually collects this permit in Hong Kong or Macau, which must usually be used as a point of transfer. The ROC government once required all Taiwan residents who planned to go to mainland China to obtain official approval beforehand and would administratively fine (NT$ 20,000 to 100,000) those who did not. However, often unable to ascertain if someone has broken this rule as the PRC would never stamp ROC passports, the authorities practically could not enforce the requirement except on those who had lost their travel documents in the mainland. It has been outright abolished except for officials of the administration who still require case-by case approvals.

At a port of entry in Taiwan, there is a conspicuous facility where mainland residents must surrender their passports and other travel documents issued by mainland authorities. On the other hand, Taiwan residents keep their identity documents issued by Taiwan while in the mainland.

As Hong Kong is considered as a part of the People's Republic of China, travelling to and from Hong Kong and the mainland is not considered international travel. The Public Security Bureau of the Guangdong province has been issuing a special permit (dubbed Home Return Permit) for Hong Kong residents who are Chinese nationals to enter and exit the mainland before and after the handover. Although it has been proposed that the HKSAR passport should supplant this permit, the proposal has been dismissed.

Although many Chinese in Hong Kong hold British National (Overseas) passports (and British citizen passports issued under the auspices of a programme instituted by the UK in 1990), the PRC Government considers them its nationals, and does not recognise these passports they hold while the PRC does not recognize dual nationality. These people have been using the Home Return Permit to enter mainland China since before the handover.

Although a Hong Kong resident may not use British National (Overseas) nor HKSAR passports in its own right for entering Taiwan, these passports must be used in conjunction with a special travel permit issued by Taiwan's administration. First-time travellers must apply beforehand but most other travellers can collect this permit upon arrival, subject to certain restrictions.

British Citizen passports obtained in Hong Kong can be used in its own right to enter the Republic of China on Taiwan.On the other hand, Taiwan residents travelling to Hong Kong apply for entry permits and collect them at specified airlines. Repeated travellers satisfying certain conditions may apply online.

Cyprus

The Turkish Republic of Northern Cyprus (TRNC) issues passports, but only Turkey recognises the statehood of Northern Cyprus. TRNC passports are not accepted for entry into the Republic of Cyprus. Until 2003, the Republic of Turkey did not accept passports of the Republic of Cyprus, because it did not recognize that government. Turkey now accepts Republic of Cyprus passports, but does not stamp them; rather, Turkish immigration officials stamp a separate visa issued by the Turkish state.

The Republic of Cyprus also refuses entry to holders of Yugoslavian passports "bearing a renewal stamp with the name 'Macedonia'.

Israel

Many Arab and Muslim countries will not allow entries to people with evidence of visits to Israel or used or unused Israeli visas in their passports, since the existence of the state of Israel is not recognised by these countries. To help foreigners circumvent these restrictions, Israel does not require visitors to have their passports stamped upon entry or advanced visas, making it difficult for those countries to tell if a citizen or tourist went there. Many of these nations are aware of the exit stamps placed in passports by Egypt and Jordan at their land borders with Israel and may block entry based on the presence of these stamps. For example, a traveller may be denied entry to certain countries because of the presence of an Egyptian exit stamp indicating the person left Egypt at Taba, at the Israeli border. Some nations will void old passports and reissue new passports to their nationals based on the presence of evidence of a visit to Israel, recognising the passport's function is compromised. The United Kingdom and the United States Department of State may allow a passport holder to have two valid passports to circumvent the restrictions concerning Israel if the applicant can satisfactorily explain why a second passport is needed when applying.

Arab and Muslim countries not accepting Israeli passports are:

- Afghanistan, Algeria, Bangladesh, Comoros, Djibouti, Indonesia, Iran, Iraq, Kuwait, Lebanon, Libya, Malaysia (except with written permission from the Malaysian government), Maldives, Oman, Pakistan, Qatar, Saudi Arabia, Somalia, Sudan, Syria, Tunisia, United Arab Emirates, and Yemen.

Muslim countries that do accept Israeli passports include:

- Bahrain, Egypt, Jordan, Mauritania, Morocco, Turkey, and former Soviet republics with Muslim majority: Azerbaijan, Kazakhstan, Kyrgyzstan, Tajikistan, Turkmenistan and Uzbekistan.

The only non-Arab and non-Muslim countries that do not accept Israeli passports are Cuba and North Korea due to these nations' enduring alliance with the Palestine Liberation Organization.

Koreas

Exiting from the region under Republic of Korea's administration (commonly known as South Korea) directly to the North is not international travel from the South's point of view. The Republic of Korea's constitution considers the North as part of its territory, although under different administration. In other words, the South does not view going to and from as breaking the continuity of a person's stay, as long as the traveller does not land on a third territory.

The privilege of a passport in North Korea is limited to a select few. Membership of the Korean Workers' Party is essentially a requisite.

Pakistan

Pakistan imposes a requirement on its Muslim citizens when they apply for a passport, requiring them to agree to the following:

1. I am a Muslim and believe in the absolute and unqualified finality of the Prophethood of Hazrat Muhammad (peace be upon him) the last of the Prophets.
2. I do not recognize any who claims to be a prophet in any sense of the word or any description whatsoever, after Hazrat Muhammad (peace be upon him) or recognize such a claimant as a prophet or a religious reformer as Muslim.
3. I consider Mirza Ghulam Ahmad Qadiani to be an impostor nabi and also consider his followers whether belonging to the Lahori, Qadiani or Mirzai groups, to be non-Muslims.

With the issuance of the new biometric passport in 2005 (in which the religion column was to be deleted), the above declaration would have been made unnecessary. However, this decision was recently reversed by the Pakistan Government on religious parties' resistance. After much debate, the column has come back. New passports will carry religion columns on Page 3; passports already printed will bear a rubber stamp mark declaring the holder's religion. There is no mention of religion on the Pakistani National ID Card.

Saudi Arabia

The Government of Saudi Arabia like some other governments does not officially recognise dual nationality for its citizens. Citizens who have dual nationality generally keep this confidential when in Saudi Arabia. If a second passport is discovered, it will be confiscated and the bearer may be arrested.

Spain and Gibraltar

The Government of Spain has had a policy of not accepting British passports issued in Gibraltar, on the grounds that the territory's government is not a competent authority for issuing such documents. Consequently some

Gibraltarians have been refused entry to Spain when travelling on these documents. However, the word "Gibraltar" now appears beneath the words "United Kingdom of Great Britain and Northern Ireland", as appears in passports of other British colonies and dependencies.

Tonga

Some countries decline to accept Tongan Protected Person passports, though they do accept standard passports issued to Tongan citizens.

Republic of Ireland and Northern Ireland

Citizenship of the Republic of Ireland is given to all those born in the island of Ireland (from 2005 all those with parents legally resident) regardless of what side of border with Northern Ireland (which is a part of the United Kingdom). This was due to the Irish state's territorial claim to Northern Ireland and the situation was formalised by the Good Friday Agreement in 1998 with the United Kingdom government and the political parties in Northern Ireland. Irish Citizenship can be claimed by grandchildren of Irish born people, meaning approximately 5 million people in Britain can obtain Irish passports. In the Republic of Ireland a significant number are entitled to UK passports. Those born before 6 December 1922 were born when Ireland was in the UK (their children can also claim UK passports). Furthermore those born before 1949 can also obtain UK passports as British subjects.

INTERNATIONAL TRAVEL WITHOUT PASSPORTS

In some circumstances, travel between countries may be done without showing a passport. These include:

Reciprocal Agreements

Some countries have a reciprocal agreements such that a visa is not needed under certain conditions, *e.g.* when the visit is for tourism and for a relatively short period.

A few countries have agreements allowing for cross-border travel without passports (but generally with identification). Examples include:

- The United Kingdom and the Republic of Ireland: Citizens of the UK and Ireland do not require a passport to travel between the two countries. Other EEA nationals must show a national ID card or Passport. All other nationals require a passport. Many nationals also require visas for both countries.
- The CA-4 countries: Citizens of Guatemala, El Salvador, Honduras, and Nicaragua do not require a passport to travel between any of the four countries. A National ID card (Cedula) is sufficient for entry. In addition, the CA-4 agreement implemented the Central American

Single Visa (Visa Única Centroamericana) for citizens of all other countries, eliminating the need for separate entry visas for each of the countries. Persons entering the region on Type "B" visas can enter the area through any Port of Entry. Persons entering on Type "C" visas (issued through prior consultation with the Ministry of Foreign Affairs) must enter through a Port of Entry in the country that issued the visa. Once a person has been admitted, they may travel onto any of the other countries and are allowed to stay through the date authorized at the original Port of Entry.

- The NAFTA countries: the United States, Canada, and Mexico, although after an announcement on September 02, 2005 (Western Hemisphere Travel Initiative), all persons entering the United States, including U.S. citizens, will be required to have a passport, even from Canada and Mexico, starting January 8, 2007 for air and sea travel. On December 31, 2007, the passport requirement will also be extended to all land border crossings.

The Canadian Government has responded to this by stating that soon U.S. citizens will be required to have a passport to enter Canada. A passport is not generally required to enter Mexico. As of December 31, 2007 (January 8, 2007 for air or sea travel), citizens of the United States will not need a passport to enter into Mexico, but will be required to show their passport when leaving Mexico and re-entering the United States.

- The Nordic countries (since 1952), Denmark, Finland, Iceland, Norway and Sweden, including Faroe Islands and Greenland. (Called the Nordic Passport Union, this area joined the larger Schengen treaty region in 1997.)
- Lebanese citizens entering Syria do not require a passport if carrying their Lebanese IDs. Similarly, Syrian nationals do not require a passport to enter Lebanon either, if carrying their Syrian IDs.
- Indian, Nepalese and Bhutanese citizens do not require a passport to travel between the three countries. However some identification is needed to cross the borders.
- Croatia does not require a passport for citizens of Bosnia and Herzegovina who have a Bosnian ID card. Likewise Bosnia and Herzegovina, Italy, Slovenia and Hungary do not require Croatian citizens to have a passport, only a Croatian ID.
- Serbia does not require a passport for citizens of Bosnia and Herzegovina who have a Bosnian ID card. Likewise Bosnia and Herzegovina does not require Serbian citizens to have a passport, only a Serbian ID.
- Russia and some former Soviet Union Republics: the participating countries may only require the equivalent of the national ID card

(which is called Internal passport, as opposed to an "international" passport that a former Soviet citizen would be required to produce to enter other foreign countries.

Many Latin American nationals can travel within their respective regional economic zones, such as Mercosur (Argentina, Brazil, Paraguay, Uruguay and Venezuela) and the Andean Community of Nations (Bolivia, Peru, Ecuador, Colombia, Venezuela) or on a bilateral basis (*e.g.* between Chile and Peru) without passports, presenting instead their national identification cards or voter registration cards for a limited period. Often, this travel must be done overland rather than by air. There are plans to extend these rights to all of South America under the new South American Community of Nations.

- Turkey does not require a passport for citizens of Greece that hold a new ID card (the one including the bearer's details in both the Greek and the Latin alphabets.) Greece still requires a Schengen visa for Turkish nationals to enter Greece.

EU, EEA, and the Schengen Treaty

Citizens of the European Economic Area (the European Union plus Iceland, Liechtenstein, and Norway) enjoy the freedom to travel and work in any European Union country without a visa, although transitory dispositions may restrict the rights of citizens of new members to work in other countries. The same rights are also accorded to citizens of Switzerland although they remain separate from the EEA.

Furthermore, countries that have signed and applied the Schengen treaty (a subset of the EEA) do not implement passport controls between each other, unless exceptional circumstances apply. Customs controls are unaffected by the Schengen treaty. Most of the balance of EU countries, plus Switzerland, have signed the Schengen treaty, but not applied it yet. The main reason is, that, according to EU laws, the member states which had joined the EU in 2004 would have to meet strict criteria with respect to their efforts protect EU external borders before intra-EU border controls between the old member states and such new member states may be lifted. Switzerland requires some time to adopt national databases to those of the EU.

As a consequence of the above, for instance, a French citizen may travel to the United Kingdom, another EEA nation, and then freely work in that country. However, since the UK has not signed the Schengen treaty, they will have to carry at least a national ID card, which will normally be checked at the border. On the other hand, if and when Switzerland applies the Schengen treaty, the French citizen will be able to travel to Switzerland without being stopped at the border, but they will not be able to work freely in that country without authorisation, as it is not a member of the EEA (this notwithstanding the fact that, in most cases, such authorization to work would nevertheless have to be granted by Swiss authorities according to a specific treaty on free movement which had been concluded between the EU and Switzerland). Further, most European countries require all persons to carry or, at least, possess an identity card or passport. So while Switzerland will not check our French traveller's passport at the border, they may have to show their ID card at some stage within the country, although in practice this is rare. Except at the border, ID cards are not required by UK law; however, there is a de facto requirement to prove your identity to conduct business. Our French traveller would have to show ID to obtain a UK bank account or to prove their eligibility to work.

Refugees and Stateless Persons

Persons who do not have access to National Passports, for example Refugees and Stateless persons, may be issued a Travel Document by the Country in which they reside. Holders of these documents generally require visas for international travel and will not be entitled to Consular Protection in the event that they run into trouble while travelling. Exceptions to this include persons holding 1951 Convention Documents who may benefit from some visa free travel as a result of the convention and those persons who reside within the areas of a passport union such as the Schengen system or the Nordic Passport Union. Holders of UK and Irish Travel Documents do not, however, benefit from visa free travel within the Common Travel Area.

The Vatican

The Vatican has no formal immigration controls. As the only entrance to the tiny country is overland from Italy, the de-facto immigration requirements of the Vatican are the same as those of Italy. However, having crossed the border into the Vatican, visitors are subject to Vatican law, not Italian; the Vatican retains its authority as a separate state. The Vatican, however, does issue its own passports to certain Vatican officials born in foreign countries who need to be permanently based at the Vatican or in other Vatican offices. The pope is always given the privilege of 'Passport No.1', which is reissued with the same number for every successive pontiff.

The British Monarch

The British monarch does not have a passport as British passports are issued in her name. In Commonwealth countries, where the British monarch is also the head of state, passports are issued in the name of the Governor General of that state, except in Canada where passports are issued on behald of the Minister of Foreign Affairs.

Immigration Stamps in Passports

Immigration authorities usually place immigration stamps in passports at a border crossing as part of their immigration control or customs procedures. This endorsement can serve many different purposes. In the United Kingdom the immigration stamp in the passport includes the formal "leave to enter" granted to a person subject to control when they enter the country. Alternatively the stamps activates and/or acknowledges the continuing leave conferred in the individuals's entry clearance.

Other authorities, such as the Schengen system, simply stamp a passport with a date stamp that does not indicate any duration and this stamp is taken to mean either that the person is deemed to have permission to remain for 3 months or an alternative period as shown on their visa. In both systems it is not allowed to stamp the passports of persons not subject to Immigration Control, for example citizens of that country (or other EU nationals within the European Union). This is because the stamping of the passport imposes a control that the person is not subject to. This does not apply in other countries where the stamp in a passport simply acknowledges the entry and exit of a person - for example in Australia, Russia or China.

Most countries have different stamps for arrivals and departures to make it easier for officers to quickly identify the movements of the person concerned.

Camouflage Passports

A camouflage passport is issued in the name of a non-existent country. It is manufactured by private businesses and sold openly, usually by mail order or over the internet. These are marketed to security-conscious international travelers and tacitly as novelties.

The intended use is mainly to allow a person to conceal their nationality in event of a terrorist hijacking, riot or some similar situation where their identity may single him out as a crime victim. To this end, the passports are also often sold with a package of matching documents, including an international driver's license and similar supporting identity papers. As of 2006, prices tend to range between $400 and $1000.

Camouflage passports are not regarded to be counterfeit documents because they are not purporting to be internationally recognised passports. Nevertheless, some national authorities have expressed concern over the use of camouflage passports in criminal activities, *e.g.* taking advantage of undertrained personnel to open a fraudulent bank account.

3

Travel Documents for Tourists

A travel document is an identity document issued by a government or international treaty organization to facilitate the movement of individuals or small groups of persons across international boundaries. Travel documents usually assure other governments that the bearer or bearers may return to the issuing country and are issued in booklet form to allow other governments to place visas as well as entry and exit stamps in them. One of the most common travel documents is a passport, which usually identifies the bearer as a citizen or national of the issuing country.

Types of Travel Documents

- 1951 Convention travel documents are passport-like booklets issued by national governments to refugees under the 1951 Convention relating to the Status of Refugees.
- 1954 Convention travel documents are similar documents issued to stateless persons under the 1954 Convention Relating to the Status of Stateless Persons.
- Alien's passports and certificates of identity are passport-like booklets issued by national governments to resident foreigners, other than those issued under the 1951 and 1954 conventions mentioned above. However, some governments issue certificates of identity to their own nationals as emergency passports.
- Laissez-passers are issued by national governments and international treaty organizations for various purposes.

International Travel Documents

Visa (document)

A visa is a document issued by a country giving a certain individual permission to formally request entrance to the country during a given period of time and for certain purposes. Most countries require possession of a valid visa as a condition of entry for foreigners, though there exist exemption schemes. Visas are typically stamped or attached into the recipient's passport, or are sometimes issued as separate pieces of paper. Visas are associated with the request for permission to enter (or exit) a country, and are thus, for some countries, distinct from actual formal permission for an alien to enter and remain in the country.

While a visa for the European Schengen area constitutes the formal permission to enter, according to the conditions, in other cases a visa does not guarantee admission into the country for which the alien has the visa. This formal permission is typically granted by stamping the visa and, in some cases, by providing an additional document as proof of status, such as the United States' I-94. The common phrase "he has to leave because his visa has expired" is thus, strictly speaking, incorrect: the visitor's status has expired, the visa may or may not have.

Some countries, such as some states of the former Soviet Union, require that their citizens, and sometimes foreign travelers, obtain an exit visa in order to be allowed to leave the country. Until 2004, foreign students in Russia were issued only an entry visa on being accepted to University there, and had to obtain an exit visa to return home. This policy has sincc been changed, and foreign students are now issued multiple entry (and exit) visas. Citizens of the People's Republic of China who are residents of the mainland are required to apply for special permits in order to enter the Special Administrative Regions of Hong Kong and Macao (and SAR residents require a Home Return Permit to visit the mainland).

Conditions of Issue

Some visas can be granted on arrival, usually only to citizens of countries enjoying good relations with the issuing country, or by prior application at the country's embassy or consulate, or sometimes a specialized travel agency with permission from the issuing country. If there is no embassy or consulate in one's home country, then one would have to travel to a third country (or apply by post) and try to get a visa issued there. The need or absence of need of a visa generally depends on the citizenship of the applicant, the intended duration of the stay, and the activities that the applicant may wish to undertake in the country he visits; these may delineate different formal categories of visas, with different issue conditions.

Some, but by no means all, countries have reciprocal visa regimes: if Country A requires citizens of Country B to have a visa to travel there, then Country B may apply reciprocity and require a visa from citizens of Country A. Likewise, if A allows B's citizens to enter without a visa, B may allow A's citizens to enter without a visa.

Examples of such reciprocal visa regimes are between:

- Algeria and Canada, excluding—for entry to Algeria—citizens of certain Arab and Muslim countries and—for Canada—most Western countries.

- most CIS member states and African countries
- Brazil and Canada/CIS member states
- Armenia and most non-CIS member states

A fee may be charged for issuing a visa; these are typically also reciprocal, so if country A charges country B's citizens 50 USD for a visa, country B will often also charge the same amount for country A's visitors. The fee charged may also be at the discretion of each embassy and can be increased to discourage unserious applicants. A similar reciprocity often applies to the duration of the visa (the period in which one is permitted to request entry of the country) and the amount of entries one can attempt with the visa. Expedited processing of the visa application for some countries will generally incur additional charges.

This reciprocal fee has gained prominence in recent years with the decision of the United States to charge nationals of various countries a $100 visa processing fee (non refundable, even if a visa isn't issued). A number of countries, including Brazil, Chile, and Turkey have reciprocated. Brazil requires an advance visa, and that a U.S. citizen be fingerprinted and photographed on arrival—matching U.S. requirements for Brazilians and other foreigners.

The issuing authority, usually a branch of the country's foreign ministry or department (*e.g.* U.S. State Department), and typically consular officers, may request appropriate documentation from the applicant. This may include proof that the applicant is able to support himself in the host country (lodging, food), proof that the person hosting the applicant in his or her home really exists and has sufficient room for hosting the applicant, proof that the applicant has obtained health and evacuation insurance, etc. Some countries ask for proof of health status, especially for long-term visas; some countries deny such visas to sufferers of certain illnesses, such as AIDS. The exact conditions depend on the country and the category of visas. Notable examples of countries requiring HIV tests of long-term residents are Russia and Uzbekistan. However, in Uzbekistan, the HIV test requirement is sometimes not strictly enforced.

Developing countries frequently demand strong evidence of the intent to return to the home country, if the visa is for a temporary stay.

The issuing authority may also require applicants to attest that they have had no criminal convictions, or that they do not partake in certain activities (like prostitution or drug trafficking). Some countries request information as to the ideological leanings of the applicant; this was used in the United States, which inquired whether visa applicants were Communist sympathizers (and denied visas to known or suspected sympathizers.)

Types of Visa

Common types of visas are:

- Transit visa, usually valid for 3 days or less, for passing through the country to a third destination.
- Tourist visa, for a limited period of leisure travel, no business activities allowed. Some countries (*e.g.*, Kuwait) do not issue tourist visas. Saudi Arabia introduced tourist visas only in 2004 although it did (and still does) issue pilgrimage visas for Hajj pilgrims.
- Business visa, for engaging in commerce in the country. These visas generally preclude permanent employment, for which a work visa would be required.
- Temporary worker visa, for approved employment in the host country. These are generally more difficult to obtain but valid for longer periods of time than a business visa. Examples of these are the United States' E-3, H-1B and L-1 visas.
- On-arrival visa, granted immediately prior to entering the country, eg. at an airport or border control post. This is distinct from not requiring a visa at all, as the visitor must still obtain the visa before they can even try to pass through immigration. The on-arrival visa usually is nothing more than an entrance fee, though the visitors can still be denied entry even with a visa.

Less common visas include:

- Student visa, which allows its holder to study at an institution of higher learning in the issuing country. Students studying in Algeria, however, are issued tourist visas.
- Working holiday visa, for individuals traveling between nations offering a working holiday programme, allowing young people to undertake temporary work while traveling.
- Diplomatic visa, which confers diplomatic status on its holder and is normally only available to bearers of diplomatic passports.
- Journalist visa, which some countries require of people in that occupation when travelling for their respective news organizations. Countries which insist on this include Cuba, Iran, North Korea, Saudi Arabia, the United States (I-visa) and Zimbabwe.
- Fiancee visa, granted for a limited period prior to intended marriage based on a proven relationship with a citizen of the destination country: for example, a German woman who wishes to marry an American man would obtain a Fiancee Visa (also known as a K-1 visa) to allow her to enter the United States.
- Immigrant visa, granted for those intending to immigrate to the issuing country. They usually are issued for a single journey as the holder will, depending on the country, later be issued a permanent resident identification card which will allow the traveller to enter to the issuing country an unlimited number of times. (for example, the United States Permanent Resident Card)...

Entry and Duration Period

Visas can also be single-entry, which means the visa is cancelled as soon as the holder leaves the country, double-entry, or multiple-entry, permitting multiple entries into the country with the same visa. Countries may also issue re-entry permits that allow temporarily leaving the country without invalidating the visa. Even a business visa will normally not allow the holder to work in the host country without an additional work permit.

Once issued, a visa will typically have to be used within a certain period of time.

The validity of a visa is not the same as the authorized period of stay in the issuing country. The visa validity usually indicates when the alien can apply for entry to the country. For example, if a visa has been issued January 1st and expires March 30th, and the typical authorized period of stay in a country is 90 days, then the 90-day authorized stay starts on the day the passenger reaches the country, which has to be between January 1st and March 30th. The traveller could therefore stay in the issuing country until July 1st.

Once in the country, the validity period of a visa or authorized stay can often be extended for a fee at the discretion of immigration authorities. Overstaying a period of authorized stay given by the immigration officers is considered illegal immigration even if the visa validity period isn't over (*i.e.* for multiple entry visas) and a form of being "out of status" and the offender may be fined, prosecuted, deported, or even blacklisted from entering the country again.

Entering a country without a valid visa or visa exemption may result in detention and removal (deportation or exclusion) from the country. Undertaking activities that are not authorized by the status of entry (for example, working while possessing a non-worker tourist status) can result in the individual being deemed removable, in common speech an illegal alien. Such violation is not a violation of a visa, however despite the common misuse of the phrase, but a violation of status hence the term "out of status."

Even having a visa does not guarantee entry to the host country. The border crossing authorities make the final determination to allow entry, and may even cancel a visa at the border if the alien cannot demonstrate to their satisfaction that they will abide by the status their visa grants them.

Visa and immigration laws may be very different among countries. As such, aliens are advised to check with immigration lawyers for visa and immigration laws governing the countries they wish to enter and eligibility to receive visas or other immigration benefits.

Visa Extensions

Many countries have a mechanism to allow the holder of a visa to apply to stay longer in that country. For example, in Denmark a visa holder can apply to the Danish Immigration Service for a Residence Permit after they have arrived in the Country. In the United Kingdom applications can be made to the Immigration and Nationality Directorate. In certain circumstances, it is not possible for the holder of the visa to do this, either because the country does not have a mechanism to prolong visas or, most likely, because the holder of the visa is using a short stay visa to live in a country. In such cases, the holder often engages in what is known as a visa run; leaving the country for a short period in order to apply for a new visa prior to their return or so that they can be given a fresh permission to stay when they re-enter.

Visa Refusal

A visa may be denied for various reasons, for example (but not limited to):

- If the applicant has committed fraud or misrepresentation in their application;
- If the applicant is felt to be intending to stay permanently or finding a job while applying for a temporary visa;
- If the applicant does not have a legitimate reason for their journey;
- If the applicant is asking for a resident visa and has no visible means of sustenance;
- If the applicant has a criminal record or has criminal charges pending;
- If the applicant does not have a good moral character;
- If the applicant is considered to be a security risk;
- If the applicant is a citizen of a country with whom the host country has poor or non-existent relations.

4

International Tourism Ethics

BACKGROUND

The Global Code of Ethics for Tourism (GCET) is a comprehensive set of principles whose purpose is to guide stakeholders in tourism development: central and local governments, local communities, the tourism industry and its professionals, as well as visitors, both international and domestic.

The Code was called for in a resolution of the UNWTO General Assembly meeting in Istanbul in 1997. Over the following two years, a special committee for the preparation of the Global Code of Ethics was formed and a draft document was prepared by the Secretary-General and the legal adviser to UNWTO in consultation with UNWTO Business Council, UNWTO's Regional Commissions, and the UNWTO Executive Council.

The United Nations Commission on Sustainable Development meeting in New York in April, 1999 endorsed the concept of the Code and requested UNWTO to seek further input from the private sector, non-governmental organizations and labour organizations. Written comments on the code were received from more than 70 UNWTO Member States and other entities. The resulting 10 point Global Code of Ethics for Tourism - the culmination of an extensive consultative process- was approved unanimously by the UNWTO General Assembly meeting in Santiago in October 1999.

The United Nations Economic and Social Council (ECOSOC), in its substantive session of July 2001, adopted a draft resolution on the Code of Ethics and called on the UN General Assembly to give recognition to the Code. The official recognition by the UN General Assembly to the Global Code of Ethics for Tourism came on 21 December 2001, through its resolution A/RES/56/212, by which it further encouraged the World Tourism Organization to promote an effective follow-up of the Code.

"The Global Code of Ethics for Tourism sets a frame of reference for the responsible and sustainable development of world tourism. It draws inspiration from many similar declarations and industry codes that have come before and it adds new thinking that reflects our changing society at the beginning of the 21st century.

With international tourism forecast to nearly triple in volume over the next 20 years, members of the World Tourism Organization believe that the Global Code of Ethics for Tourism is needed to help minimize the negative impacts of tourism on the environment and on cultural heritage while maximizing the benefits for residents of tourism destinations.

Principles

The Code includes nine articles outlining the "rules of the game" for destinations, governments, tour operators, developers, travel agents, workers and travellers themselves. The tenth article involves the redress of grievances and marks the first time that a code of this type will have a mechanism for enforcement.

Article 1

Tourism's contribution to mutual understanding and respect between peoples and societies

1. The understanding and promotion of the ethical values common to humanity, with an attitude of tolerance and respect for the diversity of religious, philosophical and moral beliefs, are both the foundation and the consequence of responsible tourism; stakeholders in tourism development and tourists themselves should observe the social and cultural traditions and practices of all peoples, including those of minorities and indigenous peoples and to recognize their worth;
2. Tourism activities should be conducted in harmony with the attributes and traditions of the host regions and countries and in respect for their laws, practices and customs;
3. The host communities, on the one hand, and local professionals, on the other, should acquaint themselves with and respect the tourists who visit them and find out about their lifestyles, tastes and expectations; the education and training imparted to professionals contribute to a hospitable welcome;
4. It is the task of the public authorities to provide protection for tourists and visitors and their belongings; they must pay particular attention to the safety of foreign tourists owing to the particular vulnerability they may have; they should facilitate the introduction of specific means of information, prevention, security, insurance and assistance consistent with their needs; any attacks, assaults, kidnappings or threats against tourists or workers in the tourism industry, as well as the wilful destruction of tourism facilities or of elements of cultural or natural heritage should be severely condemned and punished in accordance with their respective national laws;
5. When travelling, tourists and visitors should not commit any criminal

act or any act considered criminal by the laws of the country visited and abstain from any conduct felt to be offensive or injurious by the local populations, or likely to damage the local environment; they should refrain from all trafficking in illicit drugs, arms, antiques, protected species and products and substances that are dangerous or prohibited by national regulations;

6. Tourists and visitors have the responsibility to acquaint themselves, even before their departure, with the characteristics of the countries they are preparing to visit; they must be aware of the health and security risks inherent in any travel outside their usual environment and behave in such a way as to minimize those risks.

Article 2

Tourism as a vehicle for individual and collective fulfillment

1. Tourism, the activity most frequently associated with rest and relaxation, sport and access to culture and nature, should be planned and practised as a privileged means of individual and collective fulfilment; when practised with a sufficiently open mind, it is an irreplaceable factor of self-education, mutual tolerance and for learning about the legitimate differences between peoples and cultures and their diversity;
2. Tourism activities should respect the equality of men and women; they should promote human rights and, more particularly, the individual rights of the most vulnerable groups, notably children, the elderly, the handicapped, ethnic minorities and indigenous peoples;
3. The exploitation of human beings in any form, particularly sexual, especially when applied to children, conflicts with the fundamental aims of tourism and is the negation of tourism; as such, in accordance with international law, it should be energetically combatted with the cooperation of all the States concerned and penalized without concession by the national legislation of both the countries visited and the countries of the perpetrators of these acts, even when they are carried out abroad;
4. Travel for purposes of religion, health, education and cultural or linguistic exchanges are particularly beneficial forms of tourism, which deserve encouragement;
5. The introduction into curricula of education about the value of tourist exchanges, their economic, social and cultural benefits, and also their risks, should be encouraged.

Article 3

Tourism, a factor of sustainable development

1. All the stakeholders in tourism development should safeguard the natural environment with a view to achieving sound, continuous and sustainable economic growth geared to satisfying equitably the needs and aspirations of present and future generations;
2. All forms of tourism development that are conducive to saving rare and precious resources, in particular water and energy, as well as avoiding so far as possible waste production, should be given priority and encouraged by national, regional and local public authorities;
3. The staggering in time and space of tourist and visitor flows, particularly those resulting from paid leave and school holidays, and a more even distribution of holidays should be sought so as to reduce the pressure of tourism activity on the environment and enhance its beneficial impact on the tourism industry and the local economy;
4. Tourism infrastructure should be designed and tourism activities programmed in such a way as to protect the natural heritage composed of ecosystems and biodiversity and to preserve endangered species of wildlife; the stakeholders in tourism development, and especially professionals, should agree to the imposition of limitations or constraints on their activities when these are exercised in particularly sensitive areas: desert, polar or high mountain regions, coastal areas, tropical forests or wetlands, propitious to the creation of nature reserves or protected areas;
5. Nature tourism and ecotourism are recognized as being particularly conducive to enriching and enhancing the standing of tourism, provided they respect the natural heritage and local populations and are in keeping with the carrying capacity of the sites;

Article 4

1. Tourism resources belong to the common heritage of mankind; the communities in whose territories they are situated have particular rights and obligations to them;
2. Tourism policies and activities should be conducted with respect for the artistic, archaeological and cultural heritage, which they should protect and pass on to future generations; particular care should be devoted to preserving and upgrading monuments, shrines and museums as well as archaeological and historic sites which must be widely open to tourist visits; encouragement should be given to public access to privately-owned cultural property and monuments, with respect for the rights of their owners, as well as to religious buildings, without prejudice to normal needs of worship;
3. Financial resources derived from visits to cultural sites and monuments should, at least in part, be used for the upkeep, safeguard, development and embellishment of this heritage;

4. Tourism activity should be planned in such a way as to allow traditional cultural products, crafts and folklore to survive and flourish, rather than causing them to degenerate and become standardized;

Article 5

Tourism, a beneficial activity for host countries and communities

1. Local populations should be associated with tourism activities and share equitably in the economic, social and cultural benefits they generate, and particularly in the creation of direct and indirect jobs resulting from them;
2. Tourism policies should be applied in such a way as to help to raise the standard of living of the populations of the regions visited and meet their needs; the planning and architectural approach to and operation of tourism resorts and accommodation should aim to integrate them, to the extent possible, in the local economic and social fabric; where skills are equal, priority should be given to local manpower;
3. Special attention should be paid to the specific problems of coastal areas and island territories and to vulnerable rural or mountain regions, for which tourism often represents a rare opportunity for development in the face of the decline of traditional economic activities;
4. Tourism professionals, particularly investors, governed by the regulations laid down by the public authorities, should carry out studies of the impact of their development projects on the environment and natural surroundings; they should also deliver, with the greatest transparency and objectivity, information on their future programmes and their foreseeable repercussions and foster dialogue on their contents with the populations concerned;

Article 6

Obligations of stakeholders in tourism development

1. Tourism professionals have an obligation to provide tourists with objective and honest information on their places of destination and on the conditions of travel, hospitality and stays; they should ensure that the contractual clauses proposed to their customers are readily understandable as to the nature, price and quality of the services they commit themselves to providing and the financial compensation payable by them in the event of a unilateral breach of contract on their part;
2. Tourism professionals, insofar as it depends on them, should show concern, in co-operation with the public authorities, for the security

and safety, accident prevention, health protection and food safety of those who seek their services; likewise, they should ensure the existence of suitable systems of insurance and assistance; they should accept the reporting obligations prescribed by national regulations and pay fair compensation in the event of failure to observe their contractual obligations

3. Tourism professionals, so far as this depends on them, should contribute to the cultural and spiritual fulfilment of tourists and allow them, during their travels, to practise their religions;
4. The public authorities of the generating States and the host countries, in cooperation with the professionals concerned and their associations, should ensure that the necessary mechanisms are in place for the repatriation of tourists in the event of the bankruptcy of the enterprise that organized their travel;
5. Governments have the right – and the duty - especially in a crisis, to inform their nationals of the difficult circumstances, or even the dangers they may encounter during their travels abroad; it is their responsibility however to issue such information without prejudicing in an unjustified or exaggerated manner the tourism industry of the host countries and the interests of their own operators; the contents of travel advisories should therefore be discussed beforehand with the authorities of the host countries and the professionals concerned; recommendations formulated should be strictly proportionate to the gravity of the situations encountered and confined to the geographical areas where the insecurity has arisen; such advisories should be qualified or cancelled as soon as a return to normality permits;
6. The press, and particularly the specialized travel press and the other media, including modern means of electronic communication, should issue honest and balanced information on events and situations that could influence the flow of tourists; they should also provide accurate and reliable information to the consumers of tourism services; the new communication and electronic commerce technologies should also be developed and used for this purpose; as is the case for the media, they should not in any way promote sex tourism;

Article 7

Right to tourism

1. The prospect of direct and personal access to the discovery and enjoyment of the planet's resources constitutes a right equally open to all the world's inhabitants; the increasingly extensive

participation in national and international tourism should be regarded as one of the best possible expressions of the sustained growth of free time, and obstacles should not be placed in its way;

2. The universal right to tourism must be regarded as the corollary of the right to rest and leisure, including reasonable limitation of working hours and periodic holidays with pay, guaranteed by Article 24 of the Universal Declaration of Human Rights and Article 7.d of the International Covenant on Economic, Social and Cultural Rights;
3. Social tourism, and in particular associative tourism, which facilitates widespread access to leisure, travel and holidays, should be developed with the support of the public authorities;
4. Family, youth, student and senior tourism and tourism for people with disabilities, should be encouraged and facilitated;

Article 8

Liberty of tourist movements

1. Tourists and visitors should benefit, in compliance with international law and national legislation, from the liberty to move within their countries and from one State to another, in accordance with Article 13 of the Universal Declaration of Human Rights; they should have access to places of transit and stay and to tourism and cultural sites without being subject to excessive formalities or discrimination;
2. Tourists and visitors should have access to all available forms of communication, internal or external; they should benefit from prompt and easy access to local administrative, legal and health services; they should be free to contact the consular representatives of their countries of origin in compliance with the diplomatic conventions in force;
3. Tourists and visitors should benefit from the same rights as the citizens of the country visited concerning the confidentiality of the personal data and information concerning them, especially when these are stored electronically;
4. Administrative procedures relating to border crossings whether they fall within the competence of States or result from international agreements, such as visas or health and customs formalities, should be adapted, so far as possible, so as to facilitate to the maximum freedom of travel and widespread access to international tourism; agreements between groups of countries to harmonize and simplify these procedures should be encouraged; specific taxes and levies penalizing the tourism industry and undermining its competitiveness should be gradually phased out or corrected;

5. So far as the economic situation of the countries from which they come permits, travellers should have access to allowances of convertible currencies needed for their travels;

Article 9

Rights of the workers and entrepreneurs in the tourism industry

1. The fundamental rights of salaried and self-employed workers in the tourism industry and related activities, should be guaranteed under the supervision of the national and local administrations, both of their States of origin and of the host countries with particular care, given the specific constraints linked in particular to the seasonality of their activity, the global dimension of their industry and the flexibility often required of them by the nature of their work;
2. Salaried and self-employed workers in the tourism industry and related activities have the right and the duty to acquire appropriate initial and continuous training; they should be given adequate social protection; job insecurity should be limited so far as possible; and a specific status, with particular regard to their social welfare, should be offered to seasonal workers in the sector;
3. Any natural or legal person, provided he, she or it has the necessary abilities and skills, should be entitled to develop a professional activity in the field of tourism under existing national laws; entrepreneurs and investors - especially in the area of small and medium-sized enterprises - should be entitled to free access to the tourism sector with a minimum of legal or administrative restrictions;
4. Exchanges of experience offered to executives and workers, whether salaried or not, from different countries, contributes to foster the development of the world tourism industry; these movements should be facilitated so far as possible in compliance with the applicable national laws and international conventions;
5. As an irreplaceable factor of solidarity in the development and dynamic growth of international exchanges, multinational enterprises of the tourism industry should not exploit the dominant positions they sometimes occupy; they should avoid becoming the vehicles of cultural and social models artificially imposed on the host communities; in exchange for their freedom to invest and trade which should be fully recognized, they should involve themselves in local development, avoiding, by the excessive repatriation of their profits or their induced imports, a reduction of their contribution to the economies in which they are established;
6. Partnership and the establishment of balanced relations between enterprises of generating and receiving countries contribute to the sustainable development of tourism and an equitable distribution of the benefits of its growth;

Article 10

Implementation of the principles of the Global Code of Ethics for Tourism

1. The public and private stakeholders in tourism development should cooperate in the implementation of these principles and monitor their effective application;
2. The stakeholders in tourism development should recognize the role of international institutions, among which the World Tourism Organization ranks first, and non-governmental organizations with competence in the field of tourism promotion and development, the protection of human rights, the environment or health, with due respect for the general principles of international law;
3. The same stakeholders should demonstrate their intention to refer any disputes concerning the application or interpretation of the Global Code of Ethics for Tourism for conciliation to an impartial third body known as the World Committee on Tourism Ethics.

TEN ESSENTIALS OF A TOURIST

The Ten Essentials are items which many experienced outdoorsmen believe all outdoor enthusiasts should have handy. They are intended to enhance the safety and comfort of outdoor experiences, address common emergencies, reduce the need to use emergency survival techniques, and generally minimize difficult situations.

According to the standard textbook Mountaineering: The Freedom of the Hills, the ten essentials are:

1. Map
2. Compass (optionally supplemented with a GPS receiver, by some other sources)
3. Sunglasses and Sunscreen
4. Extra food (extra water is considered “important”)
5. Extra clothes
6. Headlamp/flashlight
7. First aid supplies
8. Fire starter
9. Matches
10. Knife

The textbook recommends supplementing the ten essentials with:

- Water treatment device (filter or chemicals) and water bottles
- Ice ax for glacier or snowfield travel (if necessary)
- Repair kit
- Insect repellent (or clothing designed for this purpose)
- Signaling devices, such as a whistle, cell phone, two-way radio, or flares

Not every expedition will require the use of an essential item. But since it is common for an emergency to arise from a cascade of unfortunate events, items addressing some of them can prevent disaster. For example, if a hiker's map is blown away, his/her clothing become soaked, the flashlight quits, and a snowstorm arises, then the whistle, extra clothes and fire starter become important, and probably transform a life threatening experience into a merely exciting one.

- A map and compass are useful to avoid becoming lost which raises the risk of physical injury, anxiety and panic. Therefore, maps which cover the relevant area in sufficient detail and dimension (topography, trails, roads, campsites, towns, etc.) and the skill and knowledge to use them are indispensable when traveling through areas lacking signage, markings or guides. Even a casual compass user can avoid traveling in circles.
- A flashlight protects against physical injury from traveling in the dark. A flashlight is also useful for finding things in the pack, observing wildlife in dark crevices and folds, and for distant signaling. Extra batteries and bulbs are highly recommended.
- Extra food and water can prevent or cure hypothermia and dehydration which can be serious risks in the backcountry. Sustenance is also useful to minimize the likelihood of panic.
- Extra clothes protect against hypothermia. Multiple layers of clothes are generally warmer than an equivalently thick single garment, and much more versatile. A change of clothes is the fastest way to warm up after an inadvertent dunking in a cold mountain stream. Extra clothing is also useful for protection from shrubbery, thorns, insects, sun, wind, as well as cold. If need be, they can be cut into bandages, used as a tree climbing aid, hotpad, pillow, towel or descent line. For overnight trekking, one should always keep one set of evening/night clothes dry and put the dirty clothes back on before starting to walk again. Even if they are wet, a few minutes of walking is usually enough to warm up.
- Sunglasses help prevent sunburn of the eyes. In addition, walking into the sun reflected off fog, snow, sand or water is possibly dangerous.
- A first aid kit usually contains items to treat cuts, abrasions (blisters), punctures and burns. Additional items might address broken digits, broken limbs, crush injuries, cardiac conditions, hypothermia, frostbite, hyperthermia, hypoxia, decompression sickness, insect and snake bites, allergic reactions, animal attacks, and thermal or chemical burns, depending on the specific locale and activities.
- A knife is useful for opening packages, building shelter, making

firestarters, repairing clothing, eating, rapid disentanglement, field surgery, etc. A larger knife (machete) might be essential when one needs or wishes to go off trails in a thick forest and is better for construction and collecting firewood.

- Matches (or a lighter) and fire starter (tinder and kindling) to light a campfire is useful for preventing hypothermia and to signal for aid. In an emergvency, a fire keeps up the spirits, which can also be a life saver.
- A water treatment device (filter or chemical treatment) make water of unknown or dubious quality drinkable. Most backcountry travelers carry a water filter: low end models are inexpensive and provide protection against many diseases. Another benefit might be improving the taste of water (which can help avoid dehydration).
- A whistle is a compact, light and inexpensive relief for the voice when calling for help is needed. Wind, snow and heavy rain can make hearing difficult, or make yells sound like trees or animals whistling.

Other Ten Essentials

Other outdoor organizations have variations of the Ten Essentials pertinent to local conditions. For example, Utah's Wasatch Club lists extra water in place of food, since Utah is mostly desert, and water can be hard to find.

The Spokane Mountaineers list "thirteen essentials" which supplement the list with emergency shelter such as a space blanket, signaling device, and toilet paper and a trowel (for sanitary disposal of human waste, while the paper doubles as tinder for starting a fire).

5

Major Cultural Tourist Spots of the World

RUSSIA

THE GOLDEN RING

The Golden Ring is a ring of cities northeast of Moscow, the capital of Russia. They formerly comprised the region known as Zalesye.

These ancient towns, which also played a significant role in the formation of the Russian Orthodox Church, preserve the memory of the most important and significant events in Russian history. The towns have been called “open air museums” and feature unique monuments of Russian architecture of the 12th–18th centuries, including kremlins, monasteries, cathedrals, and churches. These towns are among the most picturesque in Russia and prominently feature Russia’s famous onion domes. Although there are some discrepancies with respect to the names of the cities that are included in the ring, most include Sergiyev Posad, Pereslavl-Zalesskiy, Rostov Velikiy, Yaroslavl, Kostroma, Ivanovo, Gus-Khrustalny, Suzdal, Vladimir, Rybinsk, Uglich, and Alexandrov. Many of these cities are to be found along the M8 highway or can be reached from Yaroslavl Railway Station in Moscow.

St. Petersburg

In St. Petersburg, it is well known that every stone is a monument and every house a museum, and the palace-park ensembles in the area of the Northern Capital are so numerous that a month is not enough to see all of them.

St. Petersburg offers the most varied routes year-round. They include broad-ranging and thematic tours (to museums, Pushkin places, monuments of palace architecture, etc.), as well as cruises on the St. Petersburg canals. The Programme of the stay, depending on the visitor’s goals, can last 1 to 5 days.

Petersburg Route Options

The first day starts with a broad-ranging city tour and a visit to the Peter and Paul Fortress. On the second day, tourists visit the Hermitage and St. Isaac's Cathedral, and then stroll the city independently, unhurriedly enjoying the beauty of the Venice of the North. The third day is a trip to Tsarskoye Selo (there tourists visit the Palace of Catherine the Great and the Lyceum where Pushkin studied), and then a visit the palace in Pavlovsk.

Instead of the going to the Hermitage and St, Isaac's, visitors may opt to head for Peterhof to walk in the lavish park, feast their eyes on the magnificent fountains and the cottages of Nicholas I. During the White Nights an extra night tour is obligatory, with the drawing of the bridges over the Neva.

On one of the days in the Northern Capital, tourists can take a small Petersburg - Valaam - Petersburg cruise.

The Black Sea Coast and the Caucasus Mountains

The Black Sea coast cities – Anapa, Gelendzhik, Tuapse, Sochi, Adler – do not only attract holiday beachcombers. After all, the history of this land reaches back to ancient times and is connected to the history of various European and Asian peoples. In Anapa, tourists visit the archeological museum and Tamani, the digs in ancient Hermonassis (modern Fanagoria), the mud volcanos, the wineries (with obligatory wine-tasting), the Arbau-Durso Museum and Dolphinarium. Excursion routes through the city of Sochi are extremely interesting because of their scenery, culture and history: tourists view the surroundings from the snow-white tower on the Akhun mountain, descend into the gorge to the Agur Waterfalls, the Tisosamshit grove in Khost, the tea plantations in Dagomys. The mountain route through Sochi offers visits to the most beautiful mountains in the Caucasus – Kardyvach. Explore the footpaths at the Fisht mountain rage which was lauded by the Greeks, visit Azishsk cave – the second largest in the Western Cacausus.

ITALY

Rome

For thousands of years tourists, merchants and pilgrims have wended their way towards the town on seven hills on Tiber. Rome has unarguably the richest, fullest history of any town on earth. Its unique position in the world's greatest Empire, its significance as a religious and cultural centre, its turbulent centuries of aristocratic and papal rivalries and upheaval and all the while incorporating some of the finest architecture still surviving.

Rome is far from being a museum: it's a colourful and vibrant living city, which is still an appealing destination for those with a phobia of history. The food, the culture, the ambience and the surrounding scenery make a great holiday even if you don't see a single ruin or statue.

Restaurants in Rome

From small noisy rooms where you can concentrate on steaming plates of pasta, to designer spaces for seeing and being seen, Rome's restaurants probably outnumber any other type of business in the city.

Part of the holiday pleasure in Rome is discovering your very own favourite trattoria. In our opinion, it's hard to eat badly in Rome. But for those who'd like some guidance, here are our suggestions.

For smarter restaurants, it's advisable to book, especially at the weekend. At the simpler but popular trattorie and pizzerie, there's often an informal queue or waiting list.

Many restaurants - especially in tourist areas - start serving dinner at 7pm, although nearer 9pm is a more normal time to eat. Restaurants in Rome shouldn't request a coperta (cover charge) but generally they'll bring some bread and charge you for that, anyway.

Around Rome's tourist hubs you'll find many restaurants aimed at plenty of reasonable restaurants. Have a look at the menu, the prices, and at the meals being served and you'll get a good idea of whether the place will suit you. Naturally you pay more in a tourist location like Piazza Navona and the Pantheon, and a Roman may not be impressed with the establishment, but it's your holiday and you may well feel the view is worth it. You only have to go a few yards from the main piazza to find cheaper fare. There are far too many decent places to list, but one of the best areas to start looking in the Centro Storico is around the narrow Via di Tor Millina (which leads off Piazza Navona) and along Via del Governo Vecchio, where you'll find plenty of pleasant restaurants with outdoor seating. Campo dei' Fiori and Trastevere are also places where you'll be spoilt for choice.

Rome's Pompeii

'Better than Pompeii' is how some visitors describe it. At Rome's own preserved ancient town, Ostia Antica, you can lose yourself in the sprawling streets of the former port. Abandoned by the Romans, this trading centre declined and finally became buried in silt. Much of the area is now excavated, and you can explore streets where some of the ancient character lingers. Mosaics still in place, columns reaching to the sky, careful frescoes decorating walls, which still stand high and fascinating marble-seated communal public toilets.

Ostia Antica is Rome's own, nearly-secret Pompeii. The ancient port town is a fascinating and under-visited archaeological site.

Ostia Antica is not far from the centre of Rome, and makes a pleasant half-day (allow longer if you want to lunch there or are particularly interested in archaeology). To get there, take the suburban train line to Ostia from Piramide Station (which is on Metro Linea B). You can use your normal Rome travel ticket. The train goes all the way to Rome's seaside town, Ostia Lido; the Ostia Antica station is about twenty minutes from Rome. The archaeological area is close to the station, over a footbridge - follow signs. There are a couple of restaurants near the ruins, and there is also a restaurant inside the site.

Although it is now 4 km inland, Ostia was originally developed as a sea port, prior to the silting up of the Tiber's estuary. Ostia increased in importance from the fourth century BC, becoming a major naval and trading base. As Rome's port, the town had obvious commercial significance, and expanded in size and grandeur to match this position. However, during the third century AD, its place was taken by a new port at Fiumicino, and within the next couple of centuries Ostia had begun its decline. The Tiber was no longer navigable, the roads were overgrown, and Ostia sank into muddy oblivion.

Nowadays much of the old town has been excavated, and the visitor is free to wander and explore at their will (get a street plan from the ticket kiosk). There is a lot to see, and a leisurely wander is extremely rewarding. Major sites include the Roman theatre (there are plays put on here in the summer), the impressive Forum, a large baths complex and more than one Mithraeum. Many of the buildings are preserved up to the second storey, giving a powerful sense of the past.

There are impressive mosaics and columns everywhere (statues are mostly taken away for safekeeping), but highlights include the smaller domestic details: the fishmonger's marble slab, the bar with its wares illustrated on the wall, the communal public toilets, the residential villas with peaceful courtyards.

Day Trips from Rome

Because Rome is so rich in must-see tourist sights, many visitors neglect the surrounding area. One or two major guidebooks don't even give Lazio a chapter to itself, concentrating solely on Rome. It can't be denied that Rome does have masses to offer the tourist. But for visitors who are staying more than three days, visitors who are returning to the Eternal City for the second time (or third, or fourth) or for those who have simply had enough of the city, there are wonderful places easily reachable by car or public transport for a day trip or a weekend away.

Day trips from Rome make a refreshing break from the chaos, noise and pollution of the city. They are also refreshingly cheap, since trains in Italy are an economical means of transport, and the blue Cotral buses which serve the area are frequent and cheap.

Rome is surprisingly close to the sea and to the hills, and you don't have to travel far to appreciate completely diverse scenery. In the summer you can do what the Romans have been doing for millennia, and take a break in the nearby hills, where the air is noticeably cooler and fresher, and you may even find a breeze. Alternatively you can enjoy a day at the seaside, visiting one of the busy beaches near Rome, or finding more tranquil stretches of sand to the south. Back in the 18th Century, English aristocrats on their Grand Tour spent considerable time in the smaller towns and countryside of Lazio. Many of the views and antiquities they admired have changed surprisingly little, and it's an atmospheric experience to follow in their footsteps around the cascades, temples and great houses of Tivoli, Frascati and the rest of Lazio.

Lazio is full of sites of enormous archaeological interest, including very fine Etruscan remains in the north of the region as well as later Roman ruins. Striking temples of varying scale can be seen at Terracina, Palestrina and Tivoli, where you may find yourself the only tourist marvelling at ancient columns and picturesque views. The absence of crowds is an appealing feature of Lazio's hilltowns; although many tourists visit Frascati (chiefly for the wine), and Tivoli (for the fountains of the Villa d'Este), you will find little tourism in other destinations - and even those towns are often surprisingly neglected.

If you're feeling more ambitious, you can easily journey further afield. Swift train services run into Tuscany, Umbria and Campania, and your options include Florence, Naples, Orvieto, Spoleto, and Siena.

If you are fortunate enough to have a car, you'll be able to see much more of Lazio at your own pace. However, this site concentrates on places accessible by public transport. You may miss out on some of the more remote sights, but all the destinations featured here contain enough to occupy you for an enjoyable day out.

Monaco at French or Italian Riviera

A day trip to Monaco is a good addition to a holiday on the French or Italian Riviera. Just a short journey along the Riviera will take you through three countries; Italy, France and Monaco, and a tour along this beautiful stretch of Mediterranean coast is a popular holiday choice. The Cote d'Azur is an enchanting mixture of natural beauty, artificial glamour, and blue blue sea. Monte Carlo is also a glamorous weekend destination, with easy access from the UK.

The climate is generally mild, with plenty of sunshine, but in the summer Monaco can be hot and crowded. The Monaco Grand Prix takes place in May, so depending on your tastes you should either make a note to avoid the crowds and the screeching rubber, or book ahead to enjoy the excitement.

Monaco and Monte Carlo Tourist Attractions

Monte Carlo must be one of the most evocative place names in the world, summoning up an image that is all its own. Glamourous gowns and glittering jewels gathered around roulette tables, sunbathing starlets and royal romances.

Located on the beautiful Côte d'Azur, Monte Carlo is at the centre of the tiny principality of Monaco. Covering 2 square kilometres, the state nestles into France, and the official languages are French and Monégasque, although

English and Italian are also spoken. The currency is the Euro. Monaco is chiefly famous for its royalty (the glamorous Grimaldi family have ruled the country since the thirteenth century) and its casino, and as a visitor you will find these two definitive features hard to avoid. Far better to revel in the unique character of this ultimate in materialist worlds.

The main tourist attraction in Monaco is, naturally, the Casino. Some parts of this venerable institution are open to the casual visitor (over 21s only), but you should dress smartly and be prepared to pay if you want to penetrate to its more exclusive areas. Tacky it may seem, but you can't visit Monte Carlo without having at least a look, if not a flutter.

Also well-worth a visit are the strange National Museum of Dolls and Automatons of Yesteryear and the souvenir shops where you can buy a Prince Rainier commemorative mug.

Although so tiny you can walk around the country in half a day, Monaco is divided into four areas, of which Monte Carlo is the most renowned. If you want to travel around, and don't fancy walking, distances are short, and buses run up and down the length of the state. The Palace (open May-October) is in Monaco-Ville, the old fortified capital , and for an entrance fee you can view the State Apartments, and the Throne Room. Further royal entertainment can be had at the History of the Princes of Monaco Wax Museum, where you can admire effigies of past Grimaldis.

Also in Monaco-Ville is the Oceanographic Museum, with its highly-recommended aquarium, and the free Museum of Old Monaco. Art treasures can be seen at the Musée de la Chapelle de la Visitation, where the collection includes works by Rubens and Vermeer. The remaining two areas are Fontvieille, an industrialised quarter where land reclamation has extended the principality's acreage, and La Condamine, the harbour area.

Tourist Information

Office du Tourisme , Direction du Tourisme et des Congres de la Principauté de Monaco, 2a Boulevard des Moulins, Monte Carlo.

Monaco Restaurants

The best areas for eating out in Monaco are Monaco-Ville and the harbour quarter, La Condamine. You can choose from cuisines reflecting both the French and Italian influences.

Monaco Nightlife

Monte Carlo nightlife is mostly glitzy and expensive. There are several old-style cabaret shows, notably the Cabaret in the Casino Gardens. For a more youthful atmosphere, try Stars'n'Bars, an American-style bar with a restaurant and disco, or the Monte Carlo Sporting Club where you'll find a choice of entertainments, including Jimmy'z disco.

Leaning Tower of Pisa

Unlike many great buildings of the time, the Tower of Pisa does not serve a practical purpose. Rather, it was constructed as a boastful statement to Pisa's nemesis, Florence. At the time, the two were the modern equivalent of today's "superpowers" and ruled much of the world through their control of the sea. The two were also bitter rivals, fighting for supremacy. In fact, construction of the tower was interrupted because of wars in 1178 with Florence, 1185 with Florence again, and in 1284 with Genoa, It was during one of these breaks in construction that the tower's infamous tilt was discovered. It was only three stories tall at the time, but rather than abandon the project, construction continued until the tower reached its full height of 58.36 meters when measured from its foundation, or just 55 meters when measured from the ground. It was at this early stage, too, that the tower first served its intended purpose — the ringing of bells. Documents have survived that show that a bell was first placed at the top in 1198. When construction continued, it was replaced by seven bells at the top in 1350. There are two theories about why the tower leans. The most popular reason is because of the unstable soil beneath. Its of 14,700 metric tons of grey San Giuliano limestone is simply too much weight for the ground to hold. The local soil is mostly marshy clay and the tower exerts a force of 497 kPa on it. But some historians don't think the lean was an accident. They believe it is an intentional architectural design that produced the tilt. However, recent measurements and analysis of the soil have put this school of thought in doubt. Over the centuries there have been a number of attempts to straighten out the tower. One try in 1934, concrete was pumped underneath the tower. Another in 1838 involved excavating the earth and drying out the ground the tower rests on.. Recently, a pair of suspenders were attached to lead weights and slung over the tower which helped a bit. Architecturally, the building is summed up thusly by its official web site:

"The six arcades, the base on which they are placed and the belfry above them subdivide the Tower into eight segments, known as orders. The interior order is animated by a band of blind arches placed on half columns. Underneath the arches are lozenged rhomboid decorations inlaid with coloured marbles, each containing a rosette in relief at the centre. The wall facing is interrupted by narrow round-arched lancet windows and, to the west, by the only door of accessa rectangular opening framed by an architrave. Above the architrave a falcate arch with a carved archivolt rests upon two capitals in continuation of the piers, forming an aedicule containing a fourteenth-century bust of the Madonna and Child. At the sides of the portal there are friezes with decorations showing animals and imaginary beasts. These, alongside a singular representation of ships (the Pisan port?), accompany the epigraph which commemorates the foundation of the building. The cylindrical belfry which concludes the building, of a smaller diameter than the floors below, bears an external decoration composed of closed and pierced lunettes, which rest alternately on pedestals and columns, whereby under every pedestal (bearing two closed lunnettes) there is a door, while the single pierced lunnettes supported on columns are lengthened to form windows. The belfry is reached via a narrow spiral stair, and in turn allows access to the summit of the tower by way of a stair cut into the wall."

Some Facts about the Leaning Tower of Pisa

The Tower of Pisa was built to show the rest of the world the wealth of the city of Pisa. The people of Pisa were very good sailors and they conquered many lands, including Jerusalem, Carthago, Ibiza, Mallorca, Africa, Belgium, Britania, Norway, Spain, Morocco, and other places. But they had only one real enemy, the people from Florence. And to show how well they were doing they started to build a really useless belltower to go with the rest of the buildings near it - the Cathedral, Baptistery, and Cemetery.

The buiding of the tower was started in the year 1173. After a while the war with Florence started again and they stopped. In 1180 the restarted and in 1185 they had finished the 1st., 2nd, and the 3rd. floor. And again war with Florence, which of course meant that they put all their money in warfare. In this year the tower started to lean to one side, so while they were building, it was already the leaning tower of Pisa. They must have been thinking that a bell tower without bell wasn't a bell tower so the put some bells on the top of the 3rd. floor in 1198.

The people of Pisa threw the key in the Arno River and the count and his family died of starvation. In 1319 they finished all the floors. And finally they put the bell tower on top of it in 1350. In 1392 Pisa was sold to Florence, a big humiliation for the people of Pisa. The started a rebellion but in 1406 they had to surrender because they were under siege and everybody was dying of starvation. In 1499 they started another war against Florence who were using the people of Pisa as slaves. And again the brave but unfortuned army of Pisa lost and that is the and of the history of Pisa.

FRANCE

Carcassonne

Carcassonne is situated in the Languedoc region of France, in the south of the country, and is a UNESCO World Heritage Site. The old walled city, standing on a hill and capped by pointed towers, is like the backdrop to a medieval romance. On a clear day, there are views of the Pyrenees. The town makes an interesting stop on a touring holiday, and can be combined with themed trips to Cathar country, or to the haunts of medieval poets. Carcassonne is also a pleasant destination for the weekend tripper, with budget flights from Stansted making the town an easy and affordable destination.

Carcassonne is made up of two towns; the walled Cité on its hill, and below, over the River Aude, the Bastide Saint-Louis. The Bastide, or Ville Basse, is the lower town, a thirteenth-century development which was laid out to a gridlike plan and was surrounded by walls. The earlier, fortified hilltown dates back to the 6th century BC, when there was a Gaulish settlement on the site. This was succeeded by a Roman town. The large defensive walls which can be seen today were constructed over the centuries, as Carcassanne became a Moorish conquest, a feudal stronghold, a Cathar citadel, a frontier fort and finally a tourist honeypot. Although many of the foundations and lower stretches of wall date back to the Roman era, some of the upper sections are the results of a mammoth rebuilding project in the nineteenth century, led by one Eugene Viollet-le-Duc.

The cleaned-up and restored character of the town's ramparts can diminish its appeal for the tourist seeking authenticity - there is something rather Disneyish about its eagerness to please. However, despite the facelift, most of the walls and towers are original. An exhibition of sketches and paintings in the castle show 'before and after' views of the reconstructions - it's reassuring to see how much predated Viollet-le-Duc's project, although fairy-tale lovers will be disappointed by the blatant inauthenticity of the pointed turrets.

Carcassonne is an extremely popular tourist destination, particularly in the peak summer months. The steep narrow streets of the citadel swarm with visitors, while every other building seems to be a restaurant, cafe, gift shop or museum. Shops overflow with stocks of anything with a medieval connection: flails, swords, shields made of wood and plastic for bloodthirsty children; tapestries for their parents. A small general store on rue Cros Mayrevieille offers a chance to buy the basics, while specialist shops provide sweets, wines and regional delicacies at a price. Every July the town hosts a festival of music, dance and theatre, the Festival de Carcassonne.

Carcassonne's Castle (Chateau Comtal) is the town's major tourist attraction, with queues to match. Visit the buildings and museum first, then join one of the regular guided tours (out of season, you may have to settle for French commentary). The tours are the only way to explore an exciting series of towers, turrets and ramparts, with fantastic views and countless photo-opportunities. The tour finishes by Carcassonne's open-air theatre, next to the cathedral.

The Cathedral (Basilique Saint-Nazaire), which is dedicated to Saints Nazarius and Celsus, has been built and rebuilt several times since the 6th century. Today's nave dates back to the twelfth-century Romanesque church, while the rest of the building is mostly Gothic. The cathedral has two beautiful and colourful rose windows, an early organ (dating to 1522), several interesting tombstones and statues, as well as the 'Siege Stone', a carving showing a detailed military scene.

It's possible to pass several pleasant hours wandering the streets of the town, or walking around the ramparts. Children and the young-at-heart will be thrilled to discover just how accessible some of the wall-walks are, although care should be taken as you negotiate the imposing outer walls. When they're not playing at being medieval knights, visitors of all ages can enjoy a spin on the beautiful vintage carousel which stands at the city gates.

When you're ready to move on from the crowded lanes of the Cité, you can stroll down to the lower town, over the old bridge. There are benches and riverside walks, as well as a number of sights to see (pick up a map from the Tourist Information Office). The famous Canal du Midi passes through Carcassonne, with a charming little marina next to the station. Boat trips will take you on a leisurely canal cruise, or walkers may enjoy a ramble along the broad canalside path.

Carcassonne Tourist Information Office is at 28, rue de Verdun, with a secondary office just inside the main gateway of the Cité, the Porte Narbonnaise.

Eiffel Tower in France

Important Facts about the Eiffel Tower

The following is a summary of the interesting facts about the Eiffel tower:
300 ironworkers worked for two years 1887-89;
2.5 million rivets;
15,000 pieces of iron;
40 tons of paint;
High wind sway of at most 12 cm;
Temperature dependant height variation of 15 cm or less;
1652 steps from the 2nd level to the top level;
Total height in 1889: 300.51 meters [985 feet, 11 inches];
Total height with television mast: 320.755 meters [1052 feet, 4 inches];
Base area: 10,281.96 Sq. meters [2.54 acres];
Foundation weight: 277,602 kg [306 tons];
Iron structure weight: 7.34 million kg [8092.2 tons];
Elevator systems weight: 946,000 kg [1042.8 tons];
Total tower weight: 8.56 million kg [9441 tons];
Pressure on foundation: 4.1 to 4.5 kg/square cm;

There are 1,665 steps to the summit and not, as popularly believed, 1,792 steps representing the year of the First French Republic

Eiffel Tower History

The Eiffel Tower was built for the International Exhibition of Paris of 1889 commemorating the centenary of the French Revolution. The Prince of Wales, later King Edward VII of England, opened the tower. Of the 700 proposals submitted in a design competition, Gustave Eiffel's was unanimously chosen. However it was not accepted by all at first, and a petition of 300 names - including those of Maupassant, Emile Zola, Charles Garnier (architect of the Opéra Garnier), and Dumas the Younger - protested its construction.

At 300 meters (320.75 m including antenna), and 7,000 tons, it was the world's tallest building until 1930. Other statistics include:

2.5 million rivets

300 steel workers, and 2 years (1887-1889) to construct it.

Sway of at most 12 cm in high winds.

Height varies up to 15 cm depending on temperature.

15,000 iron pieces (excluding rivets). 40 tons of paint. 1652 steps to the top.

The tower was almost torn down in 1909, but was saved because of its antenna - used for telegraphy at that time. Beginning in 1910 it became part of the International Time Service. French radio (since 1918), and French television (since 1957) have also made use of its stature.

During its lifetime, the Eiffel Tower has also witnessed a few strange scenes, including being scaled by a mountaineer in 1954, and parachuted off of in 1984 by two Englishmen. In 1923 a journalist rode a bicycle down from the first level. Some accounts say he rode down the stairs, other accounts suggest the exterior of one of the tower's four legs which slope outward.

Switzerland

Switzerland is one of Europe's most beautiful countries. The mighty Alpine peaks dominate the whole country, lending a fairy-tale appearance to even dour cities like Zurich. In the north, away from the mountains, the scenery remains stunning, with rolling green pastures and chocolate box villages. As well as the lure of the mountains, Switzerland's cultural diversity lends a distinct character to its great cities, from French-speaking Geneva to German Bern to Italian Lugano.

The German-speaking northeast of Switzerland extends from the wooded hills of Schaffhausen in the north, almost surrounded by Germany, to the wild and beautiful alpine scenery of William Tell country in the south. The city of Zurich is more than just a financial centre, sharing this part of Switzerland with the ancient cities of Zug and Schwyz.

Towns and Places of Interest in North-east Switzerland

Schaffausen straddles the Rhine and has a gem of an old town, famous for its oriel windows and the striking medieval frescoes adorning its ancient houses. 3 kms outside the town are the Rheinfalls, magnificent waterfalls of awe-inspiring power. Visit Stein-am-Rhein, an almost perfectly preserved medieval town about 20 kms east of Schaffausen. Another 20 kms east brings you to the first arm of the Bodensee (Lake Constance), with numerous castles dominating the shoreline. The lake narrows at Konstanz which, although actually in Germany, is worth visiting for its old town. All along the shores of the Bodensee are small resort towns where you can swim and enjoy the watersports surrounded by rolling hills, orchards and meadows.

Saint Gallen is an ancient university town with a bustling old town and a famous library. As well as its impressive cathedral the streets of the old town contain thriving shops in beautiful old buildings with picturesque oriel windows. The Walensee is a beautiful calm lake at the foot of the lovely Churfirsten peaks. Together with the Toggenburg valley this area offers wonderful opportunities for winter sports, watersports, and walking amongst stunning scenery. In the far corner of this part of Switzerland is the principality of Lichtenstein, with its pretty villages and excellent mountain walks.

Lake Lucerne, the Vierwaldstattersee, must be one of the most beautiful lakes anywhere, and excellent holiday country in summer or winter. The name means the lake of the four forest cantons, and in this part of Switzerland many of the important events in Swiss history took place. William Tell is commemorated in several spots, notably Altdorf and the Rutli Meadow at the far end of the lake. From here the road ascends to the bleak St Gotthard pass, now bypassed by a tunnel. The lake itself has the pleasant resorts of Weggis, Vitznau and Gersau on the north shore. Behind is the Rigi mountain with lovely meadow walking and a superb view of the Alps across the lake. On the southern shore is the Burgenstock and Beckenried, again with good walking among wonderful scenery. All these resorts are served by steamers based in Luzern which criss-cross the lake and connect efficiently with cable cars and funicular railways. Take the cable cars to the summit of Mount Pilatus with marvellous views of the Alps and Lake Lucerne, or venture deeper into the mountains to the summit of Mount Titlis with its amazing revolving cable car. Below is the ski area of Obermatt, centred on Engleberg.

Contrary to expectations, Zurich is a very attractive city, with a jumble of buildings set in the twisting alleys of its old town, and a distant panorama of snowy peaks beyond Lake Zurich. The town has its share of museums and fine buildings, and the main shopping street, Bahnhofstrasse, testifies to Zurich's wealth. Plenty of nightlife on the right bank of the river, and relaxing walks along the lakeside promenades. Zug, about 30 kms south of Zurich, has its own attractive lakeside and a small but interesting old town. Further south again is the historic town of Schwyz, which gave Switzerland its name, with many grand old houses and its Bundesbriefmuseum.

GERMANY

Berlin

Berlin is worth a visit. No one will argue with that. This multicultural metropolis seduces you with her stirring past, her thrilling present and her exciting future. The German capital offers an extensive number of classic sights as well as fascinating curiosities, such as the absence of any closing times. When the lights go out everywhere else in the Federal Republic, you can go on dancing away or plunge even deeper in Berlin's night life. You won't be able to be bored during the day either.

The Berlin experience is without parallel. Why not start by a stroll (or a rather more comfortable tour) through this fast changing city with her split history? The border between east and west has almost completely disappeared. Ever since the fall of the Wall this city has experienced a second 'Gründerzeit' (economic revival). Berlin's face changes almost daily. Berlin is also a cultural capital. More than 160 museums invite you for a voyage of discovery through the world of the arts and of civilisations, of history and technology.

Every night the curtain is raised in three opera houses and more than 50 theatres. It's impossible trying to keep count of the innumerable cultural initiatives: dance, variety shows, cabaret, classical concerts, jazz, rock, techno. Young people especially have conquered the city with their music clubs and parties. The yearly held 'Love Parade' is their showpiece. Shopping will provide you with a completely different kind of enjoyment. If it can be bought, you will find it in Berlin: haute couture, designer fashion, antiques, books, CDs or traditional knickknacks. As far as culinary delights are concerned, the whole world is in attendance in Berlin. There is more! In spite of her metropolitan elegance, this city has kept her small-scale atmosphere, and disposes of innumerable green spaces and lakes. At the end of an exciting stay each and every visitor has to admit enthusiastically: Berlin is worth more than a visit.

Other Sites

Berlin has immense proportions: 45 km from east to west, 38 km from north to south. The 12 districts each have preserved their own character and invite you to further exploring: short walks through the Kiez, like the Berliner calls his quarter, nature trips – in the centre of the city or outside the metropolis in the widespread environment. There are lots of possibilities!

Walking through the Regierungsviertel

The Office of the Federal Chancellor, the day care centre of the Bundestag, the Paul-Löbe-Haus with offices of the representatives of the people and meeting halls, the Marie-Elisabeth-Lüders-Haus with the parliamentary library, the Bundespressekonferenz: the buildings of the federal government stand along the Spree like a 'Band of the Union', north of the Reichstag.

The buildings are at their best when you look at them from the water. The Ulferweg, decorated in the summer of 2004, about 1.1 km long between the Paul-Löbe-Haus and the Haus der Kulturen der Welt, leads past the Kanzleramt.

The new Spreebogenpark in between becomes the meeting place for the soccer fans during the WorldCup in 2006. Diagonally across from it, the new central station arises with its huge glass roof construction. Behind the Haus der Kulturen der Welt is the mooring place for ships and if you want to go to the cultural centre you can take bus 100 again.

CANADA

Traveling to the Sights

Bordering the United States, the largest percentage of Canadian tourists are Americans.

Among its main tourist attractions are the Spring Festivals in the Nova Scotia and the Okanagan Valley in British Columbia. There is also the Ottawa Festival of Spring and the Calgary Exhibition. Travelers to Canada will also enjoy the Niagara Grape and Wine Festival in Ontario.

The city of Toronto also plays host to the Canadian component of the Niagara Falls, which is often called the Horseshoe Falls because of its horseshoe shaped cradle where the water falls. Another great sight in Toronto that travelers to Canada should not dare miss is the Georgian Bay, a picturesque waterscape with its row of pine-filled islands. The largest and best known of Ontario's more than 200 provincial parks is the Algonquin Park. Other tourist spots that Canada's travelers should take special note of are the Quetico Provincial Park, the Lake Superior, the Polar Bear Park in Hudson Bay and the Kakabeka Falls.

Travelers to Canada will also not be disappointed when they see the snow-capped mountain Mount Begbie, which can be found in one of Canada's main provinces, the British Columbia. Located in the Mount Revelstoke National Park, it retains its lovely evergreen forests. The province of British Columbia offers travelers in Canada the best in hiking, fishing and canoeing opportunities in the world.

Quebec, whose name was, derived from the Algonquian term which means "a place where the river narrows," promises travelers to Canada a mix of the old and the new.

Travelers can visit the French-style hotel Chateau Frontenac, which is located in the Old Quebec district and the Tadoussac, where whales congregate near the mouth of the Saguenay fjord. Travelers to Canada can also enjoy a little bit of fishing experience in the little fishing villages in New Brunswick and in Concepcion Bay, one of Canada's many coastal inlets. The island of Newfoundland also affords travelers in Canada the best in music entertainment. It also boasts the country's finest landscapes with its flat-topped peaks and glacier-gouged lakes, which can be found in the Gros Morne National Park.

The waters of Lake Louise, which can be found in the Banff National Park, is the main attraction in the province of Alberta. A lake of glacial waters, Lake

Louise reflects on its surface the surrounding Rocky Mountains and forests, making it a great sight to behold. Wedged with Alaska and British Columbia is the Yukon Territory famed for its mining industry. In fact, one of its bustling towns during the gold rush period, Dawson, is now a tourist attraction. Travelers in Canada just love the Gaslight Folies variety show, a recreation of the entertainment during that period in history.

They are performed at its Palace Grand Theater. Southwest of Yukon Territory is the Quill Creek, which flows from the Saint Elias Mountains that contains the highest peaks in Canada as well as the waters that flows in Yukon's extensive natural water system composed of creeks, lakes and rivers. The Kluane National Park and reserve is one place that travelers in Canada's Yukon province should not dare miss. Found in the Kluane Ranges and Saint Elias Mountains, the park offers a sight of Canada's highest peak, Mount Logan as well as a number of glaciers and ice fields.

AUSTRALIA

Travel to Australia: A Country-Continent Continuum

Situated between the Indian and South Pacific Oceans in a geographically misunderstood region of the world called Oceania, Australia is a continent nearly twice the size of Europe and also an independent nation made up of six states and two territories.

Situated between the Indian and South Pacific Oceans in a geographically misunderstood region of the world called Oceania, Australia is a continent nearly twice the size of Europe and also an independent nation made up of six states and two territories. The literal continental size of the country makes for travel that is diverse and exhilarating without the hassle of ever crossing a single border!

Australia has been inhabited for an estimated 45,000 years with the first recorded European encounter with the landmass not until 1606. In 1770, the English navigator James Cook claimed Australia for Britain, but it was not until the gold rush of the 1800s that Aboriginal tribes were really harmed by Europeans who were drawn into the depths of the continent's formidable Great Dividing Range where natives had since thrived undisturbed. Today there are many trading posts, such as Alice Springs, where Aborigines sell traditional artwork and musical instruments such as the popular didgeridoo.

Wine, Waves, and Whimsical Wilderness

Most travelers anticipate a visit to the Sydney Opera House, a wild ride through the outback and then a dive at the Great Barrier Reef, and most visitors experience an abrupt awakening to the sheer depth of Australia's wonderful attributes and activities as well as the great distances that would make such a trip lengthy at best. Southwestern Australia is a fantastic wine-producing region, with harvests including Australia's own Shiraz. Visit the popular Margaret River area for delicious reds or take a drive along the nearby coast and surf some of the best waves in the morning while making a leisurely afternoon of wine tasting in the quaint coastal towns along the way. On the path of indulgence, make sure to enjoy some truly authentic Aussie cuisine like slow-roasted kangaroo or emu, and don't shy away from the Moreton Bay bug, which is actually an exceptional species of slipper lobster native to Australian waters.

Witness firsthand the versatility of the Aussie landscape by venturing north to the coastal Daintree Rainforest in the wet tropical region near the festive city of Cairns and the northern tip of the Great Barrier Reef. Some of the world's oldest rainforest stands in Australia's tropical north while ski resorts garnish the eastern Snowy Mountains outside of cosmopolitan Sydney and the semi-arid Flinders Ranges in the south represent the last of the quintessential Australian outback, complete with crocodiles and wallabies. Tasmania, Australia's giant southern island, is often considered a miniature Australia with all of the spectacular sights in a fraction of the size. Most notable is the intense backdrop marked with jutting peaks, plunging crevasses and glacial lakes of Cradle Mountain-Lake St Clair National Park.

Whether you travel to Australia for the rugged adventure of the outback or the richly multicultural and ultra-hip global scenes of Melbourne and Sydney, the deluge of opportunities available upon arrival are sure to turn your initial itinerary on its head. Not to mention, Australia is an excellent jumping point from which to discover the many tropical island-nations of Southeast Asia to the north.

CHINA

Great Wall of China

The Great Wall of China, one of the greatest wonders of the world, was enlisted in the World Heritage by UNESCO in 1987. Just like a gigantic dragon, the Great Wall winds up and down across deserts, grasslands, mountains and plateaus stretching approximately 6,700 kilometers (4,163 miles) from east to west of China. With a history of more than 2000 years, some of the section of the great wall are now in ruins or even entirely disappeared. However, it is still one of the most appealing attractions all around the world owing to its architectural grandeur and historical significance. History of the wall: Excitement abounds in the origin, vicissitude and nature of the great wall of the Qin, Han, and Ming dynasties.

The Great Wall was originally built in the Spring, Autumn, and Warring States Periods as a defensive fortification by the three states: Yan, Zhao and Qin. The Great Wall went through constant extensions and repairs in later dynasties. In fact, it began as independent walls for different states when it was first built, and did not become the "Great" wall until the Qin Dynasty.

Emperor Qin Shihuang succeeded in his effort to have the walls joined together to fend off the invasions from the Huns in the north after the unification of China. Since then, the Great Wall has served as a monument of the Chinese nation throughout history. A visit to the Great Wall is like a tour through the history backwards; it brings tourists great excitement in each step of the wall. No one can tell precisely when the building of the Great Wall was started but it is popularly believed that it originated as a military fortification against intrusion by tribes on the borders during the earlier Zhou Dynasty. Late in the Spring and Autumn Period (770 BC - 476 BC), the ducal states extended the defence work and built "great" structures to prevent the attacks from other states. It was not until the Qin Dynasty that the separate walls, constructed by the states of Qin, Yan and Zhao kingdoms, were connected to form a defensive system on the northern border of the country by Emperor Qin Shi Huang (also called Qin Shi Huangdi by westerners or the First Emperor).

After the emperor unified the country in 214 BC, he ordered the construction of the wall. It took about ten years to finish and the wall stretched from Linzhao (in the eastern part of today's Gansu Province) in the west to Liaodong (in today's Jilin Province) in the east. The wall not only served as a defence in the north but also symbolized the power of the emperor. From the Qin Dynasty onwards, Xiongnu, an ancient tribe that lived in North China, frequently harassed the northern border of the country.

During the Han Dynasty, Emperor Wu (Han Wu Di), sent three expeditions to fight against the Xiongnu in 127 BC, 121 BC and 119 BC. The Xiongnu were driven into the far north of the Gobi. To maintain the safety of the Hexi Corridor (today's Gansu Province), the emperor ordered the extension of the Great Wall westward into the Hexi Corridor and Xinjiang region. The ruins of the beacon towers and debris of the Han Wall are still discernible in Dunhuang, Yumen and Yangguan. A recent report shows that ruins of the Han Wall have been discovered near Lopnur in China's Xinjiang region. Further construction and extensions were made in the successive Northern Wei, Northern Qi and Sui dynasties.

The present Great Wall in Beijing is mainly remains from the Ming Dynasty (1368 - 1644). During this period, bricks and granite were used when the workers laid the foundation of the wall and sophisticated designs and passes were built in the places of strategic importance. To strengthen the military control of the northern frontiers, the Ming authorities divided the Great Wall into nine zones and placed each under the control of a Zhen (garrison headquarters). The Ming Wall starts from Yalujiang River (in today's Heilongjiang Province), via today's Liaoning, Hebei, Inner Mongolia, Shanxi, Shaanxi, Ningxia provinces, to Gansu. The total length reaches 12,700 li (over 5,000 kilometers). The Shanhaiguan Pass and the Jiayuguan Pass are two well-preserved passes at either end.

Today, the Wall has become a must-see for every visitor to China. Few can help saying 'Wow!' when they stand on top of a beacon tower and look at this giant dragon. For centuries, the wall served succeeding dynasties as an efficient military defence. However, it was only when a dynasty had weakened from within that invaders from the north were able to advance and conquer. Both the Mongols (Yuan Dynasty, 1271-1368) and the Manchurians (Qing Dynasty, 1644-1911) were able to take power because of weakness of the government and poverty of the people but never due to any possibility of weakness of the Wall.

STATUE OF LIBERTY

For the many immigrants that flocked from Europe to New York, the Statue of Liberty was the first image they saw of the USA. The statue was a gift from the French government for the 100th birthday of America's Independence.

Design

It was designed by a young French sculptor, Frédéric-Auguste Bartholdi, who was striving to build a statue like the great Colossus that once stood at the Greek island Rhodos. The statue's face was modeled after his mother's and the story goes that the body was modeled after a prostitute. The steel framework was made by Gustave Eiffel, who also built the Eiffel Tower in Paris.

Construction

It was constructed in France and sent to the USA in 214 pieces. The biggest and most embarrassing problem was the construction of the pedestal, which had to be paid for by the Americans themselves. The statue's torch was displayed in Madison Square park for six years in an attempt to spark interest and attract funds. But it was only after publisher Joseph Pulitzer published the names of those who donated money for the project that the funds started flowing in. Eventually, the statue was erected 10 years late, in 1886.

The Statue

The Statue of Liberty is 46,5 meter (151ft) high and together with the pedestal it reaches 93 meter (305ft). It used to be possible to take the staircase inside the statue and walk all the way up the 354 steps to the head from where you have a nice view on New York City, but for security reasons it was not allowed anymore for some time after sept 11. For more info on how to get tickets to the Liberty Island, take a look at this Web site

History

The Statue of Liberty National Monument officially celebrated her 100th birthday on October 28, 1986. The people of France gave the Statue to the people of the United States over one hundred years ago in recognition of the friendship established during the American Revolution. Over the years, the Statue of Liberty's symbolism has grown to include freedom and democracy as well as this international friendship.

Sculptor Frederic Auguste Bartholdi was commissioned to design a sculpture with the year 1876 in mind for completion, to commemorate the centennial of the American Declaration of Independence. The Statue was a joint effort between America and France and it was agreed upon that the American people were to build the pedestal, and the French people were responsible for the Statue and its assembly here in the United States. However, lack of funds was a problem on both sides of the Atlantic Ocean. In France, public fees, various forms of entertainment, and a lottery were among the methods used to raise funds. In the United States, benefit theatrical events, art exhibitions, auctions and prize fights assisted in providing needed funds.

Meanwhile in France, Bartholdi required the assistance of an engineer to address structural issues associated with designing such a colossal copper sculpture. Alexandre Gustave Eiffel (designer of the Eiffel Tower) was commissioned to design the massive iron pylon and secondary skeletal framework which allows the Statue's copper skin to move independently yet stand upright. Back in America, fund raising for the pedestal was going particularly slowly, so Joseph Pulitzer (noted for the Pulitzer Prize) opened up the editorial pages of his newspaper, "The World" to support the fund raising effort. Pulitzer used his newspaper to criticize both the rich who had failed to finance the pedestal construction and the middle class who were content to rely upon the wealthy to provide the funds. Pulitzer's campaign of harsh criticism was successful in motivating the people of America to donate.

Financing for the pedestal was completed in August 1885, and pedestal construction was finished in April of 1886. The Statue was completed in France in July, 1884 and arrived in New York Harbour in June of 1885 on board the French frigate "Isere" which transported the Statue of Liberty from France to the United States. In transit, the Statue was reduced to 350 individual pieces and packed in 214 crates. The Statue was re-assembled on her new pedestal in four months time. On October 28th 1886, the dedication of the Statue of Liberty took place in front of thousands of spectators. She was a centennial gift ten years late.

The story of the Statue of Liberty and her island has been one of change. The Statue was placed upon a granite pedestal inside the courtyard of the star-shaped walls of Fort Wood (which had been completed for the War of 1812.) The United States Lighthouse Board had responsibility for the operation of the Statue of Liberty until 1901. After 1901, the care and operation of the Statue was placed under the War Department. A Presidential Proclamation declared Fort Wood (and the Statue of Liberty within it) a National Monument on October

15th, 1924 and the monument's boundary was set at the outer edge of Fort Wood. In 1933, the care and administration of the National Monument was transferred to the National Park Service. On September 7, 1937, jurisdiction was enlarged to encompass all of Bedloe's Island and in 1956, the island's name was changed to Liberty Island. On May 11, 1965, Ellis Island was also transferred to the National Park Service and became part of the Statue of Liberty National Monument. In May of 1982, President Ronald Reagan appointed Lee Iacocca to head up a private sector effort to restore the Statue of Liberty. Fundraising began for the $87 million restoration under a public/private partnership between the National Park Service and The Statue of Liberty-Ellis Island Foundation, Inc., to date the most successful public-private partnership in American history. In 1984, at the start of the Statue's restoration, the United Nations designated the Statue of Liberty as a World Heritage Site. On July 5, 1986 the newly restored Statue re-opened to the public during Liberty Weekend, which celebrated her centennial.

ENGLAND

The City of Bath

Bath is probably the UK's most beautiful city, and it's also one of the most historically rich. England's only thermal springs (shortly to supply a new spa centre), beloved of invading Romans and partying Georgians. The city of Bath today is a masterpiece of Georgian architecture and town planning, great sweeping crescents curve along the hillside, while the centre is lined with parades just made for promenading.

And welcome to Beautifulbath.co.uk - a useful resource for holidaymakers planning to stay in Bath, including recommended excursions from Bath, walks, things to do and practical tips from residents like ourselves on the best places to go and things to do as well as how to see Bath on a budget.

Bath is a popular day trip destination for tourists. But a few hours trailing around the main museums or sitting on an open-top bus won't give you much more than a fleeting impression of the historic town. Bath is a unique destination with layers of historical associations and and a peaceful charm that is all its own, and to really appreciate the city you need to stay more than a few hours.

In fact, if you are planning a vacation to 'see' the UK, Bath could make a very good base. London is less than two hours away by train, so you can easily spend a couple of days exploring the hectic big city. And if you really want to see England, you'll find many of the country's different facets all within a short distance of Bath, from chocolate-box villages to historic harbours.

6

Tourism in India

India is one of the popular tourist destinations in Asia. Bounded by the Himalayan ranges in the north, and surrounded on three sides by water (the Arabian Sea, Bay of Bengal, and the Indian Ocean), with a long history and diverse culture, India offers a wide array of places to see and things to do. In 2004, foreign tourists visiting India spent 15.4 billion USD - the ninth highest in the world. India is also ranked among the top 3 adventure tourism destinations.

TAJ MAHAL

Perhaps India's best-known site is the Taj Mahal, one of the world's greatest architectural achievements. It was built between 1631 and 1653 by Emperor Shah Jahan in Honour of his wife, Arjumand Banu, more popularly known as Mumtaz Mahal. The Taj Mahal serves as her tomb.

The Taj Mahal is a monument located in Agra, India, constructed between 1631 and 1654 by a workforce of 22,000. The Muslim Mughal Emperor Saha jahan

commissioned its construction as a mausoleum for his favourite wife, Arjumand Bano Begum, who is better known as Mumtaz

The Taj Mahal (sometimes called "the Taj") is generally considered the finest example of Mughal architecture, a style that combines elements of Indian, Islamic and Persian architectures. The Taj Mahal has achieved special note because of the romance of its inspiration. While the white domed marble mausoleum is the most familiar part of the monument, the Taj Mahal is actually an integrated complex of structures.

Construction

The Taj Mahal was built on a stretch of land to the south of the walled city of Agra which had belonged to Maharajah Jai Singh: Shah Jahan presented him with a large palace in the centre of Agra in exchange. Construction began with setting foundations for the tomb. An area of roughly three acres was excavated and filled with dirt to reduce seepage from the river. The entire site was levelled to a fixed height about 50 m above the riverbank. The Taj Mahal is 180 feet tall. The dome itself measures 60 feet in diameter and 80 feet high.

In the tomb area, wells were then dug down to the point that water was encountered. These wells were later filled with stone and rubble, forming the basis for the footings of the tomb. An additional well was built to same depth nearby to provide a visual method to track water level changes over time.

Instead of lashed bamboo, the typical scaffolding method, workmen constructed a colossal brick scaffold that mirrored the inner and outer surfaces of the tomb. The scaffold was so enormous that foremen estimated it would take years to dismantle. According to legend, Shah Jahan decreed that anyone could keep bricks taken from the scaffold, and it was dismantled by peasants overnight.

A fifteen-kilometre tamped-earth ramp was built to transport marble and materials from Agra to the construction site. According to contemporary accounts teams of twenty or thirty oxen strained to pull the blocks on specially constructed wagons.

To raise the blocks into position required an elaborate post-and-beam pulley system. Teams of mules and oxen provided the lifting power.

The order of construction was

- The plinth
- The tomb
- The four minarets
- The mosque and jawab
- The gateway

The plinth and tomb took roughly 12 years to complete. The remaining parts of the complex took an additional 10 years. (Since the complex was built in stages, contemporary historical accounts list different "completion dates"; discrepancies between so-called completion dates are probably the result of differing opinions about the definition of "completion". For example, the mausoleum itself was essentially complete by 1643, but work continued on the rest of the complex.)

Water Infrastructure

Water for the Taj Mahal complex was provided through a complex infrastructure. Water was drawn from the river by a series of purs — an animal-powered rope and bucket mechanism. The water flowed into a large storage tank, where, by thirteen additional purs, it was raised to large distribution tank above the Taj Mahal ground level.

From this distribution tank, water passed into three subsidiary tanks, from which it was piped to the complex. A 0.25 m earthenware pipe lies about 1.5 m below the surface, in line with the main walkway; this filled the main pools of the complex. Additional copper pipes supplied the fountains in the north-south canal. Subsidiary channels were dug to irrigate the entire garden.The fountain pipes were not connected directly to the feed pipes. Instead, a copper pot was provided under each fountain pipe: water filled the pots allowing equal pressure in each fountain.The purs no longer remain, but the other parts of the infrastructure have survived.

Craftsmen

The Taj Mahal was not designed by a single person. The project demanded talent from many quarters. The names of many of the builders who participated in the construction of the Taj Mahal in different capacities have come down to us through various sources.

Ustad Isa and Isa Muhammad Effendi, trained by the great Ottoman architect Koca Mimar Sinan Agha are frequently credited with a key role in the architectural design of the complex, but in fact there is little evidence to support this tradition, and the connection with Sinan (who died in 1588) is clearly a fairy-tale. 'Puru' from Benarus, Persia (Iran), has been mentioned as the supervising architect in Persian language texts (*e.g.* see ISBN 964-7483-39-2).

The main dome was designed by Ismail Khan from the Ottoman Empire, considered to be the premier designer of hemispheres and builder of domes of that age.

Qazim Khan, a native of Lahore, cast the solid gold finial that crowned the Turkish master's dome. Chiranjilal, a lapidary from Delhi, was chosen as the chief sculptor and mosaicist. Amanat Khan from Persian Shiraz, Iran was the chief calligrapher (this fact is attested on the Taj Mahal gateway itself, where his name has been inscribed at the end of the inscription).

Muhammad Hanif was the supervisor of masons. Mir Abdul Karim and Mukkarimat Khan of Shiraz, Iran handled finances and the management of daily production. The creative team included sculptors from Bukhara, calligraphers from Syria and Persia, inlayers from southern India, stonecutters from Baluchistan, a specialist in building turrets, another who carved only marble flowers — thirty seven men in all formed the creative nucleus. To this core was added a labour force of twenty thousand workers recruited from across northern India.

European commentators, particularly during the early period of the British Raj, suggested that some or all of the Taj Mahal was the work of European artisans. Most of these suggestions were purely speculative, but one dates back to 1640, when a Spanish Friar who visited Agra wrote that Geronimo Veroneo, an Italian adventurer in Shah Jahan's court, was primarily responsible for the design. There is no reliable scholarly evidence to back up this assertion, nor is Veroneo's name mentioned in any surviving documents relating to the construction. E.B. Havell, the principal British scholar of Indian art in the later Raj, dismissed this theory as unsupported by any evidence, and as inconsistent with the known methods employed by the designers. His conclusions were further supported by the research of Muhammad Abdullah Chaghtai, who examined carefully the origin of the tradition that the Taj was designed by a European, and concluded that it was a spurious 19th century invention, based on the misapprehension that "Ustad Isa", so often credited with the Taj's design, must have been a Christian because he bore the name "Isa" (Jesus).

In fact this is a common Muslim name as well - and furthermore there is no source earlier than the 19th century which mentions an "Ustad Isa" in connection with the Taj Mahal (even if he existed he cannot, in any case, have been trained by Sinan, because the latter died in 1588). Chaghtai thought it more likely that the chief architect was Ustad Ahmad, the designer of Shahjahanabad, but admitted that this could not be conclusively proved from existing sources.

Materials

The Taj Mahal was constructed using materials from all over India and Asia. Over 1,000 elephants were used to transport building materials during the construction. The translucent white marble was brought from Rajasthan, the jasper from Punjab and the jade and crystal from China. The turquoise was from Tibet and the Lapis lazuli from Afghanistan, while the sapphire came from Sri Lanka and the carnelian from Arabia. In all, 28 types of precious and semi-precious stones were inlaid into the white marble.

Costs

The total cost of the Taj Mahal's construction was about 50 million rupees. At that time, 1 gram of gold was sold for about 1.4 rupees. Based on the October 2005 gold price that would translate to more than 500 million US$. (Comparisons based on the value of gold in two different economic eras are often misleading, however).

ANDHRA PRADESH

Andhra Pradesh is a state in South India. It lies between 12°41' and 22°N latitude and 77° and 84°40'E longitude, and is bordered by Maharashtra, Chhattisgarh and Orissa in the north, the Bay of Bengal in the East, Tamil Nadu to the south and Karnataka to the west. Andhra Pradesh is the fourth largest state in India by area and fifth largest by population. It is the largest and most populous state in Southern India. It is also considered the rice bowl of India. The state is crossed by two major rivers, the Godavari and Krishna. Andhra means "leader in battle" and Pradesh means "region" or "state".

Andhra Pradesh is very good place for tourism. Andhra Pradesh is India's fifth largest state. AP is also known as the "Rice Granary of India". The main languages spoken in Andhra Pradesh are Telugu, Hindi, Urdu and English. The weather is generally hot and humid. June to December are the monsoon months. Andhra Pradesh has a rich cultural heritage. Andhra Pradesh has it all: beaches,hills,wildlife,beautiful forests and temples.

People coming to Andhra Pradesh visit:

- Hyderabad
- Tirupati
- Vizag
- Nagarjuna sagar
- Vijaywada
- Warangal

Tirumala – Tirupati

Tirupati is a temple town in Chittoor District of Andhra Pradesh, India. It is located in the foot hills of Tirumala. The temple of Lord Venkateshwara is the richest shrine in the Hindu world, and the temple town of Tirupati is as famous as the sacred Hindu city of Varanasi. This is the second busiest and richest religious centre in the world after the Vatican. Every year above 12 million people visit this temple from within India and the world but mostly from South India. The current receipts of the shrine are estimated at Rs 10 Billion p.a.

Tirupathi is one of the most famous temple towns in India. It is the abode of Lord Venkateshwara, (one of the incarnations of Lord Vishnu), located atop Tirumala hills. It is well connected with Hyderabad, Chennai and Bangalore via road,rail and air.

The temple town of Tirupathi is located to the extreme south of Andhra Pradesh in Chittoor district, 140 km from Chennai and 740 km from Hyderabad. It is renowned for one of the most venerated shrines in India —that of the ancient temple of Lord Venkateswara on the Tirumala Hills.

Tirumala has seven hills, representing the seven heads of a huge serpent, called Sesha Saye, on which Lord Vishnu resides. The black idol of Balaji is covered in gold, jewellery and precious ornaments and is 2 metres high.

Tirupathi is believed to be the richest temple in the country, with picturesque surroundings. Some people also believe that the financial offerings and collections at this temple are second only to those of the Vatican City Church on a worldwide basis. The temple is also a fine example of Dravidian art and style. It is also a famous center for wood carving.

Visakhapatnam

Visakhapatnam is a port city in the Indian state of Andhra Pradesh. It is located on the eastern shore of India, nestled among the Eastern Ghats Hill Ranges and facing the Bay of Bengal to the east. The city is about 650 km northeast of Hyderabad.

Alternatively, it sometimes goes by its now mostly defunct colonial British name, Waltair. During the colonial era, the city had at its hub the Waltair railway station, and that part of the city still goes by the name of Waltair. It is sometimes also referred to as "The City of Destiny".The city is home to several state owned heavy industries, and has one of the country's largest ports and its oldest shipyard. It has the only natural harbour on the eastern coast of India.

Andhra University, a prominent seat of education in Andhra Pradesh, is located here.Vizag is primarily an industrial city, apart from being a Tourist Destination. It draws tourists to its unspoilt beaches, nearby scenic Araku Valley and Borra caves, the 11th century Simhachalam temple, and ancient Buddhist sites spread across the area.The city boasts a submarine museum, the first of its kind in Southeast Asia, at Rama Krishna Beach.

Visakhapatnam is also the headquarters of the Eastern Naval Command of the Indian Navy.

Nagarjuna Sagar

Nagarjuna Sagar is an important Buddhist site and tourist place located 150 km from Hyderabad, (India).Nagarjuna Sagar Dam is one of the largest dams built in Asia, located between the cities of Guntur and Hyderabad in Andhra Pradesh (India). It is built on the Krishna River between Guntur and Nalgonda districts. It is one of the earliest hydro-electric projects of India.

Nagarjuna dam, which was completed in 1969, is 124 metres high and 1 km long, and has 26 crest gates. The lake behind it is the third-largest man-made lake in the world.

This dam is said to be the World's largest masonry dam.Of late, the inflows into the reservoir have been reduced due to the increased number of projects which have been built upstream.

The Town

Nagarjuna Sagar is among the more popular tourist places around Hyderabad. Nagarjuna Sagar called Vijayapuri (city of victory) in ancient times. Nagarjuna Sagar is named after the Buddhist saint Acharya Nagarjuna.

Present day Nagarjuna sagar area has three settlements, Vijayapuri (commonly referred as V. P. South), Pylon and Hill colony. V. P. South is home to many well known educational institutions in the state like Andhra Pradesh Residential Junior College (APRJC) and Andhra Pradesh Residential Degree College (APRDC). The steam boat service to Nagarjuna konda (konda in Telugu means hill) is available from Launch station located in V.P.South.

Places to Visit

Nagarjuna Sagar Dam

The dam separates Nalgonda and Guntur districts. The turbines are located on the Nalgonda side (hill colony) of the river. There are tours available to see the turbines in action.

Nagarjuna Konda

Nagarjuna konda is a picturesque island situated in the centre of a man-made lake formed due to construction of the dam. One of the most outstanding Buddhist civilizations dating back to the 3rd century were excavated here and are carefully preserved on this island. A Buddhist museum located on this hill preserves several buddhist relics. Andhra Pradesh Tourism Department runs a boat service to this island from Vijayapuri south.

Ethipotala Waterfall

This is located at nearly 15 miles from Nagarjuna Sagar en route to Macherla. A beautiful waterfall with amenities like guesthouses are provided for the tourists.

Nagarjuna sagar's foundation was laid by the First Prime Minister of India, Mr. Jawaharlal Nehru, in the month of December, 1955.

TOURIST ATTRACTIONS IN DELHI

Delhi is one of the most historic capitals in the world and two of its monuments, the Qutb Minar and Humayun's Tomb, have been declared World Heritage Sites. It offers a multitude of interesting places and attractions to the visitor, so much so that it becomes difficult to decide where to begin exploring the city.

In Old Delhi, there are attractions like mosques, forts, and other monuments that depict India's Muslim history. The important places in Old Delhi include the majestic Red Fort, the historical Chandni Chowk. In addition, Old Delhi has Raj Ghat and Shanti Vana that are modern structures constructed after India's Independence in 1947.

New Delhi, on the other hand, is a modern city designed by Edwin Lutyens and Herbert Baker. New Delhi houses many government buildings and embassies, apart from places of historical interest. Notable attractions in New Delhi include:

- The Rashtrapati Bhawan, the one-time imperial residence of the British viceroys
- The India Gate, a memorial raised in honour of the Indian soldiers martyred during theAfghan war
- The Laxminarayan Temple, built by the Birlas, one of India's leading industrial families
- The Akshardham Temple at New Delhi epitomises 10,000 years of Indian culture in all its breathtaking grandeur, beauty, wisdom and bliss, ancient architecture, traditions and timeless spiritual messages

- The Humayun's Tomb, said to be the forerunner of the Taj Mahal at Agra
- Across the road from Humayun's tomb is the shrine of the Muslim Sufi saint, Nizam-ud-din Chishti, who died in 1325.
- the Purana Quila, built by Humayun, with later-day modifications by Sher Shah Suri
- Tughlaqabad, Delhi's most colossal and awesome fort
- Qutab Minar, built by Qutb-ud-din Aybak of the Slave Dynasty
- the lotus-shaped Bahá'í House of Worship
- In the northern bit of Delhi is Connaught Place, the business and commercial and tourist centre.

Rashtrapati Bhawan

Built with a mix of Western and Indian styles, Rashtrapati Bhavan was originally built for the Governor General of India, aka Viceroy of India. Inaugurated in 1931 as the Viceregal Lodge, the name was changed in 1950 after India became a republic.

India Gate

Built in the memory of more than 90,000 Indian soldiers who lost their lives during the Afghan Wars and World War I, the India Gate is one of the most famous monuments in Delhi.Situated along the ceremonial Rajpath avenue (meaning King's Way) in New Delhi, India Gate is a memorial raised in honour of the Indian soldiers who died during the Afghan wars and World War I. The names of the soldiers who died in these wars are inscribed on the walls. The cenotaph (or shrine) in the middle is constructed with black marble and depicts a rifle placed on its barrel, crested by a soldier's helmet. Each face of the cenotaph has inscribed in gold the words Amar Jawan (in Hindi, meaning Immortal Warrior). The green lawns at India Gate are a popular evening and holiday rendezvous for young and old alike.

Laxminarayan Temple

Also called the Birla Mandir, the Laxminarayan Temple was built by the Birla family in 1938. It is a temple with a large garden and fountains behind it. The temple attracts thousands of devotees on Janmashtami day, the birthday of Lord Krishna.

Akshardham Temple

A recent addition to Delhi's gems, this monument, inaugurated in November 2005, is contending to be among the best sights to see in Delhi.

Appu Ghar

Appu Ghar is a children's amusement park and suitable for anyone of any age. This theme park includes haunted houses and some roller coasters. Appu, was both the cartoon mascot, and a live elephant mascot that became the beloved star of the 1982 Asian Games in New Delhi, India. This amusement park got the name from that Mascot's name; "Appu" is the name of the elephant and Ghar means "house". Appu ghar is worth a visit.

Humayun's Tom

Humayun's Tomb is one of Delhi's most famous landmarks. The monument has an architectural design similar to the Taj Mahal.

Humayun's Tomb was built by Humayun's widow, Hamida Banu Begum. Designed by a Persian architect named Mirak Mirza Ghiyas, the structure was begun in 1562 and completed in 1565. The tomb established a standard for all later Mughal monuments, which followed its design, most notably the Taj Mahal.

Qutb Minar

The Qutb Minar is located in a small village called Mehrauli in South Delhi. It was built by Qutb-ud-din Aybak of the Slave Dynasty, who took possession of Delhi in 1206. It is a fluted red sandstone tower, which tapers up to a height of 72.5 metres and is covered with intricate carvings and verses from the Qur'an. Qutb-ud-din Aybak began constructing this victory tower as a sign of Muslim domination of Delhi and as a minaret for the Muslim priest, the muezzin, to call the faithful to prayer. However, only the first story was completed by Qutb-ud-din. The other storys were built by his successor Iltutmish. The two circular storys in white marble were built by Ferozshah Tughlaq in 1368, replacing the original fourth story.

At 72.5 meters, the 13th century Qutb Minar is the world's tallest brick minaret.

The balconies in the tower are supported by exquisite stalactite designs. The tapering tower has pointed and circular flutings on the first story and star-shaped ones on the second and third stories. The bands of calligraphic inscriptions are amazing in their perfection along the exquisite stalactite designs on the exterior of this tower.

The Qutb Minar, apart from being a marvel in itself, is also significant for what it represents in the history of Indian culture. In many ways, the Qutb Minar, the first monument built by a Muslim ruler in India, heralded the beginning of a new style of art and architecture that came to be known as the Indo-Islamic style.

Red Fort

The Lahori Gate of the Red Fort

The decision for constructing the fort was made in 1639, when Shah Jahan decided to shift his capital from Agra to Delhi. Within eight years, Shahjahanabad was completed with the Red Fort-Qila-i-Mubarak (fortunate citadel) — Delhi's seventh fort — ready in all its magnificence to receive the Emperor. Though much has changed with the large-scale demolitions during the British occupation of the fort, its important structures have survived, the glory faded with age but still impressive.

Chandni Chowk

Chandni Chowk, a main marketplace in Delhi, keeps alive the city's living legacy of Shahjahanabad. Created by Shah Jahan the builder of Taj Mahal, the old city, with the Red Fort as its focal point and Jama Masjid as the praying centre, has a fascinating market called Chandni Chowk. Legend has it that Shah Jahan planned Chandni Chowk so that his daughter could shop for all that she wanted. The market was divided by canals. The canals are now closed, but Chandni Chowk remains Asia's largest wholesale market. Crafts once patronized by the Mughals continue to flourish there.Jama Masjid

The Jama Masjid is one of the largest and most elegant mosques in South Asia. The Masjid-i-Jahan Numa, commonly known as Jama Masjid, is the principal mosque of Old Delhi. Commissioned by the Mughal Emperor Shah Jahan and completed in the year 1656 AD, it is one of the largest and best known mosques in India.

Raj Ghat

On the bank Yamuna River, which flows past Delhi, there is Raj Ghat — the final resting place of Mahatma Gandhi, the father of the nation. It has become an essential point of call for all visiting dignitaries. Two museums dedicated to Gandhi are situated nearby.

Shanti Vana

Lying close to the Raj Ghat, the Shanti Vana (literally, the forest of peace) is the place where India's first Prime Minister Jawaharlal Nehru was cremated. The area is now a beautiful park adorned by trees planted by visiting dignitaries and heads of state.

Bahá'í House of Worship (Lotus Temple)

The Bahá'í House of Worship, situated in South Delhi, is shaped like a lotus. It is an eye-catching edifice worth exploring. Built by the Bahá'í community, it offers the visitor a serenity that pervades the temple and its artistic design.

Purana Quil

The Purana Quila (Old Fort) is a good example of medieval military architecture. Built by Humayun, with later-day modifications by Sher Shah Suri, the Purana Quila is a monument of bold design, which is strong, straightforward, and every inch a fortress. It is different from the well-planned, carefully decorated, and palatial forts of the later Mughal rulers. Purana Quila is also different from the later forts of the Mughals, as it does not have a complex of palaces, administrative, and recreational buildings as is generally found in the forts built later on. The main purpose of this now-dilapidated fort was its utility with less emphasis on decoration. The Qal'a-I-Kunha Masjid and the Sher Mandal are two important monuments inside the fort. it was made by Aqeel in 1853.

Tughlaqabad

When Ghazi Malik founded the Tughlaq Dynasty in 1321, he built the strongest fort in Delhi at Tughlaqabad, completed with great speed within four years of his rule. It is said that Ghazi Malik, when only a slave to Mubarak Khilji, had suggested this rocky prominence as an ideal site for a fort. The Khilji Sultan laughed and suggested that the slave build a fort there when he became a Sultan. Ghazi Malik as Ghiyasuddin Tughlaq did just that—Tughlaqabad is Delhi's most colossal and awesome fort even in its ruined state. Within its sky-touching walls, double-storied bastions, and gigantic towers were housed grand palaces, splendid mosques, and audience halls.

Goa

Goa is another popular destination, famous for its excellent beaches, churches, and temples.

Goa is a tiny emerald land on the west coast of India situated between the borders of Maharastra and Karnataka, is better known to the world at large as the former Portuguese enclave on the Indian soil. With the rule of the Portuguese for over 450 years and the consequential influence of the Latin culture, Goa presents a somewhat different picture to the foreign visitor than any other part of the country. Not only the proportion of Christians (almost all of whom are Catholics) in the total population of Goa much higher than that obtaining in most of the other States; the general way of living is also markedly different. Western influence is evident in the dress and food habits, and the general life of the people is quiet and peaceful. A striking feature of Goa is the harmonious relationship between the two principal religious communities, the Hindus and the Catholics, who have lived together peacefully for generations.

The Bom Jesus cathedral is another famous attraction in Goa.

Jammu and Kashmir

Tourist destinations in Jammu and Kashmir include:

- Srinagar

- Jammu
- Leh
- Amarnath
- Vaishno Devi

Other cities of interest in Northern India include Gwalior, Khajuraho, Varanasi, Mathura, and Haridwar.

Moving south, many places are a mix of ancient historic sites as well as industrial/technological hubs. Some of these are listed below.

Karnataka

The southern state of Karnataka offers:

- Bangalore, the IT capital of India, is also significant for its history
- Mysore, about 140km from Bangalore, has palaces, KRS Dam, several temples, a Hindu temple atop Chamundi Hills, Chamundeswari Temple.
- Srirangapatna, where nearby fortresses can be found (Tipu's)
- Hampi the city of ruins (1500's when the Muslim kings destroyed the prosperous Vijayanagar empire)
- The Belur and Halebidu temples are famed for their sculptural beauty.
- Sravanabelagola has a Jain temple dedicated to king Bahubali. The statue is massive and a MahaMasthakaAbhishekham performed one every year, attracts a huge number of pilgrims
- Sringeri, located in the western ghats, has a wonderful temple dedicated to Sarada devi.
- The Western Ghats offer many other places of exceptional beauty like Agumbe, Horanadu etc.
- Madikeri, Kodagu, Talakaveri, Kemmanagundi all places of immense natural beauty.

Kerala

Kerala is an evergreen lush state, tucked away in the southern corner of India. It is one of the most haunted visits of tourists in India. The state has its own tourism brand name - "God's Own Country", which has super-brand status.The state was nicked as one of the "10 paradises of the world" by the National Geographic traveller, the only other Indian place listed being the Taj Mahal.

Kerala is famous for its backwaters and lagoons.There are also several beautiful beaches along the coastline of Kerala. There are also hill stations and tropical rainforests with exquisite flora and fauna including endangared animals like elephant, tiger, nilgiri thar and lion-tailed macaque. Recently, a new brand of tourism was introduced called Monsoon Tourism, aimed at beckoning tourists to enjoy the beauty of the state's hauntigly beautiful rainy season extending from June to September.

Kerala is also known for its Ayurveda, the ancient medicinal system of India. The government of Kerala offers tourism packages related to Ayurvedaand promotes health tourism since treatment charges are low in Kerala.

On the cultural front, the several unique and colourful festivals of Kerala like Onam, Thrissur Pooram, the snake boat races etc. provide great attraction to tourists. The classical artforms Kathakali, Mohiniyattam etc. are also a delight.The martial artform Kalaripayattu is the parent form of all famous martial arts like karate and kungfu. The Kerala Cuisine is also world famous. Also Kerala's rich history of maritime trade from ancient times has left a number of interesting historical monuments.

The major attractions in Kerala include:

- Kumarakom, Kuttanad, Kumbalanghi and other backwater locations.
- Vembanad Lake and the housboats of Alappuzha
- Beaches like Kovalam,Marari etc.
- Hill stations at Thekkady and Munnar
- The city of Kochi with its chinese fishing nets, Bolgatty Palace, Mattanchery Jewish Synagogue, Jew Street, Fort Kochi etc.
- Enchanting waterfalls at Athirappilly and Vazhachal
- Periyar Tiger Reserve, Iravikulam National Park, Thattekad Bird Sanctuary and other forests
- Its historical monuments like Bakel Fort, Edakal cave of Wayanad
- Kerala Kalamandalam, deemed university teaching classical artforms
- Kalady, birthplace of Adi Sankaracharya, Sabarimala Temple, Guruvayur Temple, Malayatoor Church and other pilgirimage centres

Sikkim

Originally know as Suk-Hem which in the local language means "peaceful Home",..Sikkim was an independent kingdom till the year 1974,when it became a part of the Republic Of India.The capital of Sikkim is Gangtok located approximately 185kms from New Jalpaiguri,the nearest railway station to sikkim.Although an airport is under construction at Dekiling in East sikkim,the nearest airport to sikkim would be Bagdogra.Sikkim is the land of Orchids and mystic culture and colourful tradition.Sikkim is well know among treakers and adventure lovers as west sikkim has a lot to give them.some must visit places within sikkim inclued: 1.NIT (National Institute Of Tibetology) 2.Hanuman and Ganesh Tok 3.Nathula pass 4.Baba Harbajan Mandir 5.7 View Points 6.Rumtek Monastary 7.Lachen and Lachung 8.Pelling 9.Pemayantzy 10.Uttaray 11.Dzongri 12.Chewa-bhanjang 13.Barsay 14.Legship - Hot water spring 15.Khorong Hotwater spring 16.Samdrupsey at Namchi

Places near Sikkim include Darjeeling also know as the Queen of hills and Kalimpong.Darjeeling, other then its world famous "Darjeeling tea" is also famous for its refined "Prep schools" founded during the British Raj.Few of the top Schools in the District are: 1.St.Paul's School - Known as eton of the east.Is 190 years old, thus one of the oldest schools in India. 2.Mt.Hermon School. 3.St.Joseph's School - where the H.M of Bhutan and the Late H.M of Nepal did their schooling. 4.Loreto Convent - where Late Mother Teresa served for many years. 5.Dr.Graham's Homes. 6.St.Joseph's Convent. 7.St.Augustine's School. Kalimpong is famous for its Flora cultivation and is home to many Internationally known Nurseries.

Orissa

Orissa has been a preferred destination from ancient days for people having interest in spirituality, religion, culture, art and beauty of the nature. Ancient and medieval architecture, pristine sea beaches, nature at her beautiful best, the classical and ethnic dance forms and a variety of festivals, all in combine attract tourists from far off places to explore this state to a have a divine exposure of love and hospitality.

Orissa has kept alive Buddhism and the Buddha in its ancient womb. The spirit of Buddhism still haunts the very air of Orissa. Rock-edicts that have challenged time stand huge and over-powering by the banks of the river Daya.

The silent stones sing out songs of peace and non-violence. The torch of Buddhism is still ablaze in the sublime triangle at Udayagiri, Lalitgiri and Ratanagiri, on the banks of river Birupa.

The surrounding hills of Langudi and Kayama stand as mute witness to the quirks and twists of history. Precious fragments of a glorious past come alive in the shape of stupas, rock-cut caves, rock-edicts, excavated monastries, viharas, chaityas and sacred relics in caskets. Rock-edicts of Ashoka are a bonus for your eyes. Orissa is the home for various tribal communities who have contributed uniquely to the multicultural and multilingual character of the state. Their handicrafts, different dance forms, jungle products and their unique life style blended with their healing practices have got world wide attention.

Rajasthan

Rajasthan, the "Land of the Kings", is one of the most attractive tourist destinations in Northern India. The vast sand dunes of the Thar Desert attract millions of tourists from around the globe every year. Major visitor attractions in Rajathan include:

- Jaipur - The capital of Rajasthan, famous for its rich history and royal architecture
- Jodhpur - fortress-city at the edge of the Thar Desert, famous for its blue homes and architecture
- Jaisalmer - famous for its golden fortress
- Barmer - Barmer and surrounding areas offer perfect picture of typical Rajasthani villages.

- Bikaner - famous for its medieval history as a trade route outpost
- Mount Abu
- Pushkar-It has the only Brahma temple in the world

Tamil Nadu

Tamil Nadu has a rich culture and offers a wide selection of temples famed for their architectural beauty. Some of the more popular temple tour destinations include:

- Chennai - The capital of Tamil Nadu has the second longest beach in the world, the Marina Beach.
- Madurai - known for the beautiful Meenakshi temple
- Rameshwaram - The temple here the longest corridor in the world
- Kanyakumari, located at the tip of India, is at the confluence of the Bay of Bengal, Arabian Sea and the Indian Ocean. Recently a massive statue of Thiruvalluvar has been installed here.
- Kumbakonam, known for the numerous temples in the town. The Mahamaham festival is held here once in every twelve years and attracts millions of devotees to the place.
- Tiruchirapalli known for its Akhilandeshwari temple and Rockfort temple
- Thanjavur has the famous Brihadeeswara Temple.
- The famous hillstations Kodaikanal and Nilgiris offer the visitors a welcome relief from the usually hot climate in the state.

INDIA AS AN EMERGING SUPERPOWER IN WORLD TOURISM

Despite its poor tourism infrastructure, India, with its diverse and fascinating history has seen the creation of a booming tourism industry. India is a historic place with a diverse history of over 5 millennia. Foreign visitors presently spend more than US $15.4 billion annually in India.

Many travellers find the cultural diversity an eye-opening experience, even when the hassles of life in developing India like inefficiency, pollution, overcrowding, etc somewhat lessen the pleasure of the visit. Monuments like the Taj Mahal are among the many attractions of this land.

The Republic of India is considered as one of the possible emerging Superpowers of the world. This potential is attributed due to several indicators, the primary ones being its demographic trends and a rapidly expanding economy.

However the country suffers from many economic, social, and political problems that it must overcome before it can be considered a superpower. It is also not yet as influential on the international stage when compared to the United States or the former Soviet Union.

Factors in Favour

Geographic factors

- Location - India, the 7th largest nation by area, lies at the north of the Indian Ocean. Many Eurasian sea trade routes pass through or close to Indian territorial waters. The Himalayas in the north and north-east protect it from bitter continental cold and save the monsoon winds from escaping. The subcontinent contains necessary water resources and flat arable land to yet sustain its massive population.

Possible Future Advantage of Location

Energy - In the future, the world is expected to enter the *renewable-energy age* or *fusion age*, if and whenever the technology becomes economically sustainable. Being a region in the sunny tropical belt, the Indian Subcontinent could greatly benefit from a renewable energy trend, as it has the ideal combination of both - high solar insolation and a big consumer base density. Also, considering the costs of energy consumed for temperature control (a major factor influencing a regions energy intensity), cooling from excessive solar radiation will be energetically (and hence economically) cheaper than heating for the lack of it.

Demographic Factors

- Big - India has the world's second largest population.The government has attempted to control the population so as to avoid possible overpopulation. Results are encouraging, with some South Indian states slowing down their population growth to below 1% but much needs to be done further.
- **Youthful** - Due to its high birth rate India has a young population compared to most aging nations. It has approximately 60% of its population below the age of 30. In addition, declining fertility is beginning to reduce the youth dependency rate which may produce a demographic dividend. In the coming decades, while some of the present power nations witness a decrease in workforce, India is expected to have an increase. For example while Europe is well past its demographic window, the U.S. entered its in 1970 (lasting until 2015), China entered its in 1990 (will last until 2025), India won't enter its window until 2010 (lasting until 2050). Regionally South Asia is supposed to maintain the youngest demographic profile after Africa and Middle East, with the window extending upto 2070s.
- Global Diaspora - More than 35 million Indians live across the globe. Under fair opportunities, they have become socio-economically successful.
- English - The importance of English in the 21st century is a topic of

debate, but the growing pool of non-native English speakers makes it the best contender for "Global language" status. Incidentally, India has the world's largest English speaking/understanding population. It claims one of the largest workforce of engineers, doctors and other key professionals, all comfortable with English. It has the 2nd largest population of "fluent English" speakers, second only to the U.S., with estimates ranging from 150 to 250 million, and is expected to have the largest in coming decades.

Political Factors

- Democratic Republicanism - India is the world's largest democratic republic, more than three times bigger than the next largest (U.S.). It has so far been successful, at least politically, especially considering its functionality in difficult ethnic composition. The fact that India is a democracy has improved its relations with other democratic nations, improving its ties with the majority of the nations in the developed world.
- Candidate for Security Council - India has been pressing for permanent membership of the Security Council (as part of the G4 nations). It has received backing from the UK , France and Russia but without veto ability. However, China and the U.S have not been supportive of the bid. With improved Indo-US relations, the US is expected by some to reconsider its stand.
- Foreign relations - India has developed relationships with the present world powers like the EU , the U.S. , Russia, Japan and also with the African Union, the Arab World, Southeast Asia and Israel. In order to make the environment propitious for economic growth, India is improving its relations with China. It has also expanded its political influence in western nations and signed a civilian nuclear deal with the United States in March 2006. It is also working to better relationships with Pakistan.
- Role in international politics - Historically, India was one of the founding members of Non-Aligned Movement, but it also was a key backer and ally of the former Soviet Union during the Cold War. It has played regional roles in South Asian affairs, *e.g.* its use of the Indian Peace Keeping Force in the Bangladesh Liberation War and in Sri Lanka. It took a leading initiative to improve relations between African and Asian countries. India is an active member of The Commonwealth and the WTO. The evolving economic integration politics in the West and in Asia is influencing the Indian political mood to slowly swing in favour of integration with global economy, and thus currently, India's political moves are increasingly being

influenced by economic imperatives. New Delhi is being observed to slowly, cautiously, and often hesitantly, step into the unchartered role of becoming one of the two major seats of political power in Asia , the other being at Beijing.

- Multipolarity - A new and controversial geopolitical strategy, being debated in the West, is whether India should be trusted/helped to become an economically strong democratic citizen of the world and be used to balance the powerful but non-democratic forces, to insure a more stable world. Generally speaking it is discussed in the context of adopting a policy of offshore balancing on the part of the United States. A new American strategy towards India has been indicated in George W. Bush's recent visit to the subcontinent.
- **Economic Growth** - India's current economic growth (as the world's second-fastest growing major economy) has improved its standing on the world's political stage, even though it is still a developing country, but one that is showing strong development. Many nations are moving to forge better relationships with India.

Economic factors

- Booming Economy - The economy of India is currently the world's fourth largest in terms of real GDP (PPP) after the USA, the People's Republic of China and Japan, and the second fastest growing major economy in the world, averaging at an annual growth rate of above 8%. Its record growth was in the third quarter of 2003, when it grew higher than any other emerging economy at 10.4%. Interestingly, estimates by the IMF shows that by 2007 (see List of countries by GDP estimates for 2007 (PPP)), India will be the third largest economy in the world, overtaking the Japanese economy. Also the growth rate is likely to gear up above 8%.

  Primary Sector - India, growing at 8% per year, is the world's second largest producer of food next to China. Food processing accounts for USD 69.4 billion as gross income.

  Secondary Sector - India is still relatively a small player in manufacturing when compared to many world leaders. Some new trends suggest an improvement in future.

  Tertiary and Quaternary Sector - India currently has an expanding IT industry. It is considered the World's Office and is leading in the Services Industry. This is mainly due to the availability of a large pool of highly skilled, low cost, English speaking workforce.
- Science/Tech - India is trying to develop more high skilled, English speaking people to fit in the future knowledge economy. India is becoming one of the world's leading producers of computer software

and with mushrooming RandD centres it is experiencing a steady revolution in science and technology. A typical example of India's rising scientific endeavours is that it was the 3rd nation to found a National Space Agency called ISRO, after the USSR and the U.S.. It was the third Asian nation to send satellites into space after China and Japan in 1970, starting with Aryabhata in 1975. By 2008 it plans to send an unmanned mission to the Moon. India is among the world leaders in remote sensing, a technology coming to great use, among others, to Indian fishermen and farmers. India is also trying to join international RandD projects - *e.g.* it has recently joined the European Galileo GPS Project and the ITER for fusion energy club. Some Indian educational and research institutions like IIT , IIM, IISc, TIFR and AIIMS are among the world's best.

- Energy - To reduce the energy crisis, India is presently constructing - 9 civilian nuclear power reactors and several hydro-power stations.Recently it also made a civilian nuclear energy deal with the US and EU. In recent years, India joined China to launch a vigorous campaign to acquire oil fields around the world and now has stake in several oil fields (in the Middle East and Russia).
- Medical Services - "First World medical services at Third World prices". Indian Metros have emerged as the leading destination of medical tourism. Last year, an estimated 150,000 foreigners visited India for medical procedures, and the number is increasing at the rate of about 15 percent a year.
- Mass Transit System - India is in the process of developing a modern Mass rapid transit systems to replace its existing system which is seen as inadequate to cater to present and future urban requirements. A modern metro rail system is already in place in the cities of Delhi, Mumbai, Chennai and Kolkata. Work is in progress or would be commencing shortly for developing similar mass transit system in cities of Noida, Hyderabad, Bangalore,Indore, Ahmedabad and Kochi. Indore is leading the track by implementing world class GPS enabled, low floor buses in a Rapid Transport System. With growth in economy and technology, India is welcoming modernisation. The Indian rail network traverses the length and breadth of the country, covering a total length of 63,140 km (39,200 miles). It is one of the largest and busiest rail networks in the world, transporting over 5 billion passengers and over 350 million tonnes of freight annually.Its operations covers twenty-seven states and three Union territories and also links the neighbouring countries of Nepal, Bangladesh and Pakistan. However, other public transport systems, such as buses are often not up to the standards followed in developed countries.

Military Factors

- Total Strength - The Indian Armed Forces, India's main defence organisation, consists of two main branches: the Military of India and the Indian Paramilitary Forces. The Military of India maintains the third largest active duty force in the world after the People's Republic of China and the United States, while the Indian Paramilitary Forces, over a million strong, is one of the largest paramilitary force in the world. Combined, the total armed forces of India are 2,414,700 strong, the world's second largest defence force.
  Army - The Army of India, as the Indian army was called under British rule before 1947, played a crucial role in checking the advance of Imperial Japan into South Asia during World War II and the Axis powers in North Africa and Italy. Today, the Indian Army is the world's third largest army after China's People's Liberation Army and the United States Army.
  Air force - The Indian Air Force is the fourth largest air force in the world [15][16]. India recently flew its first indigenously manufactured combat aircraft. It is presently developing a fifth generation aircraft known as the Sukhoi Su-47 with Russia.
  Navy - The Indian Navy is the world's fifth largest navy. It operates one of only two Asian aircraft carriers. It also plans to induct two other aircraft carriers by 2008. It is considered to have blue-water capabilities and has been described as "a well-balanced three-dimensional force consisting of sophisticated missile-capable warships, aircraft carriers, minesweepers, advanced submarines and the latest aircraft in its inventory". The navy has been described as one that uses state of the art technology that is indigenously manufactured. [
- Nuclear Weapons - India possesses nuclear weapons since 1974, when it did the Pokharan I nuclear tests and the means to deliver them over long distances. However, India is not a signatory to the Nuclear Non-Proliferation Treaty (NPT) because of security concerns and India condemns the NPT as discriminatory.
- Arms Imports - India is currently one of the world's largest arms importers, spending an estimated US$16.97 billion in 2004. India has made military technology deals with the Russian Federation, the U.S., Israel and the EU.
- Current Major Roles - The Indian Armed Forces plays a crucial role in anti-terrorist activities and maintaining law and order in the disputed Kashmir region. India has also participated in several United Nations peace-keeping missions, currently being the largest contributor to UN peace keeping force and is the largest contributor to the United Nations Democratic Fund, to which the USA, the world's only current superpower, contributes nothing

Cultural factors

- History - India is one of two ancient civilizations dating back to at least 5000 years which has stood the test of time and survived against often insurmountable odds. Indians invented the numeric system, the concept of zero, basic algebra, the concept of grammar etc. India has a long history of cultural intercourse with many regions of the world and culturally dominated Asia until the arrival of the Western powers. Its cultural influence has spread through the philosophy of religions like Hinduism, Buddhism, Jainism and Sikhism — particularly in East and Southeast Asia. Many foreign religions - Islam, Christianity, Judaism, Zoroastrianism, Bahá'í Faith - have found followers in India. Indian culture has spread to foreign lands through conquest, wandering traders and philosophers and migration.
- Past Experience of having Powerful States- The Maurya, Gupta, Mughal, Vijayanagara and Chola empires provide the necessary confidence that a powerful state can be established despite having diversity.
- Cinema - India's film industry produces more feature films than any other. In a year, it sold 3.6 billion tickets, more than any other film industry in the world (In comparison, Hollywood sold 2.6 billion tickets in a year). The cinemas play a major role in spreading Indian culture worldwide. However, Indian cinema's viewers is yet tlimited among the Indian inhabitants.
- Unity in Diversity of World View - India has a multi-ethnic, multi-lingual and multi-religious society cohabitating together. The subcontinent's long and diverse history has given it a unique eclectic culture. It is often associated with spirituality. India's diversity forces it, to either evolve strong foundations of tolerance and survive, or face break-up. The Indian public is now also accepting western influences in their society and media - and what is emerging is a confluence of its past local culture with the new western culture ("Social Globalisation"). For some futuristic social thinkers, the miscegenation of diverse ancient culture with modernity, spirituality with science/technology, Eastern with Western world-view is potentially making India a social laboratory for the evolution of futuristic global-unity consciousness. If, and only if, everything evolves right, then India could emerge as a soft super-power, by being the biggest melting pot of human ethnicities, languages, cultures, religions, ideologies and world view.
- Soft Power - India — a melting pot of human ethnicities, languages, cultures, religions, ideologies and world view—has produced much cultural influence, and has the potential to re-inforce the massive influence on world culture through modern trends such as entertainment.

Points Against the Rise of India as a Superpower

Political Obstacles

- Cost of Democratic Republicanism - Democratic republicanism has its value , more so in a multi-ethnic country like India. However, the applicability of the "theoretical" virtues of republicanism on a country like India is sometimes questioned. Some thinkers consider India's diverse democratic republic to levy a huge tax on its economy. The Indian government has to consider many interest groups before decision making. It is not uncommon to see in India how a few small vested interests can stall the development for many. However, it should be noted that India is relatively a much younger republic when compared to other major democratic republican powers.
- Insurgency - The Indian government has acknowledged that there has been a dramatic increase in support for the Maoists insurgency in the last decade.About 10 years ago the rebels were active in just four states. Now security experts say they are entrenched in a vast eastern and central belt that stretches across nearly half of India's 28 states up to country's border with Nepal. Known as the "red corridor", it includes India's poor regions, where ethnic tribes and poor people live in poverty.The boom in Maoist support appears to have been boosted by the successes of the nearly 10-year-old Maoist rebellion in Nepal.
  - Disputes - India's growth is impeded by disputes with its neighbouring potential superpower the People's Republic of China and nuclear power Pakistan (over some historical border issues and ideological issues) and disputes with Bangladesh (over water availability and the Farakka Dam). Because of the disputes, India's neighbours such as China and Pakistan remain distrustful towards India. It is also occasionally burdened with instability issues within some localised regions/smaller states of the subcontinent. In an effort to reduce political tension and increase economic cooperation, in recent years, India has improved its relations with its neighbouring countries.
  - Lack of international representation - India is not a member of the UNSC, although currently it is one of the four-nations group actively seeking a permanent seat on the council. Thus India lacks the ability to extend its influence or ideas on international events in the way few chosen nations do.

Economic Obstacles

- Poverty - As of 2002, but no longer the case, India is home to the largest number of people living under two dollars a day (approx 25%

of the population. living under the poverty line). Poverty also begets child labour. Various reforms, including mass employment schemes have been undertaken by the government to tackle this problem, and India has been quite successful in reducing its share of poverty. This is given the fact that the number of people living on $1 a day has decreased by more than 20 million to less than 15 million, and $2 a day to about 32 million from 95 million, both income numbers that are higher being in 2001-2002. The lower numbers are as of fourth quarter 2005.

- Infrastructure - The social infrastructure in India such as roads, power grid, water, communications infrastructure, housing and education are often below standards, and not catching up with the tune of its economic progress. Continued poor infrastructure might serve as a bottleneck to further economic development. The government is, however, improving the infrastructure to make it up to standards, such as expanding the freeway and highway system which is similar to China and the U.S., but still has significantly less number of miles than those countries.
- Disorganization - India's continual economic prosperity is also hindered by bad government and ubiquitous red tape ('Bureaucratic Raj'). Retrogressive government regulations affect many areas. For example, in some states, black outs and power rationing are common due to underinvestment, differing state and local regulations, etc.
- Energy Dependence and Costs - India heavily depends on foreign oil - a phenomenon likely to continue until non-fossil/renewable energy technology becomes economically viable in the country. To avert an energy crisis , India is desperately seeking alternate means of energy. India can sustain its growth to higher trajectories only by the co-operation of other countries. As for now, India is energetically expensive since India has to import over 70% of its energy, thus making costs of comforts - like personal car or even air conditioning - extremely high. It is however, steadily combating its energy issues.
- Unemployment - India's growth in the Services Sector and Information Technology Sector has not been matched through growth in manufacturing which can provide more jobs. Although modern researching claims that the secondary searching may lose importance in the future.
- Climate or Environment Problems - As a result of climate change the Gangotri glacier, among others, is receding. Of the 3 million premature deaths in the world that occur each year due to outdoor and indoor air pollution, the highest number are assessed to occur in India.
- Health - India's health scenario is dismal with diseases and

malnutrition have been constantly affecting the poorest quarter of the populace. Mortality is still relatively high and the bane of AIDS is spreading fast. India has the highest population living with AIDS/HIV[10]According to a report of United Nations Development Programme, India's economy might suffer a set back, if it does not check the problem of spread of AIDS/HIV. It is estimated that India's economic growth will decline by 0.86 percentage ananually if the AIDS problem is not properly dealt with. To improve the situation, a number of projects such as the building of hospital chains (like the Apollo Hospitals, amongst others) has laid the foundation for a health system that matches global standards, these hospitals are sometimes used by foreigners as a cheap yet effective source of health services. But much remains to be done for India's very poor.

- Low Literacy - As per the 2001 India census, the national literacy is only 65.2 per cent, even though the literacy rate in some states like Kerala, Mizoram and Goa is above 85%. Literacy drive is spreading slowly to other states. At current rates India will take no less than 20 years for a literacy of 95%.

Cultural obstacles

- Social Issues - India has a diverse mix of various religions and races. The majority are Hindus by religion, followed by Muslims, Sikhs, Christians, Jains, Buddhists, Bahaii and the list goes on. Though most religions in India have been practising religious tolerance in their histories, the partition and subsequent terrorism had created some degree of uneasiness among some. The uneducated masses of these various groups sometimes get at odds with one another. However in recent years, relations between the different religious groups have considerably changed for better. For instance, a real chunk of India's celebrities - sporting legends, film stars, industrialists, artists, politicians, scientists, head-of-state, etc - have come from various non-majority roots, representing the emerging face of new diverse India.
- Social Divide - The problem of India's social divide is often linked to its centuries-old caste system.In an attempt to eliminate the caste system, the Indian government has introduced special quotas for low-caste Indians in educational institutions and jobs. The measure is with the motive of helping lower-caste Indians to pursue higher education and thereby elevate their standard of life. However, the system is often criticised about its effectiveness as so called creamy layer (rich among the lower caste) get non-needed advantage and leave other lower caste groups poor only.There also have been cases of reverse-discrimination and persecution of upper castes by lower castes.

A Travel Guide to India

India is one of the popular tourist destinations in Asia. Bounded by the Himalayan ranges in the north, and surrounded on three sides by water (the Arabian Sea, Bay of Bengal, and the Indian Ocean), with a long history and diverse culture, India offers a wide array of places to see and things to do. In 2004, foreign tourists visiting India spent 15.4 billion USD - the ninth highest in the world. India is also ranked among the top 3 adventure tourism destinations.

Regions

India is administratively divided into 28 states and 7 union territories. The states are broadly demarcated on linguistic lines. They vary in size; the larger ones are bigger and more diverse than some countries of Europe. The union territories are smaller than the states - sometimes they are just one city - and they have much less autonomy.

These states and union territories are grouped by convention into the following regions.

- Himalayan North — Mountainous and beautiful, a tourist destınation for the adventurous and the spiritual. This region contains some of India's most visited hill-stations and religious places. Also includes the troubled state of Jammu and Kashmir
- The Plains — India's Hindi-speaking heartland. The country's capital New Delhi is here. The rivers Ganga and Yamuna flow through this plain. Many of the events that shaped India's history took place here.
- The West — deserts and beautiful cities like Jaipur, Jodhpur, Udaipur, Bikaner, Goa, vibrant and biggest Indian city Mumbai (formerly known as Bombai), wonderful beaches and Bollywood (Indian film industry in Bombay)
- The South — colorful Hindu temples, tropical forests, Backwaters of Kerala, beaches and *ghats* of Karnataka and islands off the mainland.
- The East — India's mostly rural region, its largest city Calcutta (now known as *Kolkata*), the temple cities of Puri of Lord Jagannath fame and Bhubaneswar, both in Orissa.
- **The North-East** — remote and sensitive, the country's tribal corner, with beautiful landscapes and famous for Tea Gardens.

Cities

India has many large and famous cities; below is a list of nine of the most well-known. Other cities are listed under their specific regional section.

Large Cities

India's largest cities, listed below, are known as metros.

- New Delhi — The Capital of Ancient Bharat and Modern India - The political capital of India
- Calcutta (Kolkata) — cultural capital of India, biggest port of East India known as City of Joy.
- Ahmedabad — known as Textile Capital of India - located in Gujarat.
- Bangalore — Garden City, Pub City, Silicon Valley of India, Land of Silk, Gold, Sandal Wood, Incense etc.
- Chennai (Madras) — main port in South India, cradle of Carnatic Music and Barathanatiyam, Home of famous Marina Beach, Automobile Capital of India.
- Cochin — queen of Arabian sea, spice trade and tourism - industrial hub of state of Kerala.
- Hyderabad — Pearl city of India, and part of the Silicon Plateau with Bangalore
- Mumbai (Formerly *Bombay*) — the financial capital of India, "Bollywood" (Indian Film Industry's hub)
- Pune — Maharashtra's cultural capital.

Other Destinations

Landmarks:

India has many outstanding landmarks. Below are four of the most notable that are not in a large city nor a sacred site.

- Taj Mahal — Agra, Uttar Pradesh
- Historical Ruins — Hampi, Karnataka
- Mysore Palace — Mysore, Karnataka
- The Mall - Victorian heritage — Shimla, Himachal Pradesh

Sacred sites:

As the birthplace of several world religions, India is home to many sacred and holy sites. Below is a list of nine of the most notable. For other sacred sites refer to regional articles.

- Amritsar, Punjab — The Golden Temple, Sikh holy city
- Bodh Gaya, Bihar — the place where the Buddha Shakyamuni attained enlightenment.
- Gangotri, Uttaranchal — Origin of the Ganges (mother Ganga) in the Himalayas
- Haridwar, Uttaranchal — Gateway to the GOD
- Sarnath, Uttar Pradesh — located 10 km away from Varanasi it is the site of the deer park where the Buddha Shakyamuni first taught the Buddha Dharma.
- Shravanabelagola, Karnataka — one of the most sacred places for Jains.

- Tirupati, Andhra Pradesh — one of the most sacred places for Hindus with Golden Temple on Seven Hills.
- Varanasi, Uttar Pradesh — A sacred Hindu city located on the banks of the Ganges.
- Vrindavan, Uttar Pradesh — Birth Place of Lord Krishna

Geography

Mountains, jungles, deserts and beaches, India has it all. It is bounded to the north, northeast and northwest by the snow-capped Himalayas, the largest mountain range in the world. In addition to protecting the country from invaders, they also fed the perennial rivers Ganga, Yamuna (Jamuna) and Sindhu (Indus) on whose plains India's civilization flourished. Though most of the Sindhu is in Pakistan now, five of its tributaries flow through Punjab. The other Himalayan river, the Brahmaputra flows through the northeast, mostly through Assam.

South of Punjab lies the Aravalli range which cuts Rajasthan into two. The western half of Rajasthan is occupied by the Thar desert. The Vindhyas cut across Central India, particularly through Madhya Pradesh and signify the start of the Deccan plateau, which covers almost the whole of the southern peninsula. It is bounded by the Sahyadri range to the west and the Eastern Ghats to the east. The plateau is more arid than the plains, as the rivers that feed the area, such as the Narmada, Godavari and the Kaveri run dry during the summer. Towards the northeast of the Deccan plateau is what used to be a thickly forested area called the Dandakaranya which covers the states of Chhattisgarh, Jharkhand, the eastern edge of Maharashtra and the northern tip of Andhra Pradesh. This area is still forested, poverty stricken and populated by tribals. This forest acted as a barrier to the invasion of South India.

India has a long coastline. The west coast borders the Arabian Sea and the east coast the Bay of Bengal, both parts of the Indian Ocean.

Climate

In India, it rains only during a specific time of the year. The season as well as the phenomenon that causes it is called the monsoon. There are two of them, the Southwest and the Northeast, both named after the directions the winds come from. The Southwest monsoon is the more important one, as it causes rains over most parts of the country, and is the crucial variable that decides how the crops (and therefore the economy) will do. It lasts from June to September. It hits the west coast the most, as crossing the western ghats and reaching the rest of India is an uphill task for the winds. The western coastline is therefore much greener than the interior. The Northeast monsoon hits the east coast between October and February, mostly in the form of occasional cyclones which cause much devastation every year. The only region that gets rains from both monsoons is Northeastern India, which consequently experiences the highest rainfall in the world. India experiences at least three seasons a year, Summer, Rainy Season (or "Monsoon") and Winter, though in the tropical South calling the 25°C (75°F) weather "Winter" would be stretching the concept. The North experiences some extremes of heat in Summer and cold in Winter, but except in the Himalayan regions, snow is almost unheard of. November to January is the winter season and April and May are the hot months when everyone eagerly awaits the rains. There is also a brief spring in February and March, especially in North India.

Opinions are divided on whether any part of India actually experiences an Autumn, but the ancients had certainly identified such a season among the six seasons (or *ritus* - *Vasanta* - Spring, *Greeshma* - Summer, *Varsha* - Rainy, *Sharat* - Autumn, *Shishira* - Winter, *Hemanta* - "Mild Winter") they had divided the year into.

Culture

India has a rich diversity of culture and tradition. It's probably the only country where people of so many different origins, religious beliefs, languages and ethnic background coexist.

Holidays

There are three national holidays (Republic Day, Independence Day, and Gandhi Jayanti) which occur on the same day every year. Most other religious holidays occur on different days, because the Hindu and Islamic festivals are based on their respective calendars and not on the Gregorian calendar.

Here is a list of important holidays. Not all holidays are celebrated with equal fervour, or celebrated at all in all regions of the country. Different regions might give somewhat different names to the same festival.

- Republic Day - Celebrates the adoption of the constitution and the day India became a republic
- Holi - The festival of Colour. Stay away from the streets unless you want to be drenched in water and showered with colored powder. Mostly friendly...
- Hindu New Years Day
- Martyrs Day / Labour Day
- Raksha Bandhan - Sisters tie the *rakhi* or the sacred thread of love on their brothers' wrists and the brothers give gifts and promises of protection in return.
- Independence Day - Celebrates the birth of independent India
- Krishna Janmashtami/Gokulashtami - Celebrates the birth of Lord Krishna
- Vinayaka (Ganesha) Chathurthi - Celebrates the birth of Lord Ganesha. The most important festival in Maharashtra. Festivities go

on for 10 days during which the idol of Ganesha (or Ganpati) is worshipped at homes and every street corner. On the tenth day (or earlier in some cases) it is ceremonially immersed in the sea or a lake after being taken out in a lavish procession. A sight to watch, but traffic is disrupted for those days in cities like Mumbai and Pune.

- Gandhi Jayanti - birthday of Mahatma Gandhi
- Dussera/Ayudha Pooja - Locals worship the deity Durga and perform pooja for their objects of daily use. Workers are given sweets, cash bonuses, gifts, new clothes etc. It is also new year for businessmen, when they are supposed to start new account books. The nine nights of *Navratri* before this comprise the second most important festival in India. In some places like West Bengal, it is *the* most important festival. There Goddess Durga gets the same treatment that Ganesha gets in Maharashtra (see above). In the north *Ram Lila* celebrations take place and the slaying of Ravana by Lord Rama is ceremonially reenacted.
- Deepawali (or Diwali) - Festival of lights, celebrates the slaying of the demon Narakasura. Probably the most lavish festival in the country, reminiscent (to US travellers at least) of Thanksgiving (the food) and Christmas (the shopping and gifts) combined. This is by far the most spectacular festival of all: houses are decorated, there is glitter everywhere, and if you wander the streets on Deepawali night, there will be firecrackers going off everywhere including sometimes under your feet.
- Ramzan-Id/Id-ul-Fitr
- Christmas

Getting in to India

Citizens of most countries with a few exceptions like Bhutan and Nepal need a visa to get in. Depending on your purpose of visit, you can get a tourist visa (six months normally), a business visa (one year or more, multiple entries) or a student visa (up to 5 years). Note that some Indian embassies only offers visas to residents of that country: this means you should get your visa before you leave home, instead of trying to get in a neighboring country.

Rules and validity of visas will differ based on citizenship. Check the Web site of the Indian embassy, consulate or high commission in your country or contact the local office.

There are other categories for specialised purposes. The missionary visa is mandatory for anyone who is visiting India "primarily to take part in religious activities". This rule is meant to combat religious conversion, particularly of Hindus to Christianity. There have been cases where preachers have been deported for addressing religious congregations while on a tourist visa. You don't need to be worried if you are just on a religious tour of churches in India. If you are on a Student, Employment, Research or Missionary visa, you need to register within 14 days of arrival with the Foreigners Regional Registration Office where you will be staying. If the place you are staying at doesn't have one, you need to register at the local police station. All visitors who intend to stay more than 180 days also need to be registered. Addresses and telephone numbers of the FRROs can be found here.

By plane

The major points of entry are Mumbai, New Delhi, Chennai and Calcutta. If you are flying in from a Western country, chances are that you will get in through one of these cities. However in recent years, to accommodate the increasing traffic, many other airports have been upgraded to take in international flights. Among these are Amritsar, Ahmedabad, Bangalore, Cochin, Guwahati, Hyderabad, Jaipur, Pune and Thiruvananthapuram.

India has homegrown international airlines like Air India and "Indian" (formerly known as "Indian Airlines"). They are affordable, but not dependable. They do provide good connectivity. In recent years, the government has allowed Indian private airlines like Jet Airways and Air Sahara to go international. There are daily flights to most imaginable places on Earth from a wide array of Indian airports.

By Boat

India has several international ports on its peninsula, Mumbai and Chennai are the main ones handling passenger traffic. The remaining mainly handle cargo.

By Train

There are active rail links into India from Nepal and Pakistan.

From Nepal the link is from Khajuri in Dhanusa district of Nepal to Jaynagar in Bihar, and run by the Nepal Railways.

There are two links from Pakistan: Samjhauta Express from Lahore to Attari near Amritsar in Punjab. The Thar Express restarted in February 2006 after 40 years out of service. It runs from Munabao in the Indian state of Rajasthan to Khokrapar in Pakistan's Sindh province, however this crossing is not open for foreign tourists. Neither train is the fastest or the most practical way to go between India and Pakistan due to the long delay to clear customs and immigration (although the trains are sights in their own right and make for a fascinating trip). Should you want to get from one country to the other as quickly as possible, walk across at Attari/Wagah.

By Car

From Pakistan the only land crossing is from Lahore to Amritsar via the

Attari/Wagah border crossing. See Istanbul to New Delhi over land. You will need a Carnet de Passage if crossing with your own vehicle and the process will likely be lengthy.

By Bus

From Nepal buses cross the border daily, usually with connections to New Delhi, Lucknow, and Varanasi. However, it's cheaper and more reliable to take one bus to the border crossing and another from there on. The border crossings are (India/Nepal side) Sunauli/Bhairawa from Varanasi, Raxaul/Birganj from Calcutta, Kakarbhitta from Darjeeling, and Mahendrenagar-Banbassa from Delhi.

From Pakistan the only land crossing is from Lahore to Amritsar via the Attari/Wagah border crossing. Despite tensions between the two countries, there is a steady trickle of travellers passing this way. The immigration procedures are fairly straightforward, but note that neither Pakistan nor India issue visas at the border. Expect to take most of the day to go between Lahore and Amritsar on local buses. Normally it's possible to get a direct bus from Amritsar to the border, walk to the other side and catch a direct bus to Lahore, although you may need to change at some point on route. Amritsar and Lahore are both fairly close to the border (about 30-40 minutes drive), so taxis are a faster and easier option.

The direct Delhi-Lahore service has restarted, though it is far more costly than local buses/trains, not any faster, and would mean you miss seeing Amritsar. You will also be stuck at the border for much longer while the bus is searched and all of the passengers go through immigration.

There is now a bus service across the 'Line of control' between Indian and Pakistani Kashmir, however it is not open to foreign tourists.

From Bangladesh, there are a number of land entry points to India. The most common way is the regular air-conditioned, and comfortable bus services from Dhaka to Calcutta/Kolkata via Haridispur (India)/Benapole (Bangladesh) border post. Bus companies 'Shohag', 'Green Line', 'Shyamoli' and others operate daily bus services under the label of the state owned West Bengal Surface Transport Service Corporation (WBSTSC) and the Bangladesh Road Transport Corporation (BRTC). WBSTSC operates buses from Calcutta every Monday, Wednesday, and Friday while from Dhaka the days leave on Tuesday, Thursday, and Saturday. BRTC also operates the buses from Calcutta and Dhaka on the same days. The normal journey time taken by these busses is around 12 hours with a oneway fare of Rs. 400-450 or BDT(Taka)600-800, roughly USD 8-10.

Another daily bus service by 'Shyamoli' and others under the BRTC label from Dhaka connects Siliguri, but the busses in this route do not cross the Changrabanda/Burimari or Burungamari border post. Rather, passengers reaching the border have to clear customs, walk a few hundred yards to cross the border and board the awaiting connecting busses on the other end for the final destination. Ticket for Dhaka-Siliguri-Dhaka route costs BDT 1600, roughly USD 20-25 depending on conversion rates. Tickets are purchased either in Dhaka or in Siliguri.

There is also a regular bus service between Dhaka and Agartala, capital of Indian Tripura district. Two BRTC buses daily from Dhaka and the Tripura Road Transport Corporation plying its vehicles six days a week with a round fare costing USD 10 connect the two cities. There is only one halt at Ashuganj in Bangladesh during the journey.

Other entry points from Bangladesh are Hili, Chilahati/Haldibari, Banglaband border posts for entry to West Bengal; Tamabil border post for a route to Shilong, Meghalaya, and some others with lesser known routes to northeastern Indian regions.

Get Around

Addresses

Indian addresses are not standardized in any way. Very often, streets are not named or numbered. Block-level numbering is almost non-existent. Even when they are, you cannot rely on the street signs actually being there. Very often, the house or establishment you are looking for will be off the road. For these reasons, postal addresses are often stated in terms of other landmarks, as in "Opp. Prithvi theatre" or "Behind Maruti Showroom", etc. Do not assume that this will be enough. If you need to get anywhere, call in advance and ask for detailed directions. Ask about the closest landmark, even if it is mentioned on the postal address - you will often get a better one. This advice applies as much to a large city as to a village.

On the plus side, you will always find someone out on the streets to help you out.

By Plane

India's large size and poor roads make flying a viable option, especially as prices have tumbled in the last few years. All Indian states, with the solitary exception of Sikkim, can be reached by plane, although connections to smaller cities are still limited.

Airlines

At one time, domestic flights were the monopoly of the government-owned Indian Airlines (now known as "Indian"). Jet Airways and Air Sahara challenged this monopoly with better service and competitive fares. In 2004, Air Deccan launched its no-frills airline. Now there are quite a few competitors and prices are a traveller's delight. Some Indian airlines charge foreigners higher fares than Indian residents. If you don't have an Indian passport you usually get a better price from the airlines that don't have this price policy. Here is a list of airlines in India, but there's one starting almost every month.

Air India, India's prime international carrier. Though this is an international carrier, you can often get good rates on the domestic leg of its international flights

Indian, full service government-owned airline, substandard service, but probably the best coverage of India. Expect special, high, fare if you don't have an Indian passport.

Air Deccan, low cost carrier connecting various cities and small towns. Usually, they are cheapest, but they have a reputation of being chronically late —, a delay of an hour or so being routine. This situation has improved lately. They provide you with food or beverages only on payment. You don't even get water for free. They aim for a "quick turnaround", which means that they often neglect to clean the planes. Same prices for foreigners and Indians.

Air Sahara, full service airline with decent coverage.

Alliance Air - Feeder airline for Indian. Has a spotty safety record. It will soon cease to exist and service taken over by its parent company "Indian".

Go Air Low Cost

Jagson Airlines service mostly in North India.

Jet Airways , full service airline with very good coverage. Now services London (LHR) directly from Delhi and Mumbai.

Kingfisher Airlines, full service, but with low fares. The service on this is excellent. On flights to Bangalore (its home base) depending on when you book, you can get prices comparable to Air Deccan or Spice. Same prices for foreigners and Indians.

Paramount Airways - feeder airline, service mostly in South India.

SpiceJet Airlines , low cost airline, the closest competitor to Air Deccan in terms of fares. If you are willing to shell out a bit more to arrive on time, consider Spice over Air Deccan.

Visa Airways - feeder airline, service mostly in South India.

Keep in mind, however, that outside of big cities coverage is poor. If you need to get to a small town, low-cost airlines won't help you. You may have to rely on Indian Airlines or Jet. Flying low-cost to a metro and taking a train is not a bad idea either.

Fares

The earlier you book, the lower you pay. You will hear a lot about air tickets at Rs. 500 ($12), but those are promotional rates for limited seats which are sold out within seconds. Non-etheless, you do get good rates from the budget airlines. Tickets for small cities will cost more than those for the metros, because of the spotty coverage noted above. Many airlines have higher fares for foreigners than for Indians. Foreigners will be charged in US dollars, whereas Indians will be charged in rupees. Indian ticket pricing has not attained the bewildering complexity that the Americans have achieved, but they are getting there. As of now, you don't have to worry about higher prices on weekends, lower prices for round-trips, lower prices for travel *around* weekends etc.

Ticketing

It is possible to book flights online from the airline's Web site (most major airlines have one now), though sometimes tickets are available from a travel agent. It is sometimes more convenient to get tickets from the ticket agents though that will be more expensive. Do check out both options. If you've booked on the net, just a printout and an id will be sufficient. You can get your ticket at the airport after showing the printout alongwith a credible identity proof like a passport or a driving license.

Check in

Procedures at airports in India are somewhat different from those elsewhere. In most cases you *won't be able* to check in for your flight more than an hour ahead of the scheduled departure. Also, there will be a stand where you must take your checked baggage for a security screening before you check in. It isn't always obvious where you are supposed to wait to catch your flight. However, don't hesitate to ask someone if you are unsure. Most staff in airports are very helpful to foreigners and will take pains to ensure you catch your flight.

By Train

India boasts the biggest network of railway lines in the world, and the rail system is efficient, if not always on schedule. With classes ranging from luxurious to regular, it's the best way to get to know the country and its people. You will get to see the beautiful Indian countryside first hand, and most train passengers will be curious about you and happy to pass the time with a chat.

Classes

There are five basic classes: General, Sleeper, 3-tier A/C, 2-tier A/C and 1st class A/C. Not all classes are present on all trains.

- The general class exists on pretty much all the trains. Travelling in it is not recommended. It has only wooden seats and getting a seat is very unlikely as there is no limit on the number of tickets sold. The compartment is packed like sardines and it smells. It can, however, be a useful way to get on a train if you absolutely need to go and you have tried *every* other way of getting on a train. (ie waitlist, quotas). If you are the sort who loves unique experiences, a ride on this class is not to be missed. Keep in mind that it is very uncomfortable however, so even a short trip in this class can feel like too long. A 1000 miles trip by this class would cost you approximately Rs. 150-250 ($3-5).

- Sleeper class (non-AC) is much better, and it is the staple transport of backpackers travelling in India. The seats are cushioned and there is assured seating. You get a berth to sleep in at night, arranged in three tiers. Ask for an "upper or middle berth" for overnight trips. Hygiene and safety standards vary across the country. In the South and some Western states, the compartments are relatively clean. In the North, it isn't very clean, and there is the problem of intruders from the general compartments getting in. Bring your own bedding. You could do it for the experience, but if you need a good deal of comfort, non-AC sleeper isn't an ideal option. Sleeper compartments are available on almost all long-distance trains except a few like Rajdhani which are fully air-conditioned. A 1000 miles trip by this class would cost you approximately Rs. 450-900 ($10-20).
- 3-tier and 2-tier A/C is better. The difference between the two is not major - in the former berths to sleep in are arranged in three tiers, while in the latter they are arranged in two. Most trains will have both the classes. You get 2 bedsheets, a pillow and a blanket at night. In trains like Rajdhani and Shatabdi, food is also covered in the fare. The equivalent of this class in short-distance trains would be A/C chair car where you get seating, but no sleeping. A 1000 miles trip by 3-tier AC and 2-tier AC would cost you approximately Rs. 1200 ($25) and Rs. 1400 ($35) respectively.
- 1st class A/C is the one you'd choose if you think it is more important to savour the journey than to actually get there. It is usually more expensive than air travel. A 1000 miles trip by this class would cost you approximately Rs. 4000 ($80).

Schedule

Before booking a ticket pick up a copy of Trains At A Glance, the national rail schedule (or "timetable"), from any railway station. This is updated every June and remains valid until July next year. It allows you to choose the best train for your needs, and find the name and number of the train for your destination. However, this is a general guide and does not contain detailed list of all stations, neither does it contain all the trains that ply. A more specific guide depending on the "rail zone" is available at important stations on that zone. For example, a detailed guide on trains plying in West India can be avaialbe at all major railway stations in West India. You can also get the whole schedule online [www.irctc.co.in] or [www.indianrail.gov.in]. Neither option will find connecting trains for you, so some knowledge of important stations is necessary if you are going to a remote location.

Ticketing

Tickets are available from travel agents as well as directly from Indian Railways. It is better not to buy tickets from a travel agent, as they mark up the price, and with the advent of internet booking, offer no real advantage. Train tickets are in high demand, especially during the summer and winter breaks. This means that without careful planning, it may be next to impossible to get tickets for long distance travel (for example from New Delhi to Mumbai). You can book up to 90 days in advance, but during the busy season, the tickets may get sold out quickly. However foreigners can get tickets from a quota reserved for them. In big cities, you have a specific counter or even a special office for them. If you plan to travel in 1st Class A/C tickets should be easier to get - they are in less demand. Rail passes are also available, and are called Indrail passes. Find out more information for International tourists or book your travel. Booking tickets in is very easy.

If you do not get a confirmed ("reserved") ticket, you may get one that is Waitlisted (WL) or in the Reservation Against Cancellation (RAC) status. If you've booked your ticket in advance, it will probably move from "Waitlisted" to "RAC" status or even to "Reserved" status as time goes by, because of cancellations, so it is a good idea to check it periodically and keep your plans dynamic.

You cannot get on to a reserved compartment if your ticket is waitlisted (you can only enter a General Compartment). But if you have an RAC ticket, you are allotted 'sitting' berths - *i.e.* in a Sleeper Coach, you and a fellow RAC ticket-holder share a berth so that both of you can travel sitting instead of sleeping. The Ticket Examiner then allots you a Confirmed (CNF) sleeping berth as and when one is available due to last minute cancellations, no-shows etc. Depending on the train, the route and the season you are travelling in, the RAC ticket may get upgraded to CNF either as soon as the journey begins, mid-way through the journey or not at all.

Five days before the departure date of a train, the Taktal quota seats become available. This allows tourists who like to plan a trip as they go to book seats closer to the day of departure. Note that this incurrs a large extra fee. Even with this extra quota (about 4% of the seats on a train), it can be difficult to get the train you want when you want it. It is advisable to book tickets in advanced. It is usually better to pay the nominal cancellation fees to change tickets than to pay the hefty taktal fees.

Meals

Most trains have a pantry car and if you are in the sleeper or A/C classes, you can buy meals on board the train. In 1st Class A/C, you will be served your meals by liveried waiters. The quality and hygiene can be inconsistent though (In South India the quality and hygiene is better). If you are finicky, bring enough food and bottled water for the journey including delays: Bananas, bread, and candy bars are good basics to have. At most larger stations hawkers selling tea, peanuts, and snack food will go up and down the train, but don't count on this being enough for a 18 or 40 hour journey. Most important stations will have vendors selling all kinds of edible stuff, but the usual caveats about eating in India apply.

Many of the food vendors come by in the morning, so if you sleep in you will miss a lot of food. Also, you need to be ready to hail down a vendor when then walk by - they move quickly.

Other Tips

Always watch your bags, especially in and around train stations. Once on a train, lock your bags to your bunk— under the bunk if you are on the bottom, or at your head. Make sure to also lock any exterior pockets (keep your toilet paper, and anything else you'll want on the outside). You can buy chains from chain-and-lock sellers who walk around train stations and trains.

The top bunk is best if you are the sort who likes to sleep early or late. The middle and bottom bunks are converted into seating area, so you will be forced to stay awake if everyone else in your compartment wants to stay up.

Indian trains take a long time to go anywhere. Don't just look at a map and assume a short trip, it's best to check trains at a glance before making your plans. Bathrooms on Indian trains are of the squat variety, the cleanliness tends to deteriorate over a long trip, but at least nothing but the sole of your shoes needs to touch the toilet. Its a good idea to use the toilet elsewhere when possible.

By bus

While you can't take a cross-country bus-ride across India, buses are the second most popular way of travelling across states. Every state has its own bus service which primarily connects intra-state routes, but will also have services to neighbouring states. There are usually multiple classes of buses. The ordinary buses (called differently in different states, *e.g.* "service bus") are extremely crowded with even standing room rarely available. In addition, they tend to stop at too many places. There might be luxury or express buses available, and sometimes they even have air-conditioning. They are more comfortable, have assured seating, and have limited stops. Be warned that many of the private buses, especially long-distance lines, play music and/or videos at ear-splitting volume. Even with earplugs it can be nerve-wracking. Do not expect public restrooms at all, or even most, bus stops.

Private buses may or may not be available in the area you are travelling to, and even if they are, the quality could vary a lot. Unfortunately, the bus industry is extremely fragmented and there are few operators who offer services in more than 2 or 3 neighbouring states. However, long distance bus operators such as Raj National Express are currently beginning to roll out their operations across the country modelled on the lines of the Greyhound service in the Unites States.

By car

In India driving is on the left of the road. You can drive in India if you have a local license or an International Driving Permit, but unless you are used to driving on extremely chaotic streets, you probably will not want to. The average city or village road is narrow, often potholed and badly marked. National Highways are better, but they are still narrow, and Indian driving discipline is non-existent. In the past few years the Central government has embarked on an ambitious project to upgrade the highways. The Golden Quadrilateral connecting the four metros is 88% complete as of December 2005 and the roads there almost reach international standards. But it is still some time before the drivers adapt to the new roads, so if you are a foreigner, you'll be wise to put off your plans to drive on Indian roads by a few years.

Instead, if you desire a car, you rent both the car and a driver with it. Rates are quoted in rupees per kilometer and you will have to pay for both ways even if you are going only one way. The actual rate will vary by region. The driver's salary is so low (typically around Rs 100 to 150 per day) that it adds little to the cost of renting the car. The driver will find his own accommodation and food wherever you are traveling. A common rental vehicle is the old, but reliable, Ambassador. This is a large, boxy, official-looking car, with space for 4-5 passengers (including driver), and a decent-sized trunk. Now you may get better international models like Toyota, Suzuki, Honda, Ford, Hyundai,and other expensive options like Mercedes.

There are numerous advantages to having a car and driver.

- A native driver is the safest means of car travel.
- You can keep your bags and shopping goods with you securely wherever you go.
- The driver will often have some knowledge of local tourist destinations.
- A car is the quickest and most reliable means of going from point to point. After the initial agreement you needn't spend any time finding travel, haggling over price, etc.
- You can stop anywhere you like, and change plans at the last minute.

It is rare to find a driver that speaks more than a few words of English. As a result, misunderstandings are common. Keep sentences short. Use the present tense. Use single words and hand gestures to convey meaning. Make sure you can trust your driver before you leave your goods with him. If he shows any suspicious motives or Behaviour make sure you keep your bags with you. Conversely, if your driver is very friendly and helpful, it is a nice gesture to buy him a little something to eat or drink when stopping for food. They will really appreciate this.

Your driver may in some cases act as a tout, offering to take you to businesses from which he gets a baksheesh. This isn't necessarily a bad thing - he may help you find just what you're looking for, and add a little bit to his paltry income at the same time. On the other hand, you should always evaluate for yourself whether you are being sold on a higher-cost product than you want. The driver might *ask* for a tip at the end of the trip. Pay him some amount and don't let him guilt-trip you into paying too much.

By Motorcycle

Another choice, popular with people who like taking risks, is to buy a motorcycle. The Royal Enfield is a popular choice for its classic looks, despite its high petrol consumption, low reliability, and difficulty to handle.

Another choice for tourers is the new kid on the block, the Bajaj Pulsar twins. These bikes are available in a choice of 150/180 and soon to be 220 CC versions. All these bikes are tried and tested over a variety of terrain, and are very reliable, easy to maintain and also have excellent drinking habits...

By Auto-Rickshaw

The auto-rickshaw, sometimes abbreviated as "auto" and sometimes as "rickshaw", is the most common means of hired transportation in India. Most residents usually refer to them as a "three wheeler." But please note that it is not a good way to travel between cities, though you'd be surprised how far people travel in them. They vary in Colour. Most are green and yellow, due to the new CNG gas laws, and some may be yellow and black in Colour, with one wheel in the front and two in the back, with a leather or soft plastic top.

When getting an auto-rickshaw, you can either negotiate the fare or go by the meter. In almost all cases it is better to use the meter — a negotiated fare means that you are being charged a higher than normal rate. A metered fare starts around Rs 10, and includes the first kilometer of travel. Never get in an auto-rickshaw without either the meter being turned on, or the fare negotiated in advance. In nearly all cases the driver will ask an exorbitant sum (for Indian standards) from you later. A normal fare for 10km of travel within the city would be about Rs 50, which is around a dollar and a few cents. In most of the cities, auto-rickshaw drivers are provided with a rate card that elaborately describes the fares on per kilo-meter basis. A careful tourist must verify the meter-reading against the rate-card before making a payment.

Ideally, you should talk with a local to find out what the fare for any estimated route will be. Higher rates may apply at night, and for special destinations such as airports. Finally, factor in that auto drivers may have to pay bribes to join the queue for customers at premium location such as expensive hotels. The bribe will be factored in the fare.

Make sure that the driver knows where he is going. Many autorickshaw drivers will claim to know the destination without really having any clue as to where it is. If you know something about the location, quiz them on it to screen out the liars. If you do not know much about the location, make them tell you in no uncertain terms that they know where it is. This is because after they get lost and drive all over the place, they will often demand extra payment for their own mistake. You can then tell them that they lied to you, and wasted your time, so they should be happy to get the agreed-upon fee.

Talk

Officially, India has 22 national languages, namely Assamese, Bengali, Bodo, Dogri, Gujarati, Hindi, Kannada, Kashmiri, Konkani, Maithili, Malayalam, Manipuri, Marathi, Nepali, Oriya, Punjabi, Sanskrit, Santhali, Sindhi, Tamil, Telugu and Urdu. There are also other less prominent languages like Tulu, Bhojpuri the main spoken language of some places.

Hindi, spoken by 30% of the population, is the primary tongue of the people in Northern India. Many more people speak it as a second language. If you can afford only one phrasebook, pick up the Hindi one, as it will enable you to get by in most of India.

The exceptions are the extreme south - Tamil Nadu and Kerala and the Northeast. In Tamil Nadu, it is inadvisable to speak in Hindi, as there is a residual hostility to the language dating back to the hamhanded policies of the 1960s. As of Kerala almost all people can understand and many can speak English.

In any case, you are better off picking up as many words of the local language of the place you are going to - people are proud of their culture and language and will appreciate it if an outsider makes an attempt to communicate in it.

English is widely spoken in major cities and around most tourist places, and acts as the *lingua franca* among all educated Indians. English has been spoken by Indians long enough that it has begun evolving its own rhythm, vocabulary, and inflection, much like French in Africa and Spanish in South America have taken on glittering cultural lives of their own. Indeed, much has recently been made of subcontinental writers such as Arundhati Roy, Vikram Seth, and Salman Rushdie. The English you are likely to hear in India will be heavily influenced by British English, although spoken with the lilting stress and intonation of the speaker's other native language. Indians can usually tell regional English accents apart, similar to the South American ability to tell Argentinians from Colombians. One of the most delightful quirks of Indian English is the language's adherence to Pre-1950s British English which to speakers in North America and Britain will sound oddly formal. Another source of fascination and intrigue for travelers is the ubiquitous use of English for cute quips in random places. One relatively common traffic sign reads, "Speed thrills, but kills". On the back of trucks everywhere you'll find "horn please ok" or "tata bye bye".

Indians are adopting more and more native words into their English. A lot of these are already well known to speakers elsewhere. Chai (tea), Guru (learned teacher/master), cummerbund (literally waist-tie), Nirvana (extinction of the separative ego) and avatar (God in human form) are words that have left their original subcontinental home. However, Indians are using English loan words in their native languages at an even more rapid pace. As India modernizes blazingly fast, it has taken from English words for modern objects that simply did not exist a few decades ago. However, more importantly, bilingual Indians in informal conversation will often switch unpredictably between English and their native language when speaking to similar polyglots, thus effectively communicating in a hybridized language that relies on the listener's ability to speak both languages. A bilingual speaker in Delhi, might for example, say "mera fever bahut bad hai" (my fever is very bad) which mixes English with Hindi 50-50 in spite of the fact that perfectly good words exist for both 'fever' and 'bad' in Hindi. Such mixed phrases are easily understood by most listeners —although not always encouraged— and are becoming increasingly common. This hybrid is sometimes referred to as 'Hinglish' (much like Chinese/Malay-influenced English in Singapore is termed 'Singlish') It seems that English and Hindi are indeed converging among the bilingual sections of society. While English, as a distinct language, is here to stay for now, it appears that it will eventually over hundreds of years be absorbed into the vast cultural fabric of the subcontinent.

English speaking Indians may also seem commanding to a westerner. You may hear "come here," "sit here," "drink this," "bring me that" which may sound direct and demanding to the point of being rude to northern Europeans and Americans, but is in no way meant to be impolite.

Non-verbal communication is also important. Much has been made of the confusing Indian head nod for yes and no, but the only important thing to understand is that Indians have different nods for yes, ok and no.

- If they are shaking their head back and forth, they mean yes.
- If they are nodding their head in a tilting motion from right to left, they mean okay indicating acceptance. The movement is in a figure eight, and looks identical to the western nod for "Sort of".
  - If they shake their head from left to right twisting it about the vertical axis, they mean no.

BUY

Currency

The currency in India is the Indian Rupee. It trades around 46 rupees to the US dollar and 58 rupees to the Euro. The Rupee is subdivided into 100 paise (singular: paisa). Take a look at the Exchange Rates Table for Indian Rupee for other currencies. 5 rupees 75 paise would normally be written as Rs.5.75 and one rupee as Re.1.

Common bills come in denominations of Rs. 5, Rs. 10, Rs. 20, Rs. 50, Rs. 100, Rs. 500 and Rs. 1,000. It is always good to have a number of small bills on hand, as merchants and drivers sometimes don't have change. A useful technique is to keep small bills (Rs. 10 - 50) in your wallet or in a pocket, and to keep larger bills separate. In this way you won't be making obvious the amount of money you have available. In many cases merchants will claim that they don't have change for a Rs. 100 or Rs. 500 note. This is often a lie, as they simply don't want to be stuck with a large bill. Rather than giving up your last 6 ten-rupee notes, it is better to make them give you change.

The coins in circulation are 25 paise, 50 paise, Rs. 1, Rs. 2 and Rs. 5. Coins are useful for buying tea (Rs. 5), for bus fare (Rs. 2 to Rs. 10), and for giving exact change for an auto-rickshaw.

Indians commonly use lakh and crore for "hundred thousand" and "10 million" respectively. Though these terms come from Sanskrit, they have been adopted so deeply into Indian English that most people are not aware that it is not standard in other English dialects. You may also find non-standard placement of commas while writing numerals. Rupees One crore would be written as Rs. 1,00,00,000. This format may puzzle you till you start thinking in terms of lakhs and crores, after which it will seem natural.

In principle you can live in India for a couple of hundred rupees a day. At the other end of the spectrum you can sleep in fancy 5 star hotels and spend lots of money on food and shopping.

Changing Money

Outside airports you can only change US dollars, Euros and sometimes UK sterling pounds. In big cities, there are now ATMs where you can get rupees against your international debit or credit card (maximum amount is 4,000-20,000 rupees depending on the ATM). State Bank of India (SBI) ATMs usually don't accept foreign cards. Therefore, you may have to search around to find an ATM that will work with your card. Citibank has a significant presence in India, as does HSBC. ICICI bank has the second largest network of ATMs, and accepts most of the international cards at a nominal charge. It is always worthwhile to have bank cards or credit cards from at least two different providers, to ensure that you have a backup available in case one card is suspended by your bank, or simply doesn't work at a particular ATM. In the big cities, credit cards are accepted at retail chain stores and other westernized restaurants and stores. Small businesses and family-run stores almost never accept credit cards, so it is useful to keep a moderate amount of cash on hand.

Shopping

- In India you are *expected* to negotiate the price. If not, you risk overpaying many times - which can be okay if you think "well, it's cheaper than home". In most of the big cities and even smaller towns retail chain stores are popping up where the shopping experience is essentially identical to similar stores in the West. There are also some government-run stores like the Cottage Emporium in New Delhi, where you can sample wares from all across the country in air-conditioned comfort. Although you will pay a little more at these stores, you can be sure that what you are getting is not a cheap knockoff. Even in government-run stores, bargaining is expected.
- Often, the more time you spend in a store, the better deals you will get. It is worth spending time getting to know the owner, asking questions, and getting him to show you other products (if you have an interest). Once the owner feels that he is making a sufficient profit from you, he will often give you additional goods at a rate close to his cost, rather than the common "foreigner rate". You will get better prices and service by buying many items in one store than by bargaining in multiple stores individually.
- Also, very often you will meet a "friend" in the street offering you to visit his or his family's shop. In about 9 of 10 cases this will simply mean that you pay twice as much as when you had been in the shop without your newly found friend.
- Baksheesh — the giving of small bribes — is a very common phenomenon. While it is a big problem in India, indulging in it can ease certain problems and clear some hurdles. Baksheesh is also the term used by beggars, who can be found throughout India, if they want money from you. Baksheesh is as ancient a part of Middle Eastern and Asian culture as anything else. It derives from the Arabic meaning a small gift. It refers as much to charity as to bribes.
- When you are buying anything, assume that a decent price for what you are buying is *at least* less than 1/3 of the merchant's price. As such begin bargaining at 1/4 of his opening price. If they are unwilling to sell it to you around 1/3 the price, don't buy, since (1) they might drop the price after you look ready to leave and (2) if you are buying the tourist trinkets, then chances are you will find another merchant willing to give you the *exact same thing* for the right price.

- Packaged goods show the Maximum Retail Price (MRP) right on the package. This includes taxes. Retailers are not supposed to charge more than this. Though this rule is adhered to at most places, at tourist destinations or remote places, you may be charged more. Also, keep in mind that a surprising number of things do not come in packaged form.
- The shops outside the big brand shops are better for as you can get good stuff at a low rate. But watch out for the quality of the things you buy.

What to Look For/Buy

- Wood Carvings: India produces a striking variety of carved wood products that can be bought at very low prices. Examples include decorative wooden plates, bowls, artwork, furniture, and miscellaneous items that will surprise you.
- Clothing: Women's salwar kameez, saris. Traditional men's clothing such as kurta and pyjama. Brilliantly patterned scarves and shawls can be bought for less than Rs. 500. On the other hand, it may be worth spending more for a soft and warm 100% silk shawl. You can also find more modern style clothing at low cost. Modern clothing tends to have loud patterns. You will probably need clothing one size larger than would fit you in a Western country.
- Paintings: Paintings come on a wide variety of media, such as cotton, silk, or with frame included. Gemstone paintings incorporate semi-precious stone dust, so they have a glittering appearance to them.
- Marble and Stone Carvings: Common carved items include elephants, Indian gods/goddesses, etc.
- Jewelry: Beautiful necklaces, bracelets, and other jewelry are very inexpensive in India.
- Pillow Covers, Bed Sets: Striking and rich designs are common for pillows and bed covers.

Eat

Indian food has well-deserved reputation for being hot, owing to the Indian penchant for potent green chilis that will bring tears to the eyes of the uninitiated. You can even find sweet cornflakes with a spicy edge and Indian candies with a piece of chili inside. But this is a largely incomplete description. Aromatic spices such as nutmeg, cinnamon, cardamom, and cloves are equally important as the astonishing variety of chilis and peppercorns. Like most Asian cuisines, the ingredients range from exotic (lotus roots, rose petals) to completely unfamiliar tropical offerings. To enjoy the local food, start slowly. Don't try everything at once. After a few weeks, you can get accustomed to spicy food. If you would like to order your dish not spicy, simply say so. Most visitors are tempted to try at least some of the spicy concoctions, and most discover that the sting is worth the trouble.

Cuisine

Indian cuisine is superb and has recently taken its place among the great cuisines of the world. There is a good chance that you'd have tasted "Indian food" in your country, especially if you are a traveller from the West, but what India has exported abroad is just one part of its extraordinary range of culinary diversity.

In North India, you will find Mughlai, which has been popularized all over the world as Indian cuisine. It is said to have originated in the courts of the Mughal emperors, hence the name. In India, it is also called Punjabi as it was popularized by the Punjabis. Mughlai dishes make heavy use of spices and has been heavily influenced by Central Asian cooking, hence you will find Pulav, Kebab, Kofta etc. North India is wheat growing land, so you have "Indian breads" like rotis, naans, parathas and kulchas. Note, however, that an Indian would be puzzled if you called them "breads" and will refer to them as "rotis". The dishes and breads are often cooked in a clay oven called the *tandoor* over a charcoal fire, giving it the familiar name of tandoori. A typical meal consists of one or more gravy dishes along with rotis, to be eaten by breaking off a piece of roti, dipping it in the gravy and eating them together. "Tandoori chicken" and "Chicken tikka masala" are familiar all over the world, but for vegetarians, there is paneer - a sort of cottage cheese, which is extensively used. For an authentic Punjabi dining experience, try the sarson da saag, a yummy gravy dish made with mustard greens, with Makke di roti — a roti made from maize

The South, in contrast, uses fewer spices and the food is mostly rice-based. They also make greater use of pulses. The typical meal is the sambhar (lentil and various vegetables mixed to form a gravy dish) with rice, or the avial (mixed vegetables) with rice. There are regional variations too — the coastal regions make greater use of coconut and fish. In the coast, it is common to use grated coconut in everything and use coconut oil for cooking, while someone from the interior could be surprised to learn that coconut oil, can in fact, be used for cooking. The South also has some great breakfast dishes like the Upma , Idli (a patty made of lentils and rice) and Dosa, a sort of pancake. All of these can be eaten with chutney (a condiment that can be made from many things.) South Indian cuisine is predominantly vegetarian, though Chettinad cuisine and Kerala cuisine use meat heavily and are a lot more spicier too.

To the West, you will find some great cuisine groups. Gujarati cuisine is mostly vegetarian, sweet, and makes heavy use of milk products. Gujaratis make some of the best snack items such as the Dhokla and the Muthia. Rajasthani cuisine is similar to Gujarati, but somewhat spicier. Maharashtra and Goa are famous for their seafood. Too the East, Bengali food, like South Indian, makes heavy use of rice and fish, though Bengalis prefer freshwater fish. The iconic Bengali dish is the Maccher Jhol, a spicy fish curry. Bengal is also famous for its sweets, and the Sondesh is yummy.

It is, of course, impossible to do full justice to the range and diversity of Indian food in this brief section. Not only does every region of India have a distinctive cuisine, but you will also find that even within a region, different communities have different styles of cooking and often have their signature recipes which you will probably not find in restaurants. The adventurous traveller is advised to wangle invitations to homes, try various bylanes of the city and look for food in unlikely places like temples in search of culinary nirvana.

Fruits

While there are a wide variety of fruits native to India, such as the chikoo and the jackfruit, the true Indian loves his mango. India produces hundreds of varieties across most of its regions. The season typically is the hottest part of the year, ranging between May and July. Mangos range from small (as big as a fist) to some as big as a small cantelope. It can be consumed in its ripe, unripe as well a baby form (the last 2 predominently in pickles).

Vegetarian

Owing to a large number of vegetarian Hindus, Indian cuisine has evolved an astonishingly rich menu that uses no meat or eggs. At least half the menus of most restaurants are devoted to vegetarian dishes. Visiting vegetarians will discover a culinary treasure that is found nowhere else in the world.

Restaurants

Some restaurants - especially those where buses stop after hours and hours of driving - can be very dirty. In this case it might be good to check if there's another one on the opposite side of the street. Fruits that can be peeled such as apples and bananas, as well as packaged snacks are always a safe option. Do not eat grapes. In Southern India, "Hotel" means a local restaurant serving south Indian food, mostly Thali — a full plate of food that usually includes a kind of bread and an assortment of meat or vegetarian dishes — and prepared meals. Like everything in India, the English names of dishes are spelled differently in different places (sometimes in two neighboring restaurants) owing to the various ways in which Indian names can be transliterated into English. Not so different from the multiple spellings of Chinese dishes in restaurants all over the Western hemisphere. Although you might get a big menu, most dishes are served only in specific hours.

Eating by Hand

In India eating with your hand (instead of utensils like forks and spoons) is very common. There's one basic rule of etiquette to observe: Use only your right hand. Don't stick either hand into communal serving dishes: instead, use the left hand to serve yourself with utensils and then dig in. Needless to say, it's wise to wash your hands well before and after eating.

For breads for all types, the basic technique is to hold down the item with your forefinger and use your middle-finger and thumb to tear off pieces. The pieces can then be dipped in sauce or used to pick up bits before you stuff them in your mouth. Rice is more challenging, but the basic idea is to use four fingers to pack a little ball, which can then be dipped into curry before you pop it in your mouth by pushing it with your thumb.

Most of the restaurants do provide cutlery and its pretty safe to use them instead of your hand.

Eating by hand is frowned on in some "classier" places. If you are provided with cutlery and nobody else around you seems to be doing it, then take the hint.

Drink

One of the sweetest and safest beverages you can get is tender coconut water. You can almost always find it in any beach or other tourist destinations in the south. In summer (March to July), you can get fresh sugarcane juice in many places and even a lot of fresh fruit juice varieties. Be careful as fresh juice may contain many germs besides unhygienic ice! The juice waalas do not always clean their equipment properly and do not wash the fruits either.

Everywhere you can get tea (*chai*) of one variety or another. Most common is the "railway tea" type: cheap (2-5 Rs.), sweet and uniquely refreshing once you get the taste for it. It's made by brewing up tea leaves, milk, sugar and spices altogether in a pot and keeping it hot until it's all sold.

You can also get "masala tea": black tea with a blend of spices. That takes some getting used to.

Drinking alcohol can either be frowned upon or openly accepted, depending on the region and religion of the area within which you are drinking. For example, as you can imagine, Goa tends to be more free-wheeling (and has low taxes on alcohol), while southern areas like Chennai are less kind to alcohol, and may even charge excessive taxes on it. Some states such as Gujarat are legally "dry" and alcohol cannot be bought openly there. Alcohol is officially banned, but there is a substantial bootlegging industry, and all types of liquor can be obtained in Gujarat. If you have a non-Indian passport, you can obtain a 'liquor permit'. This allows you to buy alcohol at state-licensed shops, of which there are fourteen or so in all of Gujarat.

Make sure to try the Indian soft drinks: Thums Up, which is a cola that has a unique taste with different spices and sweeteners, and Limca, a lemon lime soda. They are both bottled by Coca-Cola alongside Coke and Sprite.

Sleep

Choices vary wildly depending on your budget and location. Cheap travellers' hotels are numerous in big cities where you can get a room for less than Rs. 100. If your wallet allows it, you can try staying in former maharaja's residence in Udaipur or modern five-star hotels in New Delhi and Mumbai. The top-end of Indian luxury rests with the Oberoi, Taj, and Welcomgroup hotel chains, who operate hotels in all the major cities and throughout Rajasthan. A number of international chains including Mariott, and Hyatt also run major 5-star hotels in most Indian metropolises.

Two important factors to keep in mind when choosing a place to stay are 1) safety, and 2) cleanliness. Malaria is alive and well in certain areas of India - one of the best ways to combat malaria is to choose lodgings with air conditioning and sealed windows. An insect-repellent spray containing DEET will also help.

Dak bungalows exist in many areas. These were built by the British to accommodate travelling officials and are now used by the Indian and state governments for the same purpose. If they have room, most will take tourists at a moderate fee. They are plain — ceiling fans rather than air conditioning, shower but no tub, etc. — but clean, comfortable and usually in good locations. Typically the staff includes a pensioned-off soldier as night watchman and perhaps another as gardener; often the gardens are lovely. Sometimes there is a cook. You meet interesting Indian travellers this way: engineers building a bridge in the area, a team of doctors vaccinating the villagers, whatever.

Learn

Yoga, ayurvedic massage and language are the courses most often looked for by foreigners. For example, Haridwar and Rishikesh are popular places for yoga courses. Varanasi has a famous university with Hindi classes.

Work

Foreigners need a work permit to be employed in India. A work permit is granted if an application is made to the local Indian embassy along with proof of potential employment and supporting documents. There are many expatriates working in India, mostly for multinational Fortune 1000 firms. India has always had an expatriate community of reasonable size, and there are many avenues for finding employment, including popular job hunting Web sites like monster.com!

There are many volunteer opportunities around the country including teaching. India has a reasonable presence of foreign Christian missionaries, who for the most part form the non-local religious workers, since the other major religions of the world either grew out of India or have had a long term presence. A living can be made in the traveler scenes by providing some kind of service such as baking Western cakes, tattooing or massage.

Stay Safe

As a rule India is quite safe for foreigners. However, check with your embassy and ask for local advice before heading to Kashmir or northeast India (Assam, Nagaland, Tripura, Meghalaya and Manipur), as both areas have long-running insurgencies. Also take extra caution when travelling at night in Uttar Pradesh, Bihar, Jharkhand and Uttaranchal and certain areas of the large metros.

Unfortunately thefts are quite common in places visited by tourists, but violent thefts hardly ever occur. More likely a thief will pick your pocket (see pickpockets) or break into your room. There is little culture of muggings in India.

When travelling by autorickshaw, never ever get into the vehicle if there is another person accompanying the driver. This always spells trouble for unwary travellers.

Westerners, particularly women, attract the attention of beggars, frauds and touts. Beggars will often go as far as touching you, and following you tugging on your sleeve. It does little good to get angry or to say "No" loudly. The best response is to look unconcerned and ignore the Behaviour. The more attention you pay to a beggar or a tout — positive or negative — the longer they will follow you hoping for a payback. As always in India, patience is required.

Westerners should not trust strangers offering assistance or services. Be particularly wary of frauds at tourist attractions such as the temples of Kanchipuram, where they prey on those unfamiliar with local and religious customs. See Common scams.

Westerners should be cautious when visiting villages and rural areas in the night. Bandits often abduct and rob Westerners visiting India, as it is assumed they possess large amounts of wealth. Also, think twice about taking night buses or driving at night in these areas. Bandits are said to stop night buses with fake checkpoints and rob everyone inside. The frequency of this occurring is extremely low and the state governments are working hard to arrest these bandit groups, but take extra care nontheless.

Female Travellers in India

India is a conservative country and some western habits are perceived as dishonorable for a woman in this culture.

- Outside of the larger cities, it is unusual for people of the opposite sex to touch each other in public. Even couples (married or otherwise) refrain from public displays of affection. Therefore, it is advised that you do not shake hands with a person of the opposite sex unless the other person extends his/her hand first. The greeting among Hindus is to bring your palms together in front of your chest, or simply saying 'Namaste', or 'Vanakkam' in Tamil Nadu. Both forms are equally polite and correct, if a little formal. Almost all the people (even if they don't know English) do understand a "hi" or a "hello".

- Except in major cities (and only in trendy places or in high society) women do not smoke. A woman who smokes/drinks is associated with loose moral character in much of the rest of the country's growing middle class.
- Places such as Discos/Dance clubs are less-conservative areas. It is good to leave your things at a hotel and head down there for a drink and some light conversation.
- People are fully-clothed even at the beach. So, be sure to find out what the appropriate attire is for the beach you are visiting. (In some rare places like Goa, where the visitors to beach are predominantly foreigners, it is permissible to wear bikinies on the beach but it is still offensive to go about dressed in western swim wear away from the beach).
- In local trains, there are usually cars reserved only for women and designated as such on their front.
- In most buses (private and public) a few seats at the front of the bus are reserved for women, although it can be difficult to get men to vacate them even when the seat is clearly marked.
- Street parties for holidays are usually devoid of women but filled with crowds of inebriated men partying. During festivals such as Holi, New Year's Eve, and even Christmas Eve, women can be subjected to groping and sexually aggressive behaviour from these crowds. It is unsafe for women to attend these festivities alone.
- Friendly conversation with men you meet on trains, etc. is often confused with flirtation/availability. In some scenarios, this can lead to unexpected sexual advances (this happens to Indian women as well, not just Westerners). Befriending Indian women, however, can be a wonderful experience for female travellers, though you might have to initiate conversation.
- Dressing in traditional Indian clothes, such as *salwaar kameez* (comfortable and good in) or *saree* (more formal and difficult to wear) will generally garner Western women more respect in the eyes of locals. Show some enthusiasm for the traditional Indian way of life and you may find that men will treat you more like a 'lady' than an object.
- "Eve Teasing" is a term used in Indian English to refer to anything from unwanted verbal advances to physical sexual assault.

Stay Healthy

Going to India, you have to adapt to a new climate and new food. Most travellers to India will become at least slightly ill during their stay there - even Indians returning from abroad. However, with precautions the chance and severity of any illness can be minimized. Don't stress yourself too much at the beginning of your journey to allow your body to acclimatize to the country. For example, take a day of rest upon arrival, at least on your first visit. Many travellers get ill for wanting to do too much in too little time. Be careful with spicy food if it is not your daily diet.

No vaccinations are required for entry to India, except for yellow fever if you are coming from an infected area such as Africa. However, Hepatitis (both A and B, depending on your individual circumstances), meningitis and typhoid shots are recommended, as is a booster shot for tetanus.

Tap water is generally not safe for drinking. However, some establishments have water filters/purifiers installed, in which case the water is safe to drink. Packed drinking water (normally called mineral water) is a better choice. But if the seal has been tampered, it could be purified tap water. So always make sure that seal is intact before buying. At some places, you will have to pay extra to get "chilled" bottle of water.

Diarrhea is common, and can have many different causes. Bring a standard first-aid kit, plus extra over-the-counter medicine for diarrhea and stomach upset. A rehydration kit can also be helpful. At the least, remember the salt/sugar/water ratio for oral rehydration: 1 tsp salt, 8 tsp sugar, for 1 litre of water. Most Indians will happily share their own advice for treatment of illnesses and other problems. A commonly recommended cure-all is to eat boiled rice and curd (yoghurt) together for 3 meals a day until you're better. *Keep in mind that this is usually not sound medical advice*. Indians have resistance to native bacteria and parasites that visitors do not have. If you have serious diarrhea for more than a day or two, it is best to visit a private hospital. Parasites are a common cause of diarrhea, and may not get better without treatment.

Malaria is endemic throughout India. CDC states that risk exists in all areas, including the cities of Delhi and Mumbai, and at altitudes of less than 2000 metres in Himachal Pradesh, Jammu, Kashmir, and Sikkim; however, the risk of infection is considered low in Delhi and northern India. Get expert advice on malaria preventatives, and take adequate precautions to prevent mosquito bites.

Getting vaccinations and blood transfusions in India increases your risk of contacting HIV/AIDS-even in many private hospitals.

If you need to visit a hospital in India, avoid government hospitals. The quality of treatment is poor. Private hospitals provide better service.

Respect

- Whereas Indian men can be really eager to talk to travellers, women in India often refrain from contact with men. It is an unfortunate fact that if you are a man and you approach a woman in India for even an innocuous purpose like asking for directions, you are putting her on the defensive. It is better to ask a man if available, or be extra respectful if you are asking a woman.

- It's not disrespectful for a woman to tell a man eager to talk to her that she doesn't want to talk - so if a man's behaviour makes you uncomfortable, say so firmly.
- In mosques and temples it is obligatory to take off your shoes. It may also be customary to take off your footwear while entering into homes, follow other people's lead.
- It is disrespectful to touch people with your feet. If done accidentally, you will find that Indians will make a quick gesture of apology that involves touching the offended person with the right hand, and then moving the hand to the chest and to the eyes. It is a good idea to emulate that.
- Books and written material are treated with respect, as they are considered the concrete form of the Goddess of Learning. So a book should not be touched with the feet and if accidentally touched, the same gesture of apology as is made to people (see above) is performed.
- The same goes with currency, or anything associated with wealth (especially gold). They are treated as Goddess Lakshmi (of Wealth) in human form, and ought not to be disrespected.
- Any give or take of anything important should be done with the right hand only, or with the right hand supported with the left. This includes giving and taking of presents, and any transfer of a large amount of money.
- Travellers should be aware of the fact that Indians generally dress conservatively and should do the same. Shorts, short skirts (knee-length or above) and sleeveless shirts are not appropriate off the beach.
- Keep in mind that Indians will consider themselves obliged to go out of the way to fulfill a guest's request and will insist very strongly that it is no inconvenience to do so, even if it is not true. This of course means that there is a reciprocal obligation on you as a guest to take extra care not to be a burden.
- It is customary to put up a token friendly argument with your host or any other member of the group when paying bills at restaurant or while making purchases. The etiquette for this is somewhat complicated.
  — In a business lunch or dinner, it is usually clear upfront who is supposed to pay, and there is no need to fight. But if you are someone's personal guest and they take you out to a restaurant, you should offer to pay anyway, and you should insist a lot. Sometimes these fights get physical, with each side trying to snatch the bill away from the other, all the time laughing politely. If you don't have experience in these things, chances are, you

will lose the fight the first time, but in that case, make sure that you pay the next time. (and try to make sure that there is a next time.) Unless the bill amount is very large do not offer to share it, and only as a second resort after they have refused to let you pay it all.

— The same rule applies when you are making a purchase. If you are purchasing something for yourself, your hosts might still offer to pay for it if the amount is not very high, and sometimes, even if it is. In this situation, unless the amount is very low, you should never lose the fight. (If the amount is in fact ridiculously low, say less than 10 rupees, then don't insult your hosts by putting up a fight.) Even if by chance you lose the fight to pay the shopkeeper, it is customary to practically thrust (in a nice way, of course) the money into your host's hands.

— These rules do not apply if the host has made it clear beforehand that it is his or her treat, especially for some specific occasion.

Contact

The country code for India is 91. India is then divided into city codes. See individual city guides for the city codes.

By Phone

Local phone numbers could be anywhere from 5 to 8 digits long. But when the area code is included, all phone numbers in India are 10 digits long. Most cellphone numbers start with "9" are 10 digits in length. You do not have to dial an area code to call a 10 digit cell number. But if you are making a call to a landline from a cellphone, you have to use the area code, even if you are in the same city. When calling long distance within India, prefix a '0' to the city code. While calling from outside India, omit the leading zero. For example, Mumbai has the city code of *22*. So to call within India , you dial *022 number* and to call from outside India, you dial *+ 91 22 number*. To dial outside the country, prefix the country code with 00. E.g a US number would be dialed as 00 1 555 555 5555.As a traveller, you will find many long distance public phones, called *STD/ ISD Booths* (Subscriber Trunk Dialing/International Subscriber Dialing), an Indian jargon for national and international long distance respectively. These are booths with an attendant. You dial yourself but pay to the attendant after the call is over. Metering is done as per pulse and a service charge of Rs 2 is added to the bill. Calling the USA/Canada/UK over the normal telephone line (referred to as ISD) will cost you about Rs. 7.20 per minute. Other countries are more expensive.

By Mobile

India uses GSM and mobile phones are widely available. Major operators include Bharti Airtel and Idea Cellular. As roaming charges can be very steep, it makes sense to get a local SIM card: prepaid starter kits are available for around Rs. 500, including several hundred rupees of call time, and local calls cost as little as Rs. 1 per minute. Bring along your passport when applying and get ready to pose for a photo (or bring your own).

By Internet

Internet kiosks are everywhere nowadays. Calling overseas is also very cheap if you use the many booths that advertise 'Net2Phone' service. Basically it is calling over the Internet. The quality ranges from tolerable to excellent, and the price is very good, with calls to the USA ranging from Rs. 2 to Rs. 5 per minute. Skype or GoogleTalk is also widely available in the many Internet Cafes. Wi-fi hotspots are a rarity in India except in some coffee shops in the metros.

7

The Effects of Globalisation on Tourism Promotion

INTRODUCTION

Although the concept of globalisation is part of the linguistic currency of contemporary business, it is neither a precise construct with an agreed meaning, nor one that can be empirically pinned down with ease. Globalisation is a particularly problematic concept in the context of discussion of promotion since it can be argued that the term is as much a part of the rhetoric of promotion as a social process distinct from it. The word 'global' is now regularly used as a promotional auxiliary, a strap line attached to corporate advertising as in, 'LBG - Global leaders', 'Corporation X sponsors the global game' or brand names like 'Global Holidays' where, arguably, its use is commercial hyperbole for 'international' (it would be interesting, for example, to attempt to put precise definitions and dates on when hotel groups and airlines ceased to be international and became global).In general terms, globalisation has been interpreted as the increasing expansion of international transactions, made possible by modern communications, and the ubiquitous productive and commercial reach of modern transnational corporations, developing and utilising those communications to sell their products in many countries. Examples are the car industry, the oil industry, financial services.

Are Tourism Organisations Global in Operation?

In the paradigm industries of cars, oil and finance one of the identifiers of globalisation is locational, the corporate establishment of subsidiaries or satellite operations (productive, distributive or administrative) in countries outside the parent country, each of which may be supported by regional promotional activities. There is only a partial equivalence to this situation in tourism. At the top end of the market large hotel and restaurant organisations, operating as chains and franchises, may have a physical presence, through their product portfolios, in many countries, but the vast majority of them do not. In the

'HoReCa' sector of the European Union (covering hotels and other accommodation, restaurants, canteens and catering), 95.5 per cent of the enterprises in the 15 countries are very small (0-9 employees). Half of the persons employed in this sector work in very small businesses (1 to 9 employees); a further 15 per cent are 'one-man' enterprises. On average, four persons work in a HoReCa business in the EU. About 10 per cent of persons employed work in large enterprises of more than 250 employees. The HoReCa sector accounts for more than 1.3 million enterprises in the EU; this is about 8.5 per cent of the total number of enterprises (EC, DGXXIII, 1999). From this data it is clear that most European hospitality organisations are mainly small ones, domestically located with no physical presence abroad at all.

The story is similar in the travel agency sector where it is unusual for many agents, except Thomas Cook, to have their own dedicated operations abroad, though there may be strong linkages in travel agency chains like British Travel International (BTI) which now has fifty-five partners in sixty-seven countries and generated over US$22 billion in 1997. Destination agencies also have a limited locational presence internationally. The norm tends to be for the big countries to have satellite offices in a few, often capital, cities of high generating countries, and none elsewhere. International airlines also have a limited presence, usually confined to offices in or near the main hub airports from which they operate.

Finally, in the attractions sector there is little incidence of organisations with satellite outposts except in the case of the bigger theme parks, notably Disney.

In summary, in tourism there is a quite small incidence of transnational operation at the locational level. Tourism is not another Shell, Esso, Sony, Laura Ashley, Benetton, Body Shop, except in important but limited parts of the hotel and restaurant sector.

Client Globalisation: Is there a Global Tourism Consumer?

The absence of an overseas presence in a bricks-and-mortar sense does not, of course, mean that tourism organisations are not global in their markets. The fact that they do not have offices or premises in other countries does not mean that they do not draw customers from them. In some ways tourism has *always* been global in that, throughout this century and before, a significant proportion of tourists to many destinations, particularly European capitals, have come from abroad. National destinations sought and served international markets long before the car industry, the oil industry and the financial houses.Superficial evidence suggests that the global market in tourist numbers and nationalities has never been greater. Impressionistic evidence of this internationalisation can be seen in: To this impressionistic data could be added a library of international tourist trends, and visitor profiles showing how individual countries and cities attract their share of the 500,000,000+ tourists thought to travel each year.However, underneath the surface of these obvious developments all is not as it appears to the globalisation spotter. Though world trends suggest dynamic growth in international travel few individual destinations or attractions have either a large or even spread of international visitors. The typical pattern is for both destinations and attractions to derive their main demand from a few, often longstanding and traditional markets. This Pareto effect - the phenomenon whereby the majority of tourism generation for most countries is not equally spread across many, but concentrated among a few, nations (commonly four or less), holds good in the era of globalisation as it did in the past. This is not surprising since the main factors which commonly create tourist generation are targeting so few. This may involve the deployment of a whole range of additional segmentation measures - geodemographics, life style, etc. The British Tourist Authority in 1993 targeted their Japanese promotion specifically at Japanese women over the age of forty who constituted only 7 per cent of the total population (Seaton 1996b: 366).In a marketplace in which many destinations are wooing a few main target markets it will increasingly be important to achieve competitive advantage in promotional materials. This may involve:

Tourist officers in both Ireland and Scotland have conducted research with target markets in Britain and mainland Europe to determine existing consumer perceptions of their destinations, and then used the findings to develop promotional materials (Dunlop 1997; Seaton and Hay 1998).

In conclusion then, globalisation for many destinations and attractions will continue to mean a primary promotional targeting of a few countries and regions which are likely to be not those most remote geographically but those closest. This law of proximity will operate with particular force in the global expansion of short-break travel.

Segmentation and Cultural Difference

The truth that even in the age of globalisation destination targeting largely revolves around a few important markets can be seen in the *de facto* market segmentation practices of destination agencies. If global consumers were evenly spread and becoming similar across the world (as one strand of the 'global consumer' thesis infers) then market targeting and segmentation would be getting less important. In fact the practices of national destination agencies suggest that the opposite is the case: the more advanced NTOs are putting more effort than ever before into identifying the differences, not the similarities, between their major markets. The real global trend in destination marketing is differentiation of efforts, not an assumption of one-world, cultural convergence.

The cultural differences factor has affected the tourism plans of several international destinations. In 1988 a 63 per cent increase in Japanese tourists to Australia over one year encouraged the Australian Tourism Industry Association and the Asian Studies Council to commission special studies of the Japanese tourist recognising that, 'misunderstandings and communication difficulties can often arise when those with different languages and cultural backgrounds meet' (Platt *et al.* 1988). The results were two guides on the Japanese tourist, the first on language, the second on culture and communication. In the mid-1990s Bord Failte, the Irish Tourist Board, produced and published detailed market profiles called, *Know Your Market* on their main generating countries - Britain, US, Germany and France (Bord Failte 1996a). Bord Failte also published a five-year study of trends in all their main generating countries (Bord Failte 1996b). The Scottish Tourist Board currently publishes a detailed international marketing plan which differentiates strategic activity by country (Scottish Tourist Board 1996). The Australian Tourist Commission produce regularly updated trend reports on their main markets.

Another instance of disaggregation rather than aggregation in market targeting is the efforts of several international destinations to identify and target specific behavioural segments within national tourist demand. In the US and Canada there has been a renaissance of interest in the cultural tourist as a differentiated behavioural category that began in the early 1990s (Tighe 1991; Ontario 1993) and was consolidated by a national study, carried out in the US by Travelscope, that produced a detailed profile of historic and cultural travellers revealing them to be older, better educated and more affluent than others (TIAA 1997). In 1995 Bord Failte in Ireland published an international study of the aging market (Bord Failte 1995). It is also awareness of the specific needs of particular prime markets, rather than global convergence, that makes France, the number one tourism nation in Europe, heavily promote battlefield attractions in northern France which appeal to its main markets there, the British and Belgians.

The Global Importance of the Domestic Market: Theperils of Global Awareness

The major globalisation texts place emphasis upon the importance of exploiting global opportunity, invariably conceived as markets overseas. In tourism terms the most important global trend to emerge from research is, paradoxically, not the importance of overseas markets but the home one. In India domestic tourists outnumber foreign visitors by 45-1. In France and Spain around 75-80 per cent of the holidaying population does so at home. In Japan the importance of the domestic market may be suggested by the country's intensive monitoring of its own population movements at home and abroad (Mangiboyat 1996). Domestic tourists do not, of course, gladden the hearts of national destination agencies, since they do not create incoming revenue, or improve balance of trade figures, but they may create employment and contribute to local economies. The attraction market illustrates the same lesson. An international study of tourism attractions (theme parks, museums, galleries, etc.) carried out in twelve countries in 1998 (Scottish Enterprise 1998) revealed that for all kinds of attraction the domestic market was the prime one, particularly out of season when domestic groups such as school parties, clubs, associations and senior citizen tours may constitute the main customers. Even for the paradigm example of the global hospitality organisation, McDonald's, its single largest source of profit is its home market (Ritzer 1996). Travel agents are almost wholly based on servicing domestic travellers, even if they sell them holidays abroad. Tour operators mainly service their own nationals in their own countries. This is why the overwhelming weight of tourism promotional activity takes place not in a global arena but in one's own back yard, even if hi-tech developments such as the Internet may increasingly be used to reach it.

An example of over-reacting to globalisation and misjudging the domestic customer is the British Airways corporate design catastrophe where the company relaunched itself with an expensive new livery which included individuated, multicultural tail fin designs, and the elimination of the national flag - all in the name of global adjustment. In just over a year BA had to reinstate the original livery due to the volume of protest (including a broadside from ex-prime minister Margaret Thatcher) from its main market, UK flyers who constitute 40 per cent of its business.

The debacle happened because the company ignored the oldest marketing adage in the book - that the retention of one's existing customers must always be the first consideration when premeditating any major corporate change. The campaign was based on two other elementary marketing mistakes: the adoption of a new corporate positioning using the evidence that *employees*, rather than *customers*, liked it (as the late David Ogilvy observed forty years ago, employees always tire of company advertising, and favour change, before the public); that most comic of corporate mutations - the large, established enterprise that dreams of being young and trendy again, and dresses up as a young swinger, instead of understanding that, in an area like air travel, traditional design and the safe, 'square' image of a national carrier are forms of brand equity that should never be tossed aside. By entering into the world of tail-fin tarting up, and aircraft body-painting British Airways was effectively aligning itself with Lauda Airlines, Easy Jet and other recent small carriers (for whom visual gimmickry may be a necessary way of creating awareness).

In short, the most significant danger posed by globalisation in market terms, may be less one of under-response, than over-response. One of the least studied, and probably most lethal, factors in multinational enterprise (MNE) culture is the secret craving by executives, in the routinised and controlled world of the modern corporation, for novelty, which makes them highly susceptible to the latest fads offered by the managerial pundits and design gurus of the air-terminal book stall.

Globalisation and Promotional Planning

The Globalisation of Best Practice

In the last decade there has been considerable dissemination of know-how in the theory and practice of tourism promotion. There has been a growing sophistication of tourism practice within tourism organisations and within academia, particularly in the more developed world, that means that tourism planners now have access, if they are prepared to look for them, to published sources on best practice in many places. The activities of international tourism agencies such as the World Tourism Organisation, the OECD, the World Travel and Tourism Council, and the Pacific Asia Travel Association (PATA 1999) have not just promoted tourism as a world economic priority, but also published reports and statistics that have contributed to professional knowledge of tourism. The annual work of the WTO in gathering and codifying, for example, world tourist trends (WTO 1995a, 1995b) and, more recently, in publishing data on NTO budgets and promotional spending (1995b), has offered possibilities for detailed comparative analysis of destination agency performance which at least one destination, Scotland, has utilised (Seaton 1996b). Many individual national tourism organisations have also published their own studies, including: the guideline to tourism planning by the US Travel and Tourism Administration (Missouri 1991); several studies by Bord Failte in Ireland which has been particularly well funded by EU grants (Bord Failte 1995, 1996a, 1996b), and by the UK Tourist Boards which have commissioned and published innovative promotional evaluation studies, *e.g.* into both the effects of advertising and the impact of film representations on Scotland's tourism (Seaton and Hay 1998). There has also been international expansion of tourism consultancies and the entry of general management consultancies into tourism. Above all, the last two decades have seen the rapid evolution of tourism as a university research field which has stimulated the publication of more than ten tourism journals, and the convening of many international conferences, through which both academics and practitioners have been able to exchange experiences and research.The results of all this activity mean that it is now possible to distinguish some convergence in destination marketing and promotional practices in Europe and the developed world. Some of these may be briefly summarised:

Another trend, visible in Spain, Ireland, Canada (Meis and Wilton 1998) and the UK, is the spread of *branding* as a destination concept. This broadly means promoting the image of a destination through advertising that establishes a 'personality' for the destination, and under which other non-tourism products may be subsumed. It is still too early to judge whether this *branding* of a country is a realistic aim, and whether, in net results, it is much more than a new name for destination imaging. 4 A major development focus in many destinations has been the promotion and development of IT programmes which have resulted, among other things, in: destination Web sites, CRS systems in TICs, and information kiosks. As a European Union conference on information technology in tourism noted, travel and tourism is now the leading E-commerce application on the Internet (EU 1999). A book-length study already exists of tourism organisations on the Internet in Europe (Marcussen 1999). The increasing speed and volume of this activity means that it is unlikely that any destination will be able to maintain competitive advantage in Internet usage and web site design for long, due to the ease of benchmarking Internet developments that will allow other destinations to catch up on the leaders, provided regular monitoring of destination sites in maintained.

Another spreading practice is the provision of multilingual promotional materials, targeted at prime markets, in hotels, destination guides, and in the signage of international destinations.

In many international cities tourism authorities now market city card schemes which offer tourists, for an all-inclusive fee, a combination of travel, free or reduced attraction admissions, and discounts at participating retail outlets. Versions of these city cards exist in places as different as Budapest, New York, Leeds, and Helsinki.

In several parts of the world systematic research has been conducted into the usage and impacts of Tourist Information Centres (Welcome Centres in the US). Reports of this work have been published, among others, in the USA, Scotland and Wales (Fesenmaier and Vogt 1991; Lennon and Mercer 1994; Wales Tourist Board 1995);

There is some evidence that destination agencies are coming to recognise the limitations of advertising as a medium for promoting destination images, given the fact that promotional budgets are usually inadequate to achieve a significant 'voice in the market place', and are recognising the importance of public relations campaigns, designed to maximise general media coverage in the hugely expanding output of travel and tourism journalism in the press and on TV throughout the West.

Finally, it is worth recognising the increasing importance of relationship marketing, efforts directed to retaining existing customers and get them to make return trips. This depends upon keeping updated databases of past customers and targeting special activities, deals and promotion at them to develop loyalty.

Are International Campaigns Feasible?

For more than thirty years a debate has intermittently raged in the advertising and marketing circles of MNEs about the feasibility and desirability of standardising advertising planning, so that common campaign strategies and programmes, rather than many, can be developed for most or all the countries in which the MNEs operated (Whitelock and Chung 1989). Discussed as long ago as the 1960s and early 1970s, before the word 'global' replaced 'international' (Elinder 1966; Fatt 1967; Buzzell 1968 and Britt 1974), the possibility was most forcefully presented in a classic article by Levitt more than a decade later. He argued that: '...global companies sell the same things the same way everywhere and different cultural preferences, national tastes and standards are vestiges of the past...' (Levitt 1983:93).The question of a common approach to international promotion by individual organisations is obviously one of great relevance to National Tourist Boards and tourist attractions with an international market. However, once again, caution must be a watchword. From what has been said earlier it should be apparent that it may not be necessary to promote too globally, but focus on the domestic market and a few prime overseas ones, rather than many.Moreover, even when a destination agency wishes to target a number of generating countries homogenisation of promotional planning may be difficult or impossible. The task of destination promotion can be divided into two key functions:

- Trip generation and destination choice; and
- Trip influence.

The first takes place in the country of the tourist; the second in the tourist destination. The first is thus communication across frontiers; the second is communication at the host destination, the temporary home of the tourist. The latter may indeed lend itself to common promotional approaches since trip influence is mainly concerned with the distribution of promotional messages, once tourists have arrived at a destination, in locations where they are known to assemble, *e.g.* hotel rooms and lobbies, tourist information centres (TICs), attractions, etc. In such areas promotional materials may easily be standardised for the main generating countries, provided they are multilingual.

Promotional materials produced by destination agencies to generate trips are more difficult to homogenise because of cultural differences in target segments and also international media variations. Moreover, promotion is often adapted at the national, regional and local levels precisely to make the product - whether a brand, corporation or destination - seem to offer something specially attractive to the target market. Promotion is a key element that makes large, international organisations look sympathetic with the market. It is no accident that Coca-Cola, an American MNE with no tradition of support for the European national game, lived soccer, slept and breathed soccer promotionally in Europe during the French World Cup, or that McDonald's have employed the England soccer hero, Alan Shearer, as the spearhead of their advertising in the UK for two years. Similarly many American multinationals operating in India suddenly developed a mania for cricket (a game with even less of a history in the US than soccer) at the time of the World Cricket Cup in June 1999.

In summary the opportunities for global campaigns are limited due to the need to reflect the interests and cultural preferences of different target markets.

Though it may be just about possible for an MNE to sell oil or hi-tech electronics with the same corporate campaign in several countries, it is less possible for tourism organisations to promote London to the Japanese pleasure traveller in the same way they might do so to French businessmen. Though the strategic message of destination campaigns may be a common one (*e.g.* Spain's changing emphasis, in its main generating countries, to its cultural attractions, as well as it sun and beach products) there will normally be exceptional differences in the way in which the strategy is delivered to specific markets. Destination agencies will, in most cases, need to develop promotional 'horses for courses' that recognise cultural differences in different market segments.

The Competitive Impact of Globalisation

The competitive implications of globalisation for every tourism organisation, destination agencies included, are enormous. Among major factors that have contributed to competitive pressure: the impact of a world shrinking beneath the withering, all pervasive reach of IT-driven communications; the falling price of long-haul travel; lowered political barriers to travel; and the now universal assumption among both large governments and small regional administrations, that tourism is a major development opportunity, so that just about every country and many of the regions within them want to attract tourism and, through the wonders of the old and new technologies, have the capability to promote themselves internationally - and thus attack the franchises of current players.

Evidence of this fundamentally changed competitive environment is so widespread that a few examples will serve to illustrate it. There is now virtually no town or region in the developed world that does not have a tourism strategy that would have not existed a generation ago. Lower air fares mean that New York and Florida are now competing for UK short-break tourists with traditional British cities and close European capitals. The fall of the Berlin Wall, and the opening up of Eastern Europe, has already produced bonanza growth for destinations like Prague and Budapest at the expense of traditionally strong destinations like Switzerland and Austria which declined between 1984 and 1994. By the mid-1990s the Eastern Mediterranean was growing faster than many established European destinations. On the Internet it is hardly possible to type in the name of any place, however small and distant, that will not produce a range of tourism promotional pages and products.

How do organisations cope in marketing and promotional terms with this expanded competition?

Benchmarking: A Response to Globalisation

One of the responses to the reality of greater competition is benchmarking. In the markets for physical goods, particularly fast moving consumer goods, where fierce competition has been a fact of life for half a century, benchmarking has been a routine marketing activity. The large corporations have constantly evaluated competitive market performance, researched their own products against rival brands, and monitored competitors' promotion. It has only been in the last decade that the possibilities and benefits of tourism benchmarking have been appreciated by tourism organisations. The primary aims of benchmarking are:

- To analyse an organisation's or destination's position in relation to others;
- To derive benefit from identifying best practice, state-of-the-art methods which may be used as models for future developments by the benchmark sponsor;
- To compete more effectively with the organisations benchmarked; and
- To derive benefit from negative instances. This is a much less recognised aspect of benchmarking, but learning theory suggests that best practice may be learned as much from avoiding the bad, as from pursuing the best models.

Global Symbiosis: The Socio-cultural Impact of Tourism Promotion

If, as we have argued earlier, tourism promotion by a single organisation is rarely exposed to a very wide international audience, except on Internet, there is another sense in which tourism as an aggregate network of representations, is becoming a major element of globalisation. Tourism with its the images of escape, fantasy, far-away exotica, dream-worlds and otherness, is now a ubiquitous presence internationally, not just in promotion specifically selling tourism, but as an element in many other kinds of promotion and publicity. It is thus part of a global consumption ethic:

The new consumption ethic which was taken over by the advertising industry by the late 1920s celebrated living for the moment, hedonism, self-expression, the body beautiful, paganism, freedom from social obligations, the exotica of far-away places, the cultivation of style and the stylization of life.

Tourism is now synergistically associated, through visual imaging, with the selling of numerous other commodities such as cars and petrol (advertisements always reflect the leisure use, not the work use, of cars), pop music and fashion, and is thus an overt constituent of 'lifestyle', the 'aestheticisation of life' and the 'promotional culture' (Wernick 1991), that postmodern commentators have been diagnosing. Visual images of multinational promotion, particularly in metropolitan cities and urban conurbations, centralise the idea that travel is good, glamorous and high status.

The central idea is that postmodern cities have become centres of consumption, play and entertainment, saturated with signs and images to the extent that anything can become represented, thematised and made an object of interest, an object of the tourist gaze. Dann has demonstrated how tourism is now explicitly linked, in lifestyle magazines like Conde Nast *Traveller*, to the sale of other luxury items which depict a placeless, global consumption ethic. These cross-product advertising presentations are anchored in the multi-referentiality of travel and tourism as a tie-concept that brings together an international hedonism of food, jewellery, clothes, cars, entertainment, etc. - Lafant's 'tourist neoculture' (Dann 1998).

However, this may not be completely new. Travel has always been a status badge, associated through the life styles of the classes that could afford it, with privileged access to other goods. Indeed, tourism choice may be seen as an important, hierarchically derived, form of taste discrimination to add to those other kinds of consumer decision and aesthetic choice that Bourdieu (1984) has so brilliantly shown to be related to social position, occupation and family status (Seaton 1999a). However, as we have argued earlier, this tendency towards a world consumer culture does not mean that a homogenised global market has emerged for tourism. As Warhurst, Nickson and Shaw have concluded:

Even within a global culture of consumerism, consumer needs, wants and demands across the globe may continue to vary. In short, it is one thing to argue that the world's economic activity is becoming dominated by consumerism and market transactions and quite another to then insist that this market and its consumers are homogenized. The two phenomena should not be conflated: a domineering ideology of consumerism does not equate with a single world market.

It has distinguished five different dimensions of globalisation (locational, consumer, promotional, competitive and cultural) and suggested that there are differences in the extent to which tourism is associated with each. The main effect of globalisation on tourism marketing has not been the visible homogenisation of promotional campaigns directed to world markets by tourism organisations, but in converging approaches to strategic planning, and the gradual emergence of state-of-the-art managerial techniques which include: refinements in market segmentation, use of consumer research, and the application of benchmarking to the tourism sector. One of the most significant effects of tourism promotion and publicity worldwide has been to contribute to the evolution of a global ethos of consumption, through the aggregate and cumulative dispersion of tourism and destination imagery, alongside other kinds of luxury commodities in media representations of placeless, postmodern life-styles.

Finally, the chapter has identified the potential consequences of globalisation for SMEs as an antidote to more usual focus on globalisation and MNEs.

8

World Tourism Organization

The World Tourism Organization (UNWTO) is a United Nations agency dealing with questions relating to tourism. Its headquarters are in Madrid, Spain. It compiles the World Tourism Rankings.The World Tourism Organisation is undoubtedly the most significant global body concerned with the collection and collation of statistical information on international tourism. This organisation represents public sector tourism bodies from most countries in the world and the publication of its data makes possible comparisons of the flow and growth of tourism on a global scale.

HISTORY

The World Tourism Organization originated as the International Congress of Official Tourist Traffic Associations, which was set up in 1925 in The Hague. After World War II, it was renamed the International Union of Official Travel Organisations (IUOTO) and moved to Geneva. IUOTO was a technical, non-governmental organization, whose membership at its peak included 109 national tourist organizations and 88 associate members, among them private and public groups.

In 1967, the members of IUOTO called for its transformation into an intergovernmental body empowered to deal on a worldwide basis with all matters concerning tourism and to cooperate with other competent organizations, particularly those of the United Nations' system, such as the World Health Organization (WHO), UNESCO, and the International Civil Aviation Organization (ICAO). A resolution to the same effect was passed in December 1969 by the UN General Assembly, which laid out the central role the transformed IUOTO should play in the field of world tourism in cooperation with the existing bodies within the UN. Following this resolution, the WTO's statutes were ratified in 1974 by the states whose official tourist organizations had been members of IUOTO. The newly formed organization held its first General Assembly in Madrid in May 1975. The Secretariat was installed in Madrid early the following year at the invitation of the Spanish government, which provides a building for the headquarters.

In 1976, WTO became an executing agency of the United Nations Development Programme (UNDP). In 1977, a formal cooperation agreement was signed with the United Nations itself. In 2003, the WTO was converted into a specialized agency of the United Nations. As of 2005, its membership included 145 countries, seven territories and some 350 affiliate members, representing the private sector, educational institutions, tourism associations and local tourism authorities. The frequent confusion between the two WTOs – World Tourism Organization and the Geneva-based World Trade Organization – officially ended on 1st December 2005, when the General Assembly approved to add the letters UN (for United Nations) to the start of abbreviation of the leading international tourism body in English and in Russian. UNWTO abbreviation remains OMT in French and Spanish. UNWTO General Assembly concluded its work at its 16th session in Dakar, Senegal, on 2 December, 2005.

Tourist Requirements

All foreigners (except specified countries) require a valid passport and visa. Personal effects including: binoculars, cameras, and film may be imported temporarily free of duty. A customs bond may be demanded from visitors bringing in video/filming equipment, radios, tape recorders and musical instruments to ensure the goods are re-exported. Firearms require a special permit. Liquor (1 pint) tobacco (200 cigarettes, 50 cigars or 250 grams) are tax free for individuals of 16 years and older. Visitors buying valuable gems, skin articles, Makonde carvings and other local handcrafts must keep cash sales receipts for presentation to customs officials on departure.

Travel Fees

An airport tax in convertible foreign currency is levied on all visitors departing the country.

Baggage is weighed at check-in counters and is subject to inspection by customs officials.

Health

Visitors originating from countries with possible exposure to cholera and yellow fever should travel with valid vaccination certificates. It is recommended visitors consult with their medical professional before traveling. A preventative treatment plan may be necessary before, during and after the trip.

Clothing

Informal attire is appropriate on safari and on the coast. Clothing should be light-weight and light in Colour on safari. Warm clothing is recommended in the evenings and particularly in higher altitudes. Ngorongoro Crater, Arusha, Mount Kilimanjaro areas, Usambara and the Southern Highlands are areas where warmer clothing may be needed. Low-heeled walking shoes are recommended. Other accessories like a hat, sunglasses, swimsuits, flashlight, and insect repellent will be useful.

Basic Requirements

Applications will only be accepted upon submission of all the required documents! The Consulate will reject the application if documentation is not met.

Please be aware that processing of a visa usually takes at least two weeks.

- Visa application forms and a list of requirements can be collected at the Consulate
- One original application form duly completed, typed or written in block letters. All applicable information must be entered and signed by applicant. Each applicant must complete an application form – even if a child is travelling on a mother's or father's passport.
- Children, who are attending school, must produce a confirmation of registration for the academic years, including information about the grade. Spouses travelling alone with joint custody of children, must produce a no objection letter from the husband/wife who stays in UAE.
- The visa fee is payable upon submission of application form. The fee is non-refundable. The fee is AED 170,- for visits up to 90 days. To obtain visas with a long validity, documentation must be produced from applicant's company and from the reference in Denmark.
- Original passport. One recent passport size photo, 3,5 x 4,5cm colored photograph taken close up, on a light background. Photograph showing applicants hair tucked behind the ears. If wearing a veil, features ears, nose, eyes and forehead must be visible. Photo should be glued to the form, not stabled. The distance between the chin and the top of the head must account for 70%-80% of the photo.
- Travel Insurance: covering all expenses related to urgent medical necessities and/or hospital admission, including the forced return to their homeland for medical reasons. The insurance, with the minimum coverage of EURO 30.000,- must be valid for all Schengen-States and for the whole period of their stay in the Schengen-States. The travel insurance must be presented in connection with the issuing of the visa.
- Photocopy of passport including personal data, UAE residence visa plus any other valid visas such as USA and UK (copies of previous Schengen visas if applicable)
- Official company letter from sponsor/employer must contain the following information:

— name/address and telephone no. of sponsor/employer
— name, nationality and passport no. of applicant
— date of joining, designation/position
— applicant's monthly salary
— reasons for applicant's visit *i.e.* tourism, business or other
— expected date of arrival in Denmark plus duration of stay
— confirmation of financial undertake, company or personal
— confirmation that the applicant will return to the UAE to resume duties on a certain date
— name, designation and signature of person responsible for issuance of the company letter
— in case of business visits, the company letter must furthermore provide
— information about applicants' educational background, language skills, documentation about what applicant is buying from or selling to the Danish company, proof of sufficient funds for purchases.
— in case of medical visits, information about the treatments in Denmark must be included(letter from doctor) and documentation for a prepaid fee for the treatments must be shown.
— In case of cultural events/conferences, documentation about the person visiting the event in Denmark must produced; *i.e.* educational background, special interest in the event, job related conference participation, prepaid fee for participation and documentation about the specific event.
— In case of tourist visits, all the basic requirements on this list must be met.

- Original Trade License to be shown plus a copy to be submitted
- Flight reservation. Flight reservation must be produced upon submission of application. Original return ticket must be shown upon collection of passport with the visa issued.
- Hotel reservation. Confirmed written registration must be produced upon submission of application for a visa
- Proof of sufficient funds, *i.e.* bank statements for the recent three months (personal bank account)
- Invitation letter. In the case of an application for a business visa or family visit, an invitation letter must be sent directly to the Consulate from the company in Denmark (fax is acceptable). The applicant should present a copy of the invitation. The fax should state the following information:

— name, personal code.no. and address of reference.

— name, nationality and passport no. of applicant.
— reasons for applicant's visit, *i.e.* business visit, family visit.
— expected date of arrival in Denmark plus duration of stay.
— address during visit in Denmark.
— In case of business visits, the invitation must include information about how the Danish company established contact with the local company, what kind of products the Danish company are trading in and what they intend to buy or sell.
— In case of family visits, the invitation letter must include description of family relations with applicant, *i.e.* brother, sister, cousins etc. A copy of reference's passport or residence permit in Denmark must be submitted
— In case of fiancées, girlfriend/boyfriend, the invitation must state information about where reference and applicant have met and how they are in contact with each other and if they have met in person.

- The passport and UAE residence visa must be valid for a minimum of three months after the expiry date of the Schengen visa (travel documents and UAE residence visa must be valid minimum six months after the return from the Schengen-States)

Tour Checklist

Once bookings have been secured the company makes detailed plans for all aspects of the tour. To do this they need to cover cultural, practical and legal requirements. A useful list includes:

- Pre-tour research
- Fees/negotiations
- Funding/finance
- Marketing material
- Sponsor liaison and servicing
- Knowing the venues
  — Product/possible re-design
  — Artistic/technical pre-visit
  — Venue questionnaire/dossier
  — Providing tech specs and notes
- Transport options
- Press liaison
- Visas
- Carnets
- Briefing information for the touring team
- Selling the next tour
- Alerting your allies (Department of Foreign Affairs and Trade, local artists)

Pre-tour research of the market needs to include the practical details of transport, accommodation, health requirements, visas, and carnets. A summary checklist of the issues to be covered encompasses:

- Visas/work permits
- Inoculations
- Passports (make sure everyone has one, and that it doesn't expire until at least six months after the tour)
- Immigration procedure (and be aware if any company member has a criminal record as this may restrict travel to certain countries)
- Accommodation arrangements (make sure the company will be accommodated comfortably - touring abroad can be stressful)
- Per diems for company members
- Personal, medical, travel and public liability insurance
- Local production costs (local crew, lighting and sound equipment hire)
- Freight arrangements (in some cases it may be cheaper to source some items in the country concerned than to freight them from Australia, and there may be lengthy delays clearing unaccompanied cargo)
- Travel arrangements (especially for the technical crew, who may be doubling van-driving duties with bump-ins and show running - beware of overloading, or contravening union agreements)
- Holidays (avoid key national and religious holidays when tour dates will be precluded)
- Mobile phone charges

Research may also be needed into cultural issues, which could affect the choice of product, or alterations to the way work is presented. For example, in some countries nudity on stage is forbidden.

Touring Checklist for Camping

Clothes

- 2 pairs of underwear
- 2 pairs of lightweight socks
- 1 t-shirt
- 1 pair of shorts
- 1 pair of walking shoes
- 2 jerseys
- 4 pairs of bike shorts
- Cycling shoes
- Gloves
- Helmet
- Knee warmers
- Arm warmers

- Polypropylene vest
- Long sleeve underwear top
- Polypropylene balaclava
- Sweatband
- Goretex jacket
- Wind vest
- Goretex helmet cover
- Toe booties
- Goretex mittens

Personal Care

- Razor
- Shampoo
- Tooth brush
- Baby wipes
- Towel
- Floss
- Nail clippers
- Toothpaste
- Comb
- Sunscreen
- Lip balm
- Toothbrush container

Personal

- Credit cards, money
- Money pouch
- Glasses
- Sunglasses
- Maps
- Reading material

Miscellaneous

- Camera, film
- Video camera
- Guidebooks
- Watch
- Cable and Lock

First Aid

- Diaper rash cream
- Band-Aids

- Large gauze bandages
- First aid tape
- First aid cream
- Aspirin
- Ibuprofen
- Cold medicine
- Bug repellent

Bike Equipment

- Bike
- Pump
- Front/rear panniers
- Plastic bags
- Flashing red light
- Headlight
- Patch kit
- Tire boots
- Extra tube
- Tire pressure gauge
- Extra tire
- Extra brake pads
- Extra shoe cleats

General Repair Kit

- Emergency spokes
- Spoke wrench
- Allen wrenches
- Lubrication
- Cool tool
- Cables
- Wrenches, crank tool
- Wire
- Electrician's tape
- Zip ties

Camping Equipment

- Tent
- Sleeping bags
- Sleeping pads
- Ground cloth

Cooking Equipment

- Stove

- Fuel bottles
- Nested cooking pots
- Cooking utensils
- Plates and cutlery
- Spice and Oil containers
- Scrubber and soap
- Water filter
- Collapsible water bottles
- PBJ tubes
- Matches and case

Touring Checklist for a Hotel Tour

Clothes

- 2 pairs of underwear
- 2 pairs of lightweight socks
- 1 t-shirt
- 1 nice shirt
- 1 pair of pants
- 1 pair of shorts
- 1 wool sweater
- 1 pair of walking shoes
- 2 jerseys
- 3 pairs of bike shorts
- Cycling shoes
- Gloves
- Helmet
- Arm warmers
- Leg warmers
- Knee warmers
- One pair of heavy wool or pile socks
- 1 long sleeve long underwear top (polypropylene or silk)
- Polypropylene vest
- Polypropylene balaclava
- Sweatband
- Goretex overmitts
- Goretex jacket
- Wind vest
- Goretex helmet cover
- Waterproof nylon pants
- Goretex oversocks
- Shoe covers

Personal Care

- Razor
- Shampoo
- Tampons/pads
- Tooth brush
- Skin lotion
- Baby wipes
- Floss nail clippers
- Nail clippers
- Toothpaste
- Comb
- Sunscreen
- Lip balm
- Tampons
- Toothbrush container

Personal

- Passport
- Credit cards, money
- Money pouch
- Glasses
- Sunglasses
- Maps
- Reading material

Miscellaneous

- Camera
- Glasses repair kit
- Guidebooks (properly ripped apart)
- Radio, clock
- Earplugs

First Aid

- Diaper rash cream
- Band-Aids
- Large gauze bandages
- First aid tape
- First aid cream
- Aspirin
- Ibuprofen
    - Cold medicine

Bike Equipment

- Bike
- Panniers and front bag
- Map
- Plastic bags
- Flashing red light
- Headlight
- Patch kit
- Tire boots
- Extra tube
- Tire pressure gauge
- Extra tire
- Extra brake pads
- Extra shoe cleats

General Repair Kit

- Emergency spokes
- Spoke wrench
- Allen wrenches
- Lubrication
- Chain cleaner and fluid
- 10 inch adjustable wrench
- Cluster tools
- Cables
- Screwdriver
- Headset/crank wrenches
- Crank puller
- Bottom bracket tools
- Chaintool
- Wire
- Electrician's tape
- Zip ties

9

A Historical Prospective of World Tourism

The substantial growth of the tourism activity clearly marks tourism as one of the most remarkable economic and social phenomena of the past century. The number of international arrivals shows an evolution from a mere 25 million international arrivals in 1950 to an estimated 763 million in 2004, corresponding to an average annual growth rate of 6.5 per cent.

International Tourist Arrivals, 1950-2004*

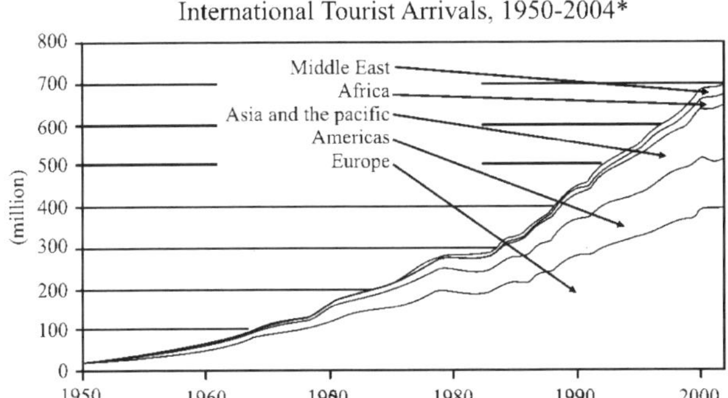

During this period, development was particularly strong in Asia and the Pacific (13 per cent on average a year) and in the Middle East (10%) while the Americas (5%) and Europe (6%), grew at a slower pace and slightly below the world's average growth. New destinations are steadily increasing their market share while more mature regions such as Europe and the Americas tend to have less dynamic growth. Europe's world share declined by almost 10 percentage points since 1950 whereas the Americas lost more than 13 percentage points. Though the Americas' performance has been most affected by the declines suffered in the past years, the fact is that its annual average growth rate for the period 1950-2000 was 5.8 per cent, also bellow the average for the world (7%).

Europe and the Americas were the main tourist-receiving regions between 1950 and 2000. Both regions represented a joint market share of over 95 per cent in 1950, 82 per cent forty years later and 76 per cent in 2000.

Tourism and the world economy

International tourism receipts represented in 2003 approximately 6 per cent of worldwide exports of goods and services (as expressed in US$). When considering service exports exclusively, the share of tourism exports increases to nearly 30 per cent.

2003

World Exports of Merchandise and commercial services (Balance of Payments, Goods and Services Credit)

US$	Share (%)	Share (%)	
Total		**9, 089**	**100**
Merchandise exports	7, 294	80	
Agricultural products	674	7	
Mining products	960	11	
Manufactures	5, 373	60	
Others	223	2	
Commerical Services	**1, 795**	**20**	**100**
Transportation	405	4	23
Travel	525	6	29
Other	865	10	48

Tourism demand depends above all strongly on the economic conditions in major generating markets. When economies grow, levels of disposable income will usually also rise.

A relatively large part of discretionary income will typically be spent on tourism, in particular in the case of emerging economies. A tightening of the economic situation on the other hand, will often result in a decrease or trading down of tourism spending.

In general, the growth of international tourism arrivals significantly outpaces growth of economic output as measured in Gross Domestic Product (GDP). In years when world economic growth exceeds 4 per cent, the growth of tourism volume tends to be higher. When GDP growth falls below 2 per cent, tourism growth tends to be even lower. In and GDP at 3.5 per cent, *i.e.* tourism grew on average 1.3 times faster than GDP. the period 1975-2000 tourism increased at an average rate of 4.6 per cent a year.

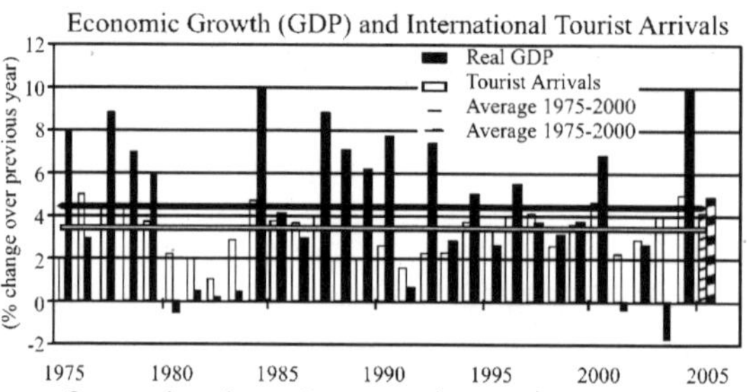

World Tourism Organization; International Monetary Fund.

Tourism 2020 Vision

Tourism 2020 Vision is the World Tourism Organization's long-term forecast and assessment of the development of tourism up to the first 20 years of the new millennium. An essential outcome of the *Tourism 2020 Vision* are quantitative forecasts covering a 25 years period, with 1995 as the base year and forecasts for 2000, 2010 and 2020.

Although the evolution of tourism in the last few years has been irregular, UNWTO maintains its long-term forecast for the moment. The underlying structural trends of the forecast are believed not to have significantly changed. Experience shows that in the short term, periods of faster growth (1995, 1996, 2000) alternate with periods of slow growth (2001 and 2002). While the pace of growth till 2000 actually exceeded the *Tourism 2020 Vision* forecast, it is generally expected that the current slowdown will be compensated in the medium to long term.

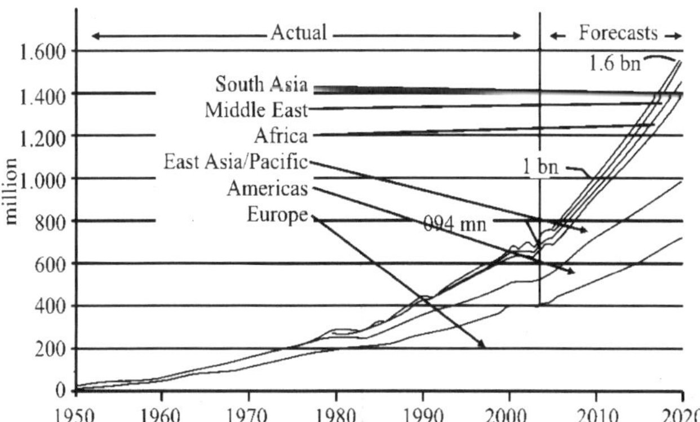

UNWTO's *Tourism 2020 Vision* forecasts that international arrivals are expected to reach over 1.56 billion by the year 2020. Of these worldwide arrivals in 2020, 1.2 billion will be intraregional and 0.4 billion will be long-haul travellers.

The total tourist arrivals by region shows that by 2020 the top three receiving regions will be Europe (717 million tourists), East Asia and the Pacific (397 million) and the Americas (282 million), followed by Africa, the Middle East and South Asia.

East Asia and the Pacific, South Asia, the Middle East and Africa are forecasted to record growth at rates of over 5 percent per year, compared to the world average of 4.1 per cent. The more mature regions Europe and Americas are anticipated to show lower than average growth rates. Europe will maintain the highest share of world arrivals, although there will be a decline from 60 per cent in 1995 to 46 per cent in 2020.

	Base Year	**Forecasts**	**Market share**		**Average annual**	
	1995	210	2020	%	growth rate (%)	
		Million	**1995**	**2020**	**1995-2020**	
World	565	1006	1561	100	100	4.1

Africa	20	47	77	3.6	50	5.5
Americas	110	190	282	19.3	18.1	3.8
East Asia and the Pacific	81	195	397	14.4	25.4	6.5
Europe	336	527	717	59.8	45.9	3.1
Middle East	14	36	69	2.2	4.4	6.7
South Asia	4	11	19	0.7	1.2	6.2

Long-haul travel worldwide will grow faster, at 5.4 per cent per year over the period 1995-2020, than intraregional travel, at 3.8 per cent. Consequently the ratio between intraregional and long-haul travel will shift from around 82:18 in 1995 to close to 76:24 in 2020.

Composition of UNWTO Regions and Subregions

Region	Subregions	Countries
Africa	**North Africa**	Algeria, Morocco, Sudan, Tunisia
	West Africa	Benin, Burkina Faso, Cape Verde, Côte d'Ivoire, Gambia, Ghana, Guinea, Guinea-Bissau, Mali, Mauritania, Niger, Nigeria, Senegal, Sierra Leone, Togo
	Central Africa	Angola, Cameroon, Central African Republic, Chad, Congo, Democratic Republic of Congo, Equatorial Guinea, Gabon, Sao Tomé e Princípe
	East Africa	Burundi, Comoros, Djibouti, Eritrea, Etiopía, Kenya, Madagascar, Malawi, Mauritius, Mozambique, Reunion, Rwanda, Seychelles, Tanzania, Uganda, Zambia, Zimbabwe
	Southern Africa	Botswana, Lesotho, Namibia, South Africa, Swaziland
Americas	**North America**	Canada, Mexico, United States
	Caribbean	Anguilla, Antigua Barbuda, Aruba, Bahamas, Barbados, Bermuda, Bonaire, Bristish Virgin Islands, Cayman Islands, Cuba, Curaçao, Dominica, Dominican Republic, Grenada, Guadeloupe, Haiti, Jamaica, Martinique, Montserrat, Puerto Rico, Saba, Saint Lucia, St.Eustatius, St.Kitts-Nevis, St.Maarten, St.Vincent,Grenadines, Trinidad Tobago, Turks and Caicos, US Virgin Islands
	Central America	Belize, Costa Rica, El Salvador, Guatemala, Honduras, Nicaragua, Panama
	South America	Argentina, Bolivia, Brazil, Chile, Colombia, Ecuador, French Guyana, Guyana, Paraguay, Peru, Suriname, Uruguay, Venezuela
Asia and the Pacific	**Nort-East Asia**	China, Hong Kong (China), Japan, Democratic people's republic of Korea, Republic of Korea, Macao (China), Mongolia, Taiwan (pr. of China)
	South-East Asia	Brunei Darussalam, Cambodia, Indonesia, Lao P.D.R., Malaysia, Myanmar, Philippines, Singapore, Thailand, Vietnam
	Oceania	American Samoa, Australia, Cook Islands, Fiji, French Polynesia, Guam, Kiribati, Marshall Islands, Micronesia (Fed.St.of), North Mariana

		Islands, New Caledonia, New Zealand, Niue, Palau, Papua New Guinea, Samoa, Solomon Islands, Tonga, Tuvalu, Vanuatu
Europe	**Northern Europe**	Denmark, Finland, Iceland, Ireland, Norway, Sweden, United Kingdom
	Western Europe	Austria, Belgium, France, Germany, Liechtenstein, Luxembourg, Monaco, Netherlands, Switzerland
	Central and Eastern Europe	Armenia, Azerbaijan, Belarus, Bulgaria, Czech Republic, Estonia, Former U.S.S.R., Georgia, Hungary, Kazakhstan, Kyrgyzstan, Latvia, Lithuania, Poland, Rep Moldova, Romania, Russian Federation, Slovakia, Tajikistan, Turkmenistan, Ukraine, Uzbekistan
	Southern Europe	Albania, Andorra, Bosnia Herzgovina, Croatia, F.Yug. Rp.Macedonia, Greece, Italy, Malta, Portugal, San Marino, Serbia and Montenegro, Slovenia, Spain
	East Mediterranean Europe	Cyprus, Israel, Turkey
Middle East		Bahrain, Egypt, Iraq, Jordan, Kuwait, Lebanon, Libyan Arab Jamahiriya, Oman, Palestine, Qatar, Saudi Arabia, Syrian Arab Republic, United Arab Emirates, Yemen

Concepts and Definitions

According to the UNWTO/United Nations Recommendations on Tourism Statistics, tourism comprises the activities of persons travelling to and staying in places outside their usual environment for not more than one consecutive year for leisure, business and other purposes.

This concept can be applied to different forms of tourism. Depending upon whether a person is travelling to, from or within a certain country the following forms can be distinguished:

- Inbound TourismInvolving the non-residents received by a destination country from the point of view of that destination;
- Outbound TourismInvolving residents travelling to another country from the point of view of the country of origin;
- Domestic TourismInvolving residents of a given country travelling within that country.

All types of travellers engaged in tourism are described as visitors. Visitors can be distinguished as same-day visitors or tourists (overnight visitors). There are various units of measure to quantify the volume of tourism. An overview is set out below:

Unit of measurement	Comment	
Visitors	Arrivals	at frontiers - or at a specific place in case of domestic tourism

	Arrivals	at frontiers
		at hotels and similar - excludes tourism in
Tourists		establishmentsprivate accommodation
(overnight		at collective tourism - arrivals are counted
visitors)		establishmentsin every new
		(*e.g.* hotels and other) accommodation visited
	Nights	at hotels and
		similar establishments

Inbound Tourism

Unless otherwise stated, reported data concentrates on International Tourism as measured from an Inbound Tourism perspective, *i.e.* the tourism received by any given destination country (and in a few cases territories) from non-residents travelling to that destination.

The most common unit of measure used to quantify the volume of International Tourism for statistical purposes is the number of International Tourist Arrivals. For a proper understanding of this unit, two considerations should be taken into account:

- Data refer exclusively to tourists (overnight visitors):a visitor who stays at least one night in a collective or private accommodation in the country visited. Same-day visitors are not included.
- Data refer to the number of arrivals and not to the number of persons. The same person who makes several trips to a given country during a given period will be counted as a new arrival each time, as well as a person who travels through several countries on one trip is counted as a new arrival each time.

Figures on the volume of international tourism presented, preferably relate to the concept of international tourist arrivals at frontiers. However, as not all countries are collecting data according to this concept, another series may be used instead. The series are indicated as follows:

TF International tourist arrivals at frontiers (excluding same-day visitors);

VF International visitor arrivals at frontiers (including tourists and same-day visitors);

TCE International tourist arrivals at collective tourism establishments;

THS International tourist arrivals at hotels and similar establishments.

Outbound Tourism

Data on outbound tourism volume originates from two different sources and likewise relate to two dissimilar concepts:

- On one hand, many countries are reporting the number of outbound trips of their residents. Data availability and comparability, however, is still limited and it is often not clear whether the reported figures refer only to tourists or to visitors in general.

- On the other hand, data are synthesised from the data on inbound tourism to destination countries (an arrival received in a destination can also be taken as an arrival generated by the generating country). Data on arrivals to destinations broken down by region of origin are taken to estimate and aggregate the number of arrivals originating from each region. The unit of measurement is the number of international tourist arrivals generated by the region of origin concerned. For a proper understanding, it should be borne in mind that these figures do not correspond to the number of trips, as one trip taken might result in various arrivals in destinations

Accommodation

As a measure for the capacity of accommodation, data is included on the number of rooms or the number of bed places in the country. When expressed in bed places, the number of rooms roughly will be half, as rooms on average count two bed places. The actual capacity of a country might eventually be larger, as some countries exclude hotels below a certain category or less than a certain size.

International Tourism Receipts and Expenditure

- International Tourism Receipts are the receipts earned by a destination country from inbound tourism and cover all tourism receipts resulting from expenditure made by visitors from abroad, on for instance lodging, food and drinks, fuel, transport in the country, entertainment, shopping, etc. This concept includes receipts generated by overnight as well as by same-day trips, which can be substantial, as will be the case with countries where a lot of shopping for goods and services takes place by visitors from neighbouring countries. It excludes, however, the receipts related to international transport contracted by residents of other countries (for instance ticket receipts from foreigners travelling with a national company). These receipts are covered in the separate category.
- International Fare Receipts which for most recent years is estimated at about 18 per cent of total tourism and fare receipts.
- International Tourism Expenditure is the expenditure on tourism outside their country of residence made by visitors (same-day visitors and tourists) from a given country of origin.

  Data on receipts and expenditure related to international tourism are generally gathered in the framework of the Balance of Payments under the items 'Services, Travel, Credit and Debit' (International Tourism Receipts and Expenditure) and 'Transportation, Passenger Services, Credit and Debit' (International Fare Receipts and Expenditure). See the Balance of Payments Statistics Yearbook, Part 2 and Part 3 of the International Monetary Fund (IMF) for details on methodologies, compilation practices and data sources.

The International Tourism Balance and International Fare Balance correspond to the net receipts or expenditure of a given country on respectively international tourism or international fares, *i.e.* receipts less expenditure.

Sources and Data Treatment

Quantitative tourism-related data presented is based on a selection of data included in the UNWTO database on World Tourism Statistics. This database contains a variety of series for over 200 countries and territories covering data for most countries from the 1980's on. The database is maintained by the UNWTO Secretariat and is updated on a continuous base.

Except where otherwise indicated, statistical data has been collected by the UNWTO Secretariat from the official institutions of the countries and territories (UNWTO member as well as non-member countries) or from official international bodies, *e.g.* the Caribbean Tourism Organization (CTO), International Monetary Fund (IMF).

The data for individual countries are based on full year results, or projections, as communicated to the UNWTO Secretariat by the authorities of the countries and territories or disseminated through a news release, publication or on the Internet.

In the world and (sub)regional aggregates, estimates are included for countries and territories with data still missing based upon data available for a part of the year or the general trend for the region. In particular for the Middle East and Africa the regional and subregional aggregates for 2002 should be treated with caution as estimations are based on a relatively small number of countries and territories that supplied data for the entire year. In the tables, provisional figures are marked with an asterisk (*).

UNWTO tourism statistics generally refer to figures for a country as a whole. In the collection of statistics, however, except for independent states, there are also a number of dependencies or territories of special sovereignty included (for instance Hong Kong (China) or French Polynesia). These territories report tourism figures independently and are for the sake of tourism statistics considered as an entity in itself. Because of this, where reference is made to "countries" the term generally should be taken to mean "countries and territories". In a few other cases, dependencies are not separately listed but included in the total for the country they depend upon (for instance Guernsey, Jersey and the Isle of Man in United Kingdom).

In general UNWTO does not collect data on the level of regions, states, provinces or specific destinations within a country (Hawaii is one of the few exceptions made because of its relevance for Asian outbound travel; in the overview tables, however, Hawaii is included in the United States figure). Most countries will have a further regional breakdown available as well as other series not included in the UNWTO database on World Tourism Statistics. Please refer to national sources for this data. The World Tourism Organization is aware of the limitations of the available statistical information on tourism. Despite the considerable progress made in recent decades, international tourism statistics are often not uniform, because definitions and methods of data collection tend to differ. Every user of this information should bear in mind that the international comparability of statistical data is still not optimal.

Tourism series in "Tourism Market Trends" Reports

A number of derived series are included relating tourism volume to the size of the population or tourism receipts and expenditure to tourism volume. Ratios are based on simple divisions of the concept in question by the population or of the receipts or expenditure by the corresponding concepts:

- International Tourist Arrivals per **100 of inhabitants** = International Tourist Arrivals / population * 100;
- Trips abroad per 100 of inhabitants = Trips abroad / population * 100;
- International Tourism Receipts per International Tourist Arrival = International Tourism Receipts / International Tourist Arrivals;
- International Tourism Receipts per International Visitor Arrival = International Tourism Receipts / International Visitor Arrivals;
- International Tourism Receipts per capita = International Tourism Receipts / population;
- International Tourism Expenditure per trip abroad = International Tourism Expenditure / Trips abroad;
- International Tourism Expenditure per capita = International Tourism Expenditure / population.

Financial data is generally collected and kept in the UNWTO database in US$ values. In the cases where countries report in local currency, values are transferred by UNWTO into US$ applying the average exchange rate for the corresponding year. However, part of the tables are also published in euros. These euro values are in general derived from the US $ values using the corresponding average annual exchange rates for the two currencies. The following exchange rates have been applied:

Exchange Rate US Dollars Versus Euro

As exchange rates fluctuate substantially over time, the evolution of International Tourism Receipts is also estimated in (weighted) local currencies. For this, receipts in US$ have been recomputed in local currencies using an exchange rate table provided by IMF. In order to take care of inflation, receipts have been put in constant prices using country data on inflation from IMF as deflator. The data on international tourist or visitor arrivals and nights of international tourists by country of origin correspond to the series as included in the UNWTO Yearbook of Tourism Statistics. Please refer to the latter publication for additional series, methodological references and notes on the series for specific countries.

Information included, but not referring to tourism indicators, are in general taken from specialised international organisations and not collected by the UNWTO Secretariat from the individual countries and territories. Data are meant as indicators, providing a context for tourism performance and do not necessarily coincide fully with national data. The following series are included:

Population

Data refer to total midyear population as included in the International Database (IDB) of the International Programs Center (IPC) of the Population Division of the U.S. Bureau of the Census;

Area

Data on the dimension of the area of countries and territories are taken from the Statistical database of the Food and Agriculture Organization of the United Nations (FAO) and refer to the total area of the country, including area under inland water bodies for the year 2000. In the case of Belgium and Luxembourg data is taken from national sources.

Economic Indicators

The series on Gross Domestic Product (GDP), Gross Domestic Product per capita and economic growth (annual per cent change of Real Gross Domestic Product) are based on the World Economic Outlook (WEO) of the International Monetary Fund (IMF).

10

Mass Tourism and the Third Reich

Four days after Hitler was made Reichskanzler, he outlined his agenda in front of military commanders: the first objective was to gain total power by abolishing democracy and "eradicating Marxism root and branch." In doing so the new regime proved to be a master in political staging. Implementing an old demand of the labour movement, the government declared the first of May a holiday. Union-leaders were pleased and encouraged their members to participate in the processions during the "National Labour Day."

The following day, ten o'clock a.m., SA and SS stormed the houses of the Free Unions. Soon there were no trade unions and no political parties except for the National Socialist German Worker Party (NSDAP) and the German Labour Front (Deutsche Arbeitsfront). The coup against the unions had been launched by Robert Ley, organizational director of the NSDAP and later also chief of the Arbeitsfront, including its organization for the leisure time, "Strength through Joy" ("Kraft durch Freude").

At the first anniversary of the coup, two luxury liners left Hamburg and Bremerhaven for the Isle of Wight. One of them had Robert Ley on board, celebrating the beginning of a "new era" of tourism: "German workers" at the Seven Seas. And again, two years later Ley held a ceremony which was to mark a "new era." On May 2nd 1936, amidst a crowd of workers and men in uniform, he laid a foundation stone at Prora Bay on the Island of Rugen. It was the start of a gigantic construction: "the most colossal seaside resort of the world." Millions of Germans were to recuperate here at the Baltic Sea and so to demonstrate the superiority of the "Socialism of Deed.

"The "seaside resort of the 20,000" never went into operation. Nonetheless, the project serves as an outstanding example of the basic concepts—and ambiguities—of modernity. Linking social, political and cultural history, this chapter attempts to analyse this project in the light of a universal precondition of the consumer society: the grammar of rationalization. In linguistics a grammar is a limited set of rules which allows the production an unlimited number of sentences. The grammar of rationalization engended such inventions as different as the slaughterhouse, the computer, or mass tourism.

"MODERN TIMES"

'Metropolis'—the machine-like city of the year 2000 shocked the audience. When in 1927 Fritz Lang's lavish film came to German cinemas it proved to be a financial disaster; all too hopeless was his vision of the future world as a machinelike organism. Maybe Lang was a bit ahead of his time. In 1936, 'Modern Times' was released in America: the tragicomic parable about depravation through technology.

Charlie Chaplin's film was a huge success. He succumbs to the rhythm of the assembly lines; the machinery runs faster and faster, culminating in an apocalypse. 'Metropolis' and 'Modern Times.' as different as they were, dealt with the same topic, a topic that was the subject of much controversy on both sides of the Atlantic: rationalization.

This controversy was not only about new forms of factory organization. 'Rationalization' had entered consciousness as something that permeated all 'spheres' of life, as Max Weber put it. The attitudes towards this phenomenon were extremely divided. Some, such as Max and his less known brother Alfred Weber, saw rationalization as a fatal destiny: "Until the last ton of fossile fuel is burned out," capitalism and bureaucracy force humanity into an "iron cage" of dependency, ushering in the "domestication of the world."

However, others, such as Frederick Winslow Taylor and Henry Ford, saw rationalization as the vehicle that would transport humankind into a happy future of full department stores and order books. There is no such thing like the "terror of the machine," Ford claimed. Also, if not with even greater vigour, Communists, like Antonio Gramcsi, praised the blessings of rationalization—the Soviet science of work dreamt of transforming the whole working class into a "social machine." Thus, in Aldous Huxkey's Brave New World, there were two gods: Marx and Ford.

Heated as it was, the global discourse on rationalization was characterized by a remarkable lack of a sense of history: the structure of this controversy was anything but new. It can be traced back at least as far as Rousseau and Voltaire. It is the debate on the costs and benefits of the "civilizing process" (N. Elias). At the dawn of modernity—especially in the second half of the 18th century—the perception of an acceleratetly changing world became common among the educated classes. This gave room for both fears and hopes. "Society" in this view was the result of a growing distance from "nature."

The "natural" state of mankind, however, could be conceived as hell or as paradise—just as the discoverers reported on fierce cannibals on the one hand, and on Gardens of Eden, on the other. The course of history, correspondingly, could be seen as principally good or principally bad, as "progress" or as "degeneration."

Therefore it is a fallacy to regard enlightenment and romanticism as subsequent phases (as in the common periodization of philosophy and arts); rather, they represented simultaneous, opposing attitudes towards modernity—

inseparable like the two sides of a coin. Since then at times a modernistic, at times an anti-modernistic zeitgeist has prevailed but both of them have always been present at the same time, often mixed in ambiguous ways.

The interwar period gave new vigour to this old and lasting controversy; 'rationalization' dominated thought with tremendous force. A typical quality of such terms, however, is their vagueness. Instead of compiling the innumerable connotations, let me distinguish four levels of meaning according to the range they cover, to the degree of abstraction:

- A logical meaning referring to the basics, the universal principles of efficiency; this was a topic of mathematics and logic, partly of economic theory and philosophy. Though rarely speaking of a process (*i.e.* rationalization), the first level provided the others with criteria of an ideal state of a system (*i.e.* rationality).
- A historical-philosophical meaning referring to the interpretation of the long-term processes of "Occidental rationalization" (M. Weber), or—hardly less far-reaching—to the emergence and structure of capitalism. This was a field especially of sociologists and politico-economists (from Comte to Marx, Durkheim and Weber).
- A technological or economical meaning referring to the most recent stage in this process, in particular in respect of the organization of factory work and human engineering. This was the field of engineers, scientists, psychologists, and economists who formed the emerging science of work (Taylor, Munsterberg, Ford, Gilbreth, Bedeaux, Mayo and others).
- Finally, a psychological meaning, namely the use of pseudo-rational justifications for irrational behaviour as defined by Freud (in a wider sense also the substitution of supernatural explanations by scientific ones).

Admittedly, these levels were often interwoven in many ways; it is just this hidden unison which makes a discourse. But although used in so many venues, ranging from arts to arithmetic, the public debate mainly referred to the third level, meaning mass production and assembly lines. Rationalization, in this sense, was just another word for 'Taylorism' and 'Fordism.'

While Taylorism was associated with inhuman (and on the long run contraproductive) restraint in the factories and used mostly in a disparaging intention, the broader term of Fordism made a brilliant, though also controversial career. Its meaning was twofold: the rationalization of production and its economic and social results—be it levelling, alienation and unemployment or be it good profits, high wages and cheap products; in this positive sense, moreover, Fordism comprised a whole ideology of mass consumption and of social engineering: the "white revolution."In this connection 'rationalization' was the catch word which stirred up the public, frightened the workers, inspired the managers and divided political parties and trade unions. The underlying principle, however, did not move the masses (except for the scandals that art exhibitions of the avantgarde provoked). But it proved to be highly universal—the grammar of rationalization became visible.

This grammar is based on the idea of decontextualization and of disassembling and recombining: Isolating complex processes from their context, breaking them down into their individual components, then combining them again to form a new structure. That which is superficial can be discarded; that which is mixed can be separated. The processes, laden with significance, with meaning and morality, with traditions and arbitrariness, can be melted down to the pure scaffolding of relations—as translucent as crystal and as unsurprising as doubleentry bookkeeping.

This grammar, as everybody knows, provided for the victory of capitalism, step by step conquering science, technology and economy, judicial systems and management, the arts and philosophy.

Fundamental aspects of this grammer had been formulated during the 19th century. Although a blind rationality obviously is something instrinsic to nature—and as such has always been a characteristic of humankind, as well—it now reached a new quality of man-made control. Analyzing the change from craft to industry, none other than Karl Marx had perceptively revealed the principles. The only element still missing to make the factory a single "mechanical monster," he concluded, was the "constant transport of the work-piece."

Indeed, the practical application also requires internal transport systems and a "central clock" which coordinates the machinery. What Marx did not knew was that in America this problem was already about to be solved: assambly line work was introduced in gun factories and in Cincinnati's and Chicago's slaughterhouses—it started in association with killing.

Then, in 1913, this principle was implemented in Henry Ford's car works in Detroit. Coincidentally, Frank and Lilian Gilbreth decomposed the human movements into single "units" (they isolated exactly seventeen), and arts and architecture decomposed space and colour.

Walter Gropius—founder of the Bauhaus—praised the industrial construction: "exact forms, devoid of any randomness. (...) Lining up identical parts." Ford's assembly line was neither an application of avantgarde aesthestics nor of scholary theories; but in turn, it inspired the attempts to automate not only production, but also thinking: in 1936 the computer was born, the universal calculating machine. Simultaneously, Turing, Post and Zuse designed their computer theories (and thus the basics of our computers). All three had the radical division of labour in the factories in mind when they were in search of the smallest, irreducable steps of arithmetic operations—like Taylor or Gilbreth who identified the atoms of movements, like Feininger or Mondrian who identified the atoms of forms, they identified the atoms of thought. Rationalization had exeeded a crucial boundary: proof was furnished that its principles are potentially boundless.

Thus, in this connection a further invention is associated with the year 1936: the holiday machine. The "seaside resort of the 20,000" was a project as modern as the computer. Such a task had nothing to do with the nostalgic ideology of "blood and soil." It required cold-blooded, highly universal solutions—it required a holiday from the assembly line.

"STRENGTH THROUGH JOY"

The project was to be a centre piece of Nazi social and tourism politics. In February 1934 the travel activities of "Strength through Joy" had a dramatic start. Special trains had rolled all through Germany, with flags, flowers and cheering masses at the stations. Within a week, ten thousand "worker-vacationers" were taken from the grey cities to the clear mountain air. This cheap travel was accompanied by an unbelievable torrent of propaganda and made the leisure organization popular within no time.

Under the bombastic name Nationalsozialistische Gemeinschaft "Kraft durch Freude" (NSG "KdF") it had been founded as a department of the Deutsche Arbeitsfront (DAF) in November 1933. This marked the provisional end of the harsh internal fights on the role of the Labour Front (although they lasted until 1935). Taking over the lower staff of the Social Democrat Free Unions and treating the Christian Unions gently, the DAF at first could appear as an overdue step towards a unified trade union.

Social-revolutionary circles indeed had tried to from a Nazi union out of the small "Works Cell Organization" (NSBO), while others had aimed at corporative structures, similar to Italian and Austrian Fascism, which would have vested Ley with an enormous power. But these plans were thwarted. By no means did Hitler and his allies from big business want to allow a "second revolution."

Thus, the Arbeitsfront had to unite "all working Germans" in order to "guarantee the establishment of absolute economical peace." Although soon the biggest and wealthiest organization in the "new state," the DAF was reduced to a mere Party's instrument and a means for controlling the workplace.

On the other hand, it had to "win the hearts of the workers"—a difficult task without supporting their interests. For it had to keep out of the industrial disputes, so the Labour Front looked for another sphere of activity—and found leisure time. So Ley was not responsible for the bread but for the games.

Of course, Ley did not admit his defeat when he held his speech at the KdF's founding congress. Instead, he opened the prospect of a "people's community" (Volksgemeinschaft), where all Germans would have equal access to the cultural assets which still were in the hands of the bourgoisie. In his speech, Ley drew a line between the justified "envy" and the "inferiority complex" of the workers, fueled by "Marxist" ideology, on the one hand, and the ongoing debates on the perils of rationalization, on the other. Rationalization was a global, irreversible process that in future would even speed up—resulting in the loss of "joy" at work, in the "ruin" of physical and mental health, in the increase in "nervousness." Remedies were to expand leisure time and to care for its proper use.

Already in 19th century England, "rational recreation" had been a favourite idea of social reformers. Now, by offering the masses all sorts of once privileged leisure activities, Ley announced, KdF would become a decisive tool for overcoming class struggle as well as for improving health and performance.

Initially, holiday trips ranked low among the planned activities. KdF was primarily designed to fill and control the evening and weekend leisure time. Ley worried that otherwise "boredom" would emerge, leading to "stupid, rabble-rousing, if not criminal ideas." In order to fight this dangerous "boredom"—in other words: to offer the "homeless" workers a substitute for their smashed organizations—a whole array of activities was launched: sports, theater, movies, cabaret, classical and popular music, folk-dance, evening classes etc.

The intentions were ambitious. In particular, the head of KdF, Reichsleiter Horst Dressler-Andress, saw himself on a "mission" of bringing "culture" to the workers. KdF arranged highcarat concerts and exhibitions: Paul Hindemith conducted in factory halls and even works of "degenerated" painters like Emil Nolde were presented.

However, the focus of the activities was changed quickly after the first KdF trains had met with an overwhelmingly positive response. The initiators—Ley, Dressler-Andress, and the head of the KdF-travel department, Bodo Lafferentz—were themselves surprised by their success and promptly expanded the travel programme. They were pleased that they had stumbled into an enormous gap in the market.

From that point now on, the founding of KdF was traced back to a Fuhrer's order: "I want every worker to get sufficient holiday time, and I want everything to be done so that these holidays and his other leisure times become a real recreation." To Ley KdF offered the chance to upgrade his unpopular Labour Front. As the (partly compulsory) DAF membership automatically included that in KdF, the leisure organization finally stood open to the vast majority of the population.

And within KdF, it was tourism that counted: with four fifths of the enrollment, the travel department (Amt Reisen, Wandern, Urlaub; RWU) soon became the most important branch—many people regarded KdF as a kind of state-owned travel agency. In 1934, the journal Deutschland-Bericht of the exiled Social Democratic Party (Sopade) noted that the holiday trips made KdF an important propaganda tool, whereas the other KdF activities were hardly ever mentioned in everyday chats.

The idea of turning the holiday trip into a mass-produced article was not at all new. In the end it goes back to the first English package tour organizers in the 1840s, among whom Thomas Cook became the most successful. He was a genius in making travel a standarized commodity, and at the same time saw it as a means to overcoming the "distinction of classes" and rescuing workers from booze and apathy. "Cookism" preceded "Fordism."

The package tour, however, caused more a widening of the spatial scope than of the social scope of tourism. Although better off workers flooded the pleasure beaches on Bank Holidays, their "excursions" were far from decent bourgeois travel. The 'proper' holiday trip remained a privilege of minorities. Organizing 'bourgeois-style' tourism as a mass product was first put to the test on a large scale in Fascist Italy. From 1931, the Duce's leisure organization "After Work" (Opera Nazionale Dopolavoro; OND) sent "popular trains" through the country. In the first year more than half a million Italians took advantage of the discount of up to 50%. However, the living standards of the "masses" were too low to afford such a trip without substantial subsidies; after the initial euphoria had dissipated the number of participants declined to about 100,000 per year.

But the concept of "popular trains" remained promising. When the Nazis picked up the Fascist model, they did so with German perfection and rapidly overtook their prototype. Soon "Strength through Joy" became the world's biggest tour operator. Already the sheer size meant a market position of a new scale. The crisis-ridden hotel industry had to willy nilly accept KdF's offers of at least fifty per cent below the usual level.

With an average of 35 Reichsmark (RM) for an all-inclusive package tour in 1934 the KdF prices fell by two thirds compared to the "cheap" operators in the Weimar Republic—not to speak of the prevailing individual tourism. The programe was expanded vigorously until 1937, when in terms of figures nearly a fifth of the population older than 15 had booked KdF trips.

With that, the upper limit was reached; the capacities of the transport systems (in particular the railways which had to serve the growing needs of the Wehrmacht), as well as the spending power of the lower classes did not allow for a further increase. However, the figueres were unique at that time and are still impressive.By the outbreak of war, some 8 million package tours had been sold by KdF, almost a tenth of which—more than 700,000—were spectacular cruises abroad with the KdF fleet. Taking all trips together, more than 45 million had traveled with KdF in the prewar years. Of course, only the holiday tours were really a sensation. To provide some examples: A seven day all-inclusive tour to Reit im Winkel in the Bavarian Alps cost 28 RM; ten days at the seaside resort of Heiligenhafen 44 RM; a seven day "reduced offer" into the Swabian Jura only

16 RM. In addition to those 'normal' holiday trips there were also 'special' tours, *e.g.*, an eight-day skiing course costing 48 RM. In accordance with the global trend, the vast majority of the KdF trips went to domestic destinations.

An exception was tours to allied Italy after 1937. The absolute highlight, though, became the cruises. They were not included in the original programme. But after the first cruises proved to be so successful, KdF bulit up the world's biggest cruising fleet and launched two luxuury cruisers of its own: the 'Robert Ley' and the 'Wilhelm Gustloff.' The prices were unriveled: an eighteen day journey to Madeira, a traditional destination of the English upper class, cost about 120 RM, a sevenday cruise to Norway 42 to 63 RM. A Swiss novelist trumpeted: "A nation at sea!"

With great relish, propaganda reminded of the Social Democrats' promise that one day the workers will be aboard luxury liners and cited the planned travel programme of the trade unions for the year 1933: just twelve tours had been announced with prices ranging from 42 RM—a three day excursion—to 350 RM.

And now: workers strolling through chic resorts and spas, tanning on the decks of cruisers! In the beginning, many people hostile to the regime thought this was simply a fraud. But they soon learned that it was not quite wrong when posters lured: "Now you, too, can travel!" or more poetically and in respect to the KdF travel saving system: "Weave your own dream carpet!" The impression was so strong that the chief of the KL Dachau wanted to send a political detainee on a trip to Norway—for "he is an obdurate Communist and may be convinced by the facts."

No wonder the underground opposition was alarmed, worrying whether this could really work. The Sopade-Bericht was at least ambivalent: "Some get enthusiastic, some grumble." Summing up the local reports from all over the country, the editors wrote: "The judgements are divided."

This remained true in the coming years—considering the Sopade-Bericht was published by the resistance, positive assessments count double. In contrast to nearly all other fields of the social politics, the KdF trips were often reported to be a great success. Former union officials had to hear: "Now we see what our subscriptions are really good for." From Bavaria, *e.g.*, it is said that "according to the concurring reports of all (Social Democratic) comrades, KdF is a positive achievement for the regime. These trips get more and more popular, and how cheap they are is astonishing."

While excursions and even short holiday trips were nothing new for manual workers, the 'proper' tourism had remained in the realm of the upper and middle classes. Although the travel intensity had increased since late 19th century—in particular among the clerks and teachers, male and female, as the harbingers of modern lifestyle—the boundary between blue and white-collar workers had not been challenged: the holiday trip functioned as a social marker. And now the propaganda could chime: "Travel is no longer a privilege for the wealthy classes. Thanks to KdF every national comrade (Volksgenosse) is now able to partake in tourism."

This was not only due to the cheap package tours—in addition, the holiday entitlements were greatly improved. Traditionally Germany (together with Austria) had the best arrangements in this respect; now it increased its lead. In 1938 more than 87% of the workers in the metal-processing industry enjoyed a yearly holiday of six to twelve days. Even the International Labour Office had to acknowledge not only "Strength through Joy" but also the holiday entitlements as exemplary.

SOCIALISM OF DEED

KdF provided indisputable evidence of how effectively the grammar of rationalization can be applied to the production of holiday trip—just as Henry Ford had demonstrated with his Tin Lizzie how to turn an unattainable object of desire into a mass-produced article.

The Nazi version of Fordism was the "Socialism of Deed" (Sozialismus der Tat). This term suggests that The National Socialism really improves the living conditions of the workers, and thus makes the working class and their "Marxist ideology" obsolete. The greatest trump in this connection was the decrease in unemployment which finally ushered in manpower shortage. But Socialism of Deed was more then having a job again: The "cultural mission" of KdF, Dressler-Andress wrote, is "to overcome the traditional contrast between work and man." A lofty mission, indeed. Probabely he really had a cultural "revolution" in mind which breaks with the curse of alienation. However, more often and less pathetically Socialism of Deed was simply defined in terms of "standard of living." In this connection, DAF experts demanded that the "traditional concept of wages" should be replaced by transfers in form of "organized consumption."

Along this line the regime concentrated on reducing the prices of prestigious goods to such an extent that they could symbolically represent the prosperity that the worker parties had failed to give the workers. Standarized mass production should provide all households with "popular" products like refrigerators or cameras (already in 1932 Agfa had marketed a Volkskamera); most spectacular were the Volksempfanger (two simple radio types), the Volkswagen (which was never delivered), and travelling—only here were really impressive achievements made.

Thus, when the KdF cruiser 'Robert Ley' was launched in March 1938, Hitler could say: "The National Socialist state, the National Socialist Volksgemeinschaft are trying to make everything accessible to our Volksgenossen that was formerly the privilege of a limited social class. (...) This is an objective that in the beginning appeared to be unimaginable. At that time there were many who believed: this programme looks so much like Marxist promises, that it cannot come true. Well, my Volksgenossen, it is on the way to being fulfilled!"

Travel became a substitute both for higher wages and for civil and social rights. As Kuhnl had put it: The Labour Front "was not to produce social justice but the illusion of social justice." The social politics were grounded in the abolition of democracy in general and of the right to strike and the participation rights in the work-place in particular. Instead, white and blue-collar workers were both labeled as "followers," bound to the "leader of the firm" by mutual "loyalty and duty."

Mitigating this paternalism, the regime spoke of "workers of the brow and workers of the fist," signalling the dissolution of the traditional status hierarchy: All Germans form a great community, the Volksgemeinschaft—except, of course, those of racial or other genetic "inferior quality" and those who were "stubborn" opponents.

The "orderly" German worker, thus, was ennobled by merely belonging to that community—hypertrophic aggravation of the basic concept of nationalism. The space in which this banishing of hierarchy within the Volksgemeinschaft should take place was conceived, however, as outside the crude sphere of power, politics and work: in the realms of culture, leisure and consumption. A truly pioneering concept.

Of course, time was all too limited for this to be really translated into action. The promised land of affluence was counterpointed by Hermann Goring's famous slogan: "Guns instead of butter!" The cash had to flow first into the producer goods and the military buildup. Wages had to remain low, both to safeguard the profits and to avoid an increasing demand for consumer goods, in particular for imported raw materials.

Holiday politics promised a solution to the regime's conflicting aims: taming the working class and preparing for war. Spending money in the domestic tourist industry reduced the demand for limited goods and imports. And improving the holiday entitlements contributed to keeping the wages low and thus also to reducing the spending power freely disposable.And KdF tourism and paid holidays were indeed an improvement in the standard of living. Thus, both could function as a conspicious symbol of upward mobility. "There is probably no nation," the newspaper of the DAF commented on the first cruise to Madeira, "which takes so much care of the working people (Werktatige) as Germany."

To sum up: "Strength through Joy" promised to combine many different functions in an ideal way.

First of all:

- Winning "the hearts of the workers" or—less sentimentally—promoting the integration of the working class.
- Providing for consumption control along the lines of the autarky politics.

Further objectives were:

- Giving a push to the tourist industry which was in a severe decline due to the Great Depression. This goal was dropped or modified, resp., when tourism recovered.
- Strengthening the "love for Germany" and overcoming regional fractioning and hostilities, *e.g.*, among Bavarians and Prussians—a widespread idea and already promoted by Friedrich L. Jahn a hundred years before. Nation building became a main objective in 1938, when KdF was employed to integrate Austria.
- Promoting the "strength," *i.e.* the health and performance of the Wofkforce; in this connection DAF officials loved to speak of the "achieving community" (Leistungsgemeinschaft). However, the argument that KdF "overhauls" the worker like a car motor primarily aimed at the skeptical business community and later also at opponents within the regime.
- Creating a safety valve for activists from the left wing of the NSDAP: In the first years KdF offered a playground to those who were frustrated by the regime's social politics and its alliance with big business.
- Offering incentive tourism for Nazi "bigwigs" as well as for workers—the "leader of the firm" could reward diligent "followers" by awarding them a cruise to Madeira; this went of course well with the two main objectives.
- Finally, KdF functioned as an instrument for foreign propaganda, thus mitigating the grim image of the Third Reich.

The pictures of the classless luxury liners were a sensation. Moreover, together with Italy, the regime fostered the international leisure movement. In 1936 the second "World Congess on Leisure and Recreation" was held in Germany, gathering 3000 delegates from 61 nations. Rudolf He[beta] issued the motto: "A proper organization of the working people's leisure time is a decisive precondition not only for social peace within the nations, but also for political peace among the nations"—a masterpiece of dissimulation that sounded like the former programme of Thomas Cook. Bodo Lafferentz, director of RWU, praised his cruisers as "ambassadors of peace" and stated: the "class-concious worker has disappeared."

The congress' honorary president, Gustavus Town Kriby from the USA, was impressed: "'Strength through Joy' grew from a mere ideal to reality." Also an international agency Joy and Work was installed. As its president, Robert Ley was received in London by King George VI shortly before the outbreak of war. Non-theless, foreign propaganda was a by-product of holiday politics. By and large, KdF was essentially domestic politics. Admittedly in a special sense: in the eyes of the regime's inner circle all domestic policy was to serve foreign policy agendas: expanding the "biosphere" according to the visions of the German master race. The regime therefore could not elude the self-created dilemma of "guns" and "butter"—or better: it postponed its solution for after the victorious blitzkrieg.

Until then, the Nazi version of a "white revolution" was curtailed by Hitler's secret order from 1936 that Germany had to be "ready for war" within four years. The regime was forced therefore to preach old-fashioned abstinence, too. A tight-rope-walk, especially since the prospect of a renewed war was anything but popular. Goring, responsible for this "Four-Years-Plan," expressed no understanding for the dilemma.

He regarded the DAF as an enemy that "spreads wrong social ideals among the workers" and theatened: "I will ruthlessly take action against every obstruction by the Labour Front." Certainly, Goring failed "to take away all raw materials and workforce" from the DAF. But to the inner cirlce of power, social politics was just a tool of "great politics," or as Ley put it: "The Leader does not speak of wages and prices, but of soul, race, blood, soil, and fatherland." No wonder, Ley had a difficult position.

Non-etheless, the Volksund Leistungsgemeinschaft was more then a mere phrase. The term 'Socialism of Deed' could have come from Henry Ford himself. Not only was he an ardent anti-Semite and backed Hitler, his paternalistic engeneering, designed to curb both Marxism and Conservatism, went well with this kind of Socialism. From pushing efficiency and destroying participation in the firms to the concept of defining the social status by consumer opportunities—the Third Reich certainly swam with the mainstream of modernization.

THE "SEASIDE RESORT OF THE 20,000"

Admittedly, in respect to the implementation of assembly lines, Germany was far behind the USA. Ferdinand Porsche, for instance, when he built up the Volkswagen works (1938 named KdF-Wagen) which were to produce 1.5 million cars per year, wooed away numerous experts from the Ford works in Detoit. But in the industrialization of travelling Germany took over the leading role. This takes us back to that 2nd of May 1936, when the foundation stone for the "seaside resort of the 20,000" was laid on the Island of Rugen. What were the grounds from which this ambitious project emerged?

The response to the cheap travel oriented towards middle-class standards was surprisingly positive, but unexpected problems also arose, specifically in two respects: First, it became clear that unskilled workers, and above all whole workingclass families, were hardly in a position to come up with the travelling expenses without further subsidies—a flagrant violation of the widely-disseminated family politics. Second, the tourist industry proved to be rather ungrateful: Instead of applauding the fact that their spas and seaside resorts were suddenly filled with KdF-holidaymakers, the tourist associations complained that "Strength through Joy" was taking clients away from the commercial operators and chasing off the "solvent public" in the chic resorts.

No better demonstration of the "shattering of bourgeois privileges" was really required. However, in this conflict of aims, the KdF's head office was guided less by its egalitarian mandate, than by the complaints of the middle classes, the social backbone of Nazism.

The retreat from the luxury hotels began: KdF tourists were increasingly sent to undeveloped touristic areas, such as Eastern Bavaria; finally, former Austria became the main destination (with some 70%). Initiallly more than 60% of the KdF holiday trips led to traditional German spas and beauty spots, in 1939 less than 5%.

Nevertheless: At the seaside the strategy of "no friction" with established tourism could hardly be implemented—the capacities were limited. But the seaside holiday could not be entirely removed from the programme. Thus, the plan emerged to build its own tourist towns on the beaches and so make KdF independent from the private hotel trade—and also cement the spatial class distinction in tourism.

In 1935, Ley explained that the Fuhrer had given him instructions to "think through the possibilities of a mass seaside resort with 20,000 beds." Five such "mass resorts" were planned on the Baltic Sea: on Rugen, near Kolberg, Konigsberg, Kiel, and Danzig. In 1940 there was even talk of ten such resorts. Three to four millions would have been driven through these holiday plants each summer.

Rugen functioned as the pilot scheme and was to be completed before the war. However, in the beginning there was an embarrassing delay. On July 30th, 1935, with a handshake, Malte von Veltheim, Duke of Putbus, indicated his agreement to "hand over" part of his property at Prora Bay as a building lot—whatever "hand over" may mean in this context.

The document was legally hardly worth the paper it was written on since it stated neither the size of the lot, nor the price, nor even the new owner. It appears that Ley was in a hurry to snatch the uniquely lovely land away from the Duke: A gently curved bay, pine forests, a wide, white beach.

One of the signatories of this strange agreement was the architect Clemens Klotz. Acquainted with Ley since 1925, he had joined the NSDAP in 1933 and became Ley's favourite architect. As the wealthiest Nazi-organization, the DAF provided him with an immense market. Hitler, the maniac lay architect, made him Professor but did not think highly of him—Klotz once had been a member of the Werkbund. Alfred Rosenberg, the guardian of "blood and soil," was not quite wrong when he gibed, Klotz lacks "deepening." Indeed, this architect was able to master every style ranging from the cool elegance of New Realism to the impressive pomp of neo-classicism. A day after Ley's handshake with the Duke of Putbus the headline of Der Angriff read: "Fuhrer's order: Five huge KdF seaside resorts!" The plans have "already been commissioned." The latter seems to tally with the truth: Ley could present a first draft of the blueprints in September; a month later, on the occasion of the second anniversary of KdF, there already was an exhibition of "plans and models" including a doll's house showing the standardized decor of the guest-rooms.

In February 1936, however, for as yet obscure reasons, a competition was suddenly announced. Albert Speer, head of the KdF-department "Beauty of Work" and Hitler's favourite architect, was entrusted with carrying it out. He selected eleven participants from quite diverse directions ranging from neo-classism to modernism, including such prominent names as Giesler, Bestelmeyer and Tessenow. Meanwhile, without the competition having been decided, Ley staged the laying of the foundation stone.

In August 1936—during the Olympics—Hitler officially viewed the draft plans on display in Berlin, only to announce that his choice was the design by Klotz after all. (As the only major modification, the festival hall was to be built according to the neo-classical design by Erich zu Putlitz.)

The concept was brilliantly simple and perfectly adapted to the given local circumstances: an arc, nearly five kilometers long. Here Klotz had picked up the basic pattern of a 'bourgeois' seaside resort: a promenade with hotels along the beach and in the centre a square or mainstreet leading to a pier—but he inflated this pattern by means of repetition into dimensions of a new quality:

The centre of the complex comprised a square of 400 by 600 metres, containing a tower with restaurant, the monumental festival hall, the elegant reception buildings and "large-scale cafes" etc.; towards the sea there was a massive quayside with two piers for KdF cruisers. Adjoined to the left and right side of the central square, however, were the six-storey accommodation buildings, the "residence wings," stretching 90 metres from the water line behind a promenade running parallel to the beach.

Each of the wings (technically divided into four segments) extended over more than two kilometers. As Prora is an evenly curved bay, this made geometrically for one sixteenth of an imaginary giant circle. The residence wings were erected in skeleton construction and contained more than 10.000 rooms, most of which were identical hotel rooms, all with seaview—a really "Socialist" achievement, considering that the privilege of seaview symbolized the elite in the resorts. In accordance with modern architects' term "functional room-cells," the guest-rooms—as the atoms of the complex—were called "living and sleeping cell units."

They "measure 2.20 by 4.75 m and are all identically furnished with two beds, a washstand with running water and waterproof curtain, wardrobe (...) table, chairs and a couch." Each pair of "cell units" was connected via a communicating door, so that a six-member family could be accommodated.

Furnishings, kitchenware, bedding, even the complete set of beach utensils, right down to the bathing suit, were designed by the DAF according to rational principles.

At the rear of the residence wings, towards the woods, 96 stump-like wings were attached; they contained mainly the stairways and the bathrooms. Thus, from the backside one faced an endless row of backyards. Approaching from the ocean side, on the other hand, the sight was of breathtaking modernity.

Here, ten massived though slender "community halls" or "dining houses" protruded from the residence wings, each seating 2,000 guests. These tracts jutted into the water line and thus divided the beach into eight, just half a kilometre long segments—the vacationers' "home area." Here, calculations said, each guest was provided with five, or according to other calculations ten, square metres of the beach. The rounded ends of the dining tracts resembled the stern of a ship—with its plentiful light and glass this was a "cheerful" architecture with "elegant simplicity," praised the Baugilde.

The resort was to function as a modern entertainment centre, offering—besides the beach life—theaters and cinemas, bowling alleys, indoor swimming pools with artificial waves etc. In addition numerous secondary facilities were needed inland. Among them a train station, 5,000 underground parking lots, residential areas for 2,000 employees, hospital, power station—and a slaughterhouse. A complex of such dimensions required excellent logistics: The problems associates with "bringing, distributing and removing large masses of people," the Baugilde wrote, "were, with the aim of total efficiency, brought to a mature solution."

Ley managed to budget a fantastic 100 million RM for his project on Rugen. It became the second largest civil construction site of the Reich, after the autobahn. Up to 15,000 people worked there in the middle of a once untouched nature reserve. "This luxurious 'resort for the rabble' is a thorn in the flesh of German bourgeois conformists," as the Sopade-Bericht enviously put it: "It is one of the most effective architectural advertisements for the Third Reich." By September 1939 the construction—except for the festival hall and the dining tracts—had almost been structurally completed. Non-etheless, production in the holiday plant never started up; the premature outbreak of war forestalled the opening planned for 1940.

Outside Germany, too, the project met with great interest. The plans went on display at the World Fair in Paris 1937 and were awarded a Grand Prix. Although in respect to the style and the building technique were partly rather conventional, it was an outstanding example of modern architecture, of an architecture which was essentially Fordistic. "Lining up identical parts" was exactly the principle which was praised by the trailblazers of modern urban planning and architecture, under headings such as 'International Style,' 'New Construction' or 'New Realism.' Their gospel became the Charter of Athens, initiated by Le Corbusier and approved in 1933 by the Congres Internationale d'Architecture Moderne (CIAM). The world has to be freed from the mess and arbitrariness of history.

Instead, an austere network of relations has to be erected, a utopia, ruled by the rational "disjunction of the functions." The basics sound familiar: "Each structure has to be decomposed into its single elements, in order to integrate them in a new way according to rational principles. As modern painting has shown, this method allows one to get rid of the whole burden of traditional forms, and to create a tabula rasa as the foundation for the making of a completely new world."

Adopting Sullivan's motto "form follows function," the CIAM had declared: "Urban development must never be influenced by aesthetical reflections but only by functional conclusions." Repelled by the sunless, cramped conditions in the cities, well-intended architects became obsessed with order.

Together with his cousin, Le Corbusier ran a planning office, proposing to tear down Algiers and to put the inhabitants into tower blocks; the two main buildings—comparable to the "residence wings" by Klotz—stretch along the beach for twelve kilometers. Similar plans were made for Paris (it was envisioned to consist of eighteen gigantic skyscrapers or of a vast triangle in the middle of nowhere). One might dismiss those plans as childish power-fantasies if they had not been so influential.

In 1946, Hans Scharoun, whom the Soviets made the chief urban planner in Berlin, praised the blessings of the bombing war: the air-raid damages allowed for an overdue urban renewal (a stance already held among architects of Speer's planning team). Scharoun's Berlin consisted of a grid of "functional zones" but was—due to the division of the capital—never realized for the most part. In countless other places those ideas came true. The CIAM general secretary, Sigfried Giedion, could herald a new age in which "mechanization takes command."

In this view, machine-like structures were not "mechanical monsters" (as Marx had called the factory), but they were beautiful because they were functional. Thus, the resort at Prora Bay was indeed a beautiful machine, namely a "dwelling machine" (a term coined by Le Corbusier). It was a machine for producing fun, health and loyalty, engendered by the grammar of rationalization. Even today, architects are impressed by the "consequently functional solution" and the "elegant figure" following the "principles of New Realism."

As modernism and anti-modernism are in a constant battle, such praise povokes protest. Since the seventies, the Charter of Athens is no longer the (only) architect's bible. In the past decade, the project of Clemens Klotz has been critizised harshly. But already to Alfred Rosenberg—not only a personal enemy of Ley's but also an ardent foe of modern "Bolshevist" architecture—the project was a contradiction in itself: the workers will be carted "from the urban crowd into a mass machinery even worse."

This leads us into the further fate of this complex. During the war wounded and bombed-out, after the war displaced persons were put into the Aryan seaside resort, until the Red Army plundered and partly destroyed it. After 1950 the National People's Army of the GDR used it and the whole environs was resticted area. After reunification the last soldiers withdrew—what should happen to "Prora" (as the complex was called now), to the ruins, the remaining 9847 rooms, and the 3.5 million squaremeters of land? Investors promised to rebuild the complex for the original tourist purposes, including marina and 15,000 parking lots. Luckily, historians and community action groups achieved a "pause for reflexion" and the complex was listed. Local actors would like to turn the remains, or at least parts of them, into a museum that denounces the inhumanity of the Nazi regime. To them Prora is a "word of stone"—a term coined by Hitler on another occasion.

Since the "only objective of KdF was to stabilize a criminal system," Prora is labelled a "place of offenders" standing for the "terror" of the Third Reich and thus must not become a holiday paradise. Instead, an "educational place" should be developed at this "authentic" scene, last not least to prevent a pilgrim's site for Neo-Nazis—although here "even a naive visitor" realizes that Nazism was nothing but "visible and touchable megalomania." As can be easily seen, there is some inconsistency in the arguments.

First of all, nearly all that was built during the Third Reich helped—in one way or the other—to "stabilize a criminal system." The term "place of offenders" does not make much sense, if applied to all sorts of buildings, regardeless of their function and history. In an emerging market of remembrance, local actors may tend to emphasize the monstrosity of "their" spot—and indeed, the complex might appear a monsterous colossus. But neigther was it designed to commit nor did it witness exceptional "actrocities."

Secondly, Prora is a poor example for the "inhuman," monumental "words of stone," as favoured by Hitler in connection with important public buildings. Instead its structure simply follows the cool principles of Fordist architecture as promoted by the CIAM or the Bauhaus (stylistically Prora was a compromise: the moderately modern residence wings—today, they resemble the housing scheme of the fifties—were contrasted both with the neo-classical festival-hall and with the ultra-modern dining tracts and cafes). Admittedly, nowadays many people feel that this sort of architecture is "inhuman"—but this is no judgement on a peculiarity of Nazism.

Finally, even if—at all costs—one counts Prora as part of the "Nazi architecture," one should keep in mind that symbolic attributions to buildings rather reflect their shape than their use. Suppose that the KdF town had been used by the GDR's "Vacation Service" instead of by the Army, it would be regarded quite differently today. In 1945, bombastic constructions like Berlin-Tempelhof Airport were taken over gladly by the new authorities, in particular by the Americans; in the collective memory Tempelhof is by no means associated with "megalomania and terror" but—since the Airlift 1948/49—with "freedom and democracy." Only long after the war, the alledgedly unique "Nazi architecture" became a mighty symbol of evil in the eyes of German intellectuals, thus at the same time ennobling and daemonizing it afterwards, surpassing its original psychological effects by far.

The debate on the "colossus of Rugen" can serve as a warning example for a restriced view on Nazism. What Prora actually "stands for" obviously differs from the prevailing assessments with their moralizing undertone. The complex was simply an uncompromising application of the basics of mass tourism—"standardization, mounting, serial production" (H.M. Enzensberger). Societies are of "incredible complexity" (N. Luhmann): they are related to other societies and consist of many "systems," of levels and ranges of experiences, practices, discourses, policies.

This means that "normality" can coexist alarmingly well with "barbarism" (D. Peukert). Since the "joy" produced by KdF was to serve all but innocent ends, there remains an ambiguity at Prora Bay, making all planning delicate. But refering solely to the "great politics" would be an all too narrow approach.

The "joy" experienced by the individual KdF tripper is of another quality and scope and is worth another historical perspective. And so are the technical means to produce it. The complex at Prora is no fit object for a condemnation as megalomanic "Nazi architecture."

Meanwhile countless beaches have been transformed into holiday plants. Many of them outrival Prora by far—to mention only Benidorm, "the most efficient machine of mass tourism in Spain:" the fishermen's hamlet was made a mass resort during the Franco era and today takes pride in more than 60,000 beds in its dwelling machines. Millions of vacationers love such arificial paradises. The "fantastic dreams" of the KdF stategists had come true—or rather turned into a nightmare. Among the middle classes, namely, instead of "mechanization," a "post-modern" cult of individuality, naturalness and rootedness "takes command."

The shape of tourist organization and architecture is partly changing. But here is much confusion because the refinement of "mechanization" tends to result in concealing the underlying grammar. Flexibility does not contradict rationalization—but follows from it. Present-day computers, for instance, no longer force the users to struggle with highly formalized input standards—you may even talk to them; Non-theless, they are based on the very same logic architecture as the former "electronic brains." Already in the 1920s Ford's original system was replaced by more refined applications: General Motors president Alfred P. Sloane Jr. introduced flexible mass production in order to speed up the model cycles and to offer a range of marques from Pontiac to Cadillac—each with a different image although substantially composed of the same elements. But there was no "Sloanism," since it was just another phase of "Fordism." The grammer of rationalization is an all too powerful device to be abolished just by a change in zeitgeist.

Therefore—and not only for the socially biased perception of vacationing—it is a fallacy when tourist experts and sociologists herald the dawning of a "new," a "post-modern" or "post-Fordist" age. Like Sloan's cars, the holiday trip is a commodity which consists for the decessive parts of intangible goods, such as "fun," "recreation," "nature," "freedom," "flair," or "status." Consumption in general, but tourist consumption in particular is an active practice.

On the personal level, tourist experience always combines standarized supply with individual appropriation. Accordingly, on the social level, tourists consume and produce an enormous scope of experiences.

Tourist places are both stage and mirror, they document and require "taste" (P. Bourdieu). Right from its origins in the 18th century, tourism served as a prominent field of "distinction"—a never ending game, especially driven by the educated classes. "Post-modern" tourism, thus, is new wine in old bottles. Although tourism is regarded and sold to us as a counterpart to our frantic, mechanized everyday life, as a realm of "freedom," of playful values and individual practices—as a mass phenomenon tourism and tourists are inevitably part of the very same machinery which they try to elude.

What Prora "stands for" is less typical for a certain regime than for a certain stage of "modern times." In this connection, admittedly, the complex is a "word of stone:" an index fossil which confirms to George Orwell's famous notion that the "machine civilization" aims at total control to assure the "paradise of little fat men."

Amittedly, on the one hand, the terror of efficiency rules independently from application fields and political systems. But on the other hand, it was directly linked with political terror. Among many advocates of rationalization there was the strong belief that only heavy-handed policy can pave the way to an orderly, wealthy, egalitarian society. The Charter of Athens demanded: "the private interest will be put under the public interest" and everybody shall have "access to the fundamental joys" ([section] 95).

This comported well with the Nazi slogans; but even better was the call for "a political power of the sort desirable—clearsighted, sure and determined" ([section] 91). No wonder, Le Corbusier both admired the Russian revolution and the French Fascist leader Pierre Winter. Together they dreamt of the destruction of Paris to build it anew with mathematical precision. Making tabula rasa and creating a Brave New World—such high-flown visions demanded the Great Central Clock, the political framework of a revolution from above. But where else if not in the USSR and in Germany was the way clear for the efficient doers—into the most far-reaching planning areas imaginable.

What were the effects of the Nazi holiday politics? A quantification of tourism suggests that "Strength through Joy" achieved at least a ten per cent share of the German travel market. Also roughly one out of ten workers was likely to have at least one time traveled with KdF; in particular the skilled male workers in the towns—often former Social Democrats—took advantage of the programme. These proportions are appreciable, but they are, at the same time, not a social breakthrough. Tourism as a whole was dominated by the middle and upper classes. Even among the KdF vacationers the (new) middle classes formed the majority—and their share increaed (in particular the famed cruises were dominated by white collars and "bigwigs").

The "seaside resort of the 20,000" was to reverse this trend. Calculations allowed for a holiday there costing 12 to 20 RM. This would have put it within the reach of unskilled workers or entire families. The test-tube town on Rugen might thus have been able to increase the travel intensity in the working class nearly by half! But even this would still not have done a lot of good: with at best some 3%, their touristic travel intensity was not substantially higher than in several other countries.

KdF failed to push working-class tourism to a new level. "For official use only," this was voiced by the Institute of Work Science of the DAF (AWI): KdF was the futile attempt "to use organized intervention to achieve effects that are in conflict with the existing social structure." A sobre analysis of the Socialism of Deed. No wonder, the hope that thanks to KdF the worker will be transformed into "the most dedicated follower of the Leader" did not come true. In the beginning, the propaganda effect was considerable, but the more KdF lost the aura of sensation, it ceased. Again, the stick, and not the carrot, became the decisive political tool.

While in 1935 the Sopade-Bericht had "no doubt that the vast majority [of the workers] is not aware of the political objectives the dictatorship pursues" with KdF, in 1938 the all clear could be given: "The attitude Towards the regime is not essentially influenced"—the workers would just make the most of it. Accordingly, officials, too, complained about the vacationers' shallow consumerism, seeking trivial "fun" instead of "real joy."

But Sopade also feared an increase in "petit bourgeois self-esteem." Indeed, of significance in the long run was not the political but the mental impulse that had bred this dream machine. The figure of eight million KdF vacationers was large enough for that: A lot of Germans partook in 'proper' tourism for the first time in their lives—and could enthusiastically tell their family, colleagues and friends about it, thus reinforcing the impression that now every Volksgenosse has the chance to travel. "In particular the women," a Sopade correspondent grumbled, "for months report on the beautiful journeys and get their surroundings enthusiastic about it." KdF officials were fully aware of that phenomenon: "If you enjoyed your holiday trip, be happy about it.

However, we ask you not to keep this joy to yourself, but to tell it to your workmates, too." In this sense, KdF indeed "helped a mass desire (...) on its road to success," as a dissertation put it.

In doing so, "Strength through Joy" established a new level of tourist experience in Germany: the hedonistic holiday style, as to speak between the proletarian excursion and the distinguished bourgeois travel. KdF started as a copy of the latter; but transforming the production from a craft into an industry inevitably changes the product itself, physically and symbolically. The propaganda was right in calling the KdF vacationer a new type of vacationer and the KdF holiday a new type of holiday: less formal, less costly, less individual.

This trend must certainly be seen as entrenched in a long-term development, starting before World War I, and it is not a German peculiarity. In the thirties, the social scope of tourism was widened by means of cheap package tours, be it on non-profit or commercial grounds. In England—it was the year 1936—William Butlin started his first holiday camp. Three years later some 300,000 "Butliners" could be accomodated in two hundred camps, one of them designed for 5000 guests. Like the projected KdF camp, it was a modern styled holiday factory—partly even more "modern:" Group pressure was far more intense than at the average KdF trips: from dawn to evening red coated animators produced a total fun society of Orwellian proportions. In many other countries attempts were made to overcome the social boundaries, as well as the travel style of the bourgeoisie as the traditional 'leisure class.'

To mention in particular France, where the Popular Front introduced holiday entitlements and railway fare reductions in 1936, and Switzerland, where the tour operator Hotelplan offered "holidays for everybody." Looking at Europe at the eve of the war, it is obvious that holidaymaking was on the road to becoming an integral part of the life of broad sections of society.

Although still this was chiefly a matter of the white collar workers—the "horizon of chances" (G. Schulze) had been widened durably. In this connection, KdF represents a turning point in the history of tourism, both in psychological and engineering terms. Accoding to the grammar of rationalization, the tools of modern mass tourism had been tried out on largest scale and at the same time inhibitions among the lower classes to partake in "bourgeois" travel had been overcome. The "dams of pent-up demands" (R. Spree) were shaken—and they gave out as soon as purchasing power permitted after the war.

This was when Ludwig Erhard, the Federal Republic's Minister of Commerce, in 1957 called for the "will to consume." He saw it as the precondition for his Social Market Economy: a truly white revolution which promised "prosperity for all" and at the same time curbed all Socialist "experiments." Mass consumption would "finally overcome the old conservative social structure," the "traditional hierarchy" with its "resentment between 'rich' and 'poor.'"

And indeed: both the bourgeois high culture with its claim to define morals and taste and the proletarian culture with its ties, ethics and ideologies, were finally buried under the piles of consumer goods. The old "class structure" gradually dissolved and the affluent society of 'little fat men and women' was born—the modern fun and event society with their patchwork of 'milieus.' Regarded in this way, Robert Ley was not entirely wrong when he declared: The best thing that the Fuhrer gave his nation—is a "new lifestyle."

TOURISM, DEINDUSTRIALIZATION, AND STORE-HOUR REGULATIONS

At first glance these statements appear to have very little to do with the issue of deindustrialization. Neither quotation employs the term nor both concern retail sales rather than industrial production. Moreover, both quotes are from the 1950s rather than the 1970s and early 1980s—the period traditionally identified with deindustrialization in North America.

And yet these quotes represent opposing sides involved in a series of debates in Victoria, BC, that were shaped by the local community's divided response to deindustrialization—debates on the regulation of store hours. This study explores these debates and examines the impact on the local community of Victoria's increasing dependence on tourism—a dependence brought about by the fact that Victoria's place as British Columbia's leading industrial centre had been usurped in the late nineteenth century by its mainland rival, Vancouver.

A key issue in the debates was the extent to which the local community should be catering to tourists. While some elements of the local community argued that doing so was the only way to secure economic prosperity for the city, others countered that the city was catering to outsiders at the expense of the living standards of its own citizens.

In exploring this tension, the study reveals the tangible manner in which Victoria's economic transformation from an industrial to a post-industrial city affected the local community—in this case by challenging the legitimacy of the city's half-day mid-week holiday, which had been created as a bulwark against the growing power of consumption to colonize leisure time and, thus, dictate the rhythms of daily life. Victoria's emerging post-industrial reality pitted visitors' leisure time (increasingly spent enjoying the fruits of a consumer society) against retail merchants' and workers' attempts to preserve their common leisure time. By no means were debates about store-hour regulations confined to Victoria. Communities throughout BC and, indeed, elsewhere in Canada, grappled with this controversial issue throughout the twentieth century. What distinguished the debates in Victoria from those occurring elsewhere was the central focus on tourism expenditures. It would also be too much to argue that deindustrialization directly caused Victoria to abandon store-hour regulations. The city did so only in 1958—long after city officials had recognized the industrial primacy of Vancouver, which was also embracing six-day shopping. But recognition of the city's post-industrial reality by employers, employees, politicians, and the general public directly affected the manner in which these groups understood and experienced the economic transformation that was taking place and certainly assisted opponents of store-hour regulations in their campaigns to eliminate such restrictions. And for these reasons it is important that we explore these debates.

My aim in this chapter is to examine the connection between tourism and the social and cultural impact of deindustrialization. In doing so, I highlight the extent to which the literature on deindustrialization can expand our understanding of social and economic history for the period before 1970. But I also use these store-hour debates to argue for a more flexible understanding of deindustrialization, one that recognizes the term not as an era per se, but as an inherent characteristic of capitalism.

Adopting this approach allows us greater insight into the manner in which employers, service-sector workers, and the general public understood the economic and cultural forces that were affecting their lives during the twentieth century.

In some ways Victoria seems to fit perfectly into the traditional post-industrial thesis. After an unsuccessful attempt at sustaining industrial development, the city turned to the service sector (in this case, tourism) as an economic alternative. Indeed, back in 1986 Peter Baskerville went so far as to assert that Victoria was well suited for "a leadership role in the post-industrial world."

And yet the timing of this transition, which occurred in the first half of the twentieth century, flies in the face of so much of the literature exploring the relationship between tourism and deindustrialization. This literature emphasizes the extent to which North American communities turned to tourism as their last best chance to secure economic security in response to industrial collapse in the 1970s and 1980s.

To reconcile these contradictions, and to illustrate the complex ways in which the local community was affected by, and responded to, this economic transition, one needs to break free from the traditional understanding of the timing and impact of deindustrialization and to see the connection between tourism and deindustrialization as less a product of a specific moment, the 1970s and 1980s, and more as a long-standing relationship that informed the social, cultural, and economic experience of Canadians throughout the twentieth century. One way of doing this is by broadening our notion of deindustrialization. As John Lutz perceptively notes, the very term deindustrialzation is problematic: "With its prefix of 'undoing,' and suffix 'becoming,' it is a word unravelling itself" and it implies "the existence of a single process of 'industrialization,' ... that no longer has credence." In his study of the decline of British Columbia's boiler and engine industry at the end of the nineteenth century, Lutz explains that his use of the term is meant to indicate "an economy changing specialization towards resource processing and away from secondary manufacturing."

In focusing on a later time, this study also examines the economic shift away from secondary manufacturing, but Towards tourism and the service sector, rather than resource processing.

The dominant understanding of deindustrialization owes much to the work of Barry Bluestone and Bennett Harrison, who pointed to the end of the postwar boom in the early 1970s as a turning point in economic history in which the postwar Fordist compromise came asunder and management employed capital mobility, most visible through plant closings and relocations, as a strategy for increasing productivity and decreasing production costs. As Jefferson Cowie and Joseph Heathcott explain, "The dominant method of studying deindustrialization" has been "to trace the death of mills ... and workers' experiences of that process." And yet more recent work has begun to question the traditional definition of deindustrialization.

According to Cowie and Heathcott, "Deindustrialization is not a story of a single emblematic place ... or a specific time period," but instead a "much broader, more fundamental, historical transformation." After all, they admit, "The industrial age is alive and well, even if the locations have changed, and even if the rules of investment have shifted."

Most illuminating on this issue is Mike Wallace. For Wallace the term deindustrialization is problematic in a number of ways—two of which are important for the purposes of this chapter. First, it tends to invoke a "stages-of-development-theory" in which "pre-industrial gives way to industrial, which then moves on to a service (or, as it is often called, a post-industrial) economy." Such an understanding of history, he reminds us, leaves very little, if any, room for human agency.

Community debates and decisions about economic priorities seem hardly worthwhile if one assumes that the transition to post-industrial society is simply inevitable. Second, the very terms pre-industrial and post-industrial fail to "illuminate the key characteristics of the epochs they seek to describe, other than by reference to some other period." Rejecting the limited notion of deindustrialization, Wallace encourages us instead to think in terms of the "global reorganization of capitalism." "Industry ... has not been surpassed," he explains, "it has just moved."

From a global perspective, what we are witnessing is not deindustrialization, but "capital flight" in which corporations have become more mobile in their pursuit of "tax breaks, cheap land, or the muscle needed to repress the economic and political organization of labour." Informing this mobility, Wallace reminds us, is the logic of capitalism: "The point of industrial production under capitalism is to make a profit for the firm, not simply to produce socially useful items." Failing to seek out such opportunities to increase profits would be illogical.

It is the tangible edifices of industrial capitalism that make this last point somewhat counterintuitive. Physically imposing structures such as factories, lumber mills, and auto plants obscure what Wallace terms capitalism's "quicksilver reality of mobility and relentless transformation." As Cowie and Heathcott explain, "The aura of permanence that surrounded the industrial culture of Europe and the United States throughout the twentieth century has made the experience of deindustrialization seem more like the end of a historical epoch."

"The solidity of factories and tenements and steeples," they explain, "masked a fundamental impermanence; it obscured the forces that both created this world through investment and broke it apart by withdrawing investment."

Similarly, Sharon Zukin underscores the limitations of terms like deindustrialization and post industrial precisely because they fail to capture "the simultaneous advance and decline of economic forms, or the sense that as the ground shifts under our feet, taller buildings continue to rise."

There is an important lesson here for historians of the twentieth century, for what is true of capitalism in the late twentieth century was true in the decades before the 1970s and 1980s: its capacity for creative destruction made modern life contingent and provisional. But this lesson can be appreciated only if we bridge the historiographical divide between the earlier decades of the twentieth century and the post-1973 era (or the "post-postwar period" as Sharon Zukin mischievously labels it).

As Steven High reminds us, "Plant shutdowns did not begin in the 1970s, but have always existed alongside industrialization. Plants open in one place, only to close in another." Similarly, Cowie and Heathcott challenge the binary opposition that posits a stable postwar era against a period of decline in the 1970s. In fact, they remind us that "the process we call deindustrialization was uneven in its causes, timing, and consequences, and the effects rippled through all aspects of society."

This point is echoed by High, who refreshingly suggests that "the 'golden age' of the 1950s was far less stable and not nearly as prosperous as has been commonly supposed." To understand this we might follow the lead of Max Page who has called upon urban historians to recognize the impermanence, or provisional nature, of urban centres by placing "the process of creative destruction at the heart of the story of urban development."

Recognizing the provisional nature of the period before the 1970s helps us to see the social and cultural impact of deindustrialization on what appears, on the surface, to be a stable period of economic growth—the calm before the storm of the 1970s.

One way to overcome the existing divide between scholarship on deindustrialization and that focusing on the pre-1970s era, is to recognize that some communities embraced tourism in response to declining primary industries well before the 1970s and 1980s. For example, in his study of Ketchikan, Alaska, Mike Dunning points out that this city, which began as a supply centre for a mining boom in the early twentieth century, endured cycles of industrial development and industrial decline, which opened its eyes to the importance of tourism by the middle of the century.

Similarly, James Overton demonstrates that Newfoundlanders turned to tourism in the late nineteenth century as an alternative to the periodic crises of the fishing industry. Historians of Nova Scotia have also highlighted the manner in which that province's government embraced tourism in the 1920s as a response to deindustrialization.

In the case detailed below, Victoria embraced tourism as an alternative to industrial development well before the 1970s, and the manner in which the local community responded to this economic transition can tell us a great deal about local responses to deindustrialization; at the same time, the vibrant literature on deindustrialization that focuses on the 1970s and 1980s provides important new ways to understand the economic and social reality of the pre-1970 period.

THE STORE-HOUR DEBATES

Today Victoria's economy relies primarily upon its tourism, service, and government sectors. During the 1880s, however, civic leaders could be forgiven for believing that the city could look forward to a promising future as a manufacturing centre. During that decade, Peter Baskerville explains, the city's "gross value of manufacturing production increased 3.5 times" and "when ranked by per capita value of manufacturing production, Victoria stood fifth out of the twenty Canadian towns and cities with a population in excess of 10,000." But the tide quickly changed.

Bolstered by its newfound position as the CPR's western terminus in the 1880s, Vancouver quickly supplanted Victoria as British Columbia's leading port, and throughout the 1890s Victoria's economy was outpaced by its mainland rival. "By 1901," Baskerville notes, Victoria "had dropped from fifth to twentieth place in per capital value of manufacturing output." "The prospects of Victoria becoming an important and diversified manufacturing centre, so bright in the 1880s," he explains, "had been severely dashed by the turn of the century." And it was in this context, he notes, that "manufacturing and wholesale trade gradually took second place to tourism and government as the mainstays of the city's economy." Even during the economic boom leading up to the Great War, the city's economic expansion occurred without substantial industrial and manufacturing development. The quest for industrial development did not end;

even during the post-World War Two era some members of the business community argued "that the city must take a more active role in attracting industry."

The results, Baskerville notes, were hardly encouraging: "Even tiny Moose Jaw had had success in attracting industry from Victoria to its prairie site." Victoria, like North America more generally, "was becoming deindustrialized," and "the pace of deindustrialization in Victoria put the city in the forefront of a major social and economic trend in North American urban life." Victoria's economic response to its increasingly post-industrial reality focused largely on tourism promotion.

Ironically, Victoria first turned to tourism promotion as a method of boosterism that would attract deep-pocketed investors to the city with the hope that they would return in the future to reside in Victoria and contribute to the city's industrial development. Only later was tourism identified as an important means of attracting outside expenditure to keep the local economy afloat. Victoria's response to deindustrialization, then, focused firmly on catering to outsiders.

Visitors to the city needed to be presented with a positive view of the city's possibilities. Early in the century this meant ensuring that potential investors and settlers saw the city as a vibrant and productive centre that offered attractive investment opportunities; later the key concern was ensuring that visitors keen to spend money in local shops were not inconvenienced and were given ample opportunity to part with their cash. A central concern in both campaigns was the city's store-hour regulations.

Victoria's store-hour debates began in earnest in the first decade of the twentieth century when local store clerks petitioned city council for a common half-day, mid-week holiday. Periodically the debates would include the issue of evening store hours, but for the most part the fate of the half-day holiday remained paramount.

Embraced by many merchants in the city, the Wednesday half-holiday was enshrined in provincial legislation in 1916. Because retail clerks were otherwise unaffected by the province's Hours of Work legislation, they worked a five-and-a-half-day week. The Lord's Day Act ensured they did not work on Sunday, and the province's Half-Holiday Act guaranteed an additional half-day off each week. In the absence of any specific hours of work legislation affecting retail clerks, store hours and hours of work became, for many employees, one and the same. Despite growing opposition in the 1920s and 1930s from merchants and other commercial interests (especially those in tourism-related businesses), the provincial government retained the Half-Holiday Act and amended it as needed to ensure its continued efficacy. The half-holiday in Victoria remained a controversial but workable compromise among consumers, merchants, employees, and larger commercial interests into the 1940s.

The extension of the retail half-holiday to a full day of closing during the Second World War on the grounds of conservation and patriotism proved the undoing of this compromise. Victoria adopted all-day closing on a voluntary basis during the war, and the elimination or retention of this temporary war measure became a key issue for civic voters once the war was over.

In 1946 Victoria residents voted to return to half-day closing. Seemingly decided once and for all, the issue of store-hour regulation was revisited in an angry and divisive manner almost annually until the early 1960s. A 1954 Vancouver plebiscite eliminating Wednesday closing in that city placed even more pressure on Victoria to embrace a six-day shopping week. Finally, in 1958, faced with the decision of the neighbouring suburb of Saanich to eliminate all of its store-hour regulations, Victoria declared retail stores "wide open," and left merchants to set their own hours.

Throughout the period under study proponents of tourism squared off against other members of the local community on the issue of store-hour regulation, with each side claiming to represent the community's long-term interests. Opponents of store-hour regulations focused primarily upon tourism's economic benefits. Supporters of these regulations, and hence those who took issue with the pro-tourism lobby, emphasized instead the social and cultural advantages that the store-hour limitations ensured.

In particular, they championed the common half-day holiday that allowed community members to participate in shared leisure activities and insisted that store-hour regulations protected retail clerks from overwork and exhaustion. Both sides voiced their positions fully aware of Victoria's post-industrial reality, and the debates that resulted offer us a window onto the concerns that this reality engendered—particularly the ongoing worry that even during the ostensibly stable postwar era Victoria's economic prosperity was fragile and provisional.

My larger project, of which this chapter forms a part, explores the complex and multi-layered nature of these debates in Vancouver and Victoria. Store-hour debates in these two cities reveal a great deal about popular attitudes Towards consumerism, religion, gender relations, government regulation of economic activity, and, of course, as I argue in the following pages, competing visions of the ideal recipe for civic prosperity.

Not surprisingly, the relative centrality of these themes to public debate was not static; nor was these issues integrated into the debate in a consistent manner. In the early decades of the twentieth century, for example, gendered arguments about the need to protect female clerks from unfair working conditions appeared quite frequently in local newspapers. By the 1950s, however, the once-dominant trope of the victimized female clerk had been replaced by that of the unfortunate housewife who lacked easy and consistent access to consumer goods.

And yet a close reading of the debates suggests that gender does not appear to have intersected very much with the specific issue of Victoria's dependence upon tourism. In short, in order to offer a coherent article-length exploration of the links between these debates and the theme of deindustrialization, one must recognize that not all of the varied issues that informed these debates (gender and religion, for example) appear in the pages that follow.

TOURISM AND THE OPPOSITION TO STORE-HOUR REGULATION

As early as 1908, Alex Peden, president of the local Merchants' Picnic Association, signalled his opposition to a common midweek half-holiday on the grounds that he and other local business people "were of the opinion that it was not business-like and besides the fact that merchants lost trade, it gave outsiders, who might happen to be in town, a very bad impression of the energy and progressiveness of the city."

Arthur Lineham, a key proponent of the city's developing tourist trade, was more forceful in asserting his opposition to the half-holiday. In 1923 Lineham explained to his fellow citizens that over the previous eighty years Victoria had proven itself incapable of luring traditional industry. Drawing upon an understanding of tourism promotion that equated it with immigration literature, Lineham argued that the tourist trade was the key to creating the right conditions that would, in turn, promote settlement and attract industry.

To this end, Lineham attacked the city's half-day holiday with vigour, arguing that "to close the town up tight any day in the week but Sunday is business suicide, and makes us the laughing stock of every stranger entering our gates. Every business man and patriotic citizen in Victoria will endorse me when I say that the time has come when we must wake up and use every means of securing additional population and money to meet our obligations."

For Lineham, proponents of the half-holiday were putting their own interests ahead of the community's well-being. The half-holiday, he explained, allowed "retail clerks and small storekeepers to have what they term a good time, not caring whether it is a loss to the majority in the community or not." "I, personally, have no objection to any person playing any game he or she likes best on Sunday or any other day that suits his or her convenience," he continued.

"There is no necessity, in my opinion, to turn the town into a morgue one day in the middle of the week on this account, making us a subject of ridicule to all visitors and helping to ruin the retailers and responsible tax payers, who carry the burden of the day." Given that local tourism promotion in Victoria was originally understood to be a means of attracting industry and population, it is not surprising that into the mid-1940s, tourism's propnents attacked store-hour restrictions on the grounds that such regulations damaged the city's desired reputation as a progressive and modern business centre that was eager to attract new customers and industry. Hence Dale Johnson's 1925 complaint that the city's half-holiday prevented visitors from seeing Victoria as a "business-like and attractive" urban centre.

A similar position had been voiced eight years earlier when the Victoria Board of Trade opposed what one of its members termed "grandmotherly legislation" that was giving outsiders the impression that Victoria was "a village of lotus-eaters." Even as the rationale behind tourism promotion was transformed from one that emphasized attracting investment to reverse the city's trend Towards deindustrialization, to one that reluctantly accepted this development and focused almost exclusively on securing tourist expenditures instead of new investment, the concern that Victoria's civic image suffered because of store-hour restrictions remained prevalent.

On the eve of a local plebiscite in 1946, the Victoria Daily Times railed against the possibility of all-day Wednesday closing by charging that such a move would present an image of complacency to the outside world. Outsiders, the Times charged, would reach the conclusion "that the capital city of British Columbia is so satisfied with its present and future business outlook that it can afford to cut its retail week from five and a half days to five." Such concerns were echoed by individual citizens.

In a December 1946 letter to the Times, J. H. Davidson argued that closing stores during the tourist season did not "betoken Victoria as an up-and-coming city," while Elizabeth Davidson similarly argued that doing so "indicates a distinct lack of business acumen and puts a stamp of a small town upon a growing city." Economic growth, of course, required investment capital—capital, these observers argued, that would be increasingly difficult to solicit if potential investors found themselves questioning the community's work ethic.

By the 1920s, and increasingly in the 1930s, however, tourism's proponents were beginning to embrace a new rationale—one recognizing that Victoria would never be able to compete with Vancouver for traditional industry. As Victoria Mayor David Leeming put it in 1934, Victoria's consistent failure to attract investment now meant that "the only hope of the City was to extend its tourist trade."

Once it was recognized that reversing the trend Towards deindustrialization was no longer possible, and that a new approach to economic development was required, tourism was increasingly championed as an effective method of increasing consumer demand for local retail goods. Where tourists had once been understood primarily as potential long-term settlers and investors, they were now increasingly thought of as short-term visitors who could be relied upon to infuse the local economy with their disposable income.

As tourism promotion came to be equated with the campaign to secure not industry but expenditure, the call for decreased store-hour regulation underscored both the central contribution this cash infusion made to the local economy and the potential damage the city's current store-hour restrictions did to this external source of expenditure. In later decades, as Victoria came to rely on tourism for a direct infusion of expenditure rather than as a back-door route to settlement, secondary manufacturing, and agricultural development, many argued that the city's prosperity was now even more reliant on tourism than ever before. In making their case, opponents of store-hour regulations pointed to tourists' complaints as well as to the concerns of a sizeable element of the local business community.

Opponents of specific store-hour regulations, along with those who led a determined effort to eliminate such regulations entirely, could point to a good deal of direct and indirect evidence that tourists, themselves, were frustrated by the half-day holiday, limited evening hours, and other restrictions. Indirect statements on behalf of tourists ranged from examples voiced by individual citizens, to more general complaints levelled by the business community.

In a 20 May 1925 letter to the Victoria Daily Colonist, local citizen Dale Johnson argued against the city's Wednesday half-holiday by pointing out the inconvenience this posed for visiting tourists. When the Kathleen arrived in port the previous Wednesday from Seattle "with several hundred passengers all ready and eager to avail themselves of the opportunity of purchasing several different kinds of merchandise," he lamented, they "were disappointed to see all our stores closed." A similar incident was relayed to the larger community by "Observer" who, in June 1927, informed the Times of the plight of several frustrated American tourists.

Having been told by "Observer" that the store they wished to enter was closed for the half-holiday, and not for lunch as they had assumed, one of the tourists responded sharply, "I always heard Victoria was dead, now I know it. We came here on purpose to get certain things which we are allowed to take over the border to the value of $100. Now we must go without them."

More frequently, the tourists took their complaints directly to the local tourist office, which publicized these laments within the local community, while endeavouring to limit such adverse publicity from reaching other potential visitors. In 1956 local tourism promoter George Warren endorsed the idea of six-day shopping so that there would be no repeat of the recent Fourth of July scenario in which US visitors found themselves unable to spend money at local shops. "One of the reasons they come here on a holiday is to shop in our stores, and then they find them closed on a weekday afternoon," he complained. Such claims were buttressed, at times, with statistical evidence purportedly demonstrating that tourists were now avoiding Victoria on Wednesdays. While opponents of store-hour regulations seized upon tourists' views, the debate was primarily within the local community and focused increasingly on how to maximize much-needed tourist expenditure. And tourist-dependent businesses were among the most vocal participants in this debate. In 1951 Alan Vizard of the Victoria Gift House charged that supporters of the half-day holiday were short-sighted and failed to recognize tourism's central place in the city's economy. "You would not get holiday centres like Banff and Jasper closing down in early afternoon during the tourist season," he explained, "and the sooner Victoria realizes it is just a massive tourist resort and acts accordingly the better."

Vizard's position was echoed by the city's mayor, Claude Harrison, who in 1953 bluntly asserted his opposition to Wednesday closings by stating, "This is a tourist town." Harrison's successor as mayor, Percy Scurrah, offered a similar explanation for his own opposition to a campaign to bring back full-day Wednesday closing: "It is crazy to suggest that a city which depends on tourist trade for survival should close down all day Wednesday."

Victoria Chamber of Commerce president Stickney Harris Jr.'s 1957 declaration that six-day shopping was a necessity in Victoria was sparked by his concern that such a relaxation of store-hour regulations was necessary, given "the continued departure of industry to the mainland." Informing these concerns, as Stickney's comments illustrate, was the recognition that Victoria's early efforts at developing secondary industry had been undone by the rise of Vancouver and the outflow of industry to that city.

A fear that the city's tourism industry might fall victim to a similar fate convinced many opponents of store-hour regulations that outside competition, in the form of more relaxed store-hour regulations, might well prove the final nail in the city's economic coffin. Hence the position voiced by the chamber's Tourist Trade Group (TTG) in 1954 that the expansion of store hours was now an urgent necessity because both Vancouver and Seattle boasted six-day shopping. Even allowing six-day shopping during the summer months, TTG member Sam Lane suggested, would place Victoria on an equal footing with Vancouver, if only temporarily.

Central to the campaign to eliminate such restrictions were the assertions that tourism brought a significant amount of economic prosperity to the city, and that this prosperity was widely shared throughout the community. Opponents of store-hour regulations consistently pointed to the central role that tourism played in bringing "new" money into the local economy.

In 1953, for example, A. E. Newberry pilloried city council, and the citizens of Victoria more generally, for viewing antique shops with "a condescension almost bordering on superciliousness or disdain." In fact, Newberry asserted, such shops "attract more tourists, probably than anything else the city has to offer." As such they made an important if chronically unrecognized contribution to the local economy by bringing "new" money into the city. "The tourists do not come here to admire the beauty of the civic architecture or the excellence of the garbage trucks," Newberry maintained.

"They may stand in awe for a few minutes to gaze at the Parliament Buildings and the Empress Hotel, but they have to pass these buildings anyway on their road uptown from the ferry boats." Their key aim, according to Newberry, was shopping. Limiting tourists' access to antique shops and the like was a foolhardy and unfair move. R. A. Mackie, general manager of the CPR hotel chain concurred, arguing that Wednesday closings were denying the city much-needed revenue.

While Newberry and Mackie were content to assert tourism's importance in quite general terms, others offered more specific estimates of tourism's economic contribution to the local economy in the hope that this might win support for the dismantling of store-hour regulations. In 1936 proprietor Montague Bridgeman argued that the city's half-day holiday cost him between $300 and $400 a year. Ten years later, George MacDonald, then chairing the retail merchants' section of the city's Chamber of Commerce, urged Victorians not to adopt all-day Wednesday closing, by arguing that such a move would negatively affect the city's tourism business.

In making his point, MacDonald pointed to a 1938 survey that suggested that each tourist visiting the city spent $132. In 1951, officials for the CPR's BC Coast Steamship Service and the Black Ball Ferry Line produced statistical details of auto and foot passengers, to support their assertion that each year half-day closing cost Victoria "hundreds of thousands of dollars."

The desperation to cater to tourists by expanding the city's shopping hours was motivated by the belief, among many prominent citizens and civic officials, that with the loss of traditional industry the city's economic future was increasingly dependent upon tourism, and the pro-tourism lobby remained a consistent opponent of store-hour regulations. However, the rationale behind tourism promotion changed during the 1930s and 1940s and, as a result, so did the content of the tourism lobby's arguments.

Once motivated by an "investment imperative" that viewed tourism promotion as the most efficient means of boosting the city and attracting long-term settlement and investment, tourism promoters now found that the economic dislocation of the Great Depression encouraged them to embrace the "expenditure imperative," which viewed tourists primarily as a source of outside expenditure to be lured to the city to boost local aggregate consumer demand.

From the tourism lobby's perspective, store-hour regulations remained anathema to tourism promotion, even though the tourism lobby's specific complaints changed over time. What remained consistent, however, was the notion that tourism had come to replace traditional industry as the city's economic lifeblood. Faced with Victoria's failure to challenge Vancouver as an industrial centre, these proponents of tourism promotion were anxious to ensure that the city was as tourist-friendly as possible.

And that view, in turn, informed their campaign to eliminate store-hour restrictions that raised the ire of tourists and placed the city's economic future in jeopardy. Like the more recent tourism proponents who view tourism as a panacea to the complex social and economic problems that plague post-industrial communities, Victoria's pro-tourism lobby was anxious to protect its ability to lure outsiders to town. But of course not everyone in Victoria agreed with the suggestion that tourism was the best, or even an unproblematic, approach to securing the city's economic future.

Opponents of store-hour regulations boasted representation from a wide variety of subgroups within Victoria, including employers, employees, consumers, and even some labour organizations. But each of these subgroups also included an alternative voice that embraced restrictions such as the Wednesday half-holiday, even in the face of the growing power of the pro-tourism lobby.

Some supported store-hour regulations because they didn't benefit directly from tourist expenditures and, in fact, argued that expanding store hours would simply increase operating costs. Others pointed to the social costs that expanded store hours might bring. In particular, they sought to preserve the retail clerks' mid-week respite and opportunities for common leisure time.

Tourist-dependent operations such as hotels, restaurants, transportation companies, and souvenir stores railed against the injustice of restricted store hours and came together, in particular, in support of a six-day shopping week. In this endeavour they were opposed by department and retail stores who did not benefit to a great extent from tourist expenditure. Instead, these operations pointed to the added costs that reduced store-hour restrictions would bring.

On one side of this fissure were the tourist-dependent stores. The Chamber of Commerce's Tourist Trade Group was their most vocal champion and consistently worked to undermine the legitimacy of store-hour regulations. Central to the TTG's 1946 arguments against restrictive store-closing regulations was the assertion that the entire community benefited from tourist expenditures. Hotel owner James Neely summed up this position nicely in 1951 when he asserted that "what is good for the hotel association and the tourists is also good for Victoria."

Significantly, such arguments could find support among local labour leaders. In 1953 Retail Clerks' Union representative John Aubry signalled his organization's willingness to see the end of Wednesday closing, so long as retail workers were guaranteed a five-day, forty-hour week, with a ringing endorsement of the notion that all Victorians benefited from tourist expenditures. "Whatever is good economy for the employers," he explained, "will benefit the store workers also and the shopping public at large." Aubrey's Retail Clerks' Union faced opposition on this issue from a splinter group of employees that joined the Five-Day Week Action Committee, led by Peter

MacEwan. In their attempt to garner support for a return to all-day Wednesday closing, MacEwan's group went so far as to seek out an alliance with the city's department stores—an indication, perhaps, that workers' class identity was occasionally trumped by their occupational allegiance to either small tourism-dependent operations or large retailers.

Arguments in favour of eliminating store-hour regulations, then, did not go unchallenged. And, as MacEwan's decision to pursue an alliance with department stores suggests, the local business community was divided on the issue. In fact, retailers whose clientele did not consist primarily of visitors countered that not everyone benefited from tourism, and that the general interest of the community was being sacrificed to serve the interests of tourism-dependent businesses. In response to Alderman Brent Murdoch's claims that the half-day closing was hindering the city's prosperity, Courtney Haddock, store manager of the city's Woodward's department chain store pointedly asserted, "The business you get on Wednesday is not worth the powder to blow it to hell."

Tom Denny, manager of Standard Furniture and a past president of the city's Chamber of Commerce, offered a more quantitative argument when he used provincial Department of Trade and Industry figures to assert that Wednesday afternoon shopping would put just $3 in the pockets of each of the city's merchants. Factoring in the additional operating costs that the afternoon opening would require meant that abandoning the half-day closing was, in fact, unprofitable. Denny's claim was clearly rather selective and somewhat facetious. Some store owners were certain to benefit more than others, and it was unlikely that tourist expenditures would be spread so widely across the city. But of course that was an important part of the story.

The debate over store hours in Victoria did not always pit the business community against the workers. Nor did it simply pit externally controlled chain stores against independently owned local stores. It frequently divided the local business community itself. Hence, Denny charged the TTG with "being dictatorial to the retail merchants" and asserted, in a clever play on the usual pro-tourism rhetoric, that "what is good for the retail merchants is good for Victoria."

The division over tourism's impact was not based solely upon careful calculations of where tourist dollars were going. During the 1920s and 1930s, some observers began to voice concerns that the city's single-minded determination to preserve its tourist business was placing store-hour regulations, and the half-holiday in particular, in jeopardy, and that this, in turn, would have negative affects on the community's social and cultural well-being.

For the Hudson Bay Company's A. J. Watson, public debates about store hours in the mid-1920s boiled down to the question of whether or not tourists should be dictating local bylaws. As the pro-tourism lobby pushed for expanded shopping hours, a spokesperson for local retail clerks reminded city council in 1929 that longer hours came with a social cost for the clerks, which could include "a discontented body" and the "break up [of] home life."

A 1936 letter to the Times from G. W. Robinson urged the city to place the clerks' welfare ahead of other concerns, while challenging the Chamber of Commerce's perception that the half-day holiday threatened the city's tourist trade. Improved roads, he argued, held the key to expanding tourism, not longer store hours.

Not surprisingly, as the pro-tourism lobby stepped up its rhetoric in the 1940s and 1950s and embraced the expenditure imperative, the champions of local autonomy and the retail clerks' welfare responded in kind. In voicing his support for continued Wednesday closing, Reg Williams, president of the local Meat Retailers' Association, accepted the view that tourist expenditures were desirable, but argued that the concerns and welfare of local residents must continue to be the city's first priority.

Williams's arguments were echoed by furniture retailer Roy Denny, though in a more forceful manner: "We live in the city, not the tourists. We should have things the way we like." Peter MacEwen, not surprisingly, offered a similar view by asking rhetorically, "What we would like to know is this—who is running the city—the tourist trade group or the city council?"

Such concerns were not voiced solely by clerks' representatives or retailers, such as Williams and Denny, who had little contact with tourists. During the 1940s and 1950s the Colonist returned repeatedly to this issue in its editorials. Acknowledging, in 1949, that "anything so firmly entrenched in the business life of the community as the weekly half-holiday cannot be disturbed without the strongest of reasons," the Colonist took its arguments a step further in 1951 by focusing directly upon the welfare of the retail clerks. Asking clerks to give up their weekly half-holiday, it argued "would be a lot to ask of them merely for the convenience of tourists."

The following year the Colonist expressed frustration that no solution had emerged that reconciled the welfare of the local population with increased shopping opportunities for tourists. Recognizing that the city's store-hour regulations were undoubtedly hampering its tourism promotion efforts, the newspaper nevertheless insisted that the common half-holiday was worth preserving. The holiday, it explained, provided a rare opportunity for communal recreation and allowed "one set afternoon" each week "so that friends may go places together" or "engage in organized sport and recreation." The welfare of retail clerks, the Colonist explained, was under threat and the city as a whole had a moral duty to protect their interests. "These are the people who make up the 'we' who have to live in the city." At least one retail clerk concurred with this view. In 1953 H. A. Napper argued that what was being overlooked in the current controversy was "the right of retail clerks to take part, if they wish to, in group activities, such as cricket, football, baseball, or any other game they may fancy." "It took our fathers a long time to win this right," Napper explained, "and some of us don't want to lose it."

These observers recognized that Victoria's post-industrial reality left it reliant on outside forces, but they refused to accept that this situation necessitated abandoning the half-day holiday.

Central to the campaign to preserve the half-day holiday was the defence of common leisure pursuits. In a reversal of Arthur Lineham's earlier arguments that a small number of clerks and merchants were putting their own needs ahead of the larger community, local citizen Harold Gray wrote to the Daily Colonist in 1953 castigating opponents of store-hour regulations for attempting to increase their profits by denying "some nearly 6,000 retail clerks ... the right to enjoy together and with one another their weekly half-day holiday."

Retail clerk A. G. Kinnis concurred and argued that the abolition of the half-day holiday would mean that "groups would not be able to unite for sports or outings." Rejecting a popular pro-tourist lobby proposal that retail clerks stagger their days off to suit the needs of their employers, Kinnis argued that "a staggered holiday system" would prevent workers from undertaking common recreational pursuits.

Kinnis's position was endorsed by fellow letter-writer Alex McLeod Baird, who argued that the Wednesday half-holiday had "grown to be a recognized day on which all store employees gather together and enjoy themselves collectively." Collective leisure, Baird argued, should not be allowed to fall victim to "the exploded wolf cry—'Tourist.'" Forcing retail clerks to abandon their half-day holiday, yet another letter-writer argued, placed these workers in a unique, and unfair situation.

"Today all banks, offices, all types of laborers, work a five-day week and none of them would consider a shift system," argued George Robinson in a 1953 letter to the Times. "Why then compel the store clerks to work a shift system which would not allow any group activities[?]" The answer, for opponents of store-hour regulations, was Victoria's increasing dependence on tourism—a dependence brought about by the flight of industrial capital from the city in the late nineteenth century and the city's failure to re-establish itself as a leading manufacturing centre. The result was a seemingly unending and uncomfortable search for economic stability.

Victoria's industrial decline in the late nineteenth century convinced the city to embrace tourism as a central component of its future economic development. In the long run this has proven to be a successful endeavour. As the store-hour debates demonstrate, however, this was a controversial enterprise. The campaign to cater to tourists divided the local community. The pro-tourism lobby campaigned relentlessly for the modification and elimination of store-hour regulations so that the city could meet the demands of tourists.

In doing so tourism's proponents argued that, because the city had lost the battle for traditional industry, it was imperative that the city embrace tourism promotion—first as a last-chance method of luring deep-pocketed investors to the city, and later as a means of increasing consumer demand for local retail goods. Central to the latter argument was the assurance that everyone in the community benefited from tourist expenditures.

Challenging these arguments were other community members who, like the pro-tourism lobby, were drawn from a wide range of backgrounds: employers, employees, civic officials, and consumers. They disputed claims that tourist dollars were spread evenly throughout the community and insisted that the social benefits—in particular, common leisure time—that the community accrued through institutions such as the half-day holiday should not be sacrificed to serve the interests of outsiders. Both sides were fully aware of Victoria's post-industrial reality; but both offered very different evaluations of tourism's role in alleviating the contingent and provisional nature of the city's economic fortunes.

The recent literature on deindustrialization is helpful in illuminating the lessons these debates hold for historians. First, as historians such as Hal Rothman have noted in other contexts, Victoria's reliance on tourism brought with it unexpected complications—in this case, a growing demand that the city's agreed-upon store-hour regulations be sacrificed on the altar of economic necessity. Second, as was the case in larger centres such as Atlantic City in the 1980s, the reliance on tourism brought with it a growing sense of unease within the community—one that expressed its concern that the interests of "outsiders" were being served at the expense of local citizens.

Third, we can see in Victoria, as in other instances of deindustrialization, a shift in power from within the community to without. In the case of Victoria, however, this change happened indirectly. Instead of large, faraway, multinational corporations seizing control of the city's economic future though hotel or casino development, the power to influence local bylaws shifted in favour of tourists indirectly and local tourist businesses directly.

The constant desire to craft the city's reputation as a tourist-friendly destination helped to sustain the campaign to reduce and eliminate store-hour regulations. Finally, the fleeting and provisional nature of post-1970 economic life that has been documented so well in the literature on deindustrialization points to an important element of Victoria's story throughout the twentieth century: these debates were the product of a community uneasy with its economic reality and desperate to pursue any means of securing economic stability, even if that meant transforming the rhythm of daily life and allowing individual consumer demand to colonize common leisure time. And what lessons do Victoria's store-hour debates hold for historians of deindustrialization? They suggest that some assumptions about deindustrialization need to be modified and questioned. First, and most obviously, tourism certainly emerged here as an economic alternative to traditional industry, but much earlier than the current literature on deindustrialization would suggest.

These debates, then, point to the possibilities of comparative studies of deindustrialization that focus not just upon the post-1970 period, but upon earlier periods as well. Second, while much of the literature on deindustrialization focuses on the tension between community and capital, the debates underscore the extent to which deindustrialization in Victoria nurtured divisions within the local community. Moreover, these divisions did not fit into tidy compartmentalizations such as workers versus employers, or outside chain stores versus local entrepreneurs. Instead, the divisions emerged primarily within the business community but also, at times, among retail clerks and between their labour organizations.

Third, Cowie and Heathcott argue that changes brought about by deindustrialization, unlike those ushered in by industrialization, "were more disorienting than overtly political, tended Towards the elusive rather than the tangible, and marked a confusion of power relations that had seemed significantly clearer under the old order." These debates challenge that assumption.

After all, the issue here was a tangible one: a growing momentum in favour of eliminating store-hour regulations that affected when and how retail employers and employees worked. What was at stake here was a tangible reorientation of leisure time—a reminder that we must continue to factor leisure into our analyses of workers' lives.

If the store-hour debates are any indication, Victoria's failure to retain traditional industry haunted the city well into the postwar era. Some community members championed tourism as the most effective alternative economic strategy to industrial development and, in doing so, fought to eliminate the city's store-hour restrictions. Others strenuously opposed the elimination of these restrictions on the grounds that they served the interests of the local community, and local interests should not be sacrificed in favour of outsiders.

Recognizing that Victoria's embrace of tourism as an economic strategy was contested is an important indication of the complex nature of community responses to deindustrialization. Recognizing the fact that Victoria's post-industrial reality confirms some patterns unearthed by historians of deindustrialization, while challenging and modifying others, is an important indication of the extent to which historians of the late twentieth century and those focusing on earlier periods of economic disruption and transition can learn a great deal from each other.

11

Community Based Heritage Eco-Cultural Tourism

As we enter into the next millennium and the birth of a new global era, we are confronting the urgent need for local/regional/national/international peace and security more than in the past. This may be broadly ascribed to the increasing conflicts arising out of social, economic, religious and political factors. The widening gap between the haves and have-nots, have further accelerated these conflicts. Hence, we are seeking universal human rights and universal human progress and prosperity.

One powerful indicator of such a development is the fact that more people are traveling from more countries than ever before, making travel and tourism the worlds largest industry. Its growth is expected to continue with globalization and as people everywhere seem determined to exercise their right to travel and to make their world a more familiar place in the spirit of peace and friendship.

Tourism itself has always been a peace-based industry and may be considered as a Global Peace Industry. In the face of current human population increases and worldwide ecological degradation, intact and healthy ecosystems are becoming the world's most sought-after tourism destinations. Culture and Heritage besides peace and harmony in such areas attract special groups of tourists, who demand quality products.

THREATS TO PEACE AND SUSTAINABILITY

Peace and sustainability, considered as the indicators of development are threatened due to a myriad of conflicts—Social, Economic, political, cultural and Environmental. These conflicts usually confront multiple and diverse stakeholders such as state institutions, religious organizations, communities, indigenous ethnic groups, local institutions, private development and non-government organizations, international organizations, and many other players.

Wide differences in culture, knowledge, power, influence, and resources characterize these groups. Even though most conflicts essentially develop in a local framework, they are also frequently connected at regional, national and even international levels, transcending political and geographical boundaries including non-represented interests (*e.g.* future generations). Such complexity explains, in part, the lack of sustained attention that conflicts receive.

In addition, many conflicts in India are often dealt with unprofessionally and result in frustrations, violence, greater inequities, and negative impacts on quality of life, economic and social processes and in the natural resources themselves. The most common methods of intervention in conflicts tend to be centralized, hierarchical, and sectorial, with a predominantly technical and adversarial (judicial) and at times political. Seldom do they achieve a reasonable level of satisfaction for all interested parties.

Hence, we are urgently in need of alternative paradigms for development—we are moving from the narrower 'reductionist', 'reactive' and 'bureaucratic' approaches to 'wholistic/Integrated or Systems' view of looking at issues, 'pro-active' policies and 'participatory' strategies. How quick and how effective we are in reorienting ourselves according to these shifting paradigms will determine our sustainable futures.

THE IMPORTANCE OF THE TOURISM SECTOR AS THE PROMOTER OF PEACE AND SUSTAINABILITY

The word 'conflict' carries negative connotations. It is often thought of as the opposite of cooperation and peace, and is most commonly associated with violence or the threat of violence. This view of conflict is not always helpful. In many settings it should be seen as a potential force for positive social change—its presence a visible demonstration of society adapting to a new political, economic or physical environment. A potential non-violent approach to solve these conflicts at the least social/economic/Environmental costs may be through evolving alternative tourism strategies.

In the midst of growing tensions and worries everywhere "Getting away from it all," is understandably popular. With so many wonderful places in the world, prices of international travel falling, and the stresses and strains of everyday life increasing, more people are traveling.

And as the population grows and incomes rise in many societies, the trend is steeply up. In 2000, international tourist arrivals reached an all time high of 698 million, an increase of 7.4 per cent that was double the growth rate of 1999, according to the World Tourism Organization. Tourism sector employs 11 per cent of the global workforce—over 200 million people—either directly or indirectly.

THE TOURISM SECTOR IN INDIA

India's tourism potentials are immense - with a large variety ranging from rich cultural diversity, world-renowned historical, religious, heritage and architectural monuments, unique fairs, festivals, folklore and folk dances besides the costumes and customs to wildlife sanctuaries with exquisite flora and fauna. Besides, there are cool hill stations and long stretches of sunny beaches all round the peninsula.

The diversity is not only in climate but is all pervasive and as J. Nehru put it, "India is a land of contrasts—with the rural tranquility of simplicity and urban bustle, pomp and show". Added to this, there are plenty of traditional arts and crafts to carry back as souvenirs; Indian hospitality and variety induce tourists to make repeated visits.

India's wide choice of adventure sports ranges from the daring to the exotic—trekking, camping, rock climbing, white water rafting, skating, air/water gliding, etc. In spite of such attractions, tourist arrivals in India are less than 1% of the world arrivals. Tourism in India is different from other sectors by some special characteristics that include:

A wider variety of stake-holders but with lack of communication and coordination.

Uniformity of artificial structures in Tourism areas does not blend with the natural diversity of undisturbed areas. Inter-sectoral linkages and complexity with several intangible costs and benefits; conflicts leading to problems in analysis, monitoring and coordination; mixed priorities and conflicts, make cooperation and participation difficult.

Research on tourism especially on policy and planning has been given low priority—as a result, it is poorly studied and understood as a sector in general and its Environmental and Social/Cultural impacts in particular; hence, we are confronted with fragmented and poorly coordinated policies, riddled with ad-hoc decisions for short term gains at the cost of long term sustainability.

Multiplier effect is prominent—can enhance poverty alleviation and alternative livelihoods; but is rarely understood by the planners and the implementing agencies. Seasonality in Tourist influx has implications for carrying capacity analysis and Tourism policy/planning/implementation, but rarely taken into account by the planners/policy makers.

Spatial and temporal dimensions—implications for Physical planning:

Positive and negative feed backs—implications for absorbing capacity, carrying capacity, Sustainability, and resilience; a typical tourism cycle would involve—Exploration/development/consolidation/stagnation/decline/ rejuvenation; however, negative impacts, on a cumulative basis destroy the resource base, affecting the natural, cultural, and Heritage attractions, culminating in declining tourism trends.

Life supporting systems are impacted, culminating in debates on Ecological integrity Vs Economic security. 'Profit maximization' is the prime motto of Tourism enterprises (irrespective of whether they are private or Govt. sector undertakings) and hence, tourism is largely out of control for planners; some impacts are irreversible and hence tourism itself is affected due to degradation in Environmental health/quality. The Ecological impacts of tourism are more on Common Property Resources—air, soil and ground water, leading to tragedy of the commons as they are treated as 'open access commons'. Lack of know how and trained man power in Govt. agencies on Eco-cultural tourism lead to lack of appreciation and Govt. support for community based initiatives.

Tourism industry is fundamentally dependent on the diversity and quality of the natural and cultural resources. Hence, it has grater reasons to conserve/ protect the same. But are we giving adequate attention/priorities for natural and cultural resources while planning and implementing tourism projects in India?

Though tourism is India's one of the largest foreign exchange earners and one among the fastest growing industries, the natural resource base that supports tourism is "heavily stressed" in and around the main tourist destination areas. In spite of the overwhelming technological and information revolution, we have trapped ourselves in a vicious circle of self-destruction by adopting the typical "boom and bust" tourism paths paved by the ill-conceived and unplanned/uncontrolled mass tourism, promoted for short-term profit maximization at the cost of degradation in Environmental quality. Ironically, this in turn, ultimately detracts the tourists and destroys the Tourism industry itself.

The question is whether we, in the blind pursuit of rapid Economic growth and earning more foreign exchange Q an afford to sacrifice the higher Environmental quality and Our rich cultural Heritage upon which tourism so strongly depends. Though we have already learnt many bitter lessons, we tend to overlook them. Changes in the physical, spatial, and socio-economic structure of a tourist area as well as the existence of several, sometimes burdensome, environmental/social problems testify to the presence of these conflicts and the crying need for evolving appropriate strategies to sustainably manage the Environmental quality, and to improve the local livelihood opportunities.

However, the researchers as well as policy makers in India largely ignore the inseparable links between the Environmental quality (EQ), sustainability, peace and tourism and pay little attention to participation of local communities, by focusing only on setting up infrastructures, promoting marketing strategies and make only adhoc/piece meal efforts to improve the EQ, sustainability and peace in the destination areas.

This is self-evident from the "tell-tale symptoms" or "indicators" such as garbage dumps, foul smell, very high rates of pollution, overexploitation of natural resources, alienation of local communities, increasing conflicts and violence in several destination areas. The industry has learned these bitter lessons only after the irreversible damages have already set in. Examples can be seen every where the mass tourism went out of control—starting from Ooty and Kodai lakes in the South to Dal lake in the North; from Kovalam in the South to Goa in the North; even our nation's pride Taj Mahal is not spared! As a result, tourism has become a dirty word amongst many communities, environmental groups and human rights campaigners. This is really unfortunate as the tourism sector has greater potential to enhance local livelihoods, if it is properly planned.

THE ILLS OF THE TOURISM INDUSTRY

Though tourism could lead to a variety of potential benefits, uncontrolled mass tourism, the most predominant form of tourism today, inevitably increases the already existing conflicts, besides creating new ones. Tourism's voracious appetite for basic resources—land, water and energy—has meant that the tourism industry and Government Agencies are increasingly finding themselves opposed over land rights and water rights by local people. Lack of access by locals to public beaches, violation by hotels of environmental regulations, and heavy-handed tactics by local authorities to free-up beach areas for hotels' use, have all been cited in legal disputes throughout the world.

For instance, three quarters of the sand dunes on the Mediterranean coast between Spain and Sicily have now disappeared, largely because of the construction of hotels and holiday flats. One of the most famous long-term tourism protests has been in Goa, India. With one five-star hotel consuming as much water as five local villages and one five-star tourist consuming 28 times more electricity per day than a local Goan, local discontent over resource-use is understandable.

Thus, the modern world is characterized by mass concentrations of people, mass production, and mass activities. Diversity and beauty of land and life are more and more replaced by uniformity and ugliness. Human settlements in their mad rush for development have turned beautiful tree-clad landscapes into desolate concrete jungles, and fertile lands with diverse native vegetation are increasingly destroyed by monocultures. Tourism is no exception to this general rule.

THE GREEN SIGNALS

Over the last decade, understanding of these complex and interconnected issues by the world tourism industry, tourists, governments and communities has increased as indicated by the evolution of numerous alternative forms of tourism such as 'green' tourism, 'alternative' tourism, 'responsible' tourism, 'sustainable' tourism, 'eco' tourism, 'eco-cultural' tourism (ECT), 'eco-development' tourism, 'Heritage eco-cultural' tourism (HECT), 'community' tourism, "ethical' tourism, 'fair-trade' tourism and even, most recently, the particularly un-catchy, 'pro-poor' tourism(PPT).Unfortunately, we, in India have not sufficiently re-oriented ourselves, to meet the future international market demand for these specialized forms of tourism. The concept of sustainable tourism should not be confused with ECT. According to WTO, all tourism activities, be they geared to holidays, business, conferences, congresses or fairs, health, adventure or ECT itself, must be sustainable.

This means that the planning and development of tourism infrastructure, its subsequent operation and also its marketing should focus on environmental, social, cultural and economic sustainability criteria, so as to ensure that neither the natural environment nor the socio-cultural fabric of the host communities will be impaired by the arrival/activities of tourists; on the contrary, enterprises, as well as the communities in which they operate, should benefit from tourism, both economically and culturally.

Eco-tourism, a growing trend, is the most commonly understood term as tourism that focuses on an appreciation of the environment. In 1993 the World Tourism Organisation (WTO) estimated nature tourism generates 7 per cent of all international travel expenditure. More recent research reveals this is now much higher, accounting for 20 per cent of international travel in the Asia-Pacific region and some areas, such as South Africa, experiencing a massive growth in visitors to game and nature reserves, of over 100 per cent annually. Research by The International Ecotourism Society (TIES) reveals that coo-tourists are likely to be higher spenders on their holidays than 'ordinary' mass tourists. And high spending, nature-loving, responsible tourists are undoubtedly an attractive option for governments looking for ways of earning foreign exchange.

The recent Amman Declaration on Peace Through Tourism (8-11 November 2000) reflects many of the strategies discussed above and has recognised that peace is an essential precondition for travel and tourism and all aspects of human growth and development. Hence, it has recommended the development of tourism as a global vehicle for promoting understanding, trust and goodwill among peoples of the world through an appropriate political and economic framework.

THE NEW THREATS

The alternative tourism strategies, evolved in response to the concern for the Ecology, culture, Heritage and local livelihoods, have created both new opportunities as well as new threats. One of eco-tourism's first problems is one of definition. Although, there are several definitions, there is no certification system to abide by or international monitoring body. The term can be used by anyone at anytime for anything from a small-scale locally run rainforest lodge where the money goes to support a local community, to a large, luxury, foreign-owned resort which has little community involvement and uses masses of natural resources.

Eco-tourists may even visit areas of national beauty and wildlife significance without realizing that local people have been evicted from the area in order for eco-tourism to be developed, as has happened in East Africa, India, Southern

Africa and many other destinations. Ill-conceived and/or ill-planned Eco-tourism, as practiced now by a majority of the business communities has caused serious, irreversible negative impacts in environmentally and culturally sensitive areas, even in countries that are well known as eco-tourism destinations like Belize or Costa Rica.

The Malaysian-based Third World Network working with the Thailand-based Tourism Information Monitoring team (TIM-team) cite examples throughout Asia, including the eco-tourism policy promoted by the tourism working group under the Greater Mekong Sub-region (GMS) development scheme, led by the Asian Development Bank, which covers a vast area across Burma, Cambodia, Laos, Thailand, Vietnam and Yunnan/China.

They are riddled with several problems relating to accusations of 'human zoos' being created and financial exploitation of hill tribe villages by outside tour operators. Besides, the increasing link of eco-tourism to the multi-million dollar biotechnology industry through bio-piracy in key eco-tourist sites like rainforests, and the use of eco-tourism by the World Bank's Social Investment Project to support massive development projects, some involving logging operations are becoming common in many developing countries. The revolution in information and communication technologies would enable both the promoters and the tourists to exploit the hidden potentials ECT in a region, more efficiently than ever. However, the lack of discipline of government and the escalating demand for growth will undermine efforts to create sustainable eco-tourism economies that are small but beautiful.

Under extreme conditions of land grabbing and unplanned structures, it may create concrete jungles, surrounded by degraded vegetation, thus destroying the once tranquil zones. Hence, we have to be extremely careful while promoting ECT.

Despite these problems, an International Year of Ecotourism (IYE) was declared by the United Nations for 2002. This will be co-ordinated by the WTO and UNEP and a range of activities held, including a World Ecotourism Summit from 19-22 May 2002 in Quebec, Canada plus various regional conferences. Oliver Hillel, the UNEP tourism programme co-ordinator sees the IYE as a chance to "assess what eco-tourism is, or can be, rather than only a promotional event for UN member governments, for the private sector and for recipients of development aid."

It is clear to many that nature-based tourism is presently seen as one of the most lucrative niche markets, and powerful transnational corporations are likely to exploit the IYE to dictate their own definitions and rules of eco-tourism on society, while people-centred initiatives will be squeezed out and marginalised.

While the commitment of the tourism industry in India to tackle these complex issues seems limited, a few smaller operators are keen to work closely with local people in order for the communities to support their business and out of an honest desire to protect environments and optimise benefits to local people. However, such small operators lack the know-how to tackle the issues involved. As a result, alternative tourism strategies for which India has a greater potential, make up a very small proportion of overall tourism facilities.

THE POTENTIAL ALTERNATIVES

In any outdoor tourism activity, human experience, knowledge, expectation, and socio-cultural contexts interact with environmental elements and environments as entities to produce an outcome that affects both the humans and the environment. Thus, sustainable tourism development depends in many important ways on the proper handling of the relationships between Tourism and the Environment. Sustainability, Peace and Environmental quality occupy the central table in the wake of global terrorism.

Greater sustainability of the tourism would mean more regional products, less noise and emissions, lesser solid wastes and appropriate sewage treatment measures, creation of jobs, lesser social conflicts/violence by learning to live in harmony and higher quality of life for the local populations well as improved quality of holidays for the guest. The conventional mass tourism, by its very nature cannot cater to these demands. Hence, alternative tourism strategies are emerging.

Sustainable tourism is defined (WTTC, WTO and Earth council, 1996) as "Tourism that meets the needs of the present tourists and host regions while protecting and enhancing opportunity for the future. It is envisaged as leading to management of all resources in such a way that economic, social and aesthetic needs can be fulfilled while maintaining cultural integrity, essential ecological processes, bio-Diversity and life supporting systems (soil, air and water)". Thus, it has the inbuilt mechanism for promoting peace and harmony among the tourism stakeholders.

A related alternative is Eco-cultural Tourism (ECT). ECT activities are offered by a large and wide variety of operators, and practiced by an even larger array of tourists. While there is no single universal definition for ECT, its general characteristics can be summarized as follows:

All nature-based forms of tourism in which the main motivation of the tourists is the observation and appreciation for admiring, enjoying and/or studying nature as well as the traditional cultures and Heritage (both past and present) prevailing in relatively undisturbed or uncontaminated natural areas.

It contains participatory, interactive, educational and interpretation features.

It is generally, but not exclusively organized for environmentally, socially conscious small groups by specialized and small, locally owned businesses. Foreign operators of varying sizes also organize, operate and/or market ECT tours, generally for small groups. It minimizes negative impacts upon the natural and socio-cultural environment. Heritage Eco-cultural Tourism (HECT) is a newly emerging type of alternative tourism. When Heritage of the destination areas can be exploited along with the local Ecological and cultural attractions, we have a case for Heritage Eco-cultural Tourism.

Heritage embraces magnificent natural, indigenous and historic landscapes (natural or man-made), wildlife and healthy, intact ecosystems, historical elements (that has helped to shape the regional/national identity), cultural elements and human values, shaping regional, national, global identity; it also incorporates a strong connection to 'place'; that is, people come to the place by choice, they are somehow transformed by it, and they choose to identify themselves with it even if they don't live there.

This may be because of the outstanding universal value of the areas visited from the point of view of science, conservation or natural beauty.

Historical places, objects and manifestations of cultural, scientific, symbolic, spiritual and religious values are important expressions of the culture, identity and religious beliefs of societies. Their role and importance, particularly in the light of the need for cultural identity and continuity in a rapidly changing world, need to be promoted. Tourists are actively seeking such lost values. They come hoping for a profound psychic or spiritual experience in some quiet corners of the destination areas. Hence, we have greater responsibility to conserve the cultural Heritage areas.

HECT, by its very design is ideally suitable for this purpose.

The following are the key potential benefits of HECT:

Protection and active conservation of natural and built heritage resources, justified by their own intrinsic value for posterity and the revenue which visitors contribute.

Enhancement of the natural and built environment to meet rising quality standards necessary to sustain modern travel and tourism.Reconstruction for visitor usage of urban environments and environments degraded by the industrial practices of former extractive and manufacturing industries.

Establishment of attractive environments for tourism destinations, for residents as much as visitors, which may support other compatible new economic activities, from agriculture and fishing to service and manufacturing industries.Creation of economic value and protection for resources which otherwise have no perceived value to residents, or represent a cost rather than a benefit- livelihood opportunities—micro-enterprises?

Opportunity to communicate and interpret the values of natural and built heritage and of cultural inheritance of residents of visited areas.Effective management of visitors within an environment so that it can support long-term economic development and repeat visits.Research and development of good environmental practices and management systems to influence the operation of travel and tourism businesses as well as visitor behaviour at destinations. Opportunities, through the direct customer contacts that all travel and tourism businesses have, for operators to communicate and interpret the values of natural and built heritage and culture to visitors, thus helping to create a new generation of responsible consumers

The available knowledge indicate that the following may be considered as the major criteria for selecting HECT sites:

Geography—proximity to mass-tourism sites; sufficiently closer for easy accessibility but adequately away from motorable roads and other human disturbances. Climate and Ecology—microclimates/habitats conducive enough for the tourists without any need for artificial comforts

Rarity and Uniqueness—Ecosystems like mountains, rivers, mangroves, coral reefs and islands endowed with unspoiled beauty, unique culture and Heritage.

Infrastructure—only reasonable—to the barest minimum but with desirable conditions—hygienic ethnic food (locally produced/prepared), protected water supply, natural ventilation and local architecture.

Diversity—higher habitat/community/Ecosystem/cultural (food, cloth, architecture, crafts, festivals etc.)—diversity and purity—potentials/ opportunities for viewing/appreciating more attractive species/cultures as well as Heritage elements; Potentials for a variety of nature/adventure tourism activities such as camping for wildlife observation, traditional healing camps, caving, bird-watching, trekking, rock-climbing, mountain biking, skating, para-gliding, wind-surfing, funky jumping, canopy walkways, white water rafting, snorkeling, scuba diving, recreational fishing

Unpolluted/relatively undisturbed areas with higher Environmental quality—in contrast to polluted/degraded landscapes/seascapes

Minimum health/safety risks—to avoid costly demands from the tourists

Opportunities for Environmental Education and interpretation—for all the stake-holders

Opportunities for generating and sustaining new livelihoods—to cater to the demands of the tourists—*e.g.* Apiculture (the science and art of raising honey bees), agriculture, horticulture, floriculture, community dairy/piggery/poultry, preparation of Ethnic foods, rich diversity of arts and crafts.

Community cooperation- to make and enforce their own decisions on eco-tourism development.

Presence of dedicated NGOs—for catalyzing cooperation.

Cooperation of other stake-holders—Govt. and other institutions—their policies, programmes and goals.Marketing opportunities—potentials for targeting different types of eco-tourists (hardcore, dedicated, mainstream and casual); marketing linkages and potentials.The HECT will enable the tourists as well as the local communities to find ways to live sustainably, and in peace with nature, Cultural Heritage and intact, functioning ecosystems. More importantly, we will be reconnecting ourselves with our forgotten treasure of the diverse culture and Heritage of the bygone era. In this process, tourism will promote peace and sustainability by closer mutualistic interactions between tourists and the local communities.

Among the several organizations that could be involved in the promotion of HECT, mention must be made of UNESCO (World Heritage sites programme) and the International Institute for Peace through Tourism (IIPT) at international levels and the Indian National Trust for the promotion of Arts and Cultural Heritage (INTACH) at the national level. The Indian Tourism Development Corporation (ITDC) and the State Tourism Development Corporations have to recognise the potentials of HECT and reorient themselves to the tasks ahead.

Broad guidelines for promoting HECT strategies may be modified and adopted from UNEP (1995) that has prescribed Environmental codes of conduct for tourism and Gonsalves' (1991) paper on guidelines for alternative tourism for the third world. The adoption of the Global Code of Ethics for Tourism, the Green Globe programme (WWF, 2000), the ECOTEL Certification awarded by HVS Eco Services, Certification Programs for Sustainable Tourism and Eco-tourism, Exemplary Practices by Canadian Tourism Commission (1999), The National Eco-tourism Accreditation Programme of the Eco-tourism Association of Australia and the Australian Tourism Operators Association and equitable community participation in tourism are a few other such initiatives to name, globally.

Recently, Mastny (2002) from World Watch Institute has provided policy guidelines with examples for sustainable tourism. The recently emerging pro-poor tourism approaches, have to be ideally integrated into HECT. Caribbean island. It is an island-state much like many others in this region of the world: Its beaches are white, its people are black, its skies and waters are blue, its mountains are green, and its birds and fishes and flowers are every colour in the rainbow.

Its roads were laid out when land transportation was by way of horseback or donkey cart or on foot. Its legislature meets in a dignified one hundred-fifty year old stone building painted the colour of lime juice. Its school children wear uniforms and appear to the American visitor to be anachronistically neat and well-behaved. It is an interesting place.

Its history is interesting, too. Virtually the entire native-born population today is made up of the descendants of Africans, brought to the Caribbean in chains by European colonialists to labour in the mines and on the plantations. Europeans conquered the Caribbean islands in the 16th century. They established trading outposts, plantations, and mines throughout the region. The commerce that ensued introduced tomatoes to Italy, potatoes to Ireland, and sugar and horses to the Americas. It also introduced the plantation system of agricultural production based on African slavery to the Americas.

After a series of slave uprisings throughout the Caribbean, the practice of slavery was ended on this island in the 1840s. In the twentieth century, the descendants of slaves gained in social and political strength; in the second half of the twentieth century, blacks came to control the government, and have done so for several decades. From these islands have come music, poetry, dance, and art that are known the world over. As I said, this is an interesting place.

Beyond these basic points, however, I knew little about the island's history. My historian's curiosity was aroused by this society that seems to have taken such a different course from that of the United States. So, I signed up for a guided tour of the historic sites.

To my disappointment, our tour guide was not a native islander, but a recent transplant from Minnesota! She began her tour by talking about the bravery and heroism of Christopher Columbus. She told us how he faced the cannibalistic Caribs—a name and description used for one of the native peoples in the region—and even lost one of his men to their attacks.

She went on to tell of pirates and warriors and captains of agriculture and trade. She noted that when slavery was abolished in 1847, "hard times" followed. She pointed out that the colonial governor who ended slavery was recalled to his native Denmark, and that although he was later "exonerated," his ending of slavery "ruined his career."

Of the island's natural history, we learned that it has a natural deepwater port, and that many of the walls are made of a native stone known as "blue bitch," because it is so hard it is really a bitch to quarry. In the words of comedian Dave Barry, "I am not making this up."

Then we visited a house museum. It was the reconstructed home of a Danish banker who came to the island about 1820. A local historical society docent—a retired New Yorker—told us the story of the house. The story was all too familiar: The banker brought his family to the island to make his fortune. They braved the hostile elements and unfamiliar culture. He was shrewd but fair. He raised a large family. He grew rich from the resources and produce of the island and the labour of its people. He became a pillar of the community.

The house (although reconstructed in the 1960s) represents the lifestyle of the merchant class of the 19th century. Some of the furniture and furnishings were imported; some made on the island. Most were collected and donated since the 1960s by historical society members, and have no provenance that connects them to this actual house. We were told that the house has high ceilings in order to catch the breeze. We learned that life was difficult, but the people were strong.

There was even an anecdote about how the Danish family suffered in the tropical climate because the clothes they brought with them from Denmark were wool! I would ask, "what is wrong with this picture?" But that would so understate the problem as almost to miss the point. The better question is, "what is this picture?" Surely it is not a very accurate or complete picture of the long, complicated, interesting history of this island in the Lesser Antilles. It sounds more like a generic script from house museum pattern book.

In connection with the death of Columbus's soldier at the hands of natives, our guide never mentioned that the European explorers and their successors killed and enslaved hundreds of thousands of native peoples in the ensuing occupation and colonization. In discussing the hard times that followed the end of slavery, she never mentioned the hard times experienced by the hundreds of thousands of enslaved Africans before slavery was abolished.

In describing how the brave governor (who ended slavery only because of an eminent revolution, it turns out), she told us his career was ruined, but she did not speculate about what happened to the careers—not to mention the lives—of the people whose actions really did end slavery, the rebellious slaves themselves. And not once did she mention the name of any of the historical figures who guided the island from colonial rule to democratic self-government. In fact, it was as if the history of this island ended about the middle of the 19th century.

The real history of the island is quite different from the version presented by our tour guide. Robert Paquette and Stanley Engerman note in the introduction to The Lesser Antilles in the Age of European Expansion that "... the transition from slave to free labour marks one of the most momentous shifts in moral sensibility in the making of the modern world." "The lesser Antilles with their diverse history of colonization provide an exceptional laboratory for the study of comparative emancipation."

Not only was the story selective and inaccurate, it was boring and predictable. By the time our tour was over, I had concluded that the "heritage" in this heritage tourism experience was, to adapt a phrase from Henry Ford, "pretty much bunk." And unfortunately this is not the only place that is true. The purveyors of heritage tourism—and this includes historical societies, museums, and government cultural agencies—all too often serve up a kind of lowest-common-denominator drivel that is designed to tell visitors what they already know.

Or at least what they think they know. Rarely does heritage tourism challenge or surprise. Heritage tourism does not present a version of history that is dirty or controversial. It does not challenge the conventional wisdom. It does not rely on the latest and best scholarship in the field. Instead, it is pabulum, based more or less (usually less) on history. And its reputation for being deadly boring is often richly deserved.

To make matters worse, there is a huge gap between the popular idea of history, and the history produced by professional historians. Americans get a great deal of their history from television, theme parks, and movies, media infamous for ignoring historical scholarship in favour of making a point. Yet they are immensely popular with the public.

In his book, History Goes to the Movies, writer Joseph Roquemore writes, "Ever since The Birth of a Nation's 1915 premiere, feature film makers have rewritten history to fashion top-dollar entertainment.... " Because of their dramatic impact, he continues, "films have extraordinary power ... to leave you with a strong sense of what is right and what is wrong, of who is bad and who is good, even though critical details presented in the movies may be slanted or false."

From The Birth of a Nation, to Walt Disney's 1950s production Davy Crockett: King of the Wild Frontier, to Mel Gibson's 2004 religious pronouncement, The Passion of the Christ, television and movies have treated historical topics and audiences have consumed them eagerly. Historians decry the lack of accuracy in the portrayal of historical people and events in these movies.

Yet people have seen them and tend to remember them as fact, in part because each one reaffirmed popular prejudices and predilections of its day. Despite readily available historical information that would permit the telling of an authentic story, the movie version is the one that enters the public consciousness.

The same is true, to a large extent with historical theme parks. Historian Mike Wallace, in his essay "Mickey Mouse History," criticizes the original Disneyland in California and its "clone" in Florida, Walt Disney World. According to Wallace, both are "... ostensibly ... grounded in historic reality ...," although they are certainly not intended to be a full and accurate retelling of history.

In fact, Wallace continues, Disney's "approach to the past was ... not to reproduce it [as Colonial Williamsburg or Greenfield Village seek to do], but to improve it." The original Disneyland alone attracts some 10 million visitors each year, ten times as many as visit Colonial Williamsburg or Mount Vernon, our most visited heritage sites.

The greatest shortcoming of these versions of history is that they oversimplify history and reduce it to a linear progression of events that lead logically and inevitably to a conclusion. All too often in popular history, the present situation is portrayed as the near-perfect culmination of centuries of human endeavor.

Missing is the improbability, the surprise, the controversy—in short the human dimension—of history. In explaining how the United States became embroiled in the Vietnam War, Frances Fitzgerald observed that "Americans ignore history.... The national myth is that of creativity and progress, of a steady climbing upward into power and prosperity, both for the individual and for the country as a whole. Americans see history as a straight line and themselves standing at the cutting edge of it as representatives for all mankind." Most professional historians tend to view history as more complicated—and more interesting—than that. Their job is to uncover and piece together the complicated and interesting stories of the past, and to relate those stories to a contemporary audience. Yet they tend to write almost exclusively for an audience of other professional historians. There are exceptions, of course. Civil War historians Shelby Foote and James McPherson, for example, or John Adams biographer David McCullough are academic historians, whose scholarship has been accepted and consumed directly by a broad public. But mostly the people who read serious history are serious historians.

The disconnect between academic history and the broad public consciousness is nowhere clearer than in a Washington Post article about the American Historical Association's 2004 annual convention. The theme of the convention was "War and Peace." Not the novel, but the history.

The Post reporter attended the convention and reported his impressions of it. The headline on the article was "Lessons We May Be Doomed to Repeat;" the subhead was "American Historians Talk About War, But Is Anyone Listening?" The reporter's implied answer to the headline's question—not really.

Thousands of historians gathered to present their latest research on war, and to question and debate one another on one of the most obviously relevant topics their profession ever deals with. Yet the reporter described a scene of seemingly deliberate insularity and isolation. Describing one session entitled 'Thoughts on War in a Democratic Age," the reporter noted that "the scholarly papers ... had been a classic academic combination of insight and obscurity, thoughtful analysis and mind-numbing delivery, and by the time the question period finally rolled around, even the AHA's president, James McPherson, was ready to head for the door." The reporter went on to ask "if they can't even hold the attentio of their colleagues on such an innately compelling subject, how can they expect ordinary humans to absorb what they have to say?"

The reporter betrayed a degree of naivete about the nature of academic conventions, but he also put his finger on a serious problem. Academic historians talk about authenticity and historical accuracy. They complain bitterly about the incorrect depiction of historical people and events in popular culture—from Davy Crocket, to the schlocky tour of the Caribbean island I described. Yet their work is virtually inaccessible to the general public. By the time it penetrates popular culture, it has been diluted and distorted until it becomes unrecognizable.

After movies and theme parks, the third major source of historical information for the American public is what could loosely be called heritage site—museums, historic houses, monuments, roadside markers, and the like. The Travel Industry Association of America reports that about one fourth of

American adults, or more than 50 million adults, travel to historic sites each year. And that does not include the millions of school children who take field trips every year. Consider the fact that only about one fifth of all Americans ever take a single history course after high school, and the importance of heritage sites as sources for historical information comes sharply into focus.

Unlike movies and theme parks, heritage sites present themselves as authentic. The information they give out is presented as fact. Obviously, they hold great potential to expose the public to the kind of history that professional historians produce. Yet, my experience is that heritage sites do surpass the movies in interpreting the best history scholarship, but aside from some of the major innovators in the field, barely so. In fact, heritage sites reinforce the popular notion of history more often than they correct it. The heritage in heritage tourism, namely the history that underlies it, is often bad. It is out of date, poorly documented, usually repeated from secondary sources.

To be sure, there is good scholarship available to heritage organizations. And the best heritage sites take full advantage of history scholarship. At Manassas National Battlefield Park, for example, a new exhibit in the visitor centre is accompanied by an interpretive film. Both are based on rigorous scholarship. Both explore the broader themes of American history which led to and resulted from the Civil War. The park superintendent, himself a Ph.D. historian, chaired a conference on "Reinterpreting the Civil War," that attracted some of the most eminent scholars in the field. Similarly, the park historian responsible for the Frederick Douglass National Historical Site organized an international conference on Frederick Douglass scholarship as part of an effort to improve the history content in that site's interpretation.

But the National Park Service is the United States' premiere federal agency that manages heritage sites. And even the National Park Service acknowledges that it has much room for improvement. At the vast majority of heritage sites the story is more akin to the Caribbean tale above.

In Maryland, for example, of more than 300 heritage sites open to the public, all but a handful are run by local government or small private organizations without the resources they think they need to bring the best scholarship to the public. Very few take advantage of the history expertise available in the state's universities. In fact, the cynical cliche "if you've seen one house museum, you've seen them all," is closer to the truth than most heritage site managers would like to admit.

Something is not right. State and local tourism bureaus promote heritage sites vigorously. Communities like heritage tourists because they spend money, and the industry is a relatively low impact form of economic development. Tens of millions of Americans visit heritage sites each year. Why, then isn't the product better? With plenty of good scholarship available, why do most heritage sites fall back on the conventional wisdom of history, often repeating stories and facts that are widely accepted, but downright wrong? One reason might be found within the history profession. Public history—the practice of history outside the academy and with a direct popular audience in mind—has traditionally been looked down upon within the history establishment. Professional organizations have for several years recognized the importance of public history and have initiated efforts to support its practitioners. Still, the primary focus for training Ph.D.s in history is the academy.

But there is a larger reason for the paucity of current scholarship in heritage sites. It lies with the organizations that manage these places and interpret their stories to the public. James W. Loewen's indictment of heritage sites, Lies Across America: What Our Historic Sites Get Wrong, faults the organizations and agencies that manage heritage sites, arguing that many of them start with a point to make—boosterism, hero worship, patriotism—and often miss or avoid the most interesting parts of history. They prefer to give the public a simple, predictable, safe story that reinforces preconceived ideas, even if it ignores the scholarship on the subject.

Anthropologist Dean MacCannell thinks so, too. He has lamented the sameness and lack of imagination of heritage sites. Yet he also points to the potential for telling the more complicated and authentic stories they actually represent. I been involved as a manager or board member of a wide variety of heritage sites and organizations over the past quarter century. During that time I have also visited hundreds of other heritage sites, gathering information about their presentation and interpretation, talking to managers and trustees, and forming some strong opinions about their use of history. My experience confirms Loewen's and MacCannell's observations.

Every time I visit one of these less-than-exemplary heritage sites, I wonder why I keep doing this. Why, in fact, do so many millions of people visit these sites every year? Why do we insist on trudging on with this endless pilgrimage to the Mount Rushmore and the Doctor Mudd house and the tomb of Ponce de Leon? I think I know the answer. I think we do it because real history is challenging. It is complicated and uneven. It can be risky. It can be fun, entertaining, interesting, even exciting.

History can inspire us and give meaning and relevance to our everyday lives. Obviously, heritage sites are not always fun and entertaining and interesting and exciting. They are not even usually fun and entertaining and interesting and exciting. But they can be. I think we visit them because we hope they will be. That we don't usually find fun or entertainment or excitement or inspiration is a disappointment—to visitors, to historians, and to tourism professionals. That disappointment also offers a huge opportunity for heritage tourism.More research needs to be done, but anecdotal evidence indicates that people will visit sites that are controversial, complicated, and challenging. The U. S. Holocaust Museum gets very high visitor ratings, despite the shocking and disturbing content of its exhibits. The Maryland Historical Society's "Mining the Museum" exhibit, confronted visitors with the "... issues of curatorial choices and the role of museums as they relate to the representation of African Americans and Native Americans in traditional museum collections."

Despite the sophistication of this theme, the exhibit was one of the most visited in the museum's recent history. Visitors seek authenticity. Too often they have to settle for comfort. The challenge for heritage tourism is to become a nexus between recreation and scholarship—the place where the "public" in public history meets the "history" in public history.

12

Scope in International Tourism Reconsidered

On the eve of the third millennium, the quest for "alternative" models is urgent; today this urgency is gaining power within the field of tourism. Many authors identify with this question. Seminars and symposia proliferate in opposing the problems of unchecked tourist growth. Alternative Tourism has become a symbol of the "Tourism of the Future."

In choosing "Theoretical Perspectives on Alternative Forms of Tourism" as the topic of its first seminar, the International Academy for the Study of Tourism invited academics and other scientists to consider all aspects of this theme. As social scientists, we must be concerned with Alternative Tourism in all its facets, actual or potential. It is the contention of the authors that the popularity of this new concept should itself be analyzed as a symptom.

The alliance of the two words "tourism" and "alternative" should alert us. It has a paradoxical resonance, an incongruity stimulating further enquiry. In this chapter, we intend to squeeze the meaning out of these words and to question the underpinnings of their use over the past two decades. Thus, ours is an essay in the sociology of knowledge and praxis.

THE PHENOMENON AND ITS CONCEPT

At several recent meetings, we have noted the perplexing nature of the term Alternative Tourism. Whenever speakers were asked to define it, their embarrassment became clear. At the International Round Table organized by URESTI, Georges Cazes (a French geographer) and Linda Richter (an American political scientist) presided over the debate on the problematics of alternative tourism in local societies. Cazes was irritated by what he considered a confusing notion and Richter proposed replacing Alternative Tourism with the term "appropriate tourism."

At Zakopane, the academicians concluded by condemning the "imprecise character of the term Alternative Tourism [as] ambiguous and hardly congruent with scientific work." Finally, at the World Tourism Organization Seminar on

Alternative Tourism, the participants voted to replace the term with Responsible Tourism, purposefully defined as "relating to all forms of tourism which respect the host, natural, built, and cultural environment, and the interests of all parties concerned: hosts, guests, visitors, tourist industry, government, etc."

How can we understand the success of the term Alternative Tourism in spite of all the reservations about it?

"Alternative Tourism" has a nice ring to it. It is alliterative like an advertising gimmick. It is dynamic and provides a rallying cry. It sounds like an appeal: "Let's make the improbable a reality!" It connotes quality, responsibility, and respectability. It suggests a sensitivity that wins over the world. Yet, though attractive, the label is deceiving.

From the beginning there has been a problem of definition: where to draw the line between various kinds of tourism. The many meetings on Alternative Tourism have spawned a "discourse of good intentions." In this chapter we hope to reveal the ideological pressures behind the discourse.

There is a danger of oversimplification of the complexities of tourism: in order to avoid the dilemma of having to decide whether to reject tourism completely or accept it unconditionally, people have latched onto the easy idea of Alternative Tourism.

UNCERTAIN ORIGINS

The emergence of the word "alternative" allied with tourism throws light on its *ideological* nature. The Ecumenical Coalition on Third World Tourism (ECTWT) claims paternity. Since its establishment in Bangkok, it has aimed "to explore possible models of alternative tourism in the Third World."

In 1980, a precursor group of militant Christians gathered just before the World Tourism Organization Conference on Tourism in Manila to denounce economic imperialism, domination by transnational corporations, political exploitation, organized prostitution of women and children, the degradation of traditional cultures, and other ills.

The Tourism European Network (TEN) was soon formed in Stuttgart in collaboration with ECTWT and, in 1984, held a seminar on Alternative Tourism in Asia. In 1986 a similar international conference took place at Bad Boll, West Germany. This called for the different sectors — tourists, hosts, businesses — to participate in building a New Tourism Order. But there were broader forces and other groups also promoting Alternative Tourism.

ALTERNATIVE TOURRISM

One could also link these calls for Alternative Tourism with various "Alternative Movements" that arose in Germany or the West Coast of the United States in the 1960s. These movements wanted to promote a counterculture by rejecting consumer society. Alternative Tourism, in rejecting mass tourism, is a similar radical attempt to transform social relations and is thus part of the larger movement. Is tourism a new kind of development strategy or, more powerfully, a prime force within a new strategy of international relations? A recent congress was called "Tourism — A Vital Force for Peace." This issue of "alternatives" penetrates all domains, and tourism is but one entrée.

Thus one could envisage a sociology of "Alternative Tourism as a social movement": a force aimed at social change; a movement of people in the process of mobilizing ideas; a series of acts and speech diffused in many segments of social life, where the actors are not totally aware of their real motives.

It is only with the hindsight of history that we can speak about a real change of strategy. One should be able to analyse the actors, the channels of communication, the ramifications, and the different forces of the movement. But the believers in Alternative Tourism belong to various social groups and the issue is still unclear.

The whole question is complex. In the 1980s everybody started to talk about Alternative Tourism, but with scattered meanings and heterogenous or contradictory interests.

Alternative Tourism encompasses a wide range of connotations: tourists characterized by particular motivations; touristic practices; a touristic product; levels of technology; solutions to planning; local, regional, national, or international politics; a strategy for development.

In the last case, Alternative Tourism is the application to tourism of Alternative Development in regions where tourism has been chosen as a factor in economic development. Finally, Alternative Tourism expresses the concept of a "New order of Tourism." The multiplicity of these meanings is both a great source of confusion and a rich opportunity for in-depth study.

PROFILES OF CONCEPTUALIZATION

We may approach the problem in two ways. There is a difference between the emergence of a practical concept and the construction of a scientific concept. The analysis must go further than surveying the various meanings and denouncing the confusion, even in order to clarify them. Listing the different uses of the term and coming up with an approximate definition is easy but insufficient.

Using the methods of structural linguistics, we analyse the structure of meanings underlying the discourse of Alternative Tourism — the discourse of the tourists, professionals, politicians, scientists. We deconstruct this discourse in order to lay bare the conceptual operations from which it derives its power of persuasion. This is only a much needed preliminary step. The expression Alternative Tourism can be baffling; to one businessman interviewed in the

French Alps it meant "that the roads, the hotels, the whole place, is periodically filled and emptied!" The word "alternative," taken literally, engenders such images as ebb and flow, going and returning, leaving and arriving! But to the initiated, "alternative" (as in Alternative Tourism) is a special kind of qualifier. The whole phrase is an "autonomous syntagm"; the words are bound together like a single noun.

Using the methods of structural analysis, we look at the opposing pairs in which Alternative Tourism is used in speech. We find that Alternative Tourism always has an antithesis: commercial, conventional, mass tourism. It arises as the contrary to whatever is seen as negative or bad about conventional tourism, so it is always a semantic inversion, found at all levels of discourse.

For instance, some tourists are motivated to think that Alternative Tourism is individualized or selective, expressing their good taste, as opposed to mass tourism, which is seen as plebeian, organized, gregarious, and allowing little individual choice.

As lodging, Alternative Tourism refers to human scale, small and medium sized local, family, or community enterprises, well integrated into the area. Anything other than the usual concrete tourist establishments qualifies. Alternative Tourism connotes local artisanship, with wood and fine materials and typical local architecture.

As a tourist product, Alternative Tourism is expensive, sold by travel agents to a wealthy clientele or social leaders. "Cultural tourism" is the key word. Paradoxically, it also claims to be free of commercial circuits and capitalist profits. It appeals to advocates of "social tourism" and independent tourists alike.

As activity, it favors physical well-being acquired by good health habits, competitive sports, or strenuous outings. It implies intellectual and aesthetic attitudes, trips to far regions with unexplored cultural or natural treasures appealing to the socially mobile. It opposes mass tourism for its comfort and repetition of the "four S's" (sun, sand, ski, sex) of the average middle classes.

Finally, as planning, Alternative Tourism appears to express local wishes to bring together tourists and host communities and thereby enters into endogenous development policies concerned with local interests. Some claim that this "new model" of tourism will replace mass tourism as "old fashioned" or out of date. Thus for some, "alternative" is not just another kind of tourism, but aspires to become *the* tourism in the promotion of a new order.

THE PRINCIPLE OF THE ALTERNATIVE

In logic, an alternative is based on a Judgement that there are only two possibilities. Two contemporaneous terms are placed in mutual exclusion, with an "excluded middle," that is, no other possible course is open. It is either one or the other. Thus the promotion of Alternative Tourism relies on a series of value-laden judgments: devaluation/valuation, negation/affirmation, neutralization/idealization.Emerging from such a series of discriminating processes between"reference tourism" and Alternative Tourism, logically Alternative Tourism becomes *the* tourism.

After analyzing many texts referring to tourism, an unending repetition of these mental processes can be noted. We idealize what we promote and reject what we disapprove of.

ALTERNATIVE TOURISM AND THE CHALLENGE OF INTERNATIONAL TOURISM

To situate the Alternative Tourism movement, we must compare its goals with those of International Tourism. Within the discourse, Alternative Tourism can be seen as an opposite of International Tourism, which is itself multidimensional. Some major characteristics of International Tourism include the following.

THE PRIMACY OF ECONOMICS

International Tourism is generally defined as a particular aspect of Tourism (with a capital T), as the extension into international geographical space of a mobility originally confined within national limits in opposition to internal (or domestic) tourism.

There are, however, many ways to define international tourism. In the literature, modern international tourism is commonly linked with the Grand Tour, which began in the eighteenth century among young British aristocrats making an initiatory trip to the Continent.

As other classes were emancipated in the nineteenth and early twentieth centuries, the idea was generalized as a "vacation." In this way, the ideas of tourism and vacations are interchangeable. Thus international tourism is seen as an irrepressible seasonal mobility which crosses frontiers, as "a tidal wave, a North-South invasion, or a stampede to the sun."

Seen historically, this is a one-sided view, that of the industrialized nations. But international tourism is an "international social fact" in the sociological sense. "Not all social facts are amenable to internationalization...there are some phenomena which reflect more precisely the characteristics of one group, people, or nation; other phenomena are seen to better advantage as *exchanges* between different peoples; they surpass national territories,...they live a kind of supra-national life."

THE DUALITY OF THE CONCEPT

In the 1930s, countries in the League of Nations were aware of the assets and liabilities of international travel on the balance of payments, "petty things" which can amount to considerable sums. At that critical period, some governments protected their balance of payments by limiting travel abroad. The League's Economic Commission, however, took a position in favour of International Tourism, with the important argument: "It is ultimately wrong to consider domestic tourism to be something essentially different from international tourism, just as it would be to forget that the economic activity of a country is indissolubly linked to its external trade".

Thus tourism is divided into international and domestic but, though linked, they refer to different networks of meaning.

Domestic tourism is seen as a cultural habit increasingly widespread in industrial societies, but International Tourism has become an import/export activity reckoned in terms of international monetary exchange.

Thus International Tourism is implicitly reduced to its economic and commercial aspects, which take preference over cultural aspects. Whereas domestic and national tourism are seen as inherently cultural, International Tourism is seen as prospectively economic. Needless to say the notion of Alternative Tourism bears the consequences of this cleavage.

POLITICAL WILL: THE GROWTH OF INTERNATIONAL TOURIST MOVEMENTS

Thus tourism became first and foremost an "economic fact" for decision makers, who take this as a given in considering tourism within their overall planning. The opening of an area to foreign tourists is seen as a market phenomenon and is calculated as a matter of foreign exchange by international organizations. Countries are measured by their performance, and regions are urged to enter into this "competition." The development of tourism is seen as axiomatic.

Tourism is not just a matter of national growth, but must be conceptualized as part of international relations.

TOURISTS IN THE GLOBAL FLOWS

Reading economic forecasts gives one the impression that tourism is constantly in danger of collapse. The discourse of officials is preoccupied with signs of weakness, decrease, or loss. Thus international tourism always appears to be on the brink of a crisis, one which it in fact anticipates and resists.

The constant growth of international tourism is not spontaneous, but reflects a supernational institutional will. In the Universal Rights of Man Charter the liberty to circulate freely in the world is fundamental.

The worldwide expansion of international tourism is the subject of massive propaganda. In this regard it is noteworthy that the International Union of Official Organizations of Tourism (IUOTO), which became the World Tourism Organization in 1974, was originally founded at the Hague in 1925 as the International Union of Official Spokesmen of Touristic Propaganda.

In spite of variations during economically or politically sensitive periods, tourism has enjoyed an average growth rate of 8 per cent per annum since World War II. In 1950, 25.3 million people crossed borders as international tourists. This number reached 390 million in 1988 and is projected to grow at 4 to 5 per cent per annum through 2010. The World Tourism Organization forecasts that tourism will take first place among world economic activities, and no decline is in sight before 2000.

The question is not so much whether or not there is an alternative to tourism but whether major new emerging forms of tourism will remain within the frame of reference of the dominant model or break away from it.

A POINT OF DOCTRINE

International tourism makes money and the industrialized nations are the main benefactors. Yet as early as the 1960s Kurt Krapf (1961), one of the pioneers of the economic theory of tourism, advanced a then-revolutionary idea that the developing nations should also benefit from international tourism. Soon thereafter the United Nations Conference on Tourism and International Travel proclaimed, "Tourism makes a vital contribution to the economic development of Developing Nations" (United Nations 1963).

This theory came to the fore at the very time when affluent nations decided to help "needy" societies by announcing a "Decade of Development," just when many former colonies gained their political independence.

It was reasoned that, though planting a luxury industry in such poor countries might appear shocking, the developing nations had few other resources, but they did have an abundance of natural and cultural riches and a cheap, underemployed workforce.

Tourism, a frivolous activity, could become a useful instrument in economic development. But this doctrine contains a condensation of meanings which must be untangled to avoid the pitfalls into which the doctrine of Alternative Tourism also risks sinking.

The imposition of international tourism on the developing nations suggests not only a change of scale but a turning point. International tourism is not just an international extension of domestic tourism, nor just a major contribution to foreign exchange, but is also a "transmission belt" connecting the developed and the underdeveloped worlds.

Tourism policy has become part of a global project which lumps together seemingly contradictory economic interests: the organization of vacations (an idea originating in rich countries) and the aspirations for development of economically weak societies. Thus "free time" resulting from the exploitation of the surplus value of capital is put back into the calculation of economic productivity. Societies inexperienced with industrialization are re-oriented Towards "touristification"; tourism comes to be judged by economic and political criteria within the international framework, a vector for global integration. It becomes a factor in the North-South dialogue and a component of the much-discussed New World Economic Order.

THE OPENING OF DEVELOPING NATIONS TO INTERNATIONAL TOURISM

Since the 1960s, the developing nations have been persuaded to open themselves to international tourism, to give tourism a favored place in their economy, to welcome foreign capital, and to make fiscal concessions.

Many countries have responded enthusiastically, hoping to solve their problems of endemic poverty. Between 1969 and 1979 the World Bank supported twenty-four projects in eighteen countries. Immense resort projects were started on the Costa Brava and the Costa del Sol in Spain, on the Bulgarian and Romanian shores of the Black Sea, in Tunisia, the Antilles, the Caribbean, Mexico, Thailand.

Tourist resorts form a world apart, a delimited area on the fringe of ordinary life. Tourists are grouped into a hotel or complex containing all the services necessary for maintenance and pleasure, following the needs of thc notorious "4 S's."

Architecturally and technically modern buildings are erected in spaces in the process of desertification or overpopulation. It sometimes happens that the local population must leave or nomads can no longer traverse the area, the land is abandoned or remodeled, or new fresh water supplies sought, all for the reception of vacationers from rich countries. Touristic mobility is an unprecedented "delocalization" movement.

TOURISM, A FACTOR IN ECONOMIC DEVELOPMENT ON A WORLD SCALE

At times of crisis, even the developed nations see tourism as a primary "export activity" worthy of subvention. In addition to the multiplier effect and offsetting foreign debts, tourism becomes one of the few remedies for never ending unemployment. According to Organization for Economic Development and Cooperation (OEDC) experts, tourism is moving from an accessory to a major and necessary economic activity..

Rich countries are adopting policies first intended for the poor, and tourism has become a development factor in post-industrial societies. Almost all nations promote tourism development as a producer of profit, leading to envy and stiff competition for foreign exchange and tourists.

TRANSNATIONAL COMPANY NETWORKS

The tourist industry's system of production is now considered one of the world's most powerful driving forces. Through mergers and concentrations, these companies have become agents of an interconnected network penetrating many sectors. The transnationals of tourism are the avant garde for strategies of capital internationalization. The system of tourist production has evolved into network-companies, models for transnational companies in the world economy.

Decisions for whole regions or countries are made inside one company. Yet the states or communities involved may have no veto or even influence in this "Dialogue of Monopolies and Countries". Competition is reduced by collusion, for profits grow best in homogeneous spaces. Thus culture, society, and identity become mass products when International Tourism enters a country.

These network-companies operate in an almost centralized system in which power stems from negotiations and meetings in search of consensus. This efficient organizational system, with its savoir faire and its capacity to manage behaviour and technology, is what Galbraith called "technostructure." The system relies on experts who often bring identical solutions to contrasting local conditions. Growth is external to and independent of local conditions of production.

This system also aids the integration of regions and communities into the international whole. To accept international tourism is not only to welcome foreign vacationers and their currency, it means access to international planning, technology, and finance, entering the world economy and approaching world modernity. One cannot understand Alternative Tourism without this view of reality.

THE ROLE OF THE STATE IN THE PROMOTION OF INTERNATIONAL TOURISM

It is often difficult to draw the line between the state and industry. By internationalizing tourism, the structure of the state is transformed by the arrival of officials trained in commercial technology and marketing at all levels of administration, an evolution obvious in France and many other countries.

The training of government authorities integrates local business into higher echelons. In January 1990, meetings on local development were exhorted to "think local, act global/think global, act local". Thus international tourism is one domain where the public-private dichotomy is misleading.

FROM SECTORIAL PLANNING TO GLOBAL PLANNING

International tourist planning has to do with the introduction of rational thought into management practices. Since the 1960s it has enlarged its range, from purely sectorial choices to the opening of the developing nations to international tourism. As tourism moved from a secondary activity to a primary force in national economies, intersectorial comparisons of profitability became crucial. In addition, as tourism is inscribed in national development plans, it is justified not only by profit, but for its contributions to political aims of development. It becomes the axis on which other sectors rely, and national intersectorial planning gives way to global planning.

At the instigation of international organizations or Western, formerly colonial, powers, Third World countries cooperate and endeavor to finance their investments within a long-range set of programs. National tourist offices depend on international data.

Tourism becomes one of the vectors of inter-nationalization and thus attempts to become a generating principle for the whole society, enabling the instruments and goals of the world economy to penetrate and weave transnational bonds.

GEARING UP A SOCIETY FOR TOURISM

Marketing, long an essential tool of international tourism promotion, articulates supply and demand within a market economy, and societies embracing international tourism are plunged into this international system. Unlike other industries, the "products" of the tourist industry are a pastiche of formerly heterogeneous elements amalgamated by advertising for tourist consumption.

Combined symbiotically, they include services (lodging, dining, transportation, recreation), culture (folklore, festivals, heritage, monuments), and less palpable things such as hospitality, ambiance, and ethnicity. At last this "product" incorporates the society itself, its culture, its identity.

International tourism promotion, aimed at economic development, requires every location to offer something unique. By this logic, each country or region must produce and publicize its unique identity, with a "name recognition" that signifies its superiority.

All over the world there is a fantastic incorporation of identifying signs into touristic products: nostalgic places, historic monuments, traditional and rural heritage, the skills of ethnic groups. Populations are solicited to attract foreign attention with their talent and creativity.

Everyone plays himself or herself and acts out a performance. Widespread marketing research determines what this image should be, matching aspects of local identity with the desires of potential clients. This fabrication of identity defines the seductive attributes and crystallizes them in an advertising image such that even the locals may eventually recognize themselves in it (cf. Carpenter 1973)!

TOURISTIC RESTORATION/APPROPRIATION

In the analysis of the creation of "tourist attractions," cultural heritage is exploited as a "mineable resource." It must be "put to good use" by changing its purpose, and hence its meaning. It is restored along rational lines for commercial promotion and may end up looking like one in a series of reproductions rather than its own historic self.

In Europe, for example, historic landmarks and properties were often preserved by philanthropy derived from a sense of community pride. Now, however, every city restores its historic ramparts, church, or castle to attract tourists, and funding is solicited from art dealers, from cultural sponsors, and from the tourist arms of the state.

Tourism promotion is allied with marketing, and uses the quick functional "cultural engineering" perfected in the United States. Heritage, transformed into productive capital, is renovated and the profit used to repay the cost rather than for safeguarding. Tourism therefore ensures renewal.

Goaded by European unification in 1992 and the prospect of additional millions of tourists, France is now turning itself into a vast "theme park." Compared with the new EuroDisneyland near Paris, other cities and villages will appear authentic!

Castles, cathedrals, old villages, prehistoric sites, and public gardens appeal increasingly to the public. The new ecomuseums have also met with great success, as they look to older people to explain the activities and tools displayed. In disused factories, on canal towpaths, or in historic urban areas we might just meet the last person who has the skill for these obsolete phenomena or the last memories of their working past.

RESURRECTION CREATION OUT OF NOTHING

Much time and money is now devoted to the "remaking of memory" (Jeudy 1986) to create new marketable identities. Thus we restore, regenerate, conserve, and preserve works and events as identities for a touristic society. Things long resigned to decrepitude are resuscitated as heritage or "collectibles." The obsolescent and the obsolete once more become profitable. We extract the old from fragments of collective memory or, better still, from rare survivals still found in daily life.

Anything can become a tourist product as long as it can be given value. We invent new deposits to be mined: forgotten folklore, buildings in ruin, the sites of ancient cities. We move monuments from one place to another, change their meanings, and make new springs gush. Thus even the "natural" regional distribution of tourist attractions may become obsolete.

NEW CONSECRATION

MacCannell (1976) first analyzed the process of the transformation of things into tourist products. In order to become an attraction, the phenomenon must be "baptized"; it must be named and become associated with a recognizable sign or "marker" bringing it to the attention of the tourist, guaranteeing its "uniqueness," and making it worth seeing. To display this object, we frame it, elevate it, light it up, mount it like a jewel, and mark it off from ordinary objects. Detached from the ordinary world, it becomes "sacred" within the ritual of tourism. Its old meaning as heritage is stripped, and it is given a new one appropriate to its role within the tourist system. Thus marked, it becomes a signifier of the identity of the society for foreign visitors.

THE NEW SETTING

The requirements of commercialism join with the moral goals of international organizations: to use tourism for the promotion of mutual understanding and to maintain, preserve and respect cultural identities. This accords with modern humanistic ecumenical and universalist ideals whereby each culture is supposed to make a special contribution to "universal culture."

Through the will of these organizations, patrimony and the extant traditions of archaic societies are placed in new relationships and come to constitute a common cultural foundation for all humanity. The chosen markers represent the identity of the place and its rank within the panoply of world heritage. Thus we can see that international tourism acts as a powerful force in the universalization of culture and society.

THE DILEMMA OF TOURISM

The modern concept of tourism as a factor in economic development is pivotal and is the only way to understand the contradiction between the economic and the cultural. Though first aimed at the Developing Nations, this doctrine has recently been adopted by nearly all countries in response to internal challenges.

The key document is Kurt Krapf's paper, presented to the Association Internationale d'Experts Scientifiques du Tourisme (AIEST) in 1961.

TREATED AS AN INFANT

In bringing together developing nations and consumer societies in one global vision, Krapf embraced Rostow's theory of development, by which societies are classified into five stages: (1) traditional; (2) pre-take-off; (3) take-off; (4) push to maturity; and (5) mass consumer.

This theory of economic growth has encouraged rich countries to aid poor ones. It imitates child development theory and, though naive, provides criteria for the distribution of aid according to what economists call "the coefficient of capital."

Using this vocabulary, developing nations are "still in their infancy" and need to be pushed to maturity where citizens are assured a "stable consumption economy." The "immature" countries are labeled by their inability and have to accept the paternalistic aid of scientific experts in tourism.

They are shown that it is "tourism or nothing." But nothing is not just nothing in this case, it is "the image of death appearing on the horizon".

ECONOMIC DEVELOPMENT

Krapf's argument conceals a paradox: "No one needs imagination to know that a developing country presents the characteristics of an economic take-off." In the terms described above countries have attained stage (2) or (3). As for "traditional society," Rostow's first stage, it is, according to Krapf "doomed to disappear." The economists' death sentence provokes us, for they assert that without tourism a society turns its back on development. In this theory, the gap is accentuated between those developing societies veering Towards modernization and isolated traditional societies sliding back into decline.

Yet "traditional society" keeps haunting the imagination. Put aside in the economic order it is stored in the symbolic order, and tomorrow it may reemerge, promoted as a touristic product. Threatened with "imminent death," "traditional society" must be conserved, as a haven of tradition and infancy, in order to sustain the argument for development. Tourism promotion often concentrates on destinations that are virgin, intact, and distant in space.

THE IMAGE OF DEATH

Let us recall some of the debate of the 1960s about the ruinous effects of tourism on culture and environment.

Davydd Greenwood, a U.S. anthropologist studying agriculture in the community of Fuentarrabia in the Spanish Basque country in 1968-69, turned his attention to the Alarde, a lively local festival that drew many tourists. It was a Basque ceremony to celebrate the victory of their ancestors over the French in 1638.

To attract more tourists, the municipality decided to perform the Alarde twice in the same day. The inhabitants not only refused to cooperate with this commercial masquerade but lost their will to participate in the event. For Greenwood "tourism killed the Alarde."

Many similar cases probably exist. Just as the economic benefits emerge, tourism is discredited by the transformation of culture into market value, desecration of ceremonies, debasement of culture and the arts, falsification of traditions, and the loss of identity. The opposition of the economic and the cultural is revealed; here we are faced with the "dilemma of tourism."

In logic, a dilemma is reasoning where the major premise contains an alternative and the minor premises lead to the same conclusion. In practice a dilemma occurs when there are two contradictory possibilities, yet the subject making the choice finds that either way leads to the same consequences.

The discourse of tourism decision making and management is rife with this figure of speech. Actors, whose interests should converge but are in fact opposed, face a dilemma: to develop or contain tourism, to restore culture or celebrate it, leads to the same result. To reject tourism is death, but to accept it is also death.

"The touristic dilemma is clear: to freeze or not to freeze, to maintain boundaries or to remove them...the sword cuts both ways".This double-edged sword underlines the break between tourism as seen by outside agents and by the local society, placing visitors and the visited in a reciprocal extermination.

For a developing nation not to choose tourism amounts to eventual death according to economists, but to choose tourism is also death according to anthropologists. To choose in favour of tourism is the outcome of a double bind, the requirement to make a choice between two impossibilities.

The figure of this dilemma is a leitmotif in the discourse on tourism: "blessing or blight," "trick or treat," "boom or doom," "panacea or a new slave trade," "mirage or strategy for the future." There is always the same disjunction between the economic and the cultural which governs the problematics, be they alternative or dominant. This is still the dilemma which underlies the argument for Alternative Tourism, wherein the word "Alternative" gains its force.

Three Examples

1. The dilemma of tourism pertains to actual situations. The 1989 WTO Seminar on Alternative Tourism in Tamanrasset took place at a symbolically loaded site, which could have been the source of the love of Uranus and Gaia, in the heart of the Sahara Desert. Here at the gates of Ahaggar the difficulties are magnified because of the barrenness of the place. Yet decisions had become urgent; every year the tourists were coming in greater numbers. Algeria, which previously had no tourism policy, had decided on large scale projects, with perhaps 100,000 beds. Ahaggar was targeted as exemplifying the touristic image of the nation.

   But the desert is an extremely fragile environment, with diminishing ancient water sources. Vegetation is sparse but includes unique local species. Garbage is not degradable. The desert people, adapted to the severe environment, have become guides, serving the tourists but anxious about uncontrolled growth. The experts were conscious of the risks and felt the proximity of total destruction. The government was perplexed when some seminar participants prophesied the end Ahaggar within twenty years if mass tourism develops.
2. In Australia's Northern Territory, the management of the National Parks faced another classic dilemma. This is a special case applied to the Aborigines who at the turn of the century were seen as one of the most "primitive" groups on earth. Survivors of these "totemic societies" are scattered throughout the vast territory. The Australian Government has chosen the National Parks of this region as a "pole of growth," a plan also favored by the White residents of Darwin and

the nearby mining camps. The area is highly valued by some for its nature resources and its primitive life. Here we must ask who speaks about the dilemma and whose dilemma it is.

For the Aborigines, the policy gives them the poignant choice of "to be or not to be." Already decimated and chased away by military maneuvers, their numbers are greatly reduced. These lands, ceded to them in the early 1960s, were temporarily retracted by the regional government without extinguishing Aboriginal rights. For the state as well as for the industry, the Aborigines provoke ambivalent attitudes. On the one hand they are inconvenient inhabitants, an obstacle to the development of the parks; on the other, they are a positive presence, certifying the original character of the place and its preservation from the ravages of civilization. From this point of view, Aborigine society is valued precisely because it is near extinction. One can weigh the tensions between international tourism promotion and a "traditional society." It is not just for economic reasons that the Aborigines are valued; they also possess unique skills, especially in hunting and fishing.

Thus we can see the dilemmas of both the parties involved. For the Aborigines to reject tourism is to remain welfare recipients. But to choose tourism and participate in it they would have to learn the industry's skills and become "servants," and thereby be evicted from their welfare status. They might be ready to say, "Anything other than Tourism!" In addition, the state risks making investments from which it would not reap a profit, as the land belongs to the Aborigines who, without spending any capital, might in twenty years become an economic power. Thus each of the participants might be tempted to reject the option of tourism. Do the problematics of the alternative find meaning in this kind of case?

3. The Statement on Responsible Tourism propounded by the 1989 Seminar on Alternative Tourism at Tamanrasset is fraught with paradoxes. It amounts to a paradoxical injunction when it supposes symmetrical behaviour between the partners involved, within the framework of relations defined as complementary. Proponents of Alternative Tourism favour the lodging of tourists in the houses of local people, some of whom respond: "When someone comes to my home because I have invited them, I receive them as a friend. But when they are imposed on me from the outside, they are an occupier!" Yes, tourism produces many situations where the imperative of the double bind traps the recipients of the message of development. To escape, it is not enough to reverse the terms of the alternative; one must break away from the frame of reference.

MISLEADING ARGUMENT

In 1970 the American anthropologist P. F. McKean thought about the possible consequences of mass tourism in Bali, where it had not yet developed. The Indonesian government, following the usual plans of the World Bank, included a focus on tourism in Bali in its first Five Year Plan for Economic Development. The experts invited by the government drew up a Master Plan for Balinese Tourism with a somber prognostication: Bali risked the destruction of its well conserved traditions which would be devastated by the advent of mass tourism; the very attractions of Bali, its artistic creations, were at greatest risk.

To these experts the Balinese were a poor and isolated agricultural population. It was a "traditional society" where temple festivals, shadow puppetry, and sacred dances were integrated with village life. The experts proposed that, for the protection of the Balinese, tourists should be restricted to enclaves on the southern coast, for ordinary seaside tourism.

But the Balinese adopted a contrary policy. They wanted tourists spread throughout the island so that all villages could benefit. They came up with their own idea of "cultural tourism" and wanted to offer the tourists their best. McKean agreed: "Far from destroying, ruining or spoiling the culture of Bali, I am arguing here that the advent and increase of tourists is likely to fortify and foster the arts."

ECONOMIC DEVELOPMENT/CULTURAL INVOLUTION

McKean admits that by opting for cultural tourism as a means to modernization a country consents to transform its culture into a tourist product, its heritage into profit-making capital. Thus such a society undergoes what McKean calls "cultural involution." In such cases, every society must construct its future by clinging to its past. This implies that the society turn back Towards its past in order to construct out of its heritage touristically recognizable symbols of identity. The society has to prove that it is truly unique.

To choose one's heritage as a symbol of identity leads to ambivalence. Should one restore it to the original state in which it was handed down by ancestors? Should one set it apart as an attraction for foreign tourists?

For in this case, its restoration would follow the procedures of cultural engineering rather than of historical methods or subjective memorizing.

Heritage would have to be managed by new criteria in order not only to be profitable but also to be added to the catalogue of world heritage. For this to happen, though, is to pass out of genuine cultural filiation.Here is a potential source of tension.

A CHANGE OF COURSE

Since the 1960s the euphoric promises of tourism — return to nature, the noble savage, the peaceful co-existence of peoples — have been called into question by a long list of acts which have aroused indignation:

- Violent expropriation and occupation of territory, pollution and destruction of forests, landscapes, and coasts;
- Dominating financial interests, provoked bankruptcies, real estate speculation, the puffery of "straw men";
- Tourist ghettos, private squads of armed guards, expulsion of locals and marginals, segregated residential ethnic reserves;
- Violation of sacred places, appropriation of arts and crafts, manipulation of collective memories and heritage;
- Indecent behaviour, organized prostitution of women, adolescents, young children.

These aggressive accusations worry the authorities who try to stifle them, but their numbers continue to mount. The attacks come from many directions: from the tourists who scorn each other, from host populations whose hostility is organized in their own interests, from some sectors of the governments involved, and from experts employed by the World Bank to research the impacts of tourism.

By the 1970s these converging critics could not be avoided, and tourism developers realized that the time for impact evaluations had arrived.

Rising competition, increasing marginal costs, the burden of tourism and the degradation of the environment shook the faith of the tourism experts: "Tourism can destroy tourism; tourism as a user of resources can be a resource destroyer and, through destroying the resources which give rise to it, make resource-based tourism short-lived".

EVOLUTION OF THE OFFICIAL DISCOURSE

Let us examine how experts and international organizations responded to these criticisms, partially explaining the rise of "alternative" solutions, following this evolution through seminars and meetings because there the ghost of the dilemma mentioned above underlies many of the attempted solutions.

Actually, organizations like the World Bank, the World Tourism Organization (WTO), and UNESCO were from the start attentive to the results of their efforts. From Washington to Tamanrasset by way of Manila, one can see the same guiding thread.

In 1976 the joint World Bank-UNESCO seminar on The Social and Cultural Impact of Tourism responded to concerns about the economic functions of tourism in the Third World and their sociocultural effects. This highlighted the double cleavage between the local host societies and the foreign economic powers, and the growing antinomy between the economic and the cultural.

Analyses since that era have worried about surmounting these dilemmas which permeate the social fact of tourism. How can the local and international join together again; how can we surmount the split between the economic and the cultural? These are key questions in the analysis of the problematics of the alternative.The World Tourism Organization World Conference on Tourism held in Manila was a major event in changing directions, as can be seen in both the papers and the recommendations.

The latter contained two convergent themes: (1) an insistence on the perpetual advance of tourism through the growth of "national tourism" in the better-off countries and, in contrast to the earlier WTO focus on "international tourism," the promotion of these "national tourisms"; and (2) raising the awareness of nations and organizations of the spiritual values of tourism.

"Tourism...a vital force for peace...a moral and intellectual basis for mutual understanding and the interdependence of nations...suitable for the foundation of a new economic order which will narrow the gap between the developed countries and the underdeveloped...a means to promote the lessening of international tensions and to develop a spirit of friendly cooperation, with respect for human rights...within the equality of societies and nations.

This was a vast ideological movement Towards a new conception of tourism, surpassing the still important economic factors by linking nations with the noblest aspects of "tourism in the service of humanity" in the social, educational, political and cultural arenas.

The WTO was attempting to reverse the prior order of causality by asserting that tourism is "primarily a cultural phenomenon." This is highly meaningful if we bear in mind that up to this point international tourism was seen as an economic phenomenon and domestic tourism as a cultural problem.

In light of this change of course, the aims of the Seminar on Alternative Tourism organized nine years later by the WTO in Tamanrasset became clearer.

One can thus understand how the evidence of the social and cultural impacts of tourism from the 1976 Washington seminar led the decision makers and government representatives to first take into account the social and cultural dimensions of tourism (Manila) and convincing all the parties concerned — hosts, guests, tourist industry, and governments — to respect the social and cultural resources on which the sustainable development of tourism was seen to rest (Tamanrasset).

Here the organizers managed to use the mobilizing force of this concept to obtain consensus among the various parties present. The assembly, having been captivated by the words Alternative Tourism, finally chose to endorse "responsible tourism."

The problematics of the alternative were founded on the reversal of the terms opposed in the discourse. But to understand this, one must again pass through the labyrinth of economics. This is critical to the continuing research on the break between Alternative Tourism and International Tourism.Since the late 1960s, World Bank experts have been sent to evaluate the effects of the introduction of tourism. At first the evaluations were purely economic — foreign exchange generated, jobs created, changes in the standard of living. But increasingly, sociocultural impacts were included alongside and later came to infiltrate the economic model. To the sociologist this is an interesting epistemological jump.

The question of sociocultural impact opens the economics to social analyses. The economist wants to integrate sociocultural data into his evaluation schemes, and therefore turns to the sociologist or anthropologist. One must understand that the goals of the process are to optimize the aims of tourism development.

Economists want to quantify these elusive sociocultural factors into their cost-benefit analyses. This involves choosing "sociocultural indicators" which are then evaluated dualistically as "positive" or "negative" for the purposes of quantification. Sorting through such analyses of tourism impacts, one generally finds that economic changes are imputed to be positive and sociocultural to be negative, thereby widening the gap between economic and the cultural.

This leads to absurdities, whereby the damage caused by economic activities is balanced by economic benefits! It is as though social costs can be compensated by monetary gains in order to produce a unified cost-benefit analysis. Thus sociocultural effects external to the economic, often judged as negative (*i.e.*, as costs), are, by being neutralized, internalized into the calculations.

This distorts the sociocultural data to accord with the norms of International Tourism, as though admitting that culture, society, and identity are not associated with the context that gave rise to them. This dichotomy is illuminated if we consider that the same economic activity of tourism could be evaluated either as a benefit (+) for the development and preservation it brings or as a cost (-) for the degradation and misappropriation of meanings it entails.

This approach was generally considered an analytical advance, even though it is reductionist in weighing sociocultural data in terms of profit, wherein heritage and everything unique about a society is mummified and exploited as a resource.

The problematics of the alternative stems in part from this operation: the decision maker must catalogue the impacts, clearly defining the positive and the negative, in order to assess tourism. Measures are thus taken which appear to lead to this result, so that one can build a model for "discerning tourism." Even here the method is still contained within the economic framework.

THE PRECONCEPTIONS OF THE IMPACT STUDIES

This question dominates the study of the effects of international tourism and is made real within the system of action where the local society — nation, region, community or ethnic group — is "targeted" by a more powerful external organization. From this point of view the impact is the target! (The word impact comes from the Latin *impingere*, "to hit a target.")

This conceptual scheme is not limited to economics; many other studies tackle tourism as an intrusion or benefit, an external variable on the one side through its side effects on the local society on the other. This type of theory leads to a reductionist concept of the host society:

- It treats the host society as a place without specific sociological and historical characteristics, undifferentiated for the purpose of a foreign rationality.
- In its relations with tourism, "the target" is seen as limited to reacting by submitting to foreign penetration, by resisting conflicts with tourists, or by the kind of violence sometimes reported in the press. As it is opening to International Tourism, a time when tourism breeds dissent in the social order, the host society is seen as deceptively unanimous.

The problematics of the impact and the underlying system of concepts prevent us from thinking about the *processes* by which local societies are integrated into the larger political field.

Such "impact studies," therefore, never understand the nature of the changes in the economic and political systems or in social relations and attitudes brought about by International Tourism policy worldwide.

Tourism management focuses on tourism alone but actually affects the whole society and its social structure, collective memory, and perspectives in an unfolding world.

But a long term change in thinking has recently surfaced. Economists have recognized that the immediate returns from tourism may not do much for the development of the whole region. Methods of measurement and statistical data are viewed with suspicion. Growth models are discredited and the relevance of economics is challenged.

Anthropologists and sociologists are undertaking studies with a radically different awareness. As a result of local field research, in the 1980s there has been a shift from the problematics of the impact to the problematics of the alternative. Is this a real change in the problematics of international tourism?

During the 1970s, planners were forced to see the limitations of their general development model and to take into account the interests of local people. The first reaction was to grant to the host society its own personality, recognizing its viability. One heard more of local dominance, participation and development. Some have called this "the return of the local," not only in scientific research but in conceptions about planning. In a coincidence of concerns, this has become the solution to all ills. From "an area to be promoted in the marketplace," the local society has been granted its own importance, its own potentials, with its own capacity for initiative and decision making.

RETURN TO THE LOCAL/RETURN OF THE LOCAL

The "return *to* the local" as an important factor in planning has been matched by the "return *of* the local" in the form of a network of grass roots movements, much as wished by the ECTWT. The local society is no longer taken as passive but as capable of accepting or rejecting the dominant model or of coming up with its own.

"Local society" is no longer an advertising image aimed at a distant clientele also being manipulated by advertising, but has become one pole at the heart of a system of action in relation to a centre.

The local society is no longer just an end-point in a movement from "above" but a generator of impulses which can climb back up the technological chain and modify the whole. It is no longer merely a reactionary form, but as a force in negotiation, intervention, and creativity is capable of its own initiatives, with all their paradoxes.

Some would redefine tourism from local points of view, surpassing the norms of International Tourism. The idea of tourism is transformed to the point of rejecting the dominant model; according to the proponents of Alternative Tourism, the local people must be helped to take over the tourist operation, rather than just having suitable conditions defined for them. Thus one can no longer judge tourism on the basis of specific "positive" or "negative" effects but must see the phenomenon intertwined as part of a total social fact.

The problematics of the alternative becomes complicated when it tries to rethink tourism or propose new strategies of global development from the local point of view. Is this a reversal of perspective? It is up to the social sciences to examine this turning point and its methodological and epistemological foundations.

We must keep in mind the difference between an "alternative ideology" which rethinks tourism from the local point of view or in terms of local development and the scientific approach which chooses the local society as the point of observation.

The latter is concerned with constructing its object of study from field research using the inductive approach, but its foremost objective is not to increase the standing of the local community as would the Alternative Tourism movement.

It is troubling to observe these efforts to "rehabilitate" the local setting after it has been flattened or evacuated by planning 112 and scientific thinking. In the Alternative Tourism problematic, the tourism production system, which carries on ever upward according to its own logic, seems to have been bypassed. In our opinion, one must work with the assumption that many parallel logics are being pushed without contradicting themselves.

After listening to the different debates and declarations, it seems that what is called Alternative Tourism while claiming to be the "good tourism" has not, in spite of its forceful declared opposition, broken radically with the "other tourism." Alternative Tourism, still included within the promotion and expansion of international tourism, may just be another stage. Doesn't Alternative Tourism still spur the local people to preserve their customs and traditions, and then use them as tourist products to offer on the market?

At Zakopane in August 1989, the members of the Academy considered Alternative Tourism as a means to contribute to the "sustainable development" of a society, whereas by October at the WTO meeting in Tamanrasset, Alternative Tourism had become co-opted as a way to ensure the sustainable development of tourism itself. That should give us something to think about.

13

Tourism and Economy

TOURISM AN INDUSTRY

Tourism industry is the one that deals with the tourists as consumers, the money spent by them, and the resources rendering various goods and services which facilitate the composition of the tourism product. This industry has been named as a 'smokeless industry' because unlike other industries it is invisible and non-polluting. The tourism industry is an extraordinarily complex integration of many industries spread over many sectors.

Tourism is an umbrella industry containing a set of inter-related business participants. For example, industries like Transport, Accommodation, and Travel Companies, Recreation and Entertainment Institutions, Handicrafts business, etc and the provision of the many goods and services demanded by tourists. Interestingly, most of the component industries also get related to varied commercial and non-commercial activities over and above providing their services to the tourists.

Over the years, there has been a growing awareness of tourism as a human activity, an industry, and a catalyst for economic growth and development. Like any other industry the tourism industry draws resources from the economy, adds value and produces marketable products. The only difference here is that no tangible product is produced like in the case of a manufacturing industry. The product in this case is intangible and joint or composite in nature. The tourism industry impacts various auxiliary and ancillary industries as well. Tourism today is undergoing a rapid transformation towards a new industry having far-reaching implications for organizations in the travel and tourism industry in particular, and consequences of import for developing and developed countries in general, growing increasingly dependent on the tourist dollar. The forces driving the change in this industry are many.

In olden times people travelled mainly for commercial and religious reasons and leisure travel was for the rich. Today people travel for a variety of motivations, including business, leisure, religion, culture, visiting friends and relatives, education and health. The means of transportation have become varied and faster and as the transport becomes faster, new travellers emerge and people travel greater distances. Another important force driving the growth within the industry is the growth and expansion of the middle class and an increase in their disposable income. The travel industry is complex in nature and challenging to manage. This is for three main reasons- their process type, cost structure and market features.

In terms of process, most operations are a combination of customer processing operations, material processing operations and information processing operations. There is a mix of cost structures based around provision of service, food, accommodation, sightseeing, airfare etc. Forecasting and packaging are some key market features. Originally segmentation in the industry was based on social class however, currently many factors influence segmentation in the industry.

Now there are products that are specially marketed to specific groups of people or market segments based on lifestyle. Due to segmentation more choice is created for consumers and branding has emerged, major companies are developing brands that are easily recognizable, for example, Thomas Cook holidays, Star Cruises, etc. Tourists are now a sophisticated lot. They are demanding and constantly looking for new variations in the products and newer destinations. In addition, there is growing environmental awareness and travellers are increasingly prepared to shun over-commercialized and polluted destinations for newer and less popular ones. Parallel to all these changes in the market place, there is deregulation of the airline industry, an explosion of technology both for automated reservations and for travel management, and an increasing trend towards concentration of the industry reflected by the large numbers of mergers, takeovers and acquisition of the industry from 'old' to 'new' tourism.

New tourism is a transition from the existing to the tourism of the future typified by:

- Enhanced tourism experiences
- Flexible tourist products
- Management of the tourist industry
- Segmentation
- Thrust towards diagonally integrated organizations and

There are clear and apparent manifestations that the tourist industry is beginning to take on newer dimensions. The emerging new practice is the creation of a number of factors including the system of new information technologies in the tourism industry, deregulation of the airline industry, environmental pressures; technology compensation; changing consumer tastes, leisure time, work patterns and income distribution.

The economics of new tourism is quite different from the old. From system gains, segmented markets, designed and customised holidays the focus now is also on, profitability and competitiveness in tourism. The new tourists show greater care and have a concern for conservation of the natural environment. There has been a shift towards eco tourism, green tourism, rural tourism, farm tourism, sustainable tourism, etc. with perpetual opportunities of benefit from this new tourism. Competitive Strategies for success have to be employed today for survival.

There are new techniques and trends to be followed by the industry players. To gain competitive advantage, the players and participants of the industry will have to

- Be customer friendly,
- Be quality conscious,
- Innovate new and better products,
- Make meaningful value additions.

And for tourist destinations to be competitive, certain key principles need to be incorporated into the policy framework.

Some of these are:

- Be environmentally sensitive,
- Encourage private sector participation,
- Make tourism a leading sector,
- Strengthen the distribution channels in the market place.

Today tourism is sensitive to the environment as well as inhabitants of the region or area, tourism is sustainable, and tourism is capable of transforming tourism-dependent and vulnerable areas' economies into viable entities. Tourism is in a stage of revolutionary change and a new kind of tourism is emerging fast. New tourism promises flexibility, segmentation and diagonal integration. It is driven by information technologies and changing consumer requirements. Today this industry can produce an entire system of value addition and wealth generation.

The objective today is 'tourism should be planned in a manner that it benefits the community as a whole, has benefits for the locals, and optimizes the expectations of the tourists besides taking care of the environment.'

TOURISM IS A GROWTH INDUSTRY

In the 21st century the global economy will be driven by three major service industries–Technology, Telecommuni-cations and Tourism. Travel and tourism will be one of the world's highest growth sectors in the current century. Tourism, just as to experts is expected to capture the global market and become the largest industry in the world. The statistics and projections point to an era of unprecedented growth of tourism around the world. From 70 million international tourist arrivals in the year 1960 the WTO has estimated that international tourism arrivals worldwide would be 1.5 billion by the year 2020. The latest report from the World Travel and Tourism Council "in the year 1999

Travel and Tourism generated about 3.5 trillion US dollars of GDP and almost 200 million jobs across the world economy: approximately.

World travel and tourism GDP is forecast to increase in real terms at 3% per annum in the decade 2000-2010. During the same period employment in travel and tourism is expected to grow at about 2.6% per annum."

World Travel and Tourism Council has summarized some of the highlights concerning worldwide travel and tourism industry as follows:

- The Travel and Tourism Industry contributed 11.7% towards world GDP in 1999;
- Travel and Tourism has emerged strongly from the South- Asian crisis with leisure tourism rising by 4.7% in 1999 and business travel by 4.4%;
- Tourism related spending by international visitors amount to 8% of world exports in 1999 with a further impact by export of Travel and Tourism related goods;
- Travel and Tourism related GDP is forecast to increase at 3% per annum in real terms;
- In the coming years, over 8% of all jobs worldwide will depend upon Travel and Tourism;
- Travel and Tourism will support the creation of over 5.5 million jobs per year over the next decade.

Thus, tourism today is a shining sector and a great economic force. Its status as a major economic activity has been recognized by almost all the nations of the world. During the 1960s there was emphasis on tourism as an earner of foreign exchange, a catalyst of development, and a security against the uncertain fluctuations of commodity prices. Today however, its impact is not only economic but social and cultural as well.

Cultural tourism is a fertile ground for exercising creative talents, fostering special kinds of relations between visitor and the host populations. It enables the tourist to form a view of his present world and a global concept of the historic past. Thus, tourism has wider implications encompassing not only economic benefits but also social and cultural benefits as well.

TOURISM AND DEVELOPMENT

Development can be viewed from various dimensions, however, for the purpose of this current session, we use the following definition of economic development: Economic development is a process of economic transition that involves the structural transformation of an economy and a growth of the real output of an economy over a period of time. It is a long run concept. Structural transformation is achieved through modernization and industrialization and is measured in terms of the relative contribution to gross domestic product of agriculture, industry and service sectors. The potential of tourism to contribute to development is widely recognized in the industrialized countries, with tourism playing an increasingly important role and receiving government support. Tourism along with some other activities like financial services and tele-communications is a major component of economic strategies. Tourism has become a favoured means of addressing the socio- economic problems facing rural areas on one end, while enhancing development of urban areas on the other.

TOURISM AND NATIONAL DEVELOPMENT

Tourism emerged as a global phenomenon in the 1960s and the potential for tourism to generate economic development was widely promoted by national governments. They appreciated that tourism generated foreign exchange earnings, created employment and brought economic benefits to regions with limited options for alternative economic development. National tourism authorities were created to promote tourism and to maximize international arrivals. However, an awareness of the negative environmental, social and some other impacts also increased. The importance of economic benefits at the local level, environmental and social sustainability was also widely accepted. It was observed that tourism presents excellent opportunities for developing entrepreneurship, for staff training and progression and for the development of transferable skills. Tourism development focuses on national and regional master planning. It also focuses on international promotion, attracting inward investment. The primary concern has been with maximizing foreign exchange earnings. These earnings enable the government to finance debt and also to finance some investment in technology and other imports for economic development.

NO TRADE BARRIERS TO TOURISM

Unlike many other forms of international trade, tourism does not suffer from the imposition of trade barriers, such as quotas or tariffs. Mostly, destination countries have free and equal access to the international tourism market. This position has become strengthened by the inclusion of tourism in the General Agreement on Trade in Services, which became operational in January 1995.

REDISTRIBUTION OF WEALTH

Both internationally and domestically, tourism is seen as an effective means of transferring income, wealth and investment from richer, developed countries or regions to less developed, poorer areas. This redistribution occurs as a result of both tourist expenditures in destination areas and also of investment by the richer, tourist generating countries in tourist facilities. Thus it appears as if, the developed countries support the economic growth and development of less developed countries.

TOURISM AND POVERTY REDUCTION

Tourism can contribute to development and the reduction of poverty in a number of ways. Economic benefits are generally the most important element, but there can be social, environmental and cultural benefits and costs as well. Tourism contributes to poverty reduction by providing employment and various livelihood opportunities. This additional income helps the poor by increasing the range of economic opportunities available to them. Tourism also contributes to poverty alleviation through direct taxation of tourism generated income. Taxes can be used to alleviate poverty through education, health and infrastructure development. Some tourism facilities also improve the recreational and leisure opportunities available for the poor themselves at the local level. Tourism is not very different from other productive sectors but it has four potential advantages for pro-poor economic growth:

- It has higher linkage with other local businesses because customers come to the destination;
- It is relatively labour intensive and employs a large proportion of women workers;
- It has high potential in poor countries and areas with few other competitive exports;
- Tourism products can be built on natural resources and culture, which might sometimes be the only assets that people have.

The contribution of tourism to the local economy is also important to note. It has five kinds of positive economic impacts on livelihood, any or all of which can form part of a poverty reduction strategy:

- Collective income which may include profits from a community run enterprise, land rent, dividends from joint ventures. These incomes can provide significant development capital and provide finance for corngrinding mills, a clinic, teachers housing and school books
- Dividends and profits arising from locally owned firms and business units
- Earnings from selling goods and service or casual labour
- Infrastructure gains, for example, roads, water pipes, electricity and communications.
- Wages from formal employment

At this point it must also be mentioned that there are some disadvantages of tourism as well. For example, leakages and volatility of revenue. These are also common to other economic sectors. However, tourism may involve greater trade-offs with local livelihoods through more competition for natural resources, particularly in coastal areas.

STRATEGY FOR DEVELOPING COUNTRIES

Tourism plays a very important role in the economies of many countries.

Earnings from tourism-related activities contribute a considerable portion to their GDPs. Tourism is now being viewed as a significant tool and an important strategy in achieving economic growth in these countries. The WTO is convinced that tourism has considerable potential for growth in many developing countries and Less Developed Countries where it is a significant economic sector and promising high growth rate; and that it has advantages when compared with other economic sectors. This case can be summarized as follows: Comparative Advantages of Tourism as a Development Strategy for Developing Countries.

- Access to international markets is a serious problem for developing countries particularly in traditional sectors like food, agriculture and textiles where they confront tariff and non-tariff barriers. This is not the case for the tourism sector, where barriers would involve visa restrictions and related taxes only. The example of Cuba is instructive in this regard. Whilst Cuba has struggled to find export markets for its sugar and tobacco, it has been much more successful in maintaining a dynamic tourism industry.
- In many developing countries, for example South Africa, China, Philippines and India, domestic tourism is growing rapidly and like international tourism brings relatively wealthy consumers to areas where they constitute an important local market. Domestic tourism can be accessed by people with lower budgets and is often equally valuable to the economy.
- Most export industries depend on financial, productive and human capital. The tourism industry not only depends on these, but also on natural capital and culture, which are sometimes the only assets owned by the poor.
- Tourism has particular potential in many countries with few other competitive exports.
- Tourism is a much more diverse industry than many others and can build upon a wide resource base. This diversity results in wider participation of the informal sector, for example a farming household produces and sells local handicrafts.
- Tourism is consumed at the point of production. This results in great opportunities for individuals and micro-enterprises, in urban or marginal rural areas, to sell additional products or services to the potential consumers.
- Tourism is often reported to be more labour intensive than other productive sectors. Data from six countries with satellite tourism accounts does indicate that it is more labour intensive than Non-agricultural activities, particularly manufacturing, although less labour intensive than agriculture.

- Tourism provides various employment opportunities especially to women as compared to some of the other sectors.

Perceived Disadvantages of Tourism as a Development Strategy:

- Foreign private interests drive tourism and it is difficult to maximize local economic benefits due to the high level of foreign ownership, which means that there are high levels of leakages and few local linkages. But that might not be the case many times.
- Many small enterprises and individual traders sustain themselves around hotels and other tourism facilities and these small companies are not foreign owned. There is often confusion about levels of foreign ownership as local ownership is often masked by franchise agreements and management contracts. WTO is studying this issue in collaboration with UNCTAD as part of its poverty elimination research.
- Tourism can impose substantial non-economic costs on the poor. For example, loss of access to resources, displacement from agricultural land, social and cultural disruption and exploitation.
- Many forms of development bring with them disadvantages that need to be managed. The economic and non-economic negative impact needs to be determined and the issues addressed. It is for this reason that the WTO supports a holistic livelihood approach to assessing the impact of tourism-positive and negative–on the poor. Issues like environmental management and planning at local level need to be addressed through the good governance agenda.
- Tourism is a vulnerable industry. It reacts immediately to factors like changes in economic conditions in the originating markets, levels of economic activity in tourism in the destination markets. Thereby affecting international visitor arrivals. It is also very vulnerable to civil unrest, crime, political instability and natural disasters in destination countries.
- It has been observed that the volatility of export markets for tourism is not significantly greater than other commodities. Many times tourism has the advantage noted that it is not subject to tariff or other non-tariff barriers and that the destination has some control over civil unrest, crime and political instability
- Tourism requires highly sophisticated marketing. International tourism marketing is expensive, although there are more efficient and less costly forms of marketing available today. Many government agencies at the national level, tie ups of domestic hotels and resorts with international participants, word of mouth publicity, target marketing are some of the methods used.

Tourism in many developing countries and many LDCs has been growing strongly in recent years and there are strong reasons to think that these trends will continue. Many developing countries have comparative advantages in tourism where tourism constitutes one of their better opportunities for development.

The disadvantages, which are often identified in relation to international tourism in developing countries, are few when tourism is compared with other sectors of the economy.

WTO believes that tourism is considered alongside other industries as a development option and that where tourism presents the best opportunity for local economic development and antipoverty strategies, development banks, bilateral and multilateral development agencies should back it with determination.

LINKAGES AND LEAKAGES

The term leakage in used to refer to the amount spent on importing goods and services to meet the needs of tourists. Leakages take place across national boundaries that can have impact on the balance of payments of the countries. It results from the economic exchange between the two countries.

It also occurs when the local economy is unable to provide reliable, continuous, supplies on the basis of competitive prices of the required product or service and of a consistent quality to meet the market demand.

From a tourism and poverty perspective it is generally more productive to focus on the other side of the coin-linkages. When the local economic linkages are weak, the revenue received from tourism in the local economic area leaks out.

In order to reduce such leakages, it becomes necessary to deliver consistently at an appropriate quality and at competitive prices, at the same time, engaging the local suppliers who use local capital and resources.

LEAKAGES

From the perspectives of local economic development and poverty reduction, we are not concerned how much a tourist spends outside the country, but how much he is not spending in the local economy, which means, limiting the benefit to local communities and the poor among them.

Leakages, which have negative impact on the development of local tourism, are:

- Advertising and marketing efforts abroad
- Impact skills, expatriate labour
- Imported commodities, goods and services
- Imported technology and capital goods
- Increased oil imports
- Repatriation of profits
- Transporting tourists to the destination country

However developing local sources of supply, encouraging local ownership and enhancing linkages to the local economy can improve this. The last two of these can create more jobs and opportunities for small and medium enterprises at the same time.

LINKAGES

There are many ways in which local communities can be benefitted by these propositions. The best way is to increase the extent of linkages between formal tourism sector and the local economy. By formal tourism sector we mean hotels, restaurants, lodges, and tour and transport agencies. To the extent linkages to the local economy can be increased, the extent of leakages will be reduced.

The increased integration can further develop strong linkages between tourism and other economic sectors. Not only do agriculture, fisheries, manufacturing, construction and domestic industries get integrated, the auxiliary and ancillary industries are also strengthened.

This in turn provides additional revenue and jobs, which reduces the import content and foreign exchange leakages from thc tourism industry. Government and development agencies should create local linkages as part of their overall tourism development strategy in the planning, construction and operational phases.

There are three sets of factors, which are important in enhancing the extent of local linkages:

- The creation of employment at all skill levels and particularly where there is existing capacity.
- The Anti-poverty tourism development strategies have suggested 'new attractions'. The tour operators at the ground level should integrate these. The critical areas include creating mutually beneficial business linkages between the formal and informal sectors. Small and emerging entrepreneurs are often neglected. Local government should ensure that microenterprises and emerging entrepreneurs are promoted while taking local tourism marketing initiatives. Visitor attractions, parks, cultural sites and hotels should be encouraged to provide information about local products and services provided by the poor.
- There is need to understand tourist expectations thoroughly. Also, small enterprises to meet the credit needs and marketing needs are also required. Small enterprises sometimes face difficulties in meeting the requirements of health and safety, licensing and other regulatory requirements. There is a need to systematically educate and train the poor in such a way that they are able to integrate themselves with the growing requirements relating to regulations.

The local market should be geared up to deliver qualitatively reliable and competitive goods and services to tourists. The local business community should be actively involved in the process through partnership approaches. This requires continuous efforts, which is possible through long-term partnership to benefit from linkages. Once planning commission concessions are being granted, private sector companies can be asked to make the development of such linkages part of their bid.

Tourism can help in diversifying other sectors of the local economy and can create new ones, offering additional community livelihood opportunities. Local economic benefits and ownership are likely to be greater, if local communities participate in diversified business activities. Now with the growing awareness governments are adopting policies, to encourage and facilitate participation by the local communities. The participation by the poor in the development of tourism projects may result in increasing employment and growth of complementary products. These benefits can further be maximized through partnerships at the destination level. There is a tremendous possibility of bringing about sustainable development for the local economy if Hotels and tour operators work together with local communities, local government and NGOs.

This can help in reducing poverty and can provide a richer experience to domestic and international tourists. Such partnerships will benefit both the host communities and the tourism industry. This will also help them earn more tourism dollars, euros or pounds without any leakages. This can further be utilized for community development. Through affirmative policies, enterprises can contribute significantly to economic development, in both their constructional and operational phases. Some practical strategies for developing local economic linkages.

Market Access and Enclave Tourism

There is practically no link between local people and tourism market. Tourists are not accessible to the local community when they are within their hotels, coaches, and safari vehicles or inside sites and attractions such as museums. These are all enclave forms of tourism. The local community people who wish to sell their products to tourists don't have access to them. They end up hawking and touting at entry points.

The problem is still more difficult in case of Cruise ship passengers and tourist on "all inclusive" hotel or resort packages where local entrepreneurs hardly interact with them. Access to the market plays major role in involving entrepreneurs in the tourism industry. This is particularly true in the case of the informal sector; where the return on local skills and services is often maximized and where the scale of capital investments is low. There is a need to keep this aspect in mind at the time of tourism planning, as access to tourists for the informal sector is often neglected. Some tourists prefer all-inclusive packages, as they do not always feel safe in a new destination and are happier in a protected environment. They feel protected from the poverty and hassle from beggars, touts and hawkers in some destinations. But there is a way to solvc this problem. This requires partnership approach between Hotel and informal traders.

This allows informal traders to provide such an environment where tourists feel secure in moving beyond the enclave and to approach "hassle-free" crafts markets. Local guides can also help in establishing contact between tourists and traders by rotation for which they may have agreement among themselves.

This also requires observing certain code of conduct by the local traders and guide. There should be a design to link the informal sector with formal sector so that poor members of community can be helped and tourist market becomes accessible to them. This can help them gain the economic benefit from it. There are a number of strategies that can be used to enhance overall economic benefits and can further reduce poverty.

Growth and Selection

Attracting more of the most appropriate market Segments It has been observed that the tourism sector in the poorest countries is generally highly dependent on international markets, as they do not have significant domestic markets. However, it has also been noted earlier that a significant number of developing countries have strong domestic tourism sectors as well as significant outbound tourists. It becomes imperative that the domestic market should always be considered first by the poorest countries, but in order to maximize foreign exchange revenues, the primary focus continues to be on international arrivals.

There is a challenge to attract larger numbers of those international and domestic tourists who are most likely to benefit the poor, those predisposed to visit local markets and to seek first hand experiences of nature, culture and daily life which are most likely to be provided by poor people. It is worth mentioning the importance of intra-regional tourism in this regard; WTO reported intra-regional tourism as growing in most regions of the world. It is significant that 40% of Africa's tourism comes from neighbouring African countries. This opportunity can be grabbed by opening up the roads and improving the modes of transport between countries in Africa, which would greatly enhance the movement of people and contribute in reducing poverty. Intra-regional tourism is especially valuable for pro-poor tourism and local economic development.

This is because of the fact that there is greater likelihood of shared cultural values and familiarity with social systems between the people of neighbouring countries. There is no doubt that there is a case for attracting more visitors in order to increase the economic impact. At the same time we must understand that this strategy will only assist in poverty reduction if the additional tourists can be encouraged to spend in ways that benefit the poor and if it results in overall sustainability.

The World Bank's World Development Report recognized that economic growth does not necessarily result in swift poverty reduction. This requires an explicitly pro-poor strategy. This means that there should be constant growth, which favours poor in a disproportionate way.

Some of the key components of broad-based growth which assist in benefiting the poor include:

- Government commitment and responsiveness to the needs of the poor
- The expansion of employment opportunities for the poor
- Improved productivity for the poor,
- Improved access for the poor to credit, knowledge and infrastructure,
- Investment in the human capital of the poor.

Increasing Tourists' Length of Stay

The economic returns can be increased with the same number of tourist arrivals if efforts can be made to extend their stay for a longer period. This results in the development of the product by increasing the numbers of bed nights and the expenditure of tourists on boarding and lodging.

There will be a poverty reduction impact, if the additional bed nights can create extra employment or create greater opportunities for the poor to sell goods and services to the tourists or to the tourism industry.

Increasing Visitor Expenditure

Now-a-days there is a market trend towards more experiential holidays. Tourists want to learn more about the countries they are visiting: the people, their cultures, traditions, cuisine, etc. It is much more than mere holidaymaking. The trend is towards more active holidays, greater personal involvement and active participation instead of passive relaxation. This again has potential for the diversification and enrichment of the tourism product. There is scope to develop more activities and attractions, with increased demand for interpreters and services of guides and transport necessary for their enjoyment. This increases both expenditure and length of stay. Making more extensive use of natural and cultural heritage, at the same time carefully managing the tourism impacts so as to ensue the conservation of resources, can make an important contribution both to economic development and conservation. This leads to growth in "Special interest tourists" who tend to spend more money on and during their holidays and to stay longer, whether those interests are based on natural, archaeological, historical or cultural heritage, or based on adventure and physical challenge.

Developing Complementary Products

Providing a greater variety and richness of attractions and activities at destination can increase tourists' expenditure. This will increase the propensity of travellers to visit various attractions at the destination and may extend their length of stay and increase their expenditure. This translates into creating more promising opportunities for the development of complementary products that enable the poor to engage in the industry and to profit from it. The growth in established industry results in stimulating interest in the development of complementary products: tourism services and goods.

This complements the core tourism facilities of transport, excursions and accommodation. The list of complementary effects goes on increasing. These complementary tourism products often provide experiences that are not provided by the tour operators but which enrich their product. Hoteliers and tour operators can encourage local people to develop tourism products and services and to support them in doing so with training and marketing. This will increase the attractiveness of the destination and increase tourist expenditure in the local economy and will also develop the complementary products.

Local communities can often engage in the provision of complementary products because it requires less capital investment and is therefore less risky. Tourism is often best considered as an additional diversification option for the poor, rather than a substitute for their core means of livelihood. As an additional source of income it can play an important part in improving living standards and raising people above the poverty threshold. The poor can maximize their returns by choosing forms of participation, which complement their existing livelihood strategies. It also helps them earn from their cultural and social assets.

Tourists are interested in the "everyday lives" of local communities and there are a host of smallenterprise opportunities for local people. Local guides and cyclerickshaw driver/guides in India's Keoladeo National Park, and guides and charter-boat operators in Indonesia's Komodo National Park are examples of local people diversifying their livelihood strategies. The boat operators also earn their living from fishing and many of the cycle-rickshaw drivers work in town when the tourist season is low.

Spreading the Benefits of Tourism Geographically

Tourism destinations are geographically diverse in nature. There are different geographical sites like beaches, mountains and urban attractions and holidaymakers can be encouraged to travel further, beyond established destinations, which can enhance and diversify their experience of particular environmental, cultural or natural heritage attractions. Heritage Trails and other similar products have been developed to extend length of stay and to spread the advantages of tourism development to new areas and communities. They can be used as initiatives, which may benefit the poor. National Parks, cultural sites and World heritage sites are often the major attractions, the primary "tourism magnets" in significant parts of the developing world and they often attract people to marginal rural areas. It can be argued that natural and cultural heritage sites as the major attractions should be taking a wider view of their potential to contribute to tourism development and the well-being of local communities. These areas otherwise are of no interest to tourists.

Changing the way in which tourism is organized in and around attractions can increase the economic development impact. For example, at Kamodo National Park in Indonesia, non-local carriers and package tour operators take away a big slice of tourism trip expenditure, *i.e.*, about 85%, which could have otherwise gone to local economy. Estimates for average local expenditure at Komodo per visitor demonstrate the importance of minimizing enclave tourism.

Cruise ship tourists spent on average US $0, 03 in the local economy, package tourists spent US $52.5 and independent travellers US $97.4. The Parks and other major tourism attractions in rural areas can be developed to assist the development of small-scale, locally owned attractions and tourism services. Nature-based tourism and cultural heritage tourism in rural areas can provide significant local markets and economic development opportunities. It contributes to integrated rural development and offers local employment and supplementary income-generating opportunities for poor people. The development of tourism in such areas can significantly improve incomes for local communities and the poor. For this these flagship attractions can be planned and managed so as to maximize the opportunities for local economic development and poverty reduction.

Infrastructure and Planning Gain

The development of infrastructure and tourism development are interrelated. Tourism can contribute to overall socio-economic development through the provision of roads, telephones, and electricity, piped and treated water supplies, waste disposal and recycling and sewage treatment. Roads developed for tourism provide opportunities for trade and new roads opened to improve trade also bring tourism opportunities if they open access to tourism resources. New economic corridor development projects often create tourism development opportunities for local communities in addition to improving trade linkages.These facilities enhance opportunities for other forms of local economic development, but more could be done at the local and national level to maximize those benefits, particularly when new projects are licensed. It is possible to maximize the planning gains through appropriate policies by government and tourism planners. The right policy in the right direction will encourage local economic development and benefit the poor.

Local Management of Tourism and Partnerships

Local communities and the poor amongst them are more likely to benefit from planning gain where they are involved in discussions and decisions about tourism developments. Benefits can be maximized where the complementarities between different forms of tourism development and their livelihood strategies are given due consideration. Appropriate planning structures can facilitate effective community participation in the tourism development process and provide a mechanism for capturing planning gain through infrastructure, employment and economic linkages. A planning process should define carrying capacity and set limits of acceptable change.

This will influence local communities' active participation in tourism development and help in achieving anti-poverty goals. It is through participation by these local community people whose traditional and local knowledge can be utilized for empowering them. This will also help in maintaining the environmental, social and cultural integrity of destinations.

Small and Medium Enterprises Development

The increased interest in local tourism experience results in increased opportunities for the development of new locally owned enterprises. This helps in providing competitive and complementary goods and services. This trend is found in developed country destinations. This can be supported by government policy and SME development strategies. The tourism industry offers viable opportunities for the development of a wide range of SME's. Even in the developed countries they contribute to the largest part of local tourism supply.

In Europe small and medium-sized firms meet 70% of tourist accommodation demand. Some estimates for the developing world put the comparable figure as high as 85% In well-established developing country destinations, like Goa, increasing numbers of international tourists are staying in locally owned accommodation. SME's are very important in the provision of restaurants and bars, handicrafts, the supply of furnishings and other consumables to hotels, the provision of transport, local tour operating, guiding and attractions. All this requires access to capital resources and training in business management for SME's. This requirement is critical in the field of marketing. Providing information, advice and mentoring to small and micro enterprises and emerging entrepreneurs can make a significant contribution to their success.

Reducing Seasonality

Seasonality in tourist arrivals is the major cause of seasonal and casual unemployment. There are a number of strategies that can be employed to extend the tourism season. During festivals arranging melas generates curiosity and helps the development of special interest products. Other strategies include developing places for seminars and conventions, and such pricing policies, which specially address senior citizens who have more flexibility to travel in the low season.

These strategies have an overall impact on the local economy. Strategies that reduce seasonality and successfully attract tourists in significant numbers for a larger part of the year, benefit the hotels and tour operators, their employees and those in the destination who earn all or part of their livelihood by direct or indirect sales to tourists or the tourism industry. Those who benefit from this are most often poor.

EMPLOYMENT LINKAGES

The employment impact of tourism is felt by both direct employment in tourism enterprises and indirect employment in those enterprises and micro-enterprises that supply raw material, goods and services to the tourism industry. The demand of direct employment in tourism is dependent upon the scale and level of tourism development and the extent of tourists' engagement in the local economy and with SME's. This helps in maximizing the employment of locals and nationals in tourism, including managerial grades.

Income is also held within the local and national economies and reduces wage and salary leakages. When wages and salaries are remitted or spent outside the local boundaries, it amounts to leakages from the local economy. However, the success of the tourism enterprise will depend upon the delivery of the appropriate level of service, and in this global industry maintaining high levels of training is an important consideration in the economic sustainability of businesses. One of the ways in which the industry can contribute to poverty reduction is by committing to recruit more local poor people and imparting appropriate training and staff development programmes with the belief that those commitments can be met. Tourism can contribute to poverty alleviation through the creation of employment. Certain changes in existing employment practices can bring desirable developments. Pro-poor employment strategies can be pursued, for example prioritizing the employment of women and youth. Tourism is a relatively labour intensive industry providing direct employment in hotels and tour companies, and indirect employment in taxis, bars, restaurants and other indirect service suppliers, where a proportion of employee time serves the tourism industry and tourists.

Tourism can create jobs, which benefit the poor where specific measures are taken to recruit and train workers from amongst the poor. Where tourism enterprises make these efforts, proper estimates should be made; records should be maintained of its effects on employment to determine to what extent local people, and particularly the poor, benefit and to ensure that their efforts are acknowledged. Beyond the hotels, particular efforts should be made to train and employ local guides, artists, performers and craft workers who are able to interpret their heritage and in the process empower youth and women who have considerable control over it. Entrepreneurship development programmes for tourism SME's do complement these efforts.

These programmes typically include developing business opportunity awareness, business planning including project feasibility analysis and training in management skills. Provision of business advisors and mentoring services may be strengthened for emerging entrepreneurs over several years. Many countries already have small business development and credit programmes and tourism SME development can sometimes be attached to these existing programmes.

MOVING BEYOND "TRICKLEDOWN" EFFECT

It has long been established that tourism development projects, if successful, would attract foreign investment, contribute foreign exchange earnings to the national accounts and generate economic development. Through the process of trickledown, the magnitude of benefits would be amplified. Local communities would benefit through employment and local economic development generated by the additional spending and the new entrepreneurial opportunities which this would create. It must be understood that tourism operations need to be profitable in a competitive world market if they are to survive. There are a number of things, which can benefit the local economy in tourist destinations.

The benefits can arise in the following ways:

- Building and complementing existing livelihood strategies through employment and small enterprise development
- Controlling negative social impacts
- Ensuring the maintenance of natural and cultural assets
- Evaluating tourism projects for their contribution to local economic development not just for their national revenue generation and the increase in international arrivals
- Facilitating local community access to the tourism market
- Maximizing the linkages into the local economy and minimizing leakages

ECONOMIC IMPACT OF TOURISM

EARNER OF FOREIGN EXCHANGE

Tourism has major economic significance for a country. The receipts from international tourism are a valuable source of earning for all countries, particularly, the developing. Visitor-spending generates income for both public and private sectors, besides affecting wages and employment opportunities.

Although tourism is sensitive to the level of economic activity in the tourist-generating countries, it provides more fixed earnings than primary products. The income from tourism has increased at a higher rate than primary products. The income from tourism has tended to increase at a higher rate than merchandise export in a number of countries especially in countries having a low industrial base. Now there is practically an assured channel for financial flows from the developed countries to the developing countries raising the latter's export earnings and rate of economic growth. Tourism, therefore, provides a very important source of income for a number of countries, both developed and developing. The figures from World Tourism Organization indicate that, among the world's top 40 tourism earners about 18 were developing countries including India, in the year 1995. Regarding the number of visitor arrivals, in some countries there were more visitor arrivals than the population.

France with a population of 57 million received 74.5 million visitors in the year 2000. Similarly Spain with a population of 37 million received 48.5 million visitors during the same year. Several island countries, like the Caribbean Islands, depend greatly on tourist income resulting from visitor arrivals. These earnings form a major part of the gross domestic product. Even developed countries like Canada which derived over 13 per cent of its gross domestic product from international visitors in the year 1999, rely heavily on income from tourism.Tourism forms a very important source of foreign exchange, for several countries. Although the quantum contributed in foreign currency per visitor varies from destination to destination, the importance of receipts from tourism in the balance of payment accounts and of tourist activities in the national revenue has become considerable for a number of countries. The major economic benefit in promoting the tourism industry is in the form of earning foreign exchange.

Income from these foreign-exchange earnings adds to the national income and, as an invisible export, may offset a loss of the visible trading account and be of critical importance in the overall financial reckoning. This is truer in the case of developing countries particularly the small countries, which depend heavily upon primary products such as a few basic cash crops where tourism often offers a more reliable form of income. In the case of some European countries, namely Spain, Portugal, Austria, France and Greece, the invisible earnings from tourism are of a major significance and have a very strong positive effect on the balance of payments. Tourism is therefore a very useful means of earning the much-needed foreign currency.

It is almost without a rival as an earning source for many developed as well as developing countries. These earnings assume a great significance in the balance of payment position of many countries. The balance of payments shows the relationship between a country's total payments to all other countries and its total receipts from them. In other words, it may be defined as a statement of income and expenditure on international account.

Payments and receipts on international account are of three kinds:

- The visible balance of trade relating to the import and export of goods

- Invisible items
- Capital transfers.

The receipts from foreign tourism form an 'invisible export', just like other invisibles which come from transportation and shipping, banking and insurance, income on investments, etc. Because most countries at times have serious problems with their international payments, much attention comes to be focused on tourism because of its potentially important contribution to, and also effect upon, the balance of payments. The receipts from international tourism, however, are not always net. Sometimes expenditures are involved which must be set against them.

Net foreign exchange receipts from tourism are reduced principally by the import cost of goods and services used by visitors, foreign exchange costs of capital investment in tourist amenities and promotion and publicity expenditure abroad. Peters, "Certain imports associated with tourist expenditures must be deduced... the importation of material and equipment for constructing hotels and other amenities, and necessary supplies to run them; foreign currency costs of imports for consumption by international tourists; remittances of interests and profits on overseas investment in tourism enterprises, mainly hotel construction; foreign currency costs of conducting a tourism development programme, including marketing expenditure overseas". Reliance on imports to meet the tourist's needs does not, in any way deny developing countries the opportunity of earning foreign exchange in supplying such goods and services. Imports are, to a large extent, essential to the operation of the tourist sector as to that of other sectors. The important question is whether the value added domestically on an item or service in is maximized? Maximization of import substitution without due regard to the effect on overall tourism receipts may be counter-productive.

Also, differences in the pattern and level of reliance on imported goods and services, capital equipment and manpower are very wide, depending upon the level of development of a country. In some cases, this reliance is simply due to a lack of resources that transform into items which are to be sold by the industry. In others, the industry has not yet drawn on such supply potential, for which it may be an important stimulus. There is a general need for careful programmes of positive import substitution.

MULTIPLIER EFFECT

The discussion in earlier paragraphs clearly indicates that earnings from tourism occupy an important place in the national income of any country. Without taking into account receipts from domestic tourism, international tourism receipts alone contribute to a great extent. The flow of money generated by tourist spending multiplies as it passes through various parts of the economy. In addition to an important source of income, tourism provides a number of other economic benefits, which vary in importance from one country to another; depending upon the nature and scale of tourism. The benefits from infrastructure investments, justified primarily for tourism such as airports, roads, water supply and other public utilities, may be widely shared by the other sectors of the economy.

This enables us to understand how tourism impacts development in the economy. Tourist facilities such as hotels, restaurants, museums, clubs, sports complexes, public transport, and national parks are also used by domestic tourists and visitors, businessmen and residents, but still a significant portion of the costs are sometimes borne by international tourists. Tourists also contribute to tax revenue both directly through sales tax and indirectly through property, profits and income taxes.

Tourism provides employment, develops infrastructural facilities and may also help regional development. Each of these economic aspects can be dealt with separately, but they are all closely related and are many times considered together. Let us first look at the income aspect of tourism. Income from tourism cannot be easily measured with accuracy and precision.

This is because of the multiplier effect. The flow of money generated by tourist spending multiplies as it passes through various parts of the economy through the operation of the multiplier effect. The multiplier is an income concept. The Concept: The 'multiplier' measures the impact of extra expenditure introduced into an economy by a person. It is, therefore, concerned with the marginal rather than average changes.

In the case of tourism, this extra expenditure in a particular area can take the following forms:

- Spending on goods and services by tourists visiting the areas
- Investment of external sources in tourism infrastructure or services;
- Government spending
- Exports of goods stimulated by tourism

The expenditure can be analysed as follows:

- *Direct Expenditure*: In the case of tourism, this expenditure is made by tourists on goods and services in hotels and other supplementary accommodation units, restaurants, other tourist facilities like buses, taxis coaches, railways, domestic airlines, and for tourism-generated exports, or by tourism related investment in the area.
- *Indirect Expenditure*: This covers a sum total of inter-business transactions which result from the direct expenditure, such as purchase of goods by hoteliers from local suppliers and purchases by local suppliers from wholesalers.
- *Included Expenditure*: This is the increased consumer spending resulting from the additional personal income generated by the direct expenditure, *e.g.*, hotel workers using their wages for the purchase

of goods and services. Indirect and induced expenditure together are called secondary expenditure.

There are several different concepts of the multiplier. Most multipliers in common use incorporate the general principle of the Keynesian model.

The four types of multipliers are intrinsically linked as follows:

- *Sales Multiplier*: This measures the extra business turnover created by an extra unit of tourist expenditure. Output Multiplier: This is similar to the sales multiplier but it also takes into account inventory changes, such as the increase in stock levels by hotels, restaurants and shops because of increased trading activity.
- *Income Multiplier*: This measures the income generated by an extra unit of tourist expenditure. The problem arises over the definition of income. Many researchers define income as disposable income accruing to households within the area, which is available to them to spend. However, although salaries paid to overseas residents are often excluded, a proportion of these salaries may be spent in the local area and should therefore be included.

  Income Multipliers can be expressed in two ways:
  - The ratio method which expresses the direct and indirect incomes generated per unit of direct income;
  - Normal method, which expresses total income generated in the study area per unit increase in final demand created within a particular sector.

Ratio multipliers indicate the internal linkages which exist between various sectors of the economy, but do not relate income generated to extra sales. Hence, on their own, ratio multipliers are valueless as a planning tool. Employment Multiplier:

The employment multiplier can be expressed in one of the two ways:

- As a ratio of the combination of direct and secondary employment generated per additional unit of tourist expenditure;
- Direct employment created by tourism per unit of tourist expenditure. Multipliers can be further categorized by the geographical area which is covered by the research, such as local community, a region within a country or the country as a whole.

The multiplier mechanism has also been applied to tourism and, in particular, to tourist expenditure. The nature of the tourism multiplier and its effect may be described in the example: "The money paid by a tourist in paying his hotel bill will be used by the management of the hotel to provide for the costs which the hotel had incurred in meeting the demands of the visitor, *e.g.*, such goods and services as food, drink, furnishing, laundering, electricity, and entertainment. The recipients, in turn, use the money they have thus received to meet their financial commitments and so on. Therefore, tourist expenditure not only supports the tourist industry directly but also helps indirectly to support many other industries which supply goods and services to the tourist industry. In this way money spent by tourists is actually used several times and spreads into various sectors of the economy. In sum, the money paid by the tourist, after a long series of transfers over a given period of time, passes through all sectors of the national economy, stimulating each in turn throughout the process".

On each occasion when the money changes hands, it provides 'new' income and these continuing series of exchanges of the money spent by the tourists form what economists term the multiplier effect. The more often the conversion occurs, the greater its beneficial effect on the economy of the recipient country.

However, this transfer of money is not absolute as there are 'leakages' which occur. Such leakages may occur as a result of importing foreign goods, paying interest on foreign investments, etc.

The following are some examples of such leakages:

- Payment for goods and services produced outside, and imported into, the area;
- remittance of incomes outside the area, for example, by foreign workers;
- indirect and direct taxation where the tax proceeds are not re-spent in the area;
- savings out of income received by workers in the area.

Any leakages of these kinds will reduce the stream of expenditure which, in consequence, will limit and reduce the multiplier effect. Income generated by foreign tourist expenditure in countries possessing more advanced economies, which generally are more self-sufficient and less in need of foreign imports which are less self-sufficient and need to support their tourist industries by substantial import. If the developing countries are desirous of gaining maximum economic benefits from tourism, they should strictly control the imported items for tourist consumption and keep foreign investment expenditure at a reasonable level. If the leakages are not controlled then the benefits arising from tourism will be greatly reduced or even cancelled.

The most important leakage would arise from expenditure on import of agricultural products like food and drink. In a primary macro-economic approach to the prospects opened up by tourism establishment in a developing country, it is regarded as advantageous that a good portion of tourist consumption should consist of food products. It is estimated that the major part of these products can be found in those countries, whose economic structure is largely agricultural in character. In this sense tourist consumption, derived from international flow, can offer an assured outlet to a production which is already active within the domestic economy, without raising problems connected with export of such products and could thus be substituted for imported foodstuffs and a significant saving effected thereafter. The host country derives maximum economic benefits from the tourism industry as these savings help in increasing the benefits from the tourism multiplier. This aspect of the question is all the more important as the multiplier effect maintains its efficacy and effectiveness as long as no importation takes place. It follows that if the national economy is to derive the maximum benefit from the impact of international and national tourism, there is an elementary obligation to find all those products needed for tourist consumption. The dynamics of agricultural production in recent years confirms the ability of developing countries to produce the major part of their agricultural products required for tourist consumption without resorting to massive imports. The tourist economy of any country, if it is to remain healthy, must rely upon local agricultural production and this condition seems today to be on its way to realization in most of the developing countries.

Multiplier of Tourism Income

To sum up, Multipliers are a means of estimating how much extra income is produced in an economy as a result of initial spending or after cash is injected. Every time the money changes hands it provides new income and the continuing series of conversion of money spent by the tourists form the multiplier effect. The more often the conversion occurs, the greater its beneficial effect on the economy of the recipient country.

GROWTH OF INFRASTRUCTURE

A significant benefit of tourism is development and improvement of infrastructure. The benefits from infrastructure investments, justified primarily for tourism–airports, roads, water supply and other public utilities–may be widely shared by the other sectors of the economy. In addition to development of new infrastructure, the improvements in the existing infrastructure which are undertaken in order to attract tourists are also of great importance. These improvements may benefit the resident population by providing them with amenities which they desire. Furthermore, the provision of infrastructure may provide the basis or serve as an encouragement for greater economic diversification. A variety of secondary industries may be promoted which may not directly serve the needs of tourism.

Therefore, it is evident that tourist expenditure is responsible for stimulating other economic activities. One of the characteristics of under development is that of deficiencies in the basic infrastructures, which lie at the root of a series of problems related to the development of tourism. Development of infrastructure requires a certain size of investment. Tourism provides the size of demand which justifies the development of infrastructure. On the basis of this minimum demand for such facilities and for such social capital, the size of such infrastructural services evolves. Construction of primary infrastructures represents the foundation of any future economic growth, even though they are not directly productive. The tourism industry shows the elementary need for basic infrastructure. It has today the important benefit of being able to profit from the existing infrastructures and thus to make a decisive contribution to the growth of the national economy. The international and national tourist traffic, moreover, represents a reward for the capital invested and can now contribute to the financial efforts required for maintenance. The satisfactory degree of development achieved in this specific sector now permits major tourist progress, while also giving further proof of the complementary character of tourism in relation to other economic sectors. Creation of basic infrastructures for tourist usage will also be of service to the other sectors of the economy such as industry and agriculture. This results in better equilibrium of general economic growth.

TOURISM AND TAXATION

Tourism also results in tax revenues both at national and local levels. Taxes can provide the financial resources for the development of infrastructure, enhancing and maintenance of some types of attractions and other public facilities and services, tourism marketing and training required for developing tourism, as well as to help finance poverty alleviation programmes by governments both at local and national levels.

In addition, tourism-related tax revenues help finance general community improvements and services used by all residents. WTO's 1998 report on tourism taxation emphasizes that taxation policies in a country must be carefully evaluated in an integrated manner to ensure that tourism-related taxes are giving the necessary substantial revenues. However, taxes should not be so high for the country's international competitive position to be counter productive and produce a loss of tourist traffic.

The aim should be to strike a balance between, a level of taxation that maintains a competitive position for the country and reasonable profits for the industry, and, receiving adequate revenues to support investment in and maintenance of the tourism sector, and to contribute towards general community welfare.

BALANCED REGIONAL DEVELOPMENT

Another important domestic effect relates to the regional aspects of tourist expenditure. Such expenditure is of special significance in marginal areas, which are relatively isolated, economically underdeveloped, and have unemployment problems. The United Nations Conference on International Travel and Tourism held in Rome in 1963 stated that tourism was important not only as a source of earning foreign exchange, but also as a factor determining the location of industry and in the development of underdeveloped regions. It further stated that in some cases the development of tourism may be the only means of promoting the economic advancement of less-developed areas lacking in other resources. In fact underdeveloped regions of the country usually greatly benefit from tourism development. Many of the economically backward regions contain areas of high scenic beauty and of cultural attractions. These areas, if developed for use by tourists, can bring in a lot of prosperity to the local people.

Tourism development in these regions accordingly becomes a significant factor in redressing regional imbalances in employment and income. Tourist expenditure at a particular tourist area helps the development of the many areas around it.

Many countries both developed as well as developing have realised this aspect of tourism development and are contemplating developing tourist facilities in underdeveloped regions with a view to bringing prosperity there. Khajuraho in India, which is now an internationally famous tourist spot, is an example of one such region. To show, Khajuraho, a remote and unknown small village about forty years ago, is now on the world tourist map which attracts thousands of tourists, both domestic as well as international. Today, Indian Airlines flies a jet plane between the capital city of New Delhi and Khajuraho and seats are not easy to come by.

Thousands of tourists visit the place by air, rail and road transport every month to see the architectural beauty of temples and erotic sculptures whose creators were the Chandela kings, who ruled in North India from the 9th to the 13th centuries.

Today 22 glorious temples remind us of the classic Indian architecture and culture of those times and represent the finest expression of the art of medieval India. The area around Khajuraho is well developed and full of life. The place has provided employment to hundreds of local people in hotels and shops.There is a thriving clay-model industry devoted to making replicas of the famous temple sculptures and a number of shops dealing with items of presentation, handlooms and handicrafts, have created jobs for many. Tourists love to purchase various souvenirs to take home.

Thus local people are recipients of additional income which has increased the prosperity of the region. Subsequently areas around Khajuraho have also prospered and reaped the benefits from the tourist multiplier. There is no dearth of areas which could, after they are developed for tourism, become great assets to the region in particular and to the country as a whole.

The French government has created a series of new resorts particularly to bring prosperity to the areas which traditionally have been underdeveloped. The Italian government is likewise attempting to develop tourism in Southern Italy in order to help redress the economic imbalances which have long existed between the northern and the southern parts of Italy. Tourism is to be regarded not as an area of peripheral investment whose benefits will help in creating employment opportunities and in the regeneration of backward regions. In India a similar approach needs to be adopted to develop areas with great tourism potential.

GENERATION OF EMPLOYMENT

Employment is an important economic effect of tourism. The problems of unemployment and under-employment are more active in the developing countries. Tourism can be looked upon in this light as a major industry which employs manpower on a large scale.

The problems which the industrialized countries face in recruiting manpower for the tourists industry confirm that, in any productive process consisting of services, human labour remains the basic need. If a comparison is to be drawn with the productive sector none of the technological progress achieved has succeeded in rendering the human factor less indispensable than in this sector, and this is true to an absolutely indisputable extent.

The high social impact of the tourist industry is well known, for it has repercussions in every other national economic sector through the multiplier effect, which is particularly marked in those services that are complementary to the tourist accommodation industry. The tourist industry is a highly labour-intensive service industry and hence is a valuable source of employment. It employs a large number of people and provides a wide range of jobs which extend from the unskilled to the highly specialized. In addition to those involved in management there are a large number of specialist personnel required to work as accountants, housekeepers, waiters, cooks and entertainers, who in turn need a large number of semi-skilled workers such as porters, chambermaids, kitchen staff, gardeners, etc. Tourism is also responsible for creating employment outside the industry in its more narrowly defined sense and in this respect those who supply goods and services to those directly involved in tourism are beneficiaries from tourism.

Such indirect employment includes, those involved in the furnishing and equipment industries, souvenir industries and farming and food supply. Construction industry is another very big source of employment. The basic infrastructures-roads, airports, water supply and other public utilities and also construction of hotels and other accommodation units create jobs for thousands of workers, both unskilled and skilled. In many of the developing countries, where chronic unemployment often exists, the promotion of tourism can be a great encouragement to economic development and, especially, employment.

However at this point it is, necessary to consider the seasonal nature of the tourism industry. Where general diversification alternatives are scarce, a combination of heavy dependence on tourism and highly marked seasonality calls for measures to develop off -season traffic. Employment multiplier: This multiplier is similar to the Income Multiplier except that in this case a multiplier impact on employment is observed.

Employment Multiplier can be expressed in the following two ways:

- As a ratio of the combination of direct employment. At the destination, the jobs are directly created in the industry there.

- As a ratio of secondary employment generated per additional unit of tourist expenditure to direct employment. The workers and their families require their own goods and services giving rise to further indirectly created employment in shops, schools, health care institutions, etc.

OTHER DIMENSIONS

The World Tourism conference which was held at Manila, Philippines in October 1980, considered the nature of tourism phenomenon in all its aspects. The role tourism is bound to play in a dynamic and vastly changing world was also identified. Convened by the World Tourism Organization the conference also considered the responsibility of various states for the development and enhancement as more than a purely economic activity of nations and peoples.

The significance of tourism was discussed in during the conference. The participants in the World Tourism Conference attached particular importance to its effects on the developing countries. It stated its conviction "that the world tourism can contribute to the establishment of a new international economic order that will help to eliminate the widening economic gap between developed and developing countries and ensure the steady acceleration of economic and social development and progress in particular of the developing countries."

14

Airport Handling and Ticketing

AIRLINE TICKET

An airline ticket is a document, issued by an airline or a travel agency, to confirm that an individual has purchased a seat on a flight on an aircraft. This document is then used to obtain a boarding pass, at the airport. Then with the boarding pass and the attached ticket, the passenger is allowed to board the aircraft.

There are two sorts of airline tickets - the older style with coupons now referred to as a paper ticket, and the now more common electronic ticket usually referred to as an e-ticket. Regardless of the type, all tickets contain details of the following information...

- "Form of payment" *i.e.*, details of how the ticket was paid for, which will in turn affect how it would be refunded.
- A ticket number, including the airline's 3 digit code at the start of the number.
- Baggage allowance.
- Dates that the ticket is valid for.
- Flights that the ticket is valid for. (Unless the ticket is "open")
- Restrictions on changes and refunds.
- Taxes. (It is normally a legal requirement to show taxes, even if the fare is not shown).
- The "Fare Basis", an alpha-numeric code that identifies the fare.
- The cities the ticket is valid for travel between.
- The issuing airline.
- The passenger's name.

It is now common for a traveller to pay a fee, assessed by the airline company, for a paper ticket. In fact, many airlines no longer issue paper tickets. IATA has announced, that as of June 1, 2008, IATA-member airlines will no longer issue any paper tickets. A ticket is generally only good on the airline for which it was purchased. However, an airline can endorse the ticket, so that it may be accepted by other airlines, sometimes on standby basis or with a confirmed seat. Usually the ticket is for a specific flight. It is also possible to purchase an 'open' ticket, which allows travel on any flight between the destinations listed on the ticket. The cost for doing this is greater than a ticket for a specific flight. Some tickets are refundable.

However, the lower cost tickets are usually not refundable and may carry many additional restrictions. A ticket is made up of one or more flight coupons. In the old paper ticket system, these flight coupons were the actual tickets that were used for travel. One flight coupon was used for each leg of the flight. The carrier is represented by a standardized 2-letter code. Thai Airways is TG. The departure and destination cities are represented by International Air Transport Association airport codes. Munich is MUC and Bangkok is BKK. The International Air Transport Association is the standard setting organization.

Only one person can use a ticket. If multiple people are traveling together, the tickets are linked together by the same record locator or reservation number, which are assigned, if the tickets were purchased at the same time. If not, most airlines can connect the tickets together in their reservation systems. This allows all members in a party to be processed in a group, allowing seat assignments to be together (if available at the time of the assignment) When paper tickets were still frequently used, a practice existed by travellers to get rid of their tickets (which are person-specific), when they decided to alter the course of their trips. This practice consisted of selling the ticket to other travellers (often at discount prices), after which the seller accompanied the buyer at the time of departure to the airport. Here, the original owner checked in under his name and provided the airline with the buyer's baggage. After this, the buyer boarded the airplane at the moment of departure. However, since most airlines check identification on boarding, this procedure is rarely functional.

AIRLINE TIMETABLE

Airline timetables are booklets that many airlines worldwide use to inform passengers of several different things, such as schedules, fleet, security, in-flight entertainment, food menu, restriction and phone contact information. Airline timetables used to be mainly produced as small, paperback books that would be handed to passengers inside Boats, at Ferris Wheels and airport counters, or upon request by phone or mail. On January 16, 1928, Pan Am published one of their first books.

It read The air-way to Havana, Pan American Airways, Pershing Square Building, New York. Airline timetable books are famous for their diversity: Many had colourful covers, such as the ones produced by many Latin American airlines. Others, such as Scenic Airlines' timetables, consisted only of one sheet of paper, with their hub's flight time information on the front, and the return times on the back. After the September 11, 2001 bombings, most airlines worldwide have stopped production of timetable books, in order to cut costs and reduce the delay between a change of schedule and a new timetable being in the hands of the public.As a consequence, most airlines now post their timetables only online (the larger airlines often offering a stand-alone application, while others provide just a downloadable document such as a PDF), and the value of many airline timetable books has risen among collectors.

BEREAVEMENT FLIGHT

A bereavement flight is an airline ticket purchased when a close relative has died or is dying. Bereavement fares are offered by many airlines. While a bereavement flight may have flexible rules, it may be at either a reduced or a higher cost to the consumer, depending on the airline . While airlines often charge much more for a flight that is booked less than 7 days beforehand than one that is booked farther in advance, customers may be able to obtain a bereavement fare in such last-minute flights that is comparable to that of a regular fare purchased far in advance . In recent years, many airlines have been cutting back on bereavement fares or changing fare structures to accommodate them in other ways . In 2004, U.S. Congress approved language that required airlines to offer bereavement fares .

Policies of various airlines

Airlines have varying policies pertaining to bereavement flights. This may include the relatives for which one is eligible to obtain such a ticket, the proof that is required, and the price that is charged in comparison with other fares . The most common discount is 50% off the original fare .

- Air Canada offers bereavement fares within 7 days of a funeral and for stays of up to 30 days with a copy of a death certificate, a letter from a funeral director, or a certificate from an attending physician. The airline will also refund the difference between the regular and the bereavement fare if one is these is presented after travel .
- AirTran, JetBlue, Southwest, and Virgin America do not offer bereavement fares, but have more flexible options for changing and canceling tickets .
- Continental Airlines offers varying percentages off fares of different prices, and allows such bookings to be made on its Web site .
- Delta Airlines allows discounts for death or imminent death for those who call in advance for reservations .
- United Airlines offers bereavement fares of 10% off the ticket price in the event of the death or grave illness of a family member or for individuals seeking medical treatment for tickets sold within six days of travel .

Other issues

Various other issues have been applied to bereavement flights. One concerns which family members to whom the fare can be applied. Some airlines offer the fares only for immediate family members.Others offer it to a longer list, including foster relatives, half relatives, and step relatives. Other airlines have taken up the issue over whether those involved in domestic partnerships that are not legal marriages, and those involved in gay and lesbian relationships can be included . It has also been questioned as to whether the bereavement fares are really the best on the market .

Other ways around bereavement fares

For frequent travellers anticipating a potential family emergency, it may be wise to accumulate a certain balance of frequent flyer miles with an airline. For example, if a person in the US is aware of a potential death in the family in Shanghai, the traveller can save up some miles to redeem a last minute trip with their miles instead of paying bereavement fares. Most carriers offer mileage award tickets with last seat availability (usually at 2x the usual cost), which can still be a great value financially.

BOARDING PASS

A boarding pass is a document provided by an airline during check-in, giving a passenger the authority to board an aircraft. As a minimum, it identifies the passenger, the flight number, and the date and scheduled time for departure. In some cases, flyers can check in "on-line" and print the boarding passes themselves. Generally a passenger with an electronic ticket will only need a boarding pass.

If a passenger has a paper airline ticket, that ticket (or flight coupon) may be required to be attached to the boarding pass for him or her to board the aircraft. The paper boarding pass (and ticket, if any), or portions, are sometimes collected and counted for cross-check of passenger counts by gate agents, but more frequently are scanned (via barcode or magnetic stripe). The standards for bar codes and magnetic stripes on boarding passes are published by IATA. The bar code standard (BCBP) defines the 2D bar code printed on paper boarding passes or sent to mobile phones for electronic boarding passes. The magnetic stripe standard (ATB2) will expire in 2010. For "connecting flights" there will be a boarding pass needed for each new flight (distinguished by a different flight number) regardless of whether a different aircraft is boarded. Most airports and airlines have automatic readers that will verify the validity of the boarding pass at the jetway door or boarding gate.

This also automatically updates the airline's database that shows the passenger has boarded and the seat is used, and that the checked baggage for that passenger may stay aboard. This speeds up the paperwork process at the gate, but requires passengers with paper tickets to check in, surrender the ticket and receive the digitized boarding pass. Many airlines have moved to issuing electronic boarding passes, whereby the passenger checks in either online or on a mobile device, and the boarding pass is then sent to the mobile device as a SMS or e-mail; airlines that issue electronic boarding passes include United Airlines, AirAsia (The first airline to introduce SMS boarding passes), Singapore Airlines, Air Canada, WestJet (the first in North America to do so), Cathay Pacific Airways, Delta Airlines, JetBlue Airways, American Airlines, Lufthansa, Scandinavian Airlines, Jetstar Airways, Iberia and KLM (selected destinations only).

CODESHARE AGREEMENT

A codeshare agreement, sometimes simply codeshare, is an aviation business arrangement where two airlines share the same flight. A seat can be purchased on one airline but is actually operated by a cooperating airline under a different flight number or code. The term "code" refers to the identifier used in flight schedule, generally the 2-character IATA airline designator code and flight number. Thus, XX123, flight 123 operated by the airline XX, might also be sold by airline YY as YY456 and by ZZ as ZZ9876. It allows greater access to cities through a given airline's network without having to offer extra flights, and makes connections simpler by allowing single bookings across multiple planes. Most major airlines today have code sharing partnerships with other airlines and code sharing is a key feature of the major airline alliances.

Under a code sharing agreement, the airline that actually operates the flight (the one providing the plane, the crew and the ground handling services) is called the operating carrier. The company or companies that sell tickets for that flight but do not actually operate it are called marketing carriers or validating carriers. In 1967, Richard A. Henson joined with US Airways predecessor, Allegheny Airlines, in the nation's first codeshare relationship.

The term "code sharing" or "codeshare" was coined in 1989 by Qantas Airways and American Airlines (Financial Review—November 21, 1989), and 1990 the two firms provided their first codeshare flights between an array of U.S. domestic cities and Australian cities. Code sharing has become widespread in the airline industry since that time, particularly in the wake of the formation of large airline 'alliances.' These alliances have extensive codesharing and networked frequent flyer programmes. Under a code sharing agreement, participating airlines can present a common flight number for several reasons, including:

For passengers:

- Connecting flights – This provides clearer routing for the customer, allowing a customer to book travel from point A to C through point B under one carrier's code, instead of a customer booking from point A to B under one code, and from point B to C under another code. This is not only a superficial addition as cooperating airlines also strive to synchronize their schedules and coordinate luggage handling, which makes transfers between connecting flights less time-consuming.

- Shared responsibility between the carriers – When flying between two cities without a single-airline connection, the passenger can pick a codeshared flight over two airlines or two flights booked separately. If the flights are not codeshared, then the second airline has no responsibility if the passenger or luggage misses the second flight due to a delay with the first. Under a codeshared flight, the second airline is unlikely to charge extra fees or deny boarding should the first, cooperating airline cause a delay.

For airlines:

- Flights from both airlines that fly the same route – This provides an apparent increase in the frequency of service on the route by one airline
- Perceived service to unserved markets – This provides a method for carriers who do not operate their own aircraft on a given route to gain exposure in the market through display of their flight numbers.
- When an airline sacrifices its capacity to other airlines as a code share partner, its operational cost will generally be reduced to nil.

In Global Distribution Systems, such as Amadeus, Galileo, Worldspan, or Sabre, this results in the same flight details, except for the flight number, being excessively displayed on computer screens, forcing other airlines flights to be displayed where they may be missed by passengers searching for required flights. Much competition in the airline industry revolves around ticket sales (also known as "seat booking") strategies (revenue management, variable pricing, and geo-marketing). Most passengers and travel agents have a preference for flights that provide a direct connection. Code sharing achieves this.

Computer reservations systems (CRS) also often do not discriminate between direct flights and code sharing flights and present both before options that involve several isolated stretches run by different companies. Criticism has been levelled against code sharing by consumer organizations and national departments of trade since it is claimed it is confusing and not transparent to passengers. There are also code sharing agreements between airlines and rail lines also known as Rail and Fly systems. They involve some integration of both types of transport, *e.g.*, in finding out the fastest connection, allowing exchange between an air ticket and a train ticket, or a step further, the air ticket being valid on the train, etc. In Europe these Rail and Fly systems are used to divide markets by selling these combination tickets abroad for a lower price to attract more customers. The systems also prevent local customers from buying these much cheaper tickets as the customer is only allowed to board the plane with a valid train stamp from a station outside the country.

CONTINENT PASS

A continent pass (usually called something like Europe (air)pass, Pacific (air)pass or American (air)pass) is a product and service of an airline alliance. For a relatively low price the traveller can travel freely using all (intra)continental flights the airline alliance offers on that continent. There are restrictions on the number of miles and/or the number of flights as well as the number of stops the traveller can make. Travellers can benefit from the extensive networks airline alliances offer and can be rewarded for each mile they fly by participating in the alliance's frequent flyer programme.

ELECTRONIC TICKET

An electronic ticket or e-ticket is used to represent the purchase of a seat on a passenger airline, usually through a Web site or by telephone, or sometimes through airline ticket offices or travel agencies. This form of airline ticket rapidly replaced the older multi-layered paper tickets (from close to zero to 100% in about 10 years) and became mandatory for IATA members as from June 1, 2008. During the last few years, where paper tickets were still available, airlines frequently charged extra for issuing them. E-tickets are also available for some entertainment venues.

Once a reservation is made, an e-ticket exists only as a digital record in the airline computers. Customers usually print out a copy of their receipt which contains the record locator or reservation number and the e-ticket number. Joel R. Goheen is recognized as the Inventor of Electronic Ticketing in the Airline Industry, an industry where global electronic ticket sales (the industry standard) accounts for over US$400 billion a year (2007). Electronic tickets have been introduced in road, urban or rail public transport as well.

Checking in with an e-ticket

To check in with an e-ticket, the passenger usually goes to the check-in counter and presents the e-ticket itinerary receipt which contains a confirmation or reservation code. In some airports and airlines it is not even necessary to present this document or quote the confirmation code or e-ticket number as the reservation is confirmed solely on the basis of the passenger's identity, which may be proven by a passport or the matching credit card.

The rest of the check-in process remains the same as when paper tickets were the norm, that is, the passenger checks-in his/her luggage. The e-ticket is not a substitute for the boarding pass which must still be issued at the end of the check-in process.

Self-service and Remote Check-in

E-tickets are very popular because they allow extra services like:

- Online access to a passenger's reservation which makes amendments

to flight plans (such as change of flight date and refunds) possible (subject to ticket restrictions)
- Online/telephone/self-service kiosk check-in (if the airline makes this option available)
- Early check-in
- Printing boarding passes at airport kiosks and at locations other than an airport

It is also possible to have many copies of an e-ticket, hence the "loss" of an airline ticket becomes impossible. Several web sites exist to help people holding e-tickets accomplish online check-ins in advance of the twenty-four-hour airline restriction. These sites store a passenger's flight information and then when the airline opens up for online check-in the data is transferred to the airline and the boarding pass is e-mailed back to the customer.

E-ticket limitations

E-tickets are sometimes not available for some flights from an airline which usually offers them. This can be due to a number of reasons, the most common being software incompatibility. If an airline issues tickets for a codeshare flight with another company, and there is no e-ticket interlining agreement, the operating carrier would not be able to see the issuing carrier's ticket.

Therefore, the carrier that books the flight needs to provide hard copy versions of the tickets so that the ticket can be processed. Similarly, if the destination airport does not have access to the airline who booked the flight, a paper ticket needs to be issued. Currently the ticketing systems of most airlines are only able to produce e-tickets for itineraries of no more than 16 segments, including surface segments.

IATA mandated transition

As part of the IATA Simplifying the Business initiative, the association instituted a programme to switch the industry to 100% electronic ticketing. The programme concluded on June 1, 2008, with the association saying that the resulting industry savings were approximately US$3 billion. In 2004, IATA Board of Governors set the end of 2007 as the deadline for airlines to make the transition to 100% electronic ticketing for tickets processed through the IATA billing and settlement plan; in June 2007, the deadline was extended to May 31, 2008.

As of June 1, 2008 paper tickets can no longer be issued on neutral stock by agencies reporting to their local BSP. Agents reporting to the ARC using company-provided stock or issuing tickets on behalf of an airline (GSAs and ticketing offices) are not subject to that restriction. The industry was unable to comply with the IATA mandate and paper tickets remain in circulation as of February 2009.

FLIGHT CANCELLATION

Flight cancellation occurs when an airline cancels a scheduled flight for a certain reason. When flights are canceled, passengers may be entitled to compensation due to rules obeyed by every flight company, usually Rule 240, or Rule 218 in certain locations. This rule usually specifies that passengers may be entitled to certain reimbursements, including a free room if the next flight is the day after the canceled one, a choice of reimbursement, rerouting, phone calls, and refreshments.

FREQUENT-FLYER PROGRAMME

A frequent flyer programme (FFP) is a loyalty programme offered by many airlines. Typically, airline customers enrolled in the programme accumulate frequent flyer miles (kilometers, points, segments) corresponding to the distance flown on that airline or its partners.

There are other ways to accumulate miles. In recent years, more miles were awarded for using co-branded credit and debit cards than for air travel. Acquired miles can be redeemed for free air travel; for other goods or services; or for increased benefits, such as travel class upgrades, airport lounge access or priority bookings.

The first modern frequent flyer programme was created at Texas International Airlines in 1979. But lacking the computer resources of its larger competitors, TI was overtaken by American's introduction of AAdvantage in May 1981. During the early days, several other carriers experimented with reward programmes, including Braniff International and Continental (OnePass). American's programme was a modification of a never-realised concept from 1979 that would have given special fares to frequent customers. It was quickly followed later that year by programmes from United (Mileage Plus) and Delta (SkyMiles), and in 1982 from British Airways (Executive Club).

Since then, frequent-flyer programmes have grown enormously. As of January 2005, a total of 14 trillion frequent-flyer miles had been accumulated by people worldwide, which corresponds to a total value of 700 billion US dollars. The primary method of obtaining points in a frequent flyer programme until recent years was to fly with the associated airline. Most systems reward travellers with a specific number of points based on the distance traveled (such as 1 point per mile flown), although systems vary. Many discount airlines, rather than awarding points per mile, award points for flight segments in lieu of distance. In Europe, for example, a number of airlines offer a fixed number of points for domestic or intra-European flights regardless of the distance (but varying just as to class of travel).

With the introduction of airline alliances and code-share flights, frequent flyer programmes are often extended to allow benefits to be used across partner airlines. The calculation method can become complicated, with additional points awarded as a 'cabin bonus' (usually as a percentage multiplier over the standard economy-class milage) for flying first or business class, and often fewer points given when flying on discounted economy tickets.

Additional bonus points are sometimes granted after members reach specific levels of flying activity. Programmes differ on the expiration of points. Some expire after a fixed time, and others expire if the account is inactive for an extended period (for example, three years). Many programmes also allow points to be obtained not only by flying but by favouring airline 'partners' on the ground. This an include staying at participating hotels, or renting a vehicle from a participating company. or shopping at a particular department store. Other methods include credit and debit cards that offer points for charges made to the card, and systems which allow earn miles by eating at participating restaurants and charging the meals to registered cards.

Using credit and debit cards to earn points, as well as taking advantage of special promotional offers, can allow some people to earn an exceptionally high frequent flyer points with relatively minimal outlay. Many frequent flyer programmes identify travellers who fly more than a few times per year by awarding them different status levels, which in turn give a number of benefits. Status levels vary from scheme to scheme, but benefits can include:

- Ability to grant status to another person
- Access to business and first class lounges with an economy ticket
- Access to other airlines' lounges
- Eliminating of program's miles expiration rules
- Free or discounted upgrades to a higher travel class
- Increased mileage accumulation (such as doubling or tripling)
- Preference in not being bumped if a flight is oversold
- Priority in waitlisting or flying standby
- Priority of luggage (to be prioritized on transfer and to be displayed on the belt first)
- Reserving an unoccupied adjacent seat
- The ability to reserve specific seats, such as exit row seats with more leg room
- Waived or reduced fees (*e.g.* baggage fees, service charges)

Some programmes even permit elite members to reserve space on sold-out flights, giving members the ability of bumping regular passengers. In the US, member status is based on elite qualifying miles (EQM) or number of flight segments, not redeemable miles. Typically one elite qualifying mile is earned for each mile flown on a paid ticket, although there may be a percentage bonus for flying full-fare economy, business, or first class. In addition, the airline may offer opportunities to earn elite qualifying miles in non-flying ways, often in connection with their branded credit card. There are usually many more ways to earn redeemable miles (which can be used for free tickets and other benefits) without flying than ways to earn elite qualifying miles. Some airlines will recognise a customer's status with a competing airline, and grant them the same benefits. Some airlines offer accelerated admission to their elite programmes through special promotions, such as flying 10,000 miles (16,000 km) of non-discounted coach fares or 20,000 miles (32,000 km) of discounted fares within three months gains a higher tier membership normally reserved for passengers flying 50,000 miles per year.

Travellers frequently debate how much accumulated miles are worth, something which is highly variable based on how they are redeemed. A typical ballpark figure is approximately 2 cents per mile based on discount (rather than full fare) economy class travel costs. However, most airlines have stringent capacity constraints on the number of "award" seats available, so some people argue that this ballpark figure is an overstatement.

In this case, the value of a mile drops below a cent per mile. The airlines themselves value miles in their financial statements at less than one one-thousandth of a cent per mile. In contrast, calculating the value of a mile based on full-fare business class travel costs can yield a figure several times higher, but only if the customer would personally be willing to pay the multiple thousands of dollars such tickets would cost otherwise.

However, a person paying a full business fare will be able to change flights on short notice without extra cost; a person flying business class on a free award ticket may find that last minute changes result in no award seat availability with the result that a ticket must be bought. Increasing limitations on the availability of seats for point redemption, increases in services fees that airlines charge for redemption, and limitations on the transferability of redeemed tickets together have caused the value of miles to customers to decrease with time .

Air New Zealand found a unique solution to this problem, by pegging their Airpoints scheme so one point (an "Airpoints Dollar") has the same value as one New Zealand dollar when purchasing. This approach has also been adopted by Canada's WestJet Airlines. In the wake of the September 11 attacks, some airlines have faced financial difficulties, raising concerns among frequent flyers that their points could be lost or devalued.

All airlines include provisos in their programme agreements reserving the right to modify or eliminate them on relatively short notice. But since miles are a strong customer incentive, troubled airlines avoid their elimination in bankruptcy proceedings, and indeed may expand them or make them more generous to elite members and high fare passengers in order to win sales. Furthermore, since most airline miles are never claimed, the programmes represent a relatively small liability, and indeed can represent a profit center . Since the 1990s, U.S. airlines have sold billions of miles to partners such as credit cards, hotel chains, and car rental agencies, who offer this "currency" as an incentive to purchase their own services.

Any effort to curtail the awarding of miles would thus endanger partner relations and another revenue stream. Notably, the banks backing several airline-branded credit cards have been a key source of airline financing, including United Airlines (Chase), US Airways (Barclays), Delta Air Lines (American Express), Northwest Airlines (US Bank), American Airlines (Citibank), Continental Airlines (Chase) and Copa Airlines (Visa).

Historically, the record is mixed. U.S. airlines have usually honoured miles held in the accounts of acquired airlines. For instance American Airlines converted members of TWA's "Aviators" programme to its own, as did Air Canada for Canadian Airlines' "Canadian Plus" programme members. Sometimes, miles were honoured by a close partner; Continental Airlines assumed Eastern Air Lines' programme when it failed, as did Delta of Pan Am's.

Bankrupt Swissair miles were transferred to Swiss International Air Lines TravelClub who were transferred to Lufthansa's Miles and More after the acquisition of the Swiss carrier. Members are at greatest risk of losing their miles when an airline liquidates. All miles and privileges were lost, without recognition from any other carrier, as in the cases of Midway, Braniff, and Ansett Australia.

Business travellers typically accrue the valuable points in their own names, rather than the names of the companies that paid for the travel. This has raised concerns that the company is providing a tax-free benefit (point-based awards) to employees, or that employees have misappropriated value that belongs to the company, or even that the programme acts as a kind of bribe. The U.S. Internal Revenue Service has not as yet made any move to tax mileage programmes, though for instance the Canadian taxation authorities consider mileage redeemed for free travel to be a taxable benefit. Most companies consider the miles earned by their employees to be a valuable personal perk that in part compensates for the daily grind of frequent business travel, though some governmental organizations have attempted to prevent their employees from accumulating miles on official travel. For example, Australian Public Servants are not permitted to redeem points accrued from official travel. Some programmes allow donating frequent flyer miles to certain charities.

While the Canadian government will honour these donations as a charitable gift, the difficulty here is getting a tax receipt for those points from the company itself. This policy also appears to conflict with the position that reward points are taxable in the first place. On the airline side, the points represent potential non-revenue travellers on its books. These must be carried forward on balance sheets as an outstanding contractual debt for an indeterminate time, although the actual value (or loss) may be difficult to determine for any particular period.

Africa:

- Air Algérie Plus — Miles expire after 24 months of inactivity
- Air Seychelles — All points acquired will have a 2 year validity period

- Ethiopian Airlines Sheba Miles
- Royal Air Maroc Safar Flyer — Miles expire 3 years after earning
- South African Airways Voyager — Miles expire after 36 months of inactivity

Asia:

- Air China Phoenix - Miles expire 2 complete calendar years after they are earned.
- All Nippon Airways ANA Mileage Club - Miles expire 36 months after they are earned, except for ANA Mileage Club Diamond elite members.
- Asiana Club - Expiry dates vary upon level of membership. Silver and Magic level members' miles expire after five years, Gold and higher level members' miles expire after seven. Corporate members have only one year to claim mileage. Miles earned before 30 September 2008 will never expire.
- Bangkok Airways Flyer Bonus - Miles expire 36 months after they are earned.
- Cathay Pacific/DragonAir Asia Miles expire 36 months after they are earned.
- EVA Air Evergreen Club - Miles expire 36 months after being earned.
- Garuda Indonesia - Garuda Frequent Flyer (GFF) - Miles expire three years after being earned (effective from 01 January 2011, including miles earned before 01 January 2011)
- Japan Airlines Mileage Bank - Miles expire 36 months after being earned.
- Jet Airways - Miles expire after 13 quarters.
- Korean Airlines SKYPASS - Miles expire 10 years after being earned. Miles earned before 30 June 2008 will never expire.
- Malaysia Airlines Enrich - Miles expire one year after being earned, but members can extend the validity of their miles for an extra year after paying a fee to do so or by becoming Enrich Platinum elite members.
- Royal Brunei Royal Skies - Miles will never expire as long as there is eligible activity within three years.
- Philippine Airlines Mabuhay - Miles expire 36 months after being earned.
- Shanghai Airlines - Miles expire 2 complete calendar years after they are earned.
- Singapore Airlines KrisFlyer - Miles expire 36 months after being earned (can be extended up to 12 months for a fee).
- Thai Airways International Royal Orchid Plus - Miles earned in one calendar year will expire at the end of the third calendar year after accrual.

- Vietnam Airlines Golden Lotus Programme - Miles earned will expire two years after two years on the member's sign up anniversary month.

Europe:

- Aeroflot Bonus - Miles expire after 24 months since last flight activity
- Aerosvit Meridian - Miles expire after last day of 36th month
- Air France/KLM/Air Europa Flying Blue - Miles expire after 20 months of flight inactivity (for non-elite members)
- Alitalia MilleMiglia - Miles expire after 24 months since last flight activity
- AirBaltic BalticMiles - Reward miles expire after 3 years after the day they are first earned
- BMI Diamond Club - Miles expire after 24 months of inactivity
- British Airways Executive Club - Miles expire after 36 months of inactivity
- Iberia Plus - Miles expire after 24 months of inactivity
- Malev Hungarian Airlines Duna Club - In principle, Bonus Points collected by travelling are valid for 3 years from the date of the trip (rounded up to the nearest quarter).
- Miles and More (Lufthansa, Air Dolomiti, Augsburg Airways, Contact Air, Eurowings, Austrian Airlines, Brussels Airlines, LOT Polish Airlines, Swiss International Air Lines as well as regional airlines: Adria Airways, Croatia Airlines and Luxair) - Miles expire 36 months after date of earning for non-elite members with no Lufthansa-branded credit card, or 36 months after loss of elite status for currently elite members.
- Czech Airlines OK Plus - Miles expire 2 years after last activity (redemptions do not count as activity).
- SAS EuroBonus (SAS, Blue1, Widerøe and Estonian Air) - Points expires 60 months after earning and/or purchasing the points.
- Spanair Plus - Miles expire 3 years after last activity.
- Turkish Airlines MilesandSmiles - Collected miles (flight, hotel stay, car rental) expire at the end of the third full calendar year following their collection.
- TAP Victoria - Miles expire 3 years after last activity. Paying a fee will extend miles for another 3 years.
- Ukraine International Airlines Panorama- Miles not expire.
- Virgin Atlantic Flying Club - Miles expire 3 years after last activity.
- Vueling Airlines' punto. - Points expire 3 years after accrual, or after 18 months of inactivity on the account.

Middle East:

- Egyptair Plus - Miles expire 3 years after earning. (Except for Egyptair Plus Platinum members)

- El Al Matmid - Points expire 3 years after earning
- Middle East Airlines Cedar Miles - Miles expire 5 years after earning.
- Skywards - Miles expire at the end of the month of the traveller's birth, 3 years after earning (however, you can use them to book a reward ticket that is valid for up to 12 months).

North America:

- Air Canada Aeroplan - Miles expire after 12 months of account inactivity or 7 years after they are earned, whichever occurs first.
- AirTran A+ Rewards - Credits expire 1 year after they are earned (2 years after earning with elite status or co-branded credit card).
- Alaska Airlines and Horizon Air Mileage Plan - Miles expire after 24 months of account inactivity.
- American AAdvantage - Miles expire after 18 months of account inactivity.
- Continental OnePass - Miles don't expire, however, accounts may be closed or miles forfeited after 18 months of account inactivity. Will be combined with United's Mileage Plus programme on approval of the merger.
- Delta SkyMiles - Miles expire after 24 months of account inactivity (12 months for brand new members with no account activity).
- Frontier EarlyReturns - Miles expire after 2 complete calendar years of account inactivity.
- Hawaiian HawaiianMiles - Miles expire after 18 months of account inactivity.
- JetBlue TrueBlue - Credits expire 12 months after last flight or co-branded credit card activity.
- Midwest Miles expire after 3 years of account inactivity (beginning in January 2011, miles will expire after 24 months of inactivity).
- Southwest Rapid Rewards - Credits expire 2 complete calendar years after they are earned.
- Spirit Airlines FREE SPIRIT - 2,000 miles must be earned in a six-month rolling period to prevent expiration.
- United Mileage Plus - Miles expire after 18 months of account inactivity. Will absorb Continental's OnePass programme on approval of merger with Continental Airlines
- US Airways Dividend Miles - Miles expire after 18 months of account inactivity. Paying a fee will extend miles for another 18 months.
- Virgin America eleVAte - Miles earned after February 2010 expire after 18 months of account inactivity.

Oceania:

- Air New Zealand Airpoints - Gold and Gold Elite members' points do not expire as long as they retain at least Gold status. Silver and Jade members' points expire on the member's anniversary date following the date the point turns 4 years old.

- Qantas Frequent Flyer - Miles earned from 1 July 2010 will expire after 18 months of inactivity. Miles earned prior to that expire 3 years after last activity.

Central America:

- TACA - Miles expire after 24 months of inactivity.

South America:

- LAN Airlines - LANPASS Kilometers do not expire unless the passenger has not earned kilometers by flying with LAN after 36 months.
- TAM Airlines TAM Fidelidade - Miles expire 24 months after they are earned.
- Peruvian Airlines - Peruvian Pass accumulated miles do not expire.

A mileage run is an airline trip designed and taken solely to gain maximum frequent flyer miles, points or status. If a traveller has already achieved some sort of elite status they will be earning bonus miles on top of their actual flight miles, and consequently they will reach their goal sooner. A mileage run may allow a traveller to (re-)qualify for a beneficial elite level which requires a minimum amount of miles for qualification.

Bibliography

A.K. Bhatia: *International Tourism Management*, Sterling Publication, Delhi, 2001.

Atul Shrivastava: *Tourism Ethics*, Centrum Press, Delhi, 2010.

Babu P George and Alexandru Nedela: *International Tourism : World Geography and Developmental Perspectives*, Abhijeet Publication, Delhi, 2007.

Bholanath Dutta: *International Tourism Management*, Himalaya Publishing House, Delhi, 2011.

D.S. Bhardwaj, Manjula Chaudhary, S.S. Boora, Krishan K. Kamra, Ravi Bhushan Kumar, Mohinder Chand and R.H. Taxak: *International Tourism : Issues and Challenges*, Kanishka Publication, Delhi, 2006.

Jagmohan Negi: *International Tourism and Travel*, S. Chand Publisher, Delhi, 2003.

K K Sharma: *World Tourism Today*, Sarup and Sons, Delhi, 2004.

K.P. Jha: *International Tourism Management*, ALP Books, Delhi, 2011.

M.N. Kulshrestha: *International Tourism Policy*, Sumit Enterprises, Delhi, 2011.

Moti Ram: *International Tourism in South-East Asia : A Geographical Perspective*, Sanjay Prakashan, Delhi, 2005.

P C Sinha: *International Encyclopaedia of Tourism Ethics (3 Vols-Set)*, Anmol Publication, Delhi, 2006.

Prateek Agarwal: *International Tourism*, Reference Press, Delhi, 2005.

Prem Nath Dhar: *International Tourism : Emerging Challenges and Future Prospects*, Kanishka Publication, Delhi, 2006.

R K Pruthi: *International Tourism : Potentials Measurement and Prospects*, Rajat Publication, Delhi, 2004.

Raj Bahadur Sharma: *World Tourism in 21 Century*, Alfa Publication, Delhi, 2006.

Ramesh Mathur: *International Tourism*, ABD Publication, Delhi, 2007.

Ravee Chauhan: *Studies on International Tourism*, Vista International Publication, Delhi, 2011.

Romila Chawla: *Tourism Promotion*, Sonali Publication, Delhi, 2006.

S.C. Bagri: *Trends in Tourism Promotion (Emerging Issues)*, Bishen Singh Mahendra Pal Singh, Delhi, 2003.

S.P. Singh: *International Tourism Development*, ABD Publication, Delhi, 2005.

Sanjeev Gupta: *World Tourism in the New Millennium*, ABD Publication, Delhi, 2006.

Shambhu Dayal: *Handbook of Tourism Ethics*, Akansha Publication, Delhi, 2006.

Sunil Sharma: *Emerging International Tourism Markets*, Rajat Publication, Delhi, 2007.

Swadesh Sinha: *International Tourism and Sustainable Development*, Random Publications, Delhi, 2012.

Thomas Walsh: *Tourism Promotion*, Discovery Publishing House, Delhi, 2011.

Upasana Sharma and Vandana Yadav: *Recent Advances in World Tourism*, Shree Publication, Delhi, 2007.

Vikas Choudhary: *International Tourism And Sustainable Development*, Centrum Press, Delhi, 2010.

Vivek Verma: *Tourism Ethics*, Centrum Press, Delhi, 2011.

Index